PLAYING OUT THE EMPIRE

PLAYING OUT THE EMPIRE

Ben-Hur and Other Toga Plays and Films,
1883–1908. A Critical Anthology.

Edited with Introductions and Notes by
David Mayer

and an essay on the incidental music for toga dramas by
Katherine Preston

CLARENDON PRESS · OXFORD

1994

Oxford University Press, Walton Street, Oxford OX2 6DP

Oxford New York Toronto
Delhi Bombay Calcutta Madras Karachi
Kuala Lumpur Singapore Hong Kong Tokyo
Nairobi Dar es Salaam Cape Town
Melbourne Auckland Madrid
and associated companies in
Berlin Ibadan

Oxford is a trade mark of Oxford University Press

Published in the United States
by Oxford University Press Inc. New York

British Library Cataloguing in Publication Data
Data available

Library of Congress Cataloging in Publication Data
Playing out the empire: Ben-Hur and other toga plays and films.
1883–1908: a critical anthology / edited with introduction and
notes by David Mayer; and an essay on the incidental music for toga
dramas by Katherine Preston.
1. Rome—History—Empire, 30 B.C.–476 A.D.—Drama. 2. English
drama—19th century. 3. English drama—20th century. 4. Historical drama, American.
5. Historical drama, English. 6. Motion picture plays.
I. Mayer, David. II. Preston, Katherine K.
PR 1255.P57   1994   822'.80358—dc20   93–21497
ISBN 0-19-811990-9

Typeset by Pure Tech Corporation, Pondicherry, India
Printed in Great Britain
on acid-free paper by
Biddles Ltd., Guildford and King's Lynn

F 463

For my parents,
Jane and Red Mayer

'Lo, I will stand at thy right hand
And keep the bridge with thee.'

Acknowledgements

My curiosity about the various permutations of toga drama goes back more than a decade. That period of time has enabled me to meet and to be advised and assisted by many wise and informed people who have answered queries, directed me to further sources, loaned me illustrative materials, read and criticized articles and papers that preceded this study, as well as commented and offered helpful suggestions as this study went through its numerous drafts. Some have furnished technical assistance. Some have generously supplied the grants that have enabled me and my colleagues on the Victorian and Edwardian Stage on Film Project to travel and to recover the early theatrical motion pictures and the theatrical texts to be found on the following pages. Some have offered reassurance, cups of tea, extended hospitality, friendship, trust, patience, and love. It has been a superb decade for me. My indebtedness to many of these friends, colleagues, benefactors, and family is acknowledged all too briefly and inadequately in the lists below. I apologize to each for such brevity even as I thank them for invaluable help.

My thanks, therefore, to the British Academy, which, on two separate occasions, provided grants which enabled me to begin and, later, to complete this study; to the Faculty of Arts at Manchester University and to the Leverhulme Trust for the funding that launched the Victorian Stage on Film Project associated with this research, and to Zoë Aldrich and Conal Percy for their research and video skills; to Gayle Harris of the Copyright Division, who provided the path through the Library labyrinth, and to Dr Patrick Loughney, who introduced me to the Paper Print (Film) Collection at the Library of Congress; to Christine Gledhill of the British Film Institute, who led me from stage to film melodrama; to art historians Dr Shearer West, Rupert Maas, and Christopher Wood for assistance in locating and interpreting pictorial sources, and to Lise Mayer, who scuttled around Manhattan in search of Ben-Hur; to Tracy Keenan Wynn, the Wheeler Opera House, and Robert Murray, all of Aspen, Colorado; to Manchester City Art Gallery, the Map Division of the Library of Congress, Blackburn Museum and Art Gallery, and the New York Public Library, for allowing me to reproduce pictures in their collection; to the Theatre Museum, the Garrick Club, the Martha Herrick Library of the Academy of Motion Picture Arts and Sciences, and the Manuscript Division of the British Library. Janet Jones and Christine Patterson assisted in transcribing manuscript texts; Peter Burton and Michael Pollard met my arbitrary and occasionally weird photographic problems.

I have been blessed with the editorship and assistance of Andrew Lockett, Jason Freeman, Elizabeth Stratford, Nicola Pike, and Nick Clarke, and with guidance from anonymous Press readers whose acerbic observations more than once made me wake up and smell the coffee. I have further gained from the assistance and/or counsel of Prof. Laurence Senelick, Prof. Bruce McConachie, Prof. Tracy Davis, Kay Hutchins, Prof. Jeffrey Richards, Dr John MacKenzie, Prof. Louis James, Dr Russell Jackson, Dr John Breuilly, Diana Kealey, Jill Edmonds, Ron Harris, David Owen, Dr John Stokes, Clare Hudson, Gillian Anderson, Matthew Scott, Richard Foulkes, Dr Sheila Stowell, Prof. Joel Kaplan, Dr Maria Wyke, Catherine Mayer, Cassie Mayer, and of my departmental colleagues Dr George Taylor, Philip Cook, Michael Holt, Vivien Gardner, and Prof. Kenneth Richards. Claudette Williams, drawing on her personal experience and wide reading, educated me in the implications and effects of colonialism which reverberate throughout my study.

This book approaches, among other issues, questions of Victorian and early twentieth-century religious faith, and I have been particularly fortunate in having drafts of my texts read and criticized by my colleague the Revd Dr Henry Rack. However, whatever faults may be found with my presentation or interpretations of toga Christianity are entirely of my own making. I wish to make it clear that I am not a member or adherent of any Christian faith. Indeed, for me a compulsory choice between Diana or Christ would not have arisen, because, given my lazy agnosticism, I would have felt more at home with laid-back Roman polytheism, and a grain of incense here or there would have been no great matter.

This project began as the task of a single author. It soon became apparent that questions of incidental music and, with *Ben-Hur*, orchestral and choral episodes demanded skill and specialized knowledge to raise well-directed issues, let alone to answer them with understanding. I therefore turned to Katherine Preston, whose work on American theatrical musicians I knew and admired. She has offered advice and wisdom beyond the confines of music, and I have gratefully incorporated these suggestions in the text. Katherine Preston, in turn, has been fortunate in being able to refer queries to Frank Cipolla and Prof. Martin Marks, and she takes this opportunity to express her thanks to them. To an equal extent, I have gained from the assistance, scholarship, and theatrical acumen of my wife Helen Day Mayer. Her involvement has been constant; she has been a source of information and judgement as well as of loving support.

Much of my research was conducted in American libraries and collections. Away from home, I was the cossetted guest of Elizabeth and Jack Buchanek, whose hospitality extended to my researchers Zoë and Conal, and of Susan and Philip Mayer and Mary Jane and Bud Bezark; such comfort, kindness, and generosity. For a time I was fortunate in having the support and excited interest of my aunt, the late Emily B. Rothschild. We would have enjoyed a large whiskey together to celebrate publication.

My thanks to all.

D.M.

Manchester
January 1993.

Foreword

The term 'toga play' is not my own. It was coined in 1895–6 and, widely understood, was in general use two years later to identify melodramas enacting conflict, persecution, and clashes in values and beliefs between early Christians or proto-Christians and their Roman oppressors. As the numerous plays described by this label disappeared from view in the 1920s, so did the term. The purpose of this volume is to present a fresh claim for the significance, variety, and quality of the popular toga drama which held public attention, achieved occasional notoriety, and earned rare critical acclaim between the mid-1880s and 1920. It is both a study and an anthology of plays and scenarios which expressed and gave vent to complex and often contradictory thoughts, emotions, myths, and ideologies of Britain and America. Equally, it is an investigation of the manner and the extent of interaction between the populace of these nations and the theatrical mode labelled the 'toga play'. In particular, toga plays ventured clandestinely into issues related to, and intertwined with, class identity, gender, religion, immigration, and imperialism, and, having ventured in, offered audiences a prismatic diffusion of interpretations and possibilities. Within a thirty-five-year span, toga dramas established a well-defined metaphoric world and a range of dramatic conventions so thoroughly understood by audiences and so completely and widely accepted as to pass from stage into motion pictures with no apparent disruption. Toga dramas, moreover, enjoyed unprecedented popularity on the stage and were seen by a wider range of audiences than had previously gathered in playhouses. The presence of these newcomers, for whom attendance at theatres—at any play or film—had hitherto been proscribed by Church elders and pastors as sinful or illicit, gave impetus and fresh audiences, but little critical approval, to melodrama, which, from the 1880s, had been tumbling into disrepute.

Although my study of toga drama queries both the toga play and toga film and identifies links between the two forms, it is necessary to stress that it is not my intention to establish a teleological connection between stage and cinema. Many film historians have assumed the resources of the Victorian stage to have been on the point of exhaustion, technically overstretched, heavily and expensively labour-intensive, starved of subject-matter, and unable to make the full leap into pictorial realism that was being demanded by audiences at the popular theatres[1] and into Naturalism required by authors and directors for the 'free' stages of Europe and America. Motion pictures, these historians insist, were the natural result of, and the happy solution to, theatrical exhaustion. This view has only a limited truth and can only be made as a *post hoc* interpretation. In the period covered by this study, popular dramatic authors and theatrical craftsmen had no evidence that the stage might be at the end of its resources, and they were largely correct. The use of electric power and lighting, well reported in the public press as well as in theatrical journals, had given fresh options to theatrical technology. Most people working in the theatre would have derided the idea that the stage play aspired to be cinema. Motion pictures were still widely perceived to be inferior to plays, and film-making was thought to be a disreputable occupation in part because film-makers flouted censorship and employed performers whose low wages undercut theatrical salaries. Theatrical producers went to law, finally taking their case all the way to the US Circuit Court of Appeals, to prevent film-makers from issuing a motion picture of *Ben-Hur*. The producers' complaint was not merely about revenue lost to a rival production, but also that the motion-picture version was so inept as to cheapen and degrade the original. This argument was convincing in 1907. It was still so in 1912, but by that date theatrical confidence was beginning to waver. Nevertheless, virtually all significant toga films from 1905—the earliest date for which I can discover evidence of such films—to 1915 are plagiarized or 'borrowed': cut-down versions of, or otherwise derived from, toga plays. The 'live' theatre was still paramount, and it is probably not an exaggeration to claim that, in these early years, film aspired to be stage play.

My approach to toga drama is therefore to examine the development of an ample set of dramatic and theatrical conventions which enjoyed success in its own right and which prepared the way for toga film by establishing a large public whose expectations had been made ready through exposure to plays and to such analogous genres as the music-hall dramatic sketch. My examples of toga films, in the main, are early and, in comparison to contemporary theatre pieces, primitive and unfinished. I well accept that toga films[2] were to take over from the

---

[1] A. Nicholas Vardac, *Stage to Screen: Theatrical Method from Garrick to Griffith* (Cambridge, Mass., 1949), and John L. Fell, *Film and the Narrative Tradition* (London, 1986).

[2] Films set in the ancient or biblical world are frequently labelled 'epic films' today, but I have preferred to apply the term 'toga film' to those motion pictures which continue in the stage tradition.

stage and that motion pictures have been the most significant art form of the twentieth century, but there was scant evidence of that significance in 1915.

Contents

List of Illustrations

Unless stated, illustrations are held in the editor's private collection.

INTRODUCTION

Toga play was a term coined in derision and acknowledgement. Derision because these plays were viewed by late Victorian critics and sophisticates as melodrama which articulated a simplistic morality, enacted formulaic plots detailing lurid events, and pandered to a species of primitive and evangelical Christianity that cannot be located within the doctrines of an identifiable sect. Acknowledgement because these same dramas constituted some of the more popular entertainments on English-speaking and European stages in the closing years of the last century and in the first decades of the present, and because, with barely a pause to adjust to technological differences, these toga plays passed into the cinema and became the toga film. We cannot speak—and yet we do—of the cinema epics of D. W. Griffith or Cecil B. DeMille without acknowledging the extent to which their artistic eyes and directorial approaches were conditioned by direct exposure to spectacular Victorian and Edwardian toga dramas. For a variety of reasons, few toga plays were published, and although theatre and cinema historians passingly acknowledge the significance of such stage and screen melodramas as *The Sign of the Cross* or *The Last Days of Pompeii* or *Quo Vadis?*, few of these historians have consulted the scripts or even accounts of the technicalities of their staging. Some of these plays are still highly stageworthy and capable of being realized—even in modern theatres which lack the labour-intensive effects and machinery of the Victorian playhouse.

If today we are largely unfamiliar with the toga drama, it is because derision and distance have done their work. We usually know this dramatic genre, if we know it at all, through a uniquely disarming parody or through occasional attempts at the genre by a handful of established poets. Thus Bernard Shaw's *Androcles and the Lion* is performed by schoolchildren who have no idea that they, too, are mocking a once-reviled dramatic species, and Stephen Phillips's *Nero* and Tennyson's *The Cup* moulder unread on the shelves of second-hand booksellers. Only Shaw's *Caesar and Cleopatra* is seen in the occasional professional production, with neither producers nor audiences realizing that this play grew from toga stock.

What the coiner[1] of the term 'toga play' probably had in mind was not a single phenomenon, but an irregular cluster of plays with a recurring set of theatrical and thematic conventions in which, like a constellation, the observer may discern a shape and pattern. Whilst there is no typical toga play, there are recognizable conventions: the toga play is therefore identifiable as an elaborately spectacular 'sensation' melodrama set somewhere in the post-republican Roman Empire. The times favoured for toga plays are the reigns of Nero, Hadrian, Julian, and Diocletian, periods remembered by the early Christian writers as times of persecution and martyrdom. Such drama depicts an empire at or past the summit of its power and influence. No question is posed about the source or the legitimacy of this power. It is a multicultural empire enriched by the Asian, African, and European nations that it has subdued, dominated, and, albeit discriminatingly, pillaged. It is thus an empire rich in possessions, in the arts, in luxury, in philosophy, and in remnants of austere stoic morality. It enfolds a world of available pleasure, immediate sensual gratification, and almost omnipresent vice. The Rome of toga drama is already poisoned and corrupted by its own conquests and by its all too accessible luxury. There is, however, a new voice raised against vice, luxury, decadence, and the arbitrary and cruel abuse of power. This voice is Christianity in its evangelical form. This Christianity is characterized by a rejection of worldliness and, equally, by its insistence on deferring pleasure to another realm or to another life. Conflict between Rome and Christianity is therefore inevitable.

In representing conflict between the established pagan Romans and the new, subversive, troublesome Christians, toga drama usually offers a vexed romance between a Christian, usually a female, and a Roman, normally a male who is powerful, noble, and wealthy. The lovers are brought together by accident, and it is a mixture of lust and compassion that turns the Roman by stages from rapist to seducer to lover to husband, whilst the Christian steadfastly clings to her faith. Her moral stance has given her the right to challenge her captors. The male, however, previously successful in his conquest of women and ready to act in the name of the Roman state, is reduced to bemused reflec-

[1] Probably H. Chance Newton, who, signing himself 'Carados', regularly wrote a column for the *Referee*. Newton, in referring to *The Sign of the Cross*, uses the term generically, with the assurance that his readers will understand the general conventions of this form.

tion. The crux of such toga drama is caught in an aside which Wilson Barrett prudently excised from an early draft of *The Sign of the Cross* when he recognized that Romans would not have thought of themselves as pagans: 'She's in the clouds, and if I do not exercise my will she'll drag me after her. If I do not make a Pagan of her, she will make a Christian of me. On some level we must meet.'[2] Courtship and romance between Roman and Christian is difficult, but not unbridgeable. Christians are outlaws; Romans must collude and participate in their persecution. The Roman hero's position invites rivalry and competition. Men envy his power and wealth; women vie for his attention and affection. The heroine may be captured; the hero must attempt rescue. The couple are threatened with death in the arena—to be consumed by lions or slain by gladiators. However, a choice is offered: all can be reconciled if the parties—for now the Roman hero has discovered some ethical core to his character and, although uninstructed except by example, is gravitating towards Christianity—sacrifice to the Roman gods. This dilemma, which focuses on conflicting strains of ideology and belief, asks audiences to weigh the values of powerful secular Rome—and, by implication, modern empires—against those of the apparently weaker Christianity.

Victorians dwelt upon this dilemma and celebrated it in other forms. A memorable example is found in a painting by Edwin Long, exhibited at the Royal Academy in 1889 and subsequently sold by Thomas Agnew as an engraving. The painting shows a young Christian female standing at the edge of an arena in a festively crowded stadium. Before the lone woman is the multi-breasted image of Diana of Ephesus and a burning altar flame. Crowding about her and masking the imminent terror of the arena are a group of Roman men, each either importuning or threatening her. She must decide between the beasts and liberty. The viewer cannot read her mind but fears that she will choose martyrdom. Long's picture is entitled *Diana or Christ? Let her cast the incense—but one grain and she is free.*[3] This choice, which draws upon an ample range of melodramatic possibilities and which, equally, probes the values of the British and American societies which created and viewed these plays, confronts toga heroines and some heroes before the drama moves to its denouement.

There are variants to this formula. One, *Ben-Hur*, takes its audience and hero on a quest through the outposts of the Empire, which is

---

[2] From Act IV. 63 of the manuscript copy deposited with the Library of Congress.

[3] This painting was known to Bernard Shaw and recurs as a topic in his non-dramatic writing. Cf., among others, his preface to *Androcles and the Lion*.

perceived as a variegated society offering diverse perils, pleasures, riches, and secular temptations. The heroine is less mobile than the hero, but she, too, may be subjected to trials of health, endurance, morality, and virtue. She may also encounter a female rival—in the parlance of the late Victorian stage, an 'adventuress'—who is less scrupulous in bestowing her favours and who, temporarily at least, will captivate the more virtuous woman's lover. Eventually, the hero must encounter the power of Roman institutions and be tested in Roman society and the Roman arena alike. He will emerge triumphant, but his quest is not ended, and thereafter he is faced with ethical and spiritual choices which transform him from Roman—or Judaean— into a Christian family man. The significance of this transformation is his renunciation of power. Morality, he realizes, is relinquishing the employment of power to a Christian God who will exercise it as He ordains. Thus the Christianity of the toga plays is limited, vague, and non-sectarian. Apart from the hymn-singing in which toga Christians indulge, toga Christianity is also dour and self-denying, but it is consistent with late Victorian morality and scientific thinking. To the degree that these dramas encourage the deferral of immediate sensual gratification and urge the substitution of intellectual or social pleasures which, 'even though . . . postponed and diminished', take account of the individual's reality, toga Christianity accords with the 'reality principle' which Sigmund Freud was to articulate within a few short years.[4] It is a Christianity which evokes neither quarrels nor threats.

It is further characteristic of toga-play Christianity that it is virtually non-doctrinal and cannot be identified with the dogma or rituals of any sect. It is not unusual to find a Roman Catholic spokesperson endorsing a toga piece with the same enthusiasm as his Church of England or evangelical counterpart,[5] and it is common to find advertisements for these plays which cite favourable reviews from a variety of denominational newspapers and journals. In fact, favourable comment from Roman Catholic sources confirms that toga plays stayed clear of disputed areas of creeds and social policy. In particular, none of the plays condemns alcohol—except in excess—or offers support to the temperance or total abstinence movements affiliated to Amer-

---

[4] Sigmund Freud, 'Some Thoughts on Development and Regression: Aetiology', in *Introductory Lectures on Psychoanalysis, 1916–17* (London, 1973), 383–403.

[5] *Theatre*, in a column commenting on *The Sign of the Cross*, reports 'a Capuchin monk telling his congregation: "those who cannot be brought to hear the Divine Word spoken in churches can often be reached and stirred to serious thought in plays of so elevating a character" and the [Church of England's], Bishop of Norwich offering dispensation to his congregation who attend this play in Lent' (27 (June 1896), 310).

INTRODUCTION 5

ican and British Protestantism. Thus the plays avoid implications of the anti-Catholicism which constituted an element in the several temperance movements' rhetorics.

As much as toga drama is shaped by its own conventions, the experience of toga drama is also controlled by the conventions and characteristics of melodrama. Melodrama describes worlds in which events happen because anti-social humans—villains—instigate actions which disturb the peace, tranquillity, and plans of individuals who are neither unsociable nor malign. In toga plays people are troubled and threatened and persecuted by Roman villains such as Tigellinus and the Emperor Nero, Messala, the Marcus of *The Charioteers*, and the Egyptian Arbaces, who act on such malign motives or disturbed psychological states as greed, lust, vanity, avarice, envy, ambition, jealousy, megalomania, and sadism. Once their lives are disturbed, the innocent parties—Mercia and Marcus Superbus, Esther and Judah Ben-Hur, Ione and Glaucus—must discover why their lives have been so altered for the worse, display their worthiness by coping with adversity, and detect and sometimes punish the villain responsible.

This picture of the world ordinarily and necessarily divides the drama's cast of characters into two morally distinct categories: the good and the evil. It is not expected that antithetical moral categories should be reconciled and it is generally accepted that they should remain distinct. Conventional—early and mid-Victorian—melodrama, which draws such distinctions, therefore enables audiences to perceive dramatic action and characters, in Peter Brooks's apposite phrase, as 'morally legible'.[6] Moral legibility consequently grants to such audiences the experience of recognizing and empathizing with the virtuous and, even though their experience of the world often contradicts dramatic formulas, the pleasure of witnessing the virtuous succeed in their endeavours. In toga plays and films the pleasures and certainties of moral legibility are far less distinct, for reasons that will be discussed further below.

The pleasures of melodrama cannot be intellectual ones. Knowledge of how the 'real world' functions is pushed aside for emotional satisfaction, and the full resources of melodramatic production are deployed in furtherance of these satisfactions. Music, always at the heart of melodrama, is essential in the performance of toga plays. Whereas words and actions are explicit and denotative, music can only be connotative; but it can instruct. It can instruct audiences in how to

---

[6] Peter Brooks, *The Melodramatic Imagination* (New Haven, Conn., 1976), 42–4.

feel and how to interpret action. The use of incidental music is central
to any consideration of toga drama, and this subject is discussed in
detail below, in Katherine Preston's essay on the music to *Ben-Hur*.
However, because music is one of the fixed conventions of melodrama
and because understanding melodrama involves recognizing a genre
reliant on formulas and conventions and emotion-led, toga melodrama
may easily and inaccurately be belittled as 'harmless escapism' or
stigmatized as bad historic fiction.

It is a perception worth challenging. Melodrama, toga melodrama
included, is always 'about something'. A serious and perhaps unanswer-
able problem lies at the core of each play, even though that problem—
covert, implied, subliminal (the terms are individually or serially
applicable)—may not be immediately apparent to the theatre audience,
who unconsciously receive the 'something' as emotional information.
Much of the dramatist's skill is applied to an actual or metaphoric
description of the problem. A melodramatist who sets characters in a
terrifying city landscape (a landscape that might be Los Angeles or
Nero's Rome) in which they must cope with brutality, official hostility,
crime, and other perils may be describing current and actual problems.
But the dramatist's city may also be a metaphor for a world in which
the spectator feels isolated and helpless and hence feels him- or herself
to be a victim, unable to understand and to solve the complex tasks of
daily living. In melodrama this metaphor and the problems contained
within it are described in rich detail so that the spectator, emotionally
if not intellectually, will be able to recognize his or her own world.
Where the melodramatist and melodrama partly—but only partly—fail
the spectator is in posing solutions to the problems raised and recognized. Having described the problem—the 'something'—with fidelity,
melodrama retreats into formulas for dramatic solutions. The problem,
once stated and elaborated, becomes conflated with the villain. The
villain becomes the problem, and the problem disappears when the
villain is identified, apprehended, and punished. In some toga melodrama, where the male protagonists may be both hero and villain or
share traits of arrogance, self-indulgence, and arbitrary use of power
with more recognizable villains, the drama's conflict must lead the
protagonist to the point at which his better nature recognizes his
potential to do harm and to stifle goodness. With his own evil before
him, the appalled hero may then take steps to effect his own punishment and redemption, and here, too, the central problem vanishes.

There is the further question of whether the spectator ever really
'escapes' by attending melodrama—or, for that matter, any fictional

representation. The spectator may turn away from what he or she recognizes as immediate and specific problems, but will nevertheless encounter another set of real problems, perhaps problems of a more general nature, disguised as the fictional dramatic world. If the spectator engages with these disguised problems, and if the problems hold meaning (even if the meaning is only understood unconsciously), he or she will become involved in a process of understanding and assenting to the complexities of his or her world. Assent is registered as interest, vicarious involvement, and applause. Dissent can be registered as inattention, dislike or indifference to the performance and performers, or open hostility. Thus theatre and film-going become not escape, but significant social processes whereby the spectator chooses to confront and to assent to—or to contradict—the world seen on stage or screen. Rome and the Roman Empire, we shall observe, is such a metaphor with a lengthy history of permitting spectators to meet, confront, and understand their own world.

Their existence—in the beginning and in their continuing favour with a variegated public—raises questions about the meaning and function of toga plays and films. It is no mere coincidence that toga plays should appear in the closing decades of the nineteenth century and that toga films should continue up to and beyond the start of the First World War. The reason for such timing and continuity lies in the late Victorian and Edwardian perception of Rome, and Roman Empire, and nascent Christianity as the focal point of almost endless contradiction, incongruity, and paradox—a parallel culture, a mirror of the audience's own contradictory, incongruous, and paradoxical world. It is a view of Rome which is expressed not exclusively in drama, but equally in the novel and poetry. This view also figures extensively in painting, and these paintings often find their way back into toga dramas, where the picture is 'realized', i.e. the subject-matter, settings, costumes, and groupings are closely reproduced within the dramatic action.[7] Victorian interpretations of the Roman world are modelled in sculpture and rebuilt into civic and domestic architecture.

On the one hand, the Victorians perceived Rome in a favourable light: a culture of civilizing laws and customs fostering stoic restraint

---

[7] This practice is fully explicated in Martin Meisel, *Realizations: Narrative, Pictorial, and Theatrical Arts in Nineteenth Century England* (Princeton, NJ, 1987). Pictorial sources are indicated in Joseph Kestner, *Mythology and Misogyny: The Social Discourse of Nineteenth Century British Classical-Subject Painting* (London, 1989), and Christopher Wood, *Olympian Dreamers* (London, 1983).

and modesty. Victorians admired Romans for their self-sufficiency, deliberate frugality, and intellectual rigour. Roman domestic life was praised for the virtue of its matrons and the rectitude of its patricians. The rhetoric of Victorian imperialism spoke openly and favourably of comparisons to Rome, enlarging upon the idea of a commercial and military British Empire stretching from Canada to the hongs of China to the Cape of Good Hope, governed from an administrative capital city where, from 1897, a ruler styled as 'Empress' reigned over numerous tribute-bearing colonies. The United States, too, had claims to empire, at first chiefly commercial, but increasingly including the annexation or conquest of mainland—then overseas—territories. Empires were viewed as expanding civilizations whose frontiers held back African, Asiatic, and barbarian darkness and savagery; colonized cultures were respected and tolerated, their gods added to a growing polyglot pantheon. My father, born in 1893 and reared on Macaulay's *The Lays of Ancient Rome*, was fond of declaiming broken stanzas of 'Horatius at the Bridge'. For him, as for so many others of his age, Rome was a locus of power, honour, bravery, and self-sacrifice, images of which permeated government and civic institutions as well as private life.

On the other hand, Victorians concurrently held an altogether different perception of late Rome and its Empire as a culture of excess and decadence. Rome seemed to proclaim its vices: self-gratification, sadism, frivolity, licence, and immodesty. It failed to tolerate alien cultures and ruthlessly suppressed Christians and those of other faiths. Virtuous republicanism had yielded to a Senate cowed by a succession of demented emperors; the army no longer secured the frontier and might at any moment march against Roman citizens. The official pantheon of Roman gods was served by a class of self-aggrandizing irreligious priests, but it was probably of no matter because the gods were powerless fictions. In place of semi-rural self-sufficiency were urban squalor and poverty. Corruption and profligacy spread downward from the imperial court and rotted civic institutions and domestic life with equal speed. In short, Rome for British and North American Victorians was one of the 'other' cultures: enticing, distant, unattainable, and strange, but, paradoxically—because aspects of Roman culture and Roman conquest were perceived to resemble comparable elements of British and American life—Rome and its Empire were painfully familiar. Unattainable Rome was both infinitely desirable and frightening. It simultaneously attracted and repelled.

One of the more complex areas of meaning and significance of toga drama lies in the association of this genre with concepts and practices of imperialism. By the final decades of the nineteenth century the concept of Rome and the identities of Roman persons, objects, and institutions had become inextricably linked to the nature and destiny of modern empires. Because imperial expansion was, in the main, successful and profitable, responses were approving. Ancient Rome had not only given these modern empires their sculpture and public architecture, but their rhetoric and, it was argued,[8] their laws, military force, and civic institutions. British colonial administrators spoke loftily of *imperium et libertas*, whilst schoolroom puns in Latin reported imperial conquests.[9] Artists such as Lawrence Alma-Tadema recast middle-class domestic life into scrupulously researched Roman settings and Roman dress, but his subjects were still recognized as 'Victorians in togas'.[10] These representations of the Victorian world in Roman settings, attire, and language wrapped European and American expansion in historical garb and imparted a sense of nationhood and patriotism. Historians are virtually unanimous in citing imperialism and uncritical imperial fervour as one of the prevailing moods by the turn of the century.

Less audible and somewhat less frequent were oblique negative responses. These, sometimes troubled and critical, were never altogether mutinous. Amidst the imperial rhetoric and display were quiet, but earnestly persuasive, expressions of doubt which infiltrated and spoilt unanimity. Contemporary historians of empire reminded readers that Rome had overreached itself and collapsed from financial and logistical overstrain, and that Britain might do likewise.[11] Poet-apologists for empire such as Kipling ruminated in more general terms that empires pass away.[12] Some writers were overtly critical. Jack London wrote in 1903:

A vast empire is foundering on the hands of . . . incapable management. And by empire is meant the political machinery which holds together the English-speaking people of the world outside of the United States . . . Blood empire is greater than political empire, and the English of the New World and the Antipodes are strong and vigorous as ever. But the political empire under

---

[8] Raymond F. Betts, 'The Allusion to Rome in British Imperialist Thought of the Late Nineteenth and Early Twentieth Centuries', *Victorian Studies*, Dec. 1971: 149–59.

[9] In 1843 the capture of Sind in Pakistan by Sir Charles Napier was reported to the War Office in a single telegraphed Latin word: 'Peccavi', 'I have sinned'.

[10] Wood, *Olympian Dreamers*, 28.

[11] Betts, 'The Allusion to Rome', 153–9.

[12] Cf. 'Recessional', *The Five Nations* (London, 1903), 214–15.

which they are nominally assembling is perishing. The political machine
known as the British Empire is running down.[13]

Jack London's optimism about America was not entirely shared by
Americans. In 1893, as the World's Columbian Exposition was opening in Chicago, speakers and writers were expressing fears that the
luxury and decadence of the American Empire, which had forsaken
Christianity, were leading the nation to Armageddon. Catastrophe
might be forestalled, the critics argued, if Christian values were pro-
mulgated (and if the World's Fair were to be closed on the Sabbath).[14]
Barbara Tuchman indicates an even more generalized opposition to
empire and American expansion, emanating, in particular, from the
New England states, where the founding principles eschewing standing armies, war, and conquest were still revered and where these
principles continued to attract immigrants from Northern and Central
Europe. These views meet and fuse with those of labour leaders and
workers opposing cheaper labour from Southern Europe, the Carib-
bean and Philippine Islands, and the Orient.[15]

Because such contradictory views underlie and permeate toga drama,
audiences sensed in the plays the contradictions and anomalies of their
own world. Values of empire and imperialism are queried. In every
toga play there is an implicit warning that empires which abuse their
power and overreach themselves can, and will, collapse. British audiences recognized in the Roman Empire their own Empire, threatened
from without by national rivalries and from within, not so much by
corruption as by serious misgivings about the justice of maintaining
an empire at the expense of other races and cultures. They heard new
political voices which declared that the British industrial worker and
the Roman plebeian were both exploited in the name of empire.[16]
The very terms 'Roman', 'empire', 'Christian', 'slave', 'freeman',
'senator', 'Judaean' and many others become almost coded references
to British counterparts. It is possible to read 'Romans' as the deployed
force of the official establishment, the Established Church included,
and to read into 'Christian' elements of dissent and opposition, including identification with the working class, Socialism, or Radicalism,

[13] Jack London, *The People of the Abyss*, quoted in Peter Keating (ed.), *Into Unknown
England, 1866–1913* (Manchester, 1976) 238.
[14] R. Reid Badger, *The Great American Fair: The World's Columbian Exposition and
American Culture* (Chicago, 1979), 96, 158–9.
[15] Barbara Tuchman, *The Proud Tower: A Portrait of the World before the War, 1890–1914*,
(London, 1980), 137–59.
[16] E. J. Hobsbawm, *Industry and Empire* (London, 1990).

with affiliation to low or disestablished or evangelical churches, and with trade-union membership. 'Senator' and 'patrician', military titles, and Roman deities named in oaths (e.g. 'Perpol', 'by Pollux') are again associated with Britain, its upper and middle classes and its empire, whereas 'Judaean' may be interpreted as 'colonial' or, more simply, 'the governed'. But these identities are only nominal and shifting, and sometimes they fuse or overlap. Toga plays in the repertoire were kept fresh and alive through current issues—as, for example, in 1902, when Parliament completed an Education Act which gave support to Church of England schools at the expense of those run by Nonconformists. However, no one claimed that toga plays were dramas to which there was an explicit key, nor insisted that the Christians of toga plays and films belonged to any real Christian sect or worshipped with a recognizable liturgy.

The very fluidity and tenuousness of meaning were advantages which some politicians recognized and which other, less aware, people merely sensed. Two examples may illustrate. Following William Gladstone's visit to Chester in 1896 for a specially arranged matinée performance of *The Sign of the Cross*, he congratulated Wilson Barrett for his lofty aims and his skill in bringing before his audiences moral and social issues.[17] In 1897 my grandmother, a Jewess, bought an expensive extra-illustrated edition of Europe's foremost toga novel, Henryk Sienkiewicz's *Quo Vadis?* Why? Although sharing the late Victorian fascination with the Roman world, it is unlikely that she was interested in Christianity. However, she may have been able to identify with the Christians' cause and with a Christian heroine because the novel's— and later the drama's—Christians were themselves closely identified with self-restraint. The fact that toga dramas appealed to spectators for whom theatre-going was proscribed as immoral or frivolous testifies to the likelihood that new audiences recognized qualities and relationships that spoke to contradictions in their own lives. The plays point to tensions seeking resolution.

These contradictions and antitheses ought, we might expect, to have nullified each other. They did not; they are not mutually exclusive. The toga drama became instead an arena that held and reconciled conflicting views. Whilst toga plays narrated the breakdown and dissolution of the secular state, the imperial state, and the religious state, they replaced these institutions with another narrative that created or spoke to eventual order, justice, liberty, truth, and survival. There is

---

[17] *Theatre*, 28 (Oct. 1896), 167.

in this narrative the discourse of change, but a discourse that stops short of stating how change will come about. Evolution is the option held open, but revolution is never altogether ruled out. Toga plays thus created space for a debate between contraries whilst depicting the world in moral terms whereby the weak opposed the strong and might claim moral victory in defeat. The various elements and issues reached the spectators on many levels to produce conscious and unconscious identification. Whilst attending a toga drama, it was beyond the spectators' power to be clear and unambivalent in personal, ideological, moral, or social beliefs. It was possible for the spectators to empathize or side with both agonists, to see themselves both as powerful winning Romans and as virtuous Christians. It is a characteristic of toga melodrama that, because it never wholly condemns either group and merely identifies individual villains amongst the Romans, it allows audiences 'to have it both ways', to select from both sides, to have knowledge of the world and still retain one's innocence, to believe or not believe, and to expect optimistic solutions. Hence the possibility that, in toga drama, an official text and a subversive text, with alternative readings, coexist.

There is a further factor which links toga drama to a confined period of time. Historians have pointed to a crisis in confidence in the final decades of the nineteenth century and have identified numerous causes for this. Three of these causes, the impact of Darwinism on religion and social institutions, the growth of political consciousness amongst the working class, and the recognition of various imperial rivalries and claims, are particularly relevant to toga drama.[18]

Darwinism, or the claim of science over religion, did not so much create a crisis of faith as proclaim the coexistence of two alternative and contrary explanations for events. Clustered around these explanations are a range of skirmishes, positions, and postures. The protracted political and legal struggle of the atheist Charles Bradlaugh to take his seat in the House of Commons focused attention on the agon, so like that between Marcus Superbus and Mercia, between rationalism and the spectrum of sectarian belief. The running battle between Humanists and Christians was fought in the playhouse and cinema as much as on the street corner and in the pulpit. A toga play was a veritable invitation to pamphleteers, but the very nature and subject-matter of the quarrel attracted new audiences amongst chapel-goers and Nonconformists to whom, previously, the theatre and cinema had been but suburbs of Gomorrah.

[18] Cf. Hobsbawm, *Industry and Empire* and Tuchman, *The Proud Tower*. See also J. F. C. Harrison, *Late Victorian Britain, 1875–1901* (London, 1990).

Class awareness is another factor. The failure of 'Rational Recreation' and other panaceas to bridge antagonisms between workers and the growing middle classes speeded the growth of the Labour movement, workers' study groups, and trade unions. Existing class divisions had long been replicated in the tiered floors, seating, and admission prices of the theatre, and it had long been possible for different segments of the same audience attending the same drama to hear different messages and to infer different conclusions. Now the means existed to express consciousness of class and class aspirations and values. Toga drama offered a parable of working-class oppression that appeared to equate the oppressed with the virtuous. Because the working-class spectator and the chapel-going Nonconformist were often the same individual, the play or film's appeal was strengthened.

As with the conflict between the claims of science and religion, the debate—and resulting ambiguity—on the subject of imperialism could not be resolved in the theatre. British and American Victorians celebrated the might of their empires, but there were questions in the rejoicing. The 'scramble for Africa' had been represented and perceived as white culture bringing the gift of civilization and Christianity to benighted dark-skinned races who could neither value nor deserve the territory they owned. The South African (Boer) War, however, was fought at vast cost in manpower and expense between white nations, both of whom had claims and well-articulated rights. Rival European empires, France, Germany, Italy, could be tolerated provided they did not make Roman Catholic converts, in which instance they had to be opposed or controlled. Britain, faced with territorial claims in the Far East, vacillated. First she supported Japan against Russia in claiming the Chinese base at Port Arthur, then she sided with Russia out of anxiety about the strength of the 'yellow peril'.

The American response to empire was equally troubled. The closing of the frontier and the end to westward expansion left the nation without a recognizable 'other' culture to oppose and subdue. The easy victories of the Spanish-American War which annexed Cuba and the Phillipines had briefly identified an apparently suitable alien 'other', but brought dissent from Americans who queried racism and conquest.

The gathering clamour of these discordant voices for or against religion, class, and empire replaced previous moral and political absolutes with a new relativism. The consequence of this relativism was to undermine the 'moral legibility' that had been so essentially characteristic of earlier melodrama. Whilst the morality of the heroine of toga melodrama remains entirely 'legible', the hero's position is no longer as readable, and it is in his potential illegibility that much of the drama lies. Moral clarity has been stripped from the hero of late nineteenth-century melodrama and has been replaced with the vision of the tormented relativist. Wilson Barrett's roles, as much as Henry Irving's, enact the protracted agonies of indecisive men whose object of desire is hedged about with moral absolutes.

Another factor lies behind American response to the toga play. The end of the nineteenth century and the early years of the twentieth were a period of high immigration and consequent competition for wealth and power amongst various ethnic groups. The need to assimilate new and potentially discordant cultures and the enactment of this assimilation are therefore close to the centre of American toga drama. Toga plays imply that a whole harmonious society can be created and maintained only if there is ascription to, and compliance with, the dominant European/Judaeo-Christian culture. The value of Christianity as an ethical core is never queried, but there is recurrent concern that the harmonizing of disparate cultures might be troubled or interrupted.

The 'Female Question' is not remote from toga drama. Whilst not directly associated with the crisis of confidence or general malaise which is held to be characteristic of the 1890s and beyond, the lengthy struggles to liberate and empower women—or to hold them in long-prescribed occupational, social, and domestic roles—continued on stage. In this respect, toga plays are not unique. They are merely a further extension, albeit addressing markedly different audiences and using significantly different theatrical means, of contemporary theatre pieces in the territories marked out by Arthur Pinero, Henry Arthur Jones, and Oscar Wilde. However, because toga plays use significantly different theatrical means from 'Society plays', they remained apart from the vilified 'Mayfair divorce comedy'. The women of toga drama are worthy of remark because it is chiefly they who act as catalysts for change in an empire that is conspicuously ruled by men. It is the Almidas, Mercias, and Lygias who speak for change and morally better lives. Like suffragettes and female suffragists, they can be urgent, sometimes strident, but they are not criticized as the suffragettes were. None is described by the vocabulary applied to the 'New Woman' of the 1890s: 'morbid', 'degenerate', 'neurotic', 'unnatural'. None is 'unlovely', but then, what heroine is? Lygia (the heroine of *Quo Vadis?*), for example, is a woman of means. But others are from what appears to be the Roman working class or lower middle class. Alike, they spurn men's wealth and luxury and seem prepared to make their own way and to live without men, placing vocation above marriage. By being Christian—and therefore critics of Rome—these women stand in opposition not only to imperialism, but to patriarchal authority.[19]

Because melodrama holds challenging and even antithetical possibilities in equilibrium, there are further possible readings of the toga heroine. She may also be perceived as an advocate for the domestic status quo in Britain and America, to the degree that her stand for moral change threatens her life or, as with Mercia in *The Sign of the Cross*, actually brings about her death. She may be an arbiter of morality, but Mercia's acceptance of her fate is passive, silent. This passivity may be a signal to some women in the audience, informing them to do their utmost to be good, to raise their children, to accept their lot—largely determined by the men in their life—and to be grateful. That way, no one is fed to the lions.

The 'adventuress', whether in toga drama or in wider spheres of melodrama, also belongs to the company of New Women. The adventuress does not even make her appearance in melodrama until women are active in seeking rights. Then, and only then—very likely as a warning paradigm of the woman who fails to observe society's tight norms and sexual taboos—did audiences observe the adventuress manipulate and seduce her way into positions of power and control. Whereas the Christian female is self-sacrificing and, to some degree, accommodating to received domestic norms, the adventuress, Roman or Egyptian, is intelligent, humorous, power-seeking, and, like some males, a source of disruption or havoc which must be subdued. Therefore, to the extent that older female stereotypes are challenged by new or refashioned stereotypes, the melodrama of the 1890s and the toga film, as much as Society plays, serve as testing-grounds for acceptable models of female behaviour.

Claims that toga plays reached new audiences are supported by evidence from detractors as well as from enthusiasts for these pieces. Indeed, it is difficult to determine from descriptions of spectators whether the reporter favours or condemns the event. What is likely is that, until the genre was recognized as distinct—1895 would be an appropriate date—toga dramas fared no better than any other class of melodrama in finding abnormally large audiences. From that date, revivals of earlier toga dramas began to find similarly predictable audiences. W. G. Wills and Henry Herman's *Claudian*, first performed

[19] Kestner, *Mythology and Misogyny*, 16.

in 1883, was regarded as an artistic achievement to be directed at more educated elements of society. Critics of the 1880s had been impressed by the artistry and the archaeological exactness of its scenery and costumes and by what they identified as the tragic grandeur of Wilson Barrett's performance in the title role. With *The Sign of the Cross*, all that changed. Clement Scott, a friend and adherent but an impartial critic of Barrett, described audiences at London's Lyric Theatre. Insisting of *The Sign of the Cross* that 'It suits the taste of a very large section of the public', Scott went on to remark:

It seems to be admitted that a considerable portion of those who witness it are people to whom the inside of a theatre is entirely unfamiliar—people who would hitherto have regarded the occupants of the pit of a playhouse as qualifying themselves with absolute certainty for that other pit whose bottomless depths are the eternal habitations of lost souls. Now, if the prejudice of such can be broken down, a distinct gain will have accrued to the drama, and in time they may be brought to visit theatres where, though the entertainment may not partake so largely of the nature of a sensational sermon, the lessons of life are pictured with more truth, and with the genuine morality of art rather than with that less respectable surface morality which usually underlies the workings of melodrama.[20]

G. W. Foote, perhaps Barrett's most clamorous adversary, who said of this play: 'General Booth should be delighted. It is a Salvation Army tragedy,' playfully noted of Barrett's audiences:

When I saw the performance at the Lyric Theatre I was struck by the novel character of the audience, which might almost be called a congregation. It seemed to be the emptyings of the churches and chapels of London. Most of the people appeared to be unused to such surroundings. They walked as if they were advancing to pews, and took their seats with an air of reverential expectation. Clericals, too, were present in remarkable abundance. There were parsons to right of me, parsons to left of me, parsons in front of me—though I cannot add that they volleyed and thundered. All the men and women, and all the third sex (as Sidney Smith called them) of clergymen, wore their best Sunday faces; and when the lights were turned very low in the auditorium, and pious opinions were ejaculated on stage, it was remarkably like a religious exercise. 'Ahs' and 'hear, hears' were distinctly audible, and I should not have been surprised at an 'amen' or a 'hallelujah'.[21]

Whilst both Scott and Foote are dryly cynical about Wilson Barrett's audiences, Barrett himself pursued this new constituency. His souvenir

[20] *Theatre*, 27 (Mas. 1896), 129.
[21] G. W. Foote, '*The Sign of the Cross*': A Candid Criticism of Mr Wilson Barrett's Play (London, 1896), 9–10.

programme for *The Sign of the Cross*, and frequent advertisements in theatrical journals cite favourable reviews in the religious press. It is equally clear, however, that Barrett was concerned to maintain a broad appeal, and he was also diligent in citing approval from the mainstream popular press. That he maintained this mix is ebulliently, perhaps excessively, described by Jerome K. Jerome: 'For once Clapham rubbed shoulders with Cadogan Square, and Palace Gardens and Belgravia took their place below South Kensington and Bloomsbury. The aristocracy of birth and the aristocracy of intellect lay jumbled hopelessly with the democracy in one friendly, admiring, and often touching sympathetic heap.'[22] Finally, what drew together these several strands of audience was the idea that they were witnessing, and enjoying as they witnessed, an enactment of history. In this respect, Barrett and others who offered toga plays were satisfying the Victorian predilection for 'rational recreation', entertainment that was edifying and 'improving' as well as pleasurable. Here, in toga dramas, were history lessons which were amusing, digestible, and moral and which purported to illustrate and to explain. In particular, toga pieces are fitful attempts to resolve within discrete dramatic narratives several centuries of conflict between worldly knowledge and Christian faith. Audiences with even a minimal knowledge of history or biblical text 'knew' that European Christianity eventually succeeded the Roman Empire, although they knew little of how this change came about. For those more familiar with historical narratives and the New Testament, there was a further history of conflict between Rome and its subject colonies, and a division emphasized between the world that belonged to the Caesars and their legions and a further world ruled by God and proclaimed by Christians.

The means employed to locate these plays within a historic frame were not new or unique. In some dramas—*Claudian* and *The Last Days of Pompeii*, for example—claims are made regarding the archaeological exactness of costumes and settings. The programme may state explicit dates. In other dramas—*The Sign of the Cross* and *Ben-Hur*, for instance—the historic past is verified by placing fictional characters in the immediate company of such genuine historical figures as the Emperor Nero, his Empress Poppaea, or the praetorian commander and fellow sensualist of Nero, Tigellinus. In the novel of *Ben-Hur* the character of Jesus appears at intervals; his actions are recorded, but his

---

[22] Jerome K. Jerome, 'The History of *The Sign of the Cross*', *Idler*, Mar. 1896: 273. For further comment about this article, see n. 50.

facial and bodily features remain indistinct to the reader. The stage and subsequent film versions of the novel manage to dramatize the presence of Jesus without incurring the censor's ban and whilst still maintaining historic credibility.

The texts to follow are of three full-length stage plays (*Claudian, The Sign of the Cross, Ben-Hur*) performed extensively in Britain and America, the brief scenario of a pyrodrama (*The Last Days of Pompeii*), again performed on both sides of the Atlantic, a scenario for a London music-hall dramatic sketch (*The Charioteers*), and two synopses with still images from two early toga films (*Ben-Hur* and *The Barbarian Ingomar*). One of the favourite subjects for toga films has been *Quo Vadis?*, adapted on each occasion from Henryk Sienkiewicz's 1896 novel of the same title. After the first version in 1913, remakes followed in 1924 and 1951. There are also two stage versions of this play, the first of which, by Stanislas Stange, was performed in New York in 1899. When the performing rights to this play were acquired by the Drury Lane management in 1900, Wilson Barrett rushed out his own version, playing the role of Petronius himself and with Maud Jeffries taking the role of Acte, Nero's freedwoman. Despite considerable publicity and a lawsuit which claimed that Barrett had plagiarized the plot of *The Sign of the Cross* from Sienkiewicz's novel, both stage adaptations of *Quo Vadis?* were only modestly successful. It was confirmed, moreover, that *The Sign of the Cross* had actually preceded Sienkiewicz's work by more than a full year and that resemblances, if more than coincidental, were in Barrett's favour. Both stage versions foundered on a sensation scene of Roman–Christian conflict which is effectively described in the novel and which can be effectively filmed— taking advantage of cutting, actors' doubles, and reverse angles—but which fails on the stage. This episode calls for Nero's vengeance to fall upon the persecuted *ingénue* Lygia, and for her to be cast into the arena, bound to the horns of a maddened aurochs. There she is rescued by Ursus, a Christian of great strength, who seizes the bull and wrestles it to the ground. Although posters for Barrett's and Stange's stage versions depict this scene, the action in the arena is merely narrated by characters who gaze into the wings and describe off-stage activity. Furthermore, the novel depends for its effect upon several plots which, although intersecting, constitute discrete narratives and which suffer in the abridgements required for stage drama, whereas such plays as *The Sign of the Cross* need no compression. In the light of these circumstances, it has been my decision to omit *Quo Vadis?* from this volume.

Toga Plays and Films

It is impossible for the scholar to point to the stage and identify the primal toga play. Toga plays were scarcely the first dramas to be set in ancient Rome, and there are many predecessors to the group described here. Mythic-historic Rome was a locale often visited by dramatists. However, the earlier Victorians preferred to take their Romans neat, undiluted by Christians, lions, or chariot-races. Joseph Addison's *Cato* (1713) is perhaps the most prominent of post-Jacobean plays on a Roman theme, and one that remained in the British and colonial repertoire for nearly a century after its début. For Addison, as for his successors, Rome was a metaphor in which audiences could recognize contemporary political issues and applaud speeches in which partisans of opposing political factions might discover reassuring sentiments and patriotic justification. Addison assumed the high-mindedness of Romans and dramatized their rhetorical eloquence, their outspokenness in the face of tyranny, and their readiness in resisting oppression to sacrifice themselves. London audiences still watched *Cato* in the final decades of the eighteenth century. George Washington, encamped with his troops at Valley Forge in the harsh winter of 1777–8, wrote that he wished he were home in Virginia to play *Cato*, which he read as a parable of liberty, in the family Christmas celebrations. James Sheridan Knowles's *Virginius* (1820) moves the Rome of Addison to the edge of the Victorian era, but refocuses on issues of conflict between social classes and on the cruel and arbitrary use of power. Like *Cato*, *Virginius* is a play in which supporters and opponents of the parliamentary reform could find speeches and actions to justify their politics and behaviour. Thus earlier nineteenth-century drama set in Rome tends to focus on issues of tyranny and liberty and on conflicts between the individual and the state. These Roman plays and/or novels are often associated with pro- or anti-republican political feeling or with ideologies and sentiments arising from the first and second Reform Bills. *Virginius* brings Rome into mid-century, and its continued presence in the repertoire confirms that audiences still found matters to applaud. What divides toga plays from this earlier tradition is decadent Romans, Christians, and lions.

Of numerous texts, only one, Edward Bulwer-Lytton's *The Last Days of Pompeii*, makes its way from the second quarter of the century into the final quarter. This outdoor pyrodrama—the term for a firework-spectacle melodrama—contained a full complement of decadent Romans, virtuous Christians, and voracious lions. *The Last Days of Pompeii*, first read as a novel in 1834, was adapted for the stage by John Baldwin Buckstone in the same year and, in 1835, in a competing version by Edward Fitzball. Neither version was sufficiently successful to keep the subject in the conventional theatrical repertoire. Thirty-seven years later, in 1872, a version by John Oxenford was a brief success but again there was no sustained interest in a conflict between Christian victims and Roman oppressors.

American experiences of plays on Roman themes are chiefly centred in the 1830s, notably with Robert Montgomery Bird's *The Gladiator* (1831) and Louisa Medina's spectacular adaptation of *The Last Days of Pompeii* (1835). The American theatre historian Bruce McConachie[23] identifies these dramas as interacting with, expressing, and partly creating the populist Democratic politics of Andrew Jackson and the Jacksonian era of American history. McConachie also associates *The Gladiator* with the theatrical and public persona of America's leading actor, Edwin Forrest, whose repertoire was built on oppositional figures of individual strength and charismatic grandeur who ultimately sacrificed themselves for cowed and leaderless populaces. McConachie cites Medina's *The Last Days of Pompeii* as expressing the affirmation of 'yeoman ideals ... working class solidarity ... and a millennial end to villainy' as it translates Bulwer-Lytton's novel into 'Bowery' spectacle. He further points out that the stage lives of these plays was finite; they were confined to a brief period of American history and were replaced by other non-Roman metaphors with the passage of time and events.

One of the first plays, British or American, to set out the scenic conventions of toga drama is Lord Alfred Tennyson's *The Cup* (1881). Henry Irving staged the play as a short poetic drama, not a full evening's entertainment by the standards of the 1880s, with himself and Ellen Terry in the principal roles. *The Cup* enacts a variant of the Bathsheba, Uriah, and David episodes of Samuel—or the Gertrude, Hamlet, and Claudius triangle—in which a loyal queen-wife (Terry) is pursued by the local Roman tetrarch (Irving), and her king-husband is slain. Unlike Gertrude and Bathsheba, *The Cup*'s queen does not succumb to her new consort, but kills herself with a poisoned draught. What distinguished the play was the artistry and 'archaeology' of the settings, designed and painted by Lawrence Alma-Tadema, and the costumes by E. W. Godwin. Together these artists created the luminous exoticism that can be observed in Alma-Tadema's Roman paintings and that became the measure of subsequent Roman stage sets.

---

[23] Bruce A. McConachie, *Melodramatic Formations: American Theatre and Society, 1820–1870*, (Iowa City, Ia., 1992), 98–155.

Edwin Long, *Diana or Christ? Let her cast the incense—but one grain and she is free,* 1889. (Blackburn Museum and Art Gallery)

Poster for *Quo Vadis?* (S. Stange's adaptation), *c*.1901

THE MUSIC OF TOGA DRAMA

Katherine Preston

A study of toga dramas cannot be complete without some discussion of the musical component, for such music was (and is) an essential element of all melodrama. It is unfortunate, therefore, that very little research has been conducted by music historians into this interesting topic. Reasons for this lacuna become abundantly clear as soon as one initiates such an investigation, for the sources are, at best, meagre.

Theatre historians often have scripts with which to commence their research, which can be fleshed out with additional information from reviews, financial records, contemporary commentary, and the like. This basic source of information, however, is often lacking for the music historian. Very little of the incidental music to theatrical works mounted in the nineteenth century was ever published, and manuscript scores are scarce. Judging by the dearth of musical manuscripts, one can only conclude that the music to such productions was rarely notated: evidence suggests that the accompaniments to many melodramas were pastiches—cobbled together from pre-existing scores.

Full scores are extant for some toga plays, however, and some incidental music survives from others. Furthermore, there are bits of information about the composers associated with toga plays, and a rich body of information about the music that accompanied early films. By pulling together these fragments, it is possible to draw some conclusions about the nature of the music associated with toga dramas.

First, however, it is essential to emphasize the importance of music to the successful production of toga plays. Melodramatic music—performed by the theatre orchestra either as background to speech, or as an accompaniment to silent events on stage (pantomime, tableaux vivants, and the like)—helped audiences to know how to react to, or interpret, the dramatic event. Music underscores and accentuates each situation and passion portrayed on the stage. Melodic fragments (known as motifs) can be assigned to specific characters, emotions, or even concepts. Through reiteration by the orchestra, the audience quickly learns which melody is connected with which character or idea. As an example of the latter, Christians in toga plays appear, move, pray, are tortured, encounter the presence of Jesus, are cured of leprosy, and die to music evocative of hymns or other religious compositions. Romans, on the other hand, make love, gamble, race chariots, plot evil deeds, and go to war to music of a frivolous, licentious, or martial character. In more specific situations, motifs can be a useful dramatic tool. For example, they can be used by the orchestra to refer to a character who is not present on the stage; they can also inform the audience that what is being said or portrayed has a subtext. For example, if a character articulates a particular idea or emotion, but is accompanied by music that is clearly associated with something else, the audience can recognize the conflict. If a character speaks words of love and truth while accompanied by music that is dissonant or unsetting, the character's veracity is called into question. (This technique, of course, is familiar to opera-lovers.) In addition, the composer of melodramatic music can employ melodic 'melos', little snippets of evocative music to highlight dramatic events. 'Hurry music', 'plaintive music', 'sneaky music', and other musical fragments that are similarly suggestive amplify whatever emotion is being portrayed. Finally, entrances by important characters are almost automatically announced in some manner by the orchestra, and, when the curtain rises, the orchestra generally performs music that is appropriate to each new scene. In some toga plays the music is almost continuous; in others it is used somewhat—but only somewhat—more sparingly. It should be clear, in any case, that the musical accompaniment to these plays is an essential part of the whole.

Of the seven toga dramas represented in this volume, there is only one for which a full score exists: *Ben-Hur*. The score is extant in both published piano-vocal and unpublished full orchestral versions, and was written in 1899 by Edgar Stillman Kelley (1857–1944), an American composer, writer, and music teacher. Kelley was awarded the commission only after Edward MacDowell (1860–1908), the most prominent American composer of the time, declined and suggested Kelley as alternative.[24]

Kelley's musical style reflects his solid training in the German school (he had studied in Stuttgart for four years). He was an admirer of Richard Wagner, as is clear from his harmonic vocabulary: the music is full of constant modulations and somewhat dissonant-sounding diminished chords, both of which create a sense of harmonic instability.

[24] Edgar Stillman Kelley, 'Great Yesterdays in Music', *Étude*, Mar. 1944: 141–52.

To modern ears, *Ben-Hur* might sound somewhat dated; to his con-
temporaries, however, the work was quite modern. The respected
Boston music critic William Apthorp, for example, described the work
as 'modern, even ultra-modern, in spirit, modern in its feeling, modern in harmony, melody, and colouring'.[25] Kelley's frequent use of
motifs (or, to use Wagner's term, *leitmotifs*) is similarly Wagnerian. In
the orchestral Prelude, for example, the composer introduces at least
three musical motifs: Ben-Hur, 'misfortune and ruin,' and 'vengeance';
all reappear at later points in the play. The Prelude itself is a vivid
musical illustration of the dramatic Prelude described in the 'Synopsis
of Scenes' and enacted without speech: it is in three parts, entitled
'The Prophecy', 'The Approach of the Magi', and 'The Star in the
East'.

Kelley's score is more unified musically and larger in scope than
standard melodramatic incidental music scores. In addition to the
Germanic characteristics, the work was written for a large symphony
orchestra rather than for a theatre orchestra. Kelley was also a skilled
contrapuntist, and his numerous choral numbers, which tend towards
the imitative, are somewhat reminiscent of the old-fashioned choral
style of Handel or Mendelssohn. Some of Kelley's melodies are ap-
propriately evocative of Middle Eastern music. None is particularly
modal in construction, and to the modern ear (accustomed to the more
authentic Eastern sound of the music of Béla Bartók and others) they
seem only mildly 'Eastern'. But the exoticism of the music must have
been more obvious at the time. A friend of the composer's wife, for
example, wrote in 1900 that she found the music to *Ben-Hur* to be 'so
thoroughly oriental in character that it did much to give the whole
production the proper atmosphere'.[26] The 'Song of Iras' (the play's
'hit' tune) is a good example of Kelley's melodic style. A paean to
Egypt, the song has a melody that is not so much modal (or 'Middle
Eastern') as excessively chromatic, with oddly shifting harmonies. As
such, it is Western in idiom, but at the same time somewhat odd- (or
'foreign') sounding.

Although *Ben-Hur* is the only toga piece of this collection to have
an extant score, most of the other works contain copious hints about
accompanimental music. Title-pages typically identify musical directors

---

[25] William Apthorp, programme notes of the Boston Symphony Orchestra, 28–9 Dec.
1900: Edgar Stillman Kelley Collection, Special Collections and Archives, Miami
University, Oxford, Ohio.

[26] Katherine Pease Norton to Jessie Stillman Kelley (autograph letter, signed), 7 Jan.
1900: Edgar Stillman Kelley Collection.

or composers; most works also have references to music ('trumpet heard' etc.) in their scripts. A quick perusal of *The Sign of the Cross*, for example, indicates clearly how vital music was to the play. On the title-page we find listed not only the musical director (and incidental-music composer), Edward Jones, but also a dancer, two vocal soloists, and the 'boys of Mr Steadman's choir'.[27] In the opening scene alone there are two music-related directions. First we are informed that 'music [is] heard off R.U.E. of Song', and then, during the subsequent on-stage performance of this song (by soloists and choir), a dance occurs. It is obvious that this song, chorus, and dance are important, but there are further logical places for music in this scene. Soon after the song, 'a trumpet is heard' when Marcus enters with his soldiers. Of course, it was routine melodramatic practice for entrances by important characters to be heralded (sometimes quite literally) by the orchestra—whether or not this direction was given in the script. It is likewise plausible that, when the curtain rose for this opening scene, the orchestra played music evocative of 'A street in Rome . . . Citizens, pedlars &c. grouped about the stage.' And certain portions of the dialogue might have been spoken over melodramatic music, despite the absence of such directions in the script.

Of particular interest in *The Sign of the Cross*, however, is the crucial role of music in one of the pivotal scenes (III. iii): an orgy in Marcus's house (represented musically by the Romans' performance of the 'Song of Love') is interrupted—and subsequently vanquished—by the Christians' hymn, 'Shepherd of Souls'. Edward Jones's hymn (a rather straightforward and harmonically tame parlour tune with two verses), in fact, functions as something of a *leitmotif* for the Christians throughout the play. It keeps popping up in reference to these per-secuted individuals: in Act II, scene iii, when Christians are worship-ping in the grove; in Act III, scene iii, when the hymn is heard but faintly; and, finally, in the closing scene of the play, when the martyrs sing the hymn as they march into the arena to be devoured by lions.

Most of the toga dramas that lack full scores were accompanied by some composed incidental music (like that written by Edward Jones) as well as by the typical 'melos' that were the stock-in-trade of all theatre orchestras of the time. The importance of these 'melos'—

[27] Edward Jones, a prominent theatre musician and conductor in late 19th-century London, was musical director at the Court, Princess's, Adelphi, Duke of York's, and Lyric Theatres in London; he wrote incidental music to many stage plays, extravaganzas, comic operas, and musical farces. During his collaboration with Wilson Barrett, he wrote incidental music to both *Claudian* and *The Sign of the Cross*.

which were readily available from theatre-music publishers—has been amply demonstrated elsewhere.[28] Another source of musical accompaniment for toga plays, however, was music composed for other purposes: symphonic works, operas and operettas, dance music, and popular songs. Although there is little information about the use of such music for staged toga plays, there is now a new body of scholarly research on the music of early films—some of which were versions of toga plays—that we can utilize.[29] There should be few doubts concerning the close connections between the musical conventions of staged melodramas and those of early films. As one correspondent to the periodical *Moving Picture World* wrote in 1914: 'I am an old repertoire pianist and have little trouble "playing-up" to dramatic pictures, as I accompany them much as I would similar situations in plays.'[30]

For some films (but only for the longest and most important), full scores were commissioned; these circulated along with the film (sometimes with touring orchestras as well). This, however, was far from the norm. Much more common was the practice of assembling a musical pastiche from pre-existing sources. Information about these pastiches was disseminated by means of cue-sheets: lists of appropriate musical selections (in the order in which they are to be performed), and the suggested length of the 'cut' from the selection, and the relevant cues in the film. These sheets began to appear in the second decade of the twentieth century.[31] Cue-sheets were sometimes circulated by the distributor along with the film. They were also published regularly in *Moving Picture World*, where sometimes they represented the suggestions of the periodical's music columnist and at other times the recommendations of readers (sometimes local music-theatre directors). Performance manuals began to appear at about the same time. These were books of musical compositions arranged into various

[28] See e.g. Anne Dhu Shapiro, 'Action Music for American Pantomime and Melodrama, 1730–1913', *American Music*, 2/4 (Winter, 1984), 49–72; David Mayer and Matthew Scott, *Four Bars of 'Agit': Incidental Music for Victorian and Edwardian Melodrama* (London, 1983); David Mayer, 'The Music of Melodrama', in *Performance and Politics in Popular Drama* (Cambridge, 1980); and Katherine K. Preston, *Music for Hire: A Study of Professional Musicians in Washington, 1877–1900* (New York, 1992), ch. 3, 'Theater Work'.

[29] For much of my information on the music of early films I am greatly indebted to Martin Marks, whose *Music in the Silent Film: Contexts and Case Studies* (New York, 1993) deals in depth with this subject.

[30] *Moving Picture World*, 31 Jan. 1914: 534.

[31] The first film version of *Ben-Hur* (1907) and D. W. Griffith's *The Barbarian Ingomar* were too early for cue-sheets.

categories: 'Biblical or Sacred Scenes', 'Roman Music', 'Egyptian Music', 'Historical Subjects', and the like.[32]

The pre-composed selections suggested in such sources provide specific clues as to the nature of music considered appropriate for certain toga drama scenes. From the performance manuals we learn that, for 'Biblical pictures', 'any music that can be called grandioso, stately or heavy, [can] be played'; that 'Roman music' might include such selections as 'Ballet, Queen of Sheba' by Charles Gounod, 'Coronation March' by Giacomo Meyerbeer, or 'Roman Sketches' by Charles Griffes; and 'Egyptian' musical selections could include 'Nubian Face of the Nile' by Charles Wakefield Cadman, 'Egyptian Ballet' by Alexandre Luigini, or 'Ballet, Hérodiade' by Jules Massenet.[33] Extant cue-sheets from the films *Quo Vadis?*, *Cabiria*, and *Antonio e Cleopatra* suggest a similar eclectic mixture of known and unknown compositions and composers: selections from works by Felix Mendelssohn (*Fingal's Cave*), Richard Wagner (*Parsifal, The Ring*), Gioachino Rossini (*The Italian Girl in Algiers* and *William Tell*), Edvard Grieg (*Peer Gynt*), Giacomo Puccini (*Tosca*), as well as works by other 'mainstream' composers (Claude Debussy, César Cui, Pyotr Tchaikovsky, Camille Saint-Saëns, Franz von Suppé, and Charles Gounod), are mixed in with works by composers completely forgotten today, men named Rossi, Shelley, Langley ('Hurry Music No. 2'), Axt ('Allegro Misterioso'), Vannah, Lorraine, Cobb, and Ganne, who were probably exclusively theatre-music composers.[34] It might be worth pointing out that many of these 'classical' excerpts were familiar to audiences. As such, they came equipped with emotional connotations that could be used for evocative purposes.

The music of toga plays, therefore, could come from a variety of sources. It could be a combination of newly written music with

[32] Performance manuals: W. Tyacke George, *Playing to Pictures: A Guide for Pianists and Conductors of Motion Picture Theatres*, 2nd edn. (London, 1914); May Meskiman Mills, *The Pipe Organist's Complete Instruction and Reference Work on the Art of Photo Playing* (Philadelphia, 1922); Erno Rapée (comp.), *Encyclopaedia of Music for Pictures* (New York, 1970). Some later manuals are actually anthologies of musical scores, arranged in similar categories to those used in the performance manuals. See e.g. Erno Rapée (arr.), *Motion Picture Moods for Pianists and Organists: A Rapid-Reference Collection of Selected Pieces Adapted to Fifty-Two Moods and Situations* (New York, 1924; repr. 1970).

[33] For 'Biblical pictures', see George, *Playing to Pictures*, 17; 'Roman' music, see Mills, *The Pipe Organist's Instruction*, 50; 'Egyptian' music, see Rapée (arr.), *Motion Picture Moods*, 192.

[34] Sources of cue-sheets: *Quo Vadis?* is in the cue-sheet collection of the Theatre Arts Library at UCLA; a photocopy of the *Cabiria* cue-sheet is in the private collection of Martin Marks; suggestions for *Antonio e Cleopatra* are from *Motion Picture World*, 29 Aug. 1914.

pre-existing compositions, and it could include a liberal dose of 'melos'. Most toga plays—especially as mounted by touring companies in small or provincial theatres—were undoubtedly accompanied by a combination of these styles of music. What is crucial to our understanding of these plays, however, is a thorough recognition of the fact that music—in some guise—always had some significance in the production of these dramatic works.

CLAUDIAN
A Play in a Prologue and Three Acts
W. G. Wills and Henry Herman

The earliest toga drama to attract widespread public interest and to stimulate the divided critical response which attended many toga pieces is *Claudian* (1883), the product of a collaboration among four men: Henry Herman, who devised the play's structure and narrative, the poet-dramatist W. G. Wills, who provided the dialogue, E. W. Godwin, who again provided 'the archaeology of costumes &c.', and the actor-manager Wilson Barrett,[35] who produced the drama and performed the eponymous leading role. Herman had previously collaborated with Barrett on the text of an earlier successful play for the Princess's Theatre, *The Silver King* (1882), and now devised scenic machinery intended to simulate an earthquake. This earthquake was the motive for writing *Claudian*, and the effect made the end of the second act memorably exciting.

Unlike *The Last Days of Pompeii*, however, with its long-awaited sensational cataclysm, *Claudian* is not a play of scenic effects, but a drama of a man under a sentence that is at once righteous and appalling, a curse so terrible and unforgiving that critics and spectators wondered at its theological justness. But it was precisely this uncertain justice, weighted against unassuageable guilt and remorse, 'fettered to a never-ending melancholy',[36] that fascinated and drew sympathy more than it repelled. In this respect, *Claudian* resembles Barrett's earlier success as Wilfred Denver in *The Silver King*, who is plunged into a maelstrom of self-deception, flight, and disguise because he believes, wrongly, that he has committed a murder. Denver is innocent of the crime, but his life thereafter becomes an act of expiation and atonement, a search for 'pardon, forgiveness, peace'. The role is memorable for its line, 'O Lord, put back thy universe and give me yesterday'— Denver's recognition that a single headstrong act has changed his life

---

[35] Wilson Barrett's life (1846–1904) and career have been well documented by James Thomas, *The Art of the Actor Manager: Wilson Barrett and the Victorian Theatre* (Ann Arbor, Mich., 1984).

[36] Clement Scott, *Theatre*, 3 (Jan. 1884), 46.

for ever. Even more than Denver, Claudian suffers for his rash act of will and self-gratification. Here is pagan—Christian conflict, but with no space for resolution. Claudian is rapacious and decadent, but the drama leaves scant room for Roman and Christian to be reconciled, except at the expense of one or the other.

The curse follows from his own vanity, lust, and headstrong will when Claudian pursues a young married Christian woman to a sanctuary outside the city of Charydos, a Roman settlement in Asia Minor. Despite her attempt to take refuge with the resident holy man, Claudian abducts her, fatally assaults the hermit, and so shocks the young woman that she, too, dies. Before he dies, Holy Clement calls down a curse with no escape but one:

Be young forever through the centuries. See generations born, and age and die, and all who flattered, loved, or served thee—dust. Thy course like baneful star against the sky shall blight and wither all upon thy track. To love thee—or to be beloved by thee alike—shall poison, maim or kill. The innocent sunshine shall die out before thee, and the black shadow of misfortune follow. Thy soul shall hanker, thirst, and famish to do good and try in vain to do it. The happiness as pure and crystal at the well, touched by thy lips, shall muddy at its source. Thy pity shall envenom what 'twould soothe, be poison to the wound—till thou couldst pray for the hard heart again thou hadst today. Thy charity, which might have comforted one half the kingdom's poor, breed pestilence and ruin—until the vaulted rocks be split, a gulf be struck twixt thee and me, then thou shalt choose either to die or live accurst till doom. From dying lips this curse from heaven is fallen.

A century later, Claudian is still a young man.

Claudian is recognizable as a variant of the Wandering Jew or Flying Dutchman myth, or even as a distortion of the Midas legend, for whatever Claudian touches with love he destroys. But whereas the mythic fugitives suffer and move on, atonement for Claudian seems beyond reach. Thus the earthquake which kills so many people, the prophesied splitting of the vaulted rocks, is at first a calamity because it has excluded Claudian: 'And I alone cannot die.' But it at last allows choice and expiation. Picking himself from the wreckage of his home (the woman whom he has loved but feared to touch, swept away), Claudian may now sacrifice his own life to bring life and sight to Almida.

Critics found Herman and Wills's drama at times stilted and ungainly. The male characters were praised as effectively drawn, but the female roles were thought to be thin and occasionally silly. The play's eccentric theology was frequently questioned: what sort of holiness does Holy Clement represent? Is it holy to kill so many innocents, to maim and blind to avenge one sinner's transgressions? Is divine vengeance a part of Christian thought? There was admiration, however, for the play's evocation of an empire and its powerful ruling class which had become confused in their objectives and functions, and of a society which had misplaced compassion and had lost the capacity to govern itself. There was also praise for Wilson Barrett's performance which appeared to override objections to Claudian's behaviour. Clement Scott spoke for these audiences:

Morally considered, Claudian the Pagan is indefensible; but is there a woman in the audience who does not in her heart admire the grandeur of this man's hungry selfishness? Why then is the part so played? Not to advocate the lust of Claudians but to show what Claudians were when Byzantium became a second Rome under the sway of Constantine. It is a true picture . . . This Claudian is a flesh and blood realization of old Rome.[37]

Soon afterwards Scott was to write of Claudian: 'Such a play ought to be printed.'[38] But his enthusiasm was not to endure. When Claudian was returned to Barrett's repertoire to run with The Sign of the Cross, Scott began to criticize the play for awkwardnesses and infelicities of construction and characterization so especially evident in the comic scenes.

It was in Claudian that E. W. Godwin made an innovation that was to affect the appearance of heroes in future toga plays and films. Previous stage Romans wore the toga, which restricted gesture, or a short-sleeved garment terminating in a knee-length skirt not dissimilar to a gym-slip. Godwin devised for Barrett an abbreviated Roman costume, a short, close-fitting jewelled tunic, open at the chest, worn with fleshings and high boots, which became an athletic alternative to the toga. Barrett was to wear variants of this garment for the remainder of his career.[39]

Claudian remained in Wilson Barrett's London and touring repertoire and was seen in American cities when he toured there in 1886. As Barrett's management prospered, he sent out 'A' and 'B Company'

---

[37] Ibid. 47.
[38] Ibid., Apr. 1884: 220.
[39] Maria Wyke identifies the lightly clad Roman strong-men heroes of early Italian toga films ('Maciste') as objects of homoerotic interest, and goes on to describe classical 'beef-cake' cinema as a locus for homosexual viewing: 'Herculean Muscle: The Classicizing Rhetoric of Bodybuilding', in J. Porter (ed.), Constructing the Classical Body (Ann Arbor, Mich., forthcoming). Whilst there may have been a covert following of homosexuals for Barrett's Claudian or his other toga roles, there is no evidence that Barrett was aware of, or exploited, this possible aspect of his appeal.

tours of his repertoire and, still later, leased *Claudian* to other actor-
managers. A year after Barrett's death in July 1904, whilst London
audiences were attending *The Charioteers* (q.v.) at the Coliseum and
whilst early toga films were shown to music-hall spectators, *Claudian*,
with William McLaren as Claudian and Lilly C. Bandmann as Almida,
was on tour to Leicester and Sheffield, moving to the North of
England in November on a circuit that included a week each at
Bradford, Wigan, Burnley, and Hull.

Barrett's success as *Claudian* was an inducement for him to seek
other toga roles, which he alternated with such parts as Hamlet,
Wilfred Denver in *The Silver King*, the Revd Frank Thornhill in
George R. Sims's *The Golden Ladder*, and Dan in *Ben My Chree*—'girl
of my heart'—a drama of modern life set on the Isle of Man. Between
these roles, Barrett added a revival of *Junius* by Bulwer-Lytton in 1885,
Clito, which Barrett co-wrote with Sidney Grundy and in which he
played the eponymous sculptor, in 1886, and an adaptation by Addison
Bright of *Virginius* in 1893.

From the earliest of these toga plays Barrett had assembled a group
of professional colleagues—actors, artists, and musicians—who were
to be instrumental in shaping the genre. His supporting actress and
leading lady through the 1880s and early 1890s was Mary Eastlake,
who left Barrett only when he hesitated to marry her. Edward S.
Willard was especially effective when playing calculating villains, and
was somewhat squandered as Holy Clement. Charles Hudson, who
moved from Barrett's toga dramas into other West End toga pieces,
sustained the parts of Roman officials, and Barrett's brother George
specialized in low-comedy roles. George Barrett's disrespect for the
solemnity of toga drama was fearsome; he had the reputation of being
able to subvert painstaking 'archaeology' with sudden contemporary
ad libs. Responsibility for design remained with E. W. Godwin until
his death in 1886. Godwin in turn supervised the scene-painters Stafford
Hall and Walter Hann, and William Telbin. Lawrence Alma-Tadema
joined Barrett in 1893 to produce the set designs for *Virginius*. Incidental melodrama music was composed chiefly by Edward Jones, but
occasional songs were contributed by Sir Julius Benedict. The overall
cohesion of this group doubtless paved the way for the success of
The Sign of the Cross.

The text of *Claudian* used in this edition is that of the licensing copy
(Add. MS 53304-K) deposited with the Lord Chamberlain in October
1883. The text published here differs from the performance version to

the extent that, in the latter, Scenes 1 and 2 of Act I were conflated and placed in a single setting, the 'Vineyard near Charydos'. Spelling and punctuation have been regularized. Despite Clement Scott's repeated praise for the play, *Claudian* was never published.

The programme for the first production at the Royal Princess's Theatre described this as 'an entirely new and original play' and acknowledged the following: the plot, story, and construction of the play by Henry Herman; dialogue by W. G. Wills; Harvest Song in Act I by Sir Julius Benedict (soloist, Miss Eva Harrison); the scenery by Walter Hann, Stafford Hall, and William Telbin; the 'archaeology of costumes' by E. W. Godwin; the incidental music by Edward Jones (Almida's Song); the 'new tableau curtains' by Stafford Hall; and the production and direction of Wilson Barrett.

    The cast and settings (with designers) were as follows:

In the Prologue:
Claudian Andiates, a rich noble
    of Byzantium   Mr WILSON BARRETT
The Holy Clement   Mr E. S. WILLARD
Theorus, a sculptor   Mr FRANK COOPER
Zosimus, a schoolmaster   Mr F. HUNTLEY
Volpas, a patrician   Mr NEVILLE DOONE
Symachus, a tradesman   Mr C. FULTON
Sesiphon, a slave-dealer   Mr W. A. ELLIOTT
Demos, a gladiator   Mr H. EVANS
Captain of the Scythians   Mr PHILLIP MATTHEWS
Serena, a slave, the wife of Theorus Miss EMMELINE ORMSBY
Caris her child   Miss PHOEBE CARLO

Scene 1: Byzantium, AD 362 (WALTER HANN).

Scene 2: The Cave in the Forest near Byzantium (WALTER HANN).

A hundred years are supposed to elapse between the Prologue and the Play

In the Play: Mr WILSON BARRETT
Claudian Andiates   Mr CLIFFORD COOPER
Alcares, a wealthy farmer   Mr GEORGE BARRETT
Belos, a young farmer
Thariogalus, the Tetrarch of the
    province of Charydos   Mr CHARLES HUDSON

Agazil, a blacksmith	Mr WALTER SPEAKMAN
Rhamantes, Claudian's steward	Mr C. POLHILL
Officer of the Herculeans	Mr H. DE SOLLA
Goths of the Tetrarch's Guard	Messrs BURNAGE and BELTON
Edessa, daughter of Alcares	Miss HELEN VINCENT
Threna and Clia, peasant girls	Miss GARTH and Miss NELLIE PALMER
Galena, a tramp	Mrs HUNTLEY
Hera, her daughter	Miss MARY DICKENS
Sabella, Gratia, and Cloris, slaves in Claudian's palace	Miss HELEN BRUNO, Miss ALICE COOK, and Mr H. BESLEY
Almida, daughter of Alcares	Miss EASTLAKE

Act I: Vineyard near Charydos (WILLIAM TELBIN);

Act II: Scene 1: The City of Charydos in Bithnyia (STAFFORD HALL);

Scene 2: The Chamber in the Walls (STAFFORD HALL);

Scene 3: Claudian's Palace (WALTER HANN);

Act III: Claudian's Palace (WALTER HANN).

Persons Represented in the Prologue

CLAUDIAN ANDIATES, a rich noble of Byzantium

VOLPAS, a patrician

THEORUS, a sculptor

SYMACHUS and ZASIMUS, citizens of Byzantium

SESIPHON, a slave-dealer

DEMOS, a gladiator

THE HOLY CLEMENT

THE HERMIT

SERENA, a slave, wife of Theorus

CARENOS, her boy

Scene: Byzantium; Time: AD 360.

PROLOGUE

Scene 1

[SCENE: *A slave market outside the public baths of Byzantium. The entrance to the baths, at back of street leading downhill, approaches stage from L., whilst panorama R. partly shows the Bosporus and the Asiatic shore. Continual movement of citizens to and fro. As the scene opens, a patrician lady is carried past in her palanquin—a train of slaves, black and white, following—a party of Goths—soldiers—cross, entering the public baths, and half a dozen public dancers cross with their musical instruments. At the left side of the entrance to the baths about twelve or fifteen slaves of both sexes, but principally young (about two or three among them being black), are arranged. Some are standing, others are sitting in front of them.* SESIPHON, *the slave-dealer, is busy arranging them to the best advantage, whilst passers-by stop, look at, and sometimes examine them.* DEMOS, *the gladiator, lies half-asleep in the downstage R. of the passing crowd.* SYMACHUS *looks on, carelessly watching* SESIPHON]

SYMACHUS Well, friend Sesiphon, Valerian's death must needs be thy profit? These are his slaves is it not so?

SESIPHON Profit! Yes! But small account withal—Valerian spent his sustenance on his marbles, and flesh and blood was not much in his way for one so rich as he.

SYMACHUS 'Tis said he would have freed his slaves had he but lived— but weak with age and sad infirmity, was quite unable to endorse the scrolls and thus he died, and they are to be sold. His heirs will profit by it, and his soul will be the poorer.

[*Enter excitedly* ZASIMUS (*a stout tradesman of the period, broad and jovial in his manner*). *He crosses to* SESIPHON, *whom he slaps upon the shoulder*]

ZASIMUS He is coming! He'll pass here. He's even now upon his way to meet the prefect at the baths.

SYMACHUS Who, friend?

ZASIMUS Who? Why the greatest man in all Byzantium and the happiest—Claudian!

SYMACHUS He is powerful—how know you that he is happy?

ZASIMUS Why, what is happiness? He has money at will, youth, health, fame. He's like a sorcerer. Whatever he covets lies in his hand. He bids a palace rise, gardens, palm trees, forests—straight up they spring as the clouds lift up. They spring as the clouds lift from the vapoury south. You see these slaves. If he but raise a finger they are his.

DEMOS [*who has been listening, lazily raises himself on his elbow*] You talk of Claudian?

ZASIMUS [*not attending to him*] Slaves! We are his slaves. Scythian nobles and Eastern princes are his servitors. Not a province in his empire but where he claims estates. Now I'm a philosopher and a schoolmaster, and I tell you that contentment and learning are the highest good, but, when I see his chariot roll by, I shift uneasily in my stone chair—I press my weary forehead, and I envy him with all my heart. There's no power on earth like boundless wealth.

SYMACHUS There is greater power than wealth, friend Zasimus, a greater happiness. What say I? Wealth is but a curse unless 'tis used in heaven's service, and that being true—this Claudian should be wretched.

ZASIMUS What? In his purple robes and in his palace? Ah, now thou'st coming o'er us with my philosophy of content, merit and schooling.

SYMACHUS There is a littler chamber here, the heart. He may dwell in a palace, a temple built of gold and ivory, and yet that little chamber may be a vault or a torture room.

[*Enter* THEORUS]

ZASIMUS I know not. This I know—if he is wretched, would I had his misery. What say you Theorus? You are smiling.

THEORUS Well—I have reason. What's the question?

ZASIMUS Who is the happpest man in all this world?

THEORUS I know the happiest man.

ZASIMUS Well?

THEORUS I'll tell you presently. Go on! Go on!

DEMOS [*who has risen*] The happiest man! By Hercules! Surely it is Claudian. Firstly, you see he hath nothing to do but drink and feast and sleep. Pretty slaves to bear down the goblets, rattle the cymbals and play the pipes. That's what I call the first state of happiness. Secondly, he can kill. He has an enemy, say a hundred leagues away. He lifts his aim, so, points in his direction and puff! His foe disappears like a cloud of dust in the arena. Look you here, and mark it. Woe to the mortal man that stands in Claudian's way—who dares to let his shadow fall upon his path. Ye gods! Make me for an hour as strong as Claudian. I know whom I would kill.

ZASIMUS Well, Theorus—

THEORUS Wait. Let's hear the pious Symachus.

SYMACHUS The happiest man is he who does most good. The power from heaven that bids the dying child arise and live, that is the truest power my friends. Outside our holy city lives a holy man in a desert cave. His food is herb and water. His prayer can heal the sick, can stay the pestilence, can bring the rain upon the parching land. Those whom he blesses, they are blessed indeed. Each of his days is filled with good works, and he lives in communion with his god. That is true happiness. He is the happiest man in all the world.

ZASIMUS Theorus! You are smiling still. Come tell us. Who is the happiest?

THEORUS I am that man [laughing]. Claudian's wealth is naught to me. He has been rich too long. The happy man is he who has just won the inestimable prize, as I have done today. The holy man might bless. Can you make sunshine brighter by adding light? My cup of happiness is brimming over. Add no more drops for me.

ZASIMUS What if it broke—even in your hand?

THEORUS I'll drain it first. My wife Serena, till today a slave—today she will be mine and mine only. A week ago her master died. Today, as is by law ordained, his slaves are thrown upon the mart, and I buy my love.

DEMOS Then you are rich. She'll fetch a goodly price.

THEORUS Aye, I know it, for she is beautiful. To look on her makes other women plain. To hear her voice—all music after soundeth harsh. But I can buy her freedom. I've worked. I've slaved to earn the price! And, as I moulded at my clay, her face was ever present. When I would shape another form, still her beloved features came against my will. Under my chisel dawned her beauty even in the pure marble—and the world came to buy. As I first put by my savings, day by day, I murmured: 'One day she shall be mine alone—heaven in my arms.' Now I have a home for her among the vineyards yonder. She knows it not, but this evening she and my child shall enter it. I claim it. Friends, I am the happiest man alive. See! Here she comes!

      [Enter SERENA and her boy CARENOS. THEORUS and SERENA embrace]

THEORUS Mine own! I have waited for thee. The seconds seemed hours, and they will be centuries to me until you are mine alone.

SERENA I feared you might be late; I lingered, love, to make sure you would be here. I feared the shock to find myself alone, standing for sale. You have the money? All that was demanded?

THEORUS I will place it in the hands of Sesiphon forthwith. [*Catches up child and swings it in his arms*] Welcome little free man! You shall have flowers to cull, bright butterflies to chase and rosy apples dropping at your feet and rainbow fountains leaping in the court that you shall splash in, and green, boundless hills.

SYMACHUS God's blessing on ye both and on your child.

THEORUS I thank thee friend—

ZASIMUS And my best wishes also go with thee, and if ever thou shouldst be in need, the schoolmaster and the philosopher had the worldly wisdom to be thrifty of that same base gold that philosophy scorns, and would willingly make thee a sharer. My hand upon it friend, and my heart's best wishes go with thee.

THEORUS To thee my best thanks also. My happiness makes a coward of me. Excuse me, sirs. [*To* SERENA] Now for the form that makes you quite my own. [*Calls* SESIPHON] Have you prepared the scroll?

SESIPHON Sir, I would have you bridle your patience—these things take time, and she must stand among the rest awaiting your bidding, and the form and closing of the sale. Thus saith the statue. There is no other way.

THEORUS Then hasten, friend. You'll find included here, besides the 600 drachmas which you have demanded, a liberal gratuity. I am the only bidder that must be. Let it conclude at once.

SESIPHON Sir, if I must be plain with you—there is no other way—she must stand there, and you must wait. Besides, my patron, the great Claudian, passes here, and this, my poor batch today, needs the attraction of her beauty.

THEORUS Claudian! The profligate!

SESIPHON Fear not! He comes not as a purchaser.

THEORUS Nay, not one moment! There's danger.—Before he comes! Be done before he comes!

SERENA Don't fear love! I'll take my stand. A moment's humiliation to give a relish to our pride, and the gladness which follows close at hand.

THEORUS Joy makes a coward of me. I feel this moment, whilst I hold thee fast, as if I fain must be with thee, ne'er lose my grasp till we have reached our home, our happy home.

DEMOS Take heart my friend, there is no danger.

THEORUS There's danger in delay. He might be tempted.

ZASIMUS Fut, man! Why should he who boasts a flock envy thee thy poor ewe lamb.

SYMACHUS He'll pass here as he always does, and take no note of thee
or her.

THEORUS [to SERENA] Stand there out of sight behind the others.
There's a shadow on my heart.

[Enter CLAUDIAN and his retinue. His Scythian guards precede and
follow him. Two slaves with peacock fans attend him. With him, a
cringeing old sycophant of the patrician order, VOLPAS, is gaudily
dressed. CLAUDIAN is dressed richly but in the best of taste. General
sensation. Everybody stands aside. The crowd bow low]

CLAUDIAN [sees DEMOS] What! My old acquaintance, Demos.

DEMOS Patron, my humble service.

CLAUDIAN You are idle. No plates to break or cups to crack. Mischief
and idleness are dangerous mates.

DEMOS Give me a task, patron! Bid me thrash an enemy or slit a
wizzen or some such light and fancy work, and I am your servant.

CLAUDIAN Dost thou fight at the coming games?

DEMOS I am in training, patron.

CLAUDIAN In training! Why, thou hast drunk an amphora of wine
before sunrise. Then baked in the sun till noon like a walrus. Now
thou will swell thyself with beans till thou dost find some one who'll
pay for thy drink till sunset. Then brawl and orgy until midnight.
When thou comest to fight, thou'll have as much wind as old
Silenus on his ass.

DEMOS No, by Hercules, patron, you do me wrong. I am a pious
ruffian enough. I run and wrestle and swim all the morning. Of
evenings I play in the temple, that I might take mine enemy
unawares and have him under the rib. Here I stand, patron. Do me
the honour to knock me down. I like it.

CLAUDIAN Another amphora of wine will lay thee on thy back.

DEMOS Now—now—feel my sword arm, patron—springy as a cock.
Feel that!

CLAUDIAN [pointing to VOLPAS] Here is a great patron of thy sword.

DEMOS Feel here, little sir.

VOLPAS [feeling his arm] Very fine creature. Ah, good fellow, I had an
arm once. Hah! Hah! Hah! [Strikes DEMOS a blow on the chest]

DEMOS Ho! Ho! [Hits VOLPAS a little playful tap and VOLPAS staggers
back]

VOLPAS Ha! Thou'rt a stout fellow.

CLAUDIAN Thou wert almost knocked down by the wind of his fist.
Come, give him a gold piece for his good office.

VOLPAS Illustrious! Of late I have so much cost in thy train.

CLAUDIAN Why, thou miser—the mouth of thy purse is as close as an oyster when thy shouldst give, and as loose as a gudgeon's mouth when thou wouldst receive. Thy bounty is as costive as a frost—thy greediness as an artesian well, never to be filled.

DEMOS My obedient thanks, patron, for thy favours.

CLAUDIAN I'll meet thee later in the circus, and do a favour to the world.

DEMOS What's that, patron?

CLAUDIAN Kill you!

VOLPAS Good, good, wondrous witty—by Bacchus, wondrous witty.

DEMOS [rather taken aback] I thank you humbly, patron.

CLAUDIAN [giving him money] Till then, get drunk.

[DEMOS looks at the money and exits L.U.E.]

VOLPAS You speak like Apollo. You should have a temple most illustrious.

CLAUDIAN Call it the temple of Mammon. Thou shalt to the High Priest—and steal the offerings.

VOLPAS The worshippers shall be women.

CLAUDIAN Now love forfend! I'd sooner be yelped at by the street dogs. A worshipping woman would reduce the strongest brain to pulp within the two moons.

VOLPAS What epigram! The beauty of a god. Grace and wit in every word.

CLAUDIAN [interrupting] Stay, old caterpillar. I tire of your crawling. Feed on the green leaf at your will, but no more shine. [Sees SESIPHON] Why, Sesiphon. What a small lot today.

[VOLPAS occupies himself by examining the slaves]

SESIPHON These are the slaves of old Valerian, patron, who died last week. Will your honour wait?

CLAUDIAN No! I am in no humour for such paltry bargains. Come sirs.

[Exit with retinue. VOLPAS remains]

THEORUS Thank heaven—he's gone.

[VOLPAS, who has been examining the slave girls, suddenly spies SERENA, who has been hiding herself behind the others]

VOLPAS [to SESIPHON] Ah—what is this? You hide your choicest goods.

SESIPHON [intentionally looking another way] This woman, sir?

VOLPAS [pointing to SERENA, who stands panting with fright] No rogue! That one! Why, she is so beautiful.

SESIPHON [curtly] Oh, she's not for sale.

VOLPAS Why is she here then?

[SESIPHON *does not reply, but tries to walk away*]

VOLPAS [*catches him by the shoulder*] Nay, I insist. She is for sale. I know it. Her price?

SESIPHON Since you must—600 drachmas.

VOLPAS I give 700.

SERENA [*sinks on her knees*] Merciful heaven, help me now.

THEORUS I buy her, sir. Although a slave, she is my wife.

VOLPAS Your wife! You really mean it, sir. Gently my young friend. She goes to him who thinks her worth the most. 700 drachmas I have offered. What is your bidding, sir?

THEORUS [*to* ZASIMUS] Help me, friend, in my despair. These 600 drachmas were all the money I had saved, but I have goods, a house, and can work. I'll give thee any bond that thou mayst choose, myself, my life, my liberty—if that thou will demand—but money, money, money—I must have money—lend me money.

ZASIMUS I'll do it—and gladly too. Here is this purse, thoult find 200 drachmas. I hope thou mayst succeed.

THEORUS [*to* SESIPHON] 800 drachmas will I give—a hundred more than he. [*To* VOLPAS] Surely, sir, this is most cruel sport. Your age should teach you to respect the happiness of youth. Let it end.

VOLPAS The happiness of youth! Are we to grovel in the dust when we are old and chew the cud of misery? 'Zounds, man! The blood still courses hotly in these veins, and beauty still gives zest to life. 800 say you. 900 will I give and think the price but small.

THEORUS [*to* ZASIMUS] 200 more. Lend me 200 more.

ZASIMUS [*after a pause*] Well! I will be bond for thee.

THEORUS You hear this, Sesiphon? 1,000 drachmas is my bidding—400 more than you did ask for her. Come—be satisfied. Conclude the sale.

VOLPAS Nay, stay—

THEORUS No, not a moment—

VOLPAS Stay me, friend—I must speak another word.

[CLAUDIAN *has re-entered with his retinue during the finish of this scene*]

CLAUDIAN [*to* VOLPAS, *who tries to sneak away*] What is this? The old spider caught in the cobweb. Old Volpas caught by a woman—and by Mercury! The patron of all roguery—here's a diamond among the glass beads. Stand aside, Volpas. The jackal is not served before the lion.

SESIPHON Are you in earnest, patron?

THEORUS [*to* CLAUDIAN] This woman is my wife. You know me, sir, Theorus is my name.

CLAUDIAN [*politely*] Byzantium knows thee well.

THEORUS I purchase her.

CLAUDIAN But she is not yet sold.

THEORUS Nothing remains but the last form to complete the sale.

CLAUDIAN But she is not yet sold.

THEORUS [*excitedly*] To all intents. Sesiphon has agreed to take my gold.

CLAUDIAN But she is not yet sold.

THEORUS O sir, you will not hinder.

CLAUDIAN Assuredly not. Why should you lose heart?

THEORUS You yield?

CLAUDIAN No.

THEORUS [*helplessly*] What do you mean?

CLAUDIAN Outbid me.

THEORUS I am but poor. The saving of my life and what I borrowed from my friend but barely meets the sum. What can I do?

CLAUDIAN There again you fail in resource. Spend the money. I care not. I offer 2,000 drachmas for this woman.

[THEORUS *stands aghast and paralysed*]

SERENA [*to* CLAUDIAN] O sir, this is some dreadful pleasantry.

CLAUDIAN It might have been no more, but thou art pretty—I like thee, and I will buy thee.

SERENA But sir, I am a mother and a wife. A happy home awaits me.

CLAUDIAN Aye, it does, pretty one. A palace—music and feasting [and] jewels. These are what a praying woman thinks of through her prayers, whate'er her lips may utter.

THEORUS [*hotly*] Once again! I am her husband.

CLAUDIAN Oh, thou art her husband. Let me look at thee. [*To his retinue*] What think you, gentlemen? A husband is not the word to conjure by with me. How by the radiant Venus who first made 'husband' sound ridiculous, this husband giveth relish to my prize. 'Tis like the ruddy cross upon the sheep that's marked for sale. [*To* SERENA] I will relieve thee of one bond today, if not two. [*To* SESIPHON] See her sent to my villa within the hour.

SERENA [*throws herself at his feet*] O sir—great sir—you have not heard aught. I am all but free. 'Twas like a birth of freedom in my beloved husband's home. You cannot see how piteous is our cause. We have no advocate to plead for us with passionate eloquence, or you would melt. This day was longed for—year by year. 'Twas the one solace in my slavery—that and my child. Come [*to* CARENOS]. Kneel with me.

CLAUDIAN Most eloquent! Now wert thou struck in marble in thy husband's chisel, then I could worship thee, but beauteous flesh and blood I can but love. I have been moved by supplicating grief upon a tablet. But tears upon a soft cheek, a heaving bosom but stimulates the sale. [*To* SESIPHON] Come, I will double you my offer. I must own her. She is mine.

SERENA [*rising*] I thought it was the privilege of power to aid the friendless, but not to trample on them. I will appeal for justice to the town.

CLAUDIAN [*laughing*] Why, what to do is this? Hearken my girl. See how these gentlemen uplift their brows at all these charges—cruelty, injustice. [*With sudden sternness*] Are you for sale? Your silence makes confession. You stand in the market. This old gentleman bid for you—I come in and have outbid and bought you.

SERENA Oh, let me—

CLAUDIAN [*interrupting*] Slaves should be mute—eyes, hands—no tongue. Conclude the sale.

THEORUS Hear, sir—

CLAUDIAN I'm weary of this squabble. [*To* VOLPAS] Give him that diamond on thy finger!

VOLPAS What? This invaluable stone! A gift from thy gracious self—its only value.

CLAUDIAN Give it.

[VOLPAS *gives it reluctantly.* THEORUS *pitches it away.* VOLPAS *tries to find it but fails*]

THEORUS Perish thou brash, thou robber of a jewel, which all thy wealth can never equal. I will not fawn or supplicate. I'll tell thee what thou art. A profligate whose impious will stops not at sacrilege and mocks at all that's good and pure and just. Take the defiance of a desperate man, whose hopes on earth thou wouldst destroy—whose home is desolate—his hearth defiled. I know her. She will pine and, timeless die, and so escape her bondage, cruel tyrant.

CLAUDIAN A prophet! Ah good fellow, you don't know women. That diamond which you tossed away so scornfully, would put you from her memory. I watched her longing eye that followed it.

THEORUS [*pushing at him*] Liar, too!

CLAUDIAN [*holds him with one hand as with a vice*] Fool! To measure thy waspish strength with mine. You'd better grip a tiger in the arena—I'll not punish thee. See her sent to my villa straight, and you, my Scythians, guard her thither.

[*Six or eight of the Scythians surround* SERENA]

CLAUDIAN Come, gentleman. More worthy sport awaits us at the circus.

[*Exeunt* CLAUDIAN, VOLPAS, *and retinue, except Scythians who guard* SERENA. *Citizens begin to gather*]

THEORUS [*rising*] Those arms are nerveless that should strangle him, and yet my cause should blunt the Scythian swords upraised against me. Is there no aid, no justice? Must I lose the light of my life, my patient hands glued to my side?

ZASIMUS It is the law—be patient.

THEORUS Patient! With tearing pincers at my heart! Ho! Zasimus! Symachus! Friends, citizens of Byzantium. Will ye look on the while a silk-clad tyrant tramples down the fellow citizen and outrages his home? They tear my wife from me. Ye who have wives, sisters, and mothers—will ye stand here and see it? If ye are dumb, these stones will cry out. She goes to bondage, shame, and death.

CROWD Shame! Shame! Shame!

THEORUS Aye, they cry shame and will not stir. [*To soldiers*] Surrender her to me, and all this gold I'll fling amongst you from my own hands.

ZASIMUS They dare not do it. You know well. Lead her away.

[*The Scythians make an attempt to drag her away. The crowd gets more and more excited as* SERENA *is subjected to ill-usage*]

THEORUS Help me or not! Single-handed I will rescue her or die upon their swords.

[THEORUS *makes a short rush.* ZASIMUS *stops him. In the mean time the child tries to rush to his mother and is knocked over by one of the Scythians. The crowd push at the Scythian, knock him over and disarm him, and one of the crowd drags the child away. The guards again attempt to drag* SERENA *away. The crowd, now furious, shout 'Brutes', 'Let her go', and finally rush at the Scythians.* THEORUS *snatches up his child, and drags* SERENA *from them.* ZASIMUS, SYMACHUS, *and the crowd overpower the Scythians*]

THEORUS [*to* SERENA] Fly to sanctuary! To the Holy Clement! It is your only chance! I will guard our child. Not a word! Claudian may return. Haste! Fly! [*as they move off*]

[*Scene changes*]

Scene 2

[SCENE: *Cavernous ruins in the midst of a dense forest. A flight of rocks leads like steps down to the stage. Moonlight. Enter* SERENA *down rocks, calling as she proceeds*]

SERENA Father! Father! Father! Oh, rescue! A poor slave, I come to ask for sanctuary. Father! Father!

[*Enter* CLEMENT, *a venerable old man*]

CLEMENT A woman's troubled cry. [*She kneels*] What wouldst thou, daughter?

SERENA Father, I am pursued. If ever there were need to interpose in mercy, it is the hour.

CLEMENT [*lifts her*] Who art thou?

SERENA Thou knowst the poor slave Serena. Often thy counsels have brought aid and comfort to my Theorus.

CLEMENT I know thy history. What is thy trouble, daughter?

SERENA The wreck of my life! Claudian the Pagan had bought me in the market above my hapless husband. The happiest sun that ever dawned on earth will set on our destruction unless thy saintly power can rescue us.

CLEMENT Be comforted! Take breath! Here thou art safe awhile! Thou art pursued?

SERENA I know not. But my terror made every sound a step. Hush!

CLEMENT [*kindly*] There's nothing.

SERENA How hath this cruel man the power to work such evil.

CLEMENT Unto the wicked man is often granted time to fill up the measure of his guilt.

SERENA He may yet fulfil it. Then we are lost.

CLEMENT Be patient, and be trustful, not in man.

SERENA Hast thou not power to save me—by thy word and thy uplifted hand?

CLEMENT My strength is not my own. The feeble voice of age were powerless to save thee, as the wind-tossed seagull's cry to stay a storm—this hand a wand of willow against the man of violence and wrong. It is the might above inspires my voice. In that we both must trust. Be of good cheer. All that I can do, I will. I give thee refuge. Few dare intrude in holy sanctuary.

SERENA Hark! A step! A heavy step?

[CLEMENT *rises and listens*]

SERENA If I be seized by him, I'll pray for death to free me. [*Goes L.*]

CLEMENT Comfort thee, daughter, and be calm!

[*Enter* CLAUDIAN]

CLAUDIAN So, I tracked thee down, most mutinous beauty. I'll clip your wings henceforth.

CLEMENT This is sanctuary! Respect it!

CLAUDIAN Aye, as I would thy church's. Sanctuary! No—not Diana's temple.

CLEMENT Sir, this woman you pursue is ringed around and shielded by the sacred name of 'wife'—which even pagans treat with reverence.

CLAUDIAN This woman is my slave. That name annuls the sacredness of wife. And who art thou to break thy country's laws, and hide away my bondswoman?

[CLEMENT *stands between*]

CLEMENT I am a humble servant of a god unknown to thee, but I am fellow man, and I would move thy pity.

CLAUDIAN I pity thee, old man. A smile of pity. Stand aside.

CLEMENT Not till you add another crime to all the reckless score. Whilst I have life to stand 'twixt her and her destroyer, I'll oppose thee. Do not approach!

CLAUDIAN Stout for a greybeard! So thou dost work miracles! It is the fitting moment. It seems, old man, my gods, Venus and Mars, who give her to my hands, are mightier than thine. A morning gossamer might easier baulk my step to that I own. [*Mockingly*] Why dost thou not call the lighting back from heaven to strike me where I stand?

CLEMENT If I could call the lighting, I'd forbear—nor send thee sin-laden to thine account.

CLAUDIAN I am much bounden to thee for thy forbearance. [*Mockingly*] But why not strike a gulf between us now, or bid the vaulted rocks to split and fall, and mass themselves between us a granite barrier? The echo of my laughter in their crannies would be thy only answer. I advance. Beware!

CLEMENT Not while I live shalt thou commit sacrilege.

CLAUDIAN Aside, thou dotard! Or call on thy deity. Try if he shield thy bosom from this strike! [*Stabs him*] Old meddler! On thy head doth rest thy blood. [*Raises the fainting figure of* SERENA] Now, thou pale beauteous thing, I hold thee safe. [*Kisses her*] Ah, to command such bliss perennial, would I were young forever.

CLEMENT [*raising himself to his full height*] Be young for ever through the centuries. See generations born, and age, and die, and all who flattered, loved, or served thee—dust. Thy course like baneful star across the sky shall blight and wither all upon thy track. To love thee or to be beloved by thee alike shall poison, maim or kill. The innocent sunshine shall die out before thee, and the black shadow of misfortune follow. Thy soul shall hanker, thirst, and famish to do good, and try in vain to do it. The happiness as pure and crystal at the well, touched by thy lips, shall muddy at its source. Thy pity shall envenom what 'twould soothe. Be poison to the wound—till thou couldst pray for the hard heart again thou hadst today. Thy charity, which might have comforted one half of the kingdom's poor, breed pestilence and ruin—until the vaulted rocks be split, a gulf be struck 'twixt thee and me, then thou shalt choose either to die or live accurst till doom. From dying lips this curse from heaven is fallen.

[CLEMENT *dies*]

CLAUDIAN [*violently agitated*] Mercy! Mercy! Revoke it! O revoke it! O revoke thy curse on me. My heart stands still! My blood runs icy! An awful shadow seems to hang above me like an eclipse. My pride of life is dead. [*Looks towards* SERENA] She revives! 'Tis in my power to do one deed of mercy.

SERENA [*faintly*] Spare us!

CLAUDIAN [*in violent agitation*] Spare thee? I'll give thee back all thou hast lost to thine husband's arms again, thou poor wronged one, if thou wilt grant me pardon. I will pour gentle benefits upon thee like blessings year by year—wealth, honour, service—and [*breaking down*] thou wilt pray for me. Pray to thy god that he will pardon. That I too may share the blessings of his forgiveness. [*Aside*] How white she grows!

SERENA I forgive thee all.

CLAUDIAN Then here is thy first blessing. Thou art free.

SERENA [*faintly*] O happy—[*falls back dead*]

CLAUDIAN [*looking at her*] Dead! [*horror-stricken*] My first good deed, like a poisonous snake hath struck her dead. Mercy! Mercy! Mercy! The curse is on me.

[*Curtain*]

Wilson Barrett as Claudian, photograph *c.*1890.

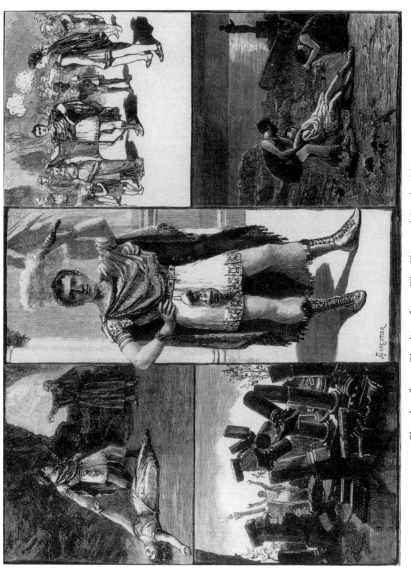

Sketches from *Claudian*, from *The Illustrated London News*,
December 13, 1883.

Wilson Barrett as Claudian. Cartoon ridiculing Barrett's abbreviated costume.
Watercolour by S. H. Beaumont, *c.*1900.

Characters in the Play

CLAUDIAN ANDIATES a rich noble of Byzantium
THARIOGALUS Tetrarch of the province of Charydos
ALCARES a farmer
AGAZIL a smith
BELOS a young farmer
OFFICER
RHAMANTES Claudian's steward
PEASANTS
ALMIDA and, EDESSA daughters of Alcares
THRENA a peasant girl
GALENA a tramp
HERA her daughter
GIRL
SOLDIERS, PEASANTS, etc.

ACT I

Scene 1

[SCENE: *A village farm near Charydos. Full summer glow at harvest time at the rising of the curtain.* THRENA *and two girls are standing on a stone seat on tiptoe, looking off*]

THRENA They're coming! They're coming! I can see them. And the others are bringing a wagon and it is so full—so full!

[*Harvest Song heard in the distance. The Harvest Song is sung partly off, partly as the harvest procession crosses the stage, and then partly off again. During this song the procession crosses the stage.* ALCARES *and* EDESSA *join the group of girls and the other peasants with them, all in full swing of joy. Six girls precede the procession, dancing, then six boys with pipes, also dancing, then six girls with musical instruments, then peasant girls and children and men, singing the Vintage Song. These group themselves to let the Vintage Wagon pass. Then the Vintage Wagon, dragged by twelve young fellows, headed by the farm steward and the overseers, goes past, and the choristers fall in again and exeunt singing. All are decked out with flowers, leaves, and grapes*]

ALCARES The harvest's safe, my friends, and a right good harvest 'tis. Am I not blest in my goods and in my children. For they are good children, both of them. My heart is full, my heart is full. [*Goes up*] [*They all exeunt except* THRENA, EDESSA, *and one or two others.* THRENA *has been standing talking to* EDESSA, *who is on the swing*]

THRENA I always told you so. Almida will never marry Thariogalus. You know well, Edessa, she loves another.

EDESSA And he is mute. The poor smith stands agaze and dare not say 'Almida be my wife'—the easiest thing said in the world, except the natural rejoinder, 'Yes, dear Agazil'.

THRENA Hush! Hush! You'll be heard.

EDESSA No, indeed I won't hush. Here is the Tetrarch of the province at her feet. Oh, if I had the chance. Chariots! A great house! Servants! Oh, how my mouth waters. If it were I—

THRENA Poor Belos! Surely you would not desert him so—

EDESSA Belos! He is the vainest, most swaggering coward in the province. Yet he is always bragging of his valour. How I wish I had the rich Tetrarch in one scale and Belos in the other: all the farmhouses in the country would be as light as thistledown. Up they'd go for me. [*Enter* BELOS. EDESSA *hides behind* THRENA]

EDESSA Now look at him. Now he'll try to anger me by making loving eyes at you. Take no notice. [BELOS *bows ridiculously at* THRENA] There it is. Now he's going to smile at you like an ape at a melon. There's the smile. How do you like it? [*To* BELOS] Oh, you're there, are you?

BELOS Yes. I'm here. How's the Tetrarch? I saw you carrying notes to him.

EDESSA O did you! Well, that's all over. Almida won't marry him.

BELOS Just my luck. Now if I had a tetrarch for a brother-in-law, I'd stand a chance one day of being a captain or a general. I was born to be a solider.

EDESSA You? Why, only the other day you ran away from a wasp.

BELOS O did I? Well the wasp wouldn't fly away from me. Was I to stand still and be stung? I'm not such a fool as you look.

EDESSA You mean, you don't look such a fool as you are.

THRENA There you are, you two, always the same. And you know you love one another dearly—you have loved one another since both of you were no bigger than my arm. [*Goes up laughing*]

BELOS She's always going on at me. A stout country girl who ought to be milking or grinding at the mill or [with] a pitcher on her giddy little head to steady it.

EDESSA O you wretch—

BELOS Why, you are steady and plump enough when you are eating or working, but the moment Master Tetrarch enters, your head goes niddle-noddle and your tongue goes twitter-twatter till I'm ashamed of you.

EDESSA And you, when nobody's by, daren't frown at a mouse, but, when Almida enters, your legs go swigger-swagger, and your tongue goes bubble-gubble till I feel ill.

BELOS And she likes it, fool—she admires me.

EDESSA You indeed! Ogling and sighing at Almida. Why, it's like a dog baying at the moon.

BELOS Why, the Tetrarch regards you no more than a fly on his nose. And the company you keep, as if you were above an honest farmer, bowing to the steward, gossiping with every soldier who comes into the village, screwing up your lips as if you were going to whistle.

EDESSA Don't talk of the company I keep—from the company you keep I always think you're going to grunt.

BELOS I'd make as good a gentleman as you. Look you here—if you were a man! If even the Tetrarch himself said that to me, he'd take his measure on the ground.

EDESSA Here he comes. I'll tell him.

BELOS O for the lord's sake. Edessa, good Edessa—sweet Edessa—you know how I love you.

EDESSA That for your love.

[BELOS *slinks away. Enter* THARIOGALUS]

THARIOGALUS Ah! Fair Edessa. [*He tips her under the chin*] Well, hast thou spoken to thy beauteous sister? Ha! Pretty pretty! [*Tips her under her chin again*] You're her sister. Now I look at thee, a monstrous comely maid.

EDESSA O sir! Illustrious sir [*simpering*].

THARIOGALUS Did you deliver my present?

EDESSA With all the pretty speeches, but she would not accept it.

THARIOGALUS Not accept it? Oh, I must assure her in person of my condescension.

[*Enter* ALCARES]

EDESSA Here is my father. I humbly thank you, most illustrious sir.

[*Exit* EDESSA]

ALCARES Most illustrious—I greet you.

THARIOGALUS Good day, farmer, good day, day . . . aha. You had my message.

ALCARES You've done me great honour, Illustrious.

THARIOGALUS What does your daughter say to it? Overcome no doubt?

ALCARES Excellence, I understand my cows. I know the character of a heifer to a caper. I could tell you what a fat ewe is thinking of, but a maiden's fancies are as far beyond me as the Milky Way.

THARIOGALUS Aha! The position I offer is one well beyond the dreams of a farmer's daughter—chariots and horses, silks of Tarsus.

ALCARES Most maidens would be dazzled—but my girl, I cannot reckon up. If it please you—meet her yourself, and learn from her own lips. What I can think sweet mayn't suit her palate.

[*He beckons. Enter* ALMIDA. ALCARES *goes up*]

THARIOGALUS Maiden, no doubt you are acquainted—I see it in your modest bearing—of your marvellous, incredible conquest of a man of station and power. Such an—an—an—an—arrangement as a marriage between a farmer's daughter and a gentleman in confidence with the Emperor hath not taken place, I wot, within the century.

ALMIDA Nor will it. Illustrious sir, all humble thanks. I refuse the honour.

THARIOGALUS Impossible!

ALMIDA It is impossible, illustrious sir. I am beneath you.

THARIOGALUS I condescend to lift you up, by making you my wife— my wife, girl, my wife.

ALMIDA Sir, I am determined if I marry, to mate with my equals. With all humble thanks from your poor servant, illustrious sir, I salute you.

[Exit]

THARIOGALUS This is past all belief. No one ever dreamed, even in madness, of such insolence. Ah, there's a smith called Agazil who moons about this audacious wench. I have a sniff—let him look to it. The Tetrarch bearded by a peasant! I am sick with wrath—I'll— I'll—I'll—have it out with you.

[*Exit* THARIOGALUS. ALCARES *comes down*]

ALCARES There's an end to that. He's gone away in a temper. I hope no ill luck may come through it. There's my honest friend the smith. The bravest man in all the countryside, he's the proper husband for my daughter.

[*Enter* AGAZIL]

ALCARES Agazil, come hither. Thou hast almost lost her by thy dallying.

[ALCARES *sits*]

AGAZIL O sir, have I lost her?

ALCARES Yes: what think you? The Tetrarch has asked her hand from me.

AGAZIL Sir! The Tetrarch has asked her hand?

ALCARES Even so. She hath refused it plump.

AGAZIL She hath refused a wealthy noble, and what have I to offer—a poor village smith! She's far above me as a twinkling star above a glow-worm grub.

ALCARES Ah, I don't think so. She hath refused wealth and station for thy sake!

AGAZIL For my sake! Do you think for my sake?

ALCARES Of course, man—as far as I can know. I see her yonder watching thee. Speak bluntly.

AGAZIL I'll be off home.

[Escapes, is brought back by ALCARES by the ear]

ALCARES No, thoult not escape, coward. Come—come—come.

AGAZIL I'm not a coward—but suppose you ask her first.

ALCARES Tut! I leave my daughter fancy free. Maidens despise those who fear them.

AGAZIL Sir, I worshipped her. I've spent a morning, while I've shaped the white-hot iron and the merry sparks flew out, in framing in my mind a pretty phrase to greet her in the evening, but when I stumbled out some sheepish saying—still she smiled on me. Sir, think you she would smile now in good earnest if I asked her to be my wife?

ALCARES I'll warrant it. Here she comes.

AGAZIL I'll hie me home. My work awaits me.

ALCARES No, not if I can hold thee, oaf! Here she is, and smiling. Courage!

[Exit ALCARES. Enter ALMIDA]

ALMIDA You were looking for me, Agazil? Don't be frightened.

AGAZIL That's a hard, ugly fist, Almida.

ALMIDA Well, it's not pretty, Agazil.

AGAZIL And that little hand of thine is beautiful.

ALMIDA You've often told me that.

AGAZIL Beshrew my tongue. It's swelling in my mouth. [Aloud] You guess what I would say. Won't you help me?

ALMIDA I know what I would wish you to say.

AGAZIL [aside] I grow giddy. [Aloud] Almida, I—I—I—[bursting out] I love you! Let all the world hear me say it. I love you. I care not, because it is honest truth—it's truth I'd fight for, die for—I love you! What does that tearful eye mean to tell me—a sorrowful refusal? [*Anticipating* ALMIDA's *reply and speaking in* ALMIDA's *voice*] No, I can't? I've told thee how I love thee, Almida. And if you cannot love a rough man like me, say it, and I will bear up. Tell me the secret truth if you heard the very word you heard now whispers to you.

ALMIDA You'd hear the very words? 'This Almida yon ought to be a proud maid. A good, honest, brave man loves thee. Tell him you have loved him for two years and had begun to doubt his love. You shed tears because you doubted it often and often.'

AGAZIL That's what it's saying?

ALMIDA Listen to it.

AGAZIL That I will—let it say it pressed against mine. What, this soft hand is mine now? [*Embraces her*]

ALMIDA Quite your own—own—

AGAZIL [*wiping a tear*] What a poor cowardly fool I was! What have I lost through all the year that's gone? I envy no man—not the Emperor. There is no trouble now before me. Every pain and fear is purged with joy. My happiness is so large I could give enough in shares to fill the world, yet leave sufficient for us two. I'm a miser. I'll not give a scrap of it. Its my first day of joy—I'll own it all.

[*Exeunt* AGAZIL *and* ALMIDA. *Enter* BELOS, EDESSA, *and* ALCARES]

ALCARES Quarrelling again. Tut! Tut! Leave me alone. Which of you is at fault, eh? Both—both—I'd rather have a blight in my wheat than quarrels at my hearthside.

BELOS [*sobbing*] She insulted me, sir, and she threw doubts on my unquestioned valour.

EDESSA He hath said that I affected the lady and was stout.

BELOS [*talking very fast*] She said that I swigger-swaggered and worse—that I bubble-gubbled and that I had been living with the pigs.

EDESSA He said that I twitter-twattered.

ALCARES Cease! Enough! You're a pair of fools, and here I solemnly and for ever break off the betrothal between you. Dog and cat can never pair.

EDESSA [*suddenly changing tune*] What! Just when Almida was going to be married, Father? And Belos and I betrothed a month?

BELOS Just when I've got the little cottage by the forest all snug.

EDESSA The dear little cottage which some great man who has come into the country forced the Tetrarch to disgorge. Father [*half-crying*], you're a cruel man.

BELOS You think nothing of blighting young innocent hearts.

ALCARES Well, well, if that be so, I'll let you blight the young hearts among yourselves. You're going the straight way. Marry and thrive. I'll help to furnish you. I'll give you both a yoke of cattle to draw you to church. To thee, Belos, I will give twelve fat ewes to cut thy grass and teach thee gentle manners.

EDESSA His face would frighten the sheep.

BELOS Now then, look you—you have a sample of her there. 'Frighten the sheep'. You heard her.

ALCARES You shall marry when it lists you.

BELOS That's if she gives up her airs.

EDESSA That's if Belos mends his manners.

ALCARES Go—go—I've done with you.

[*Exeunt squabbling. Enter* CLAUDIAN. *Repetition of the Harvest Song, and laughter heard in the distance*]

CLAUDIAN Laughter! Yes, 'tis vintage time. Laughter to me is sadder than a sigh. I passed and heard the laughter of their grandsires, and I shall hear their children's children laugh when they are dust. A century's dead have passed me, and the scythe of death sweeps on and leaves me the one venom'd thing standing alone. Still in my mirror is the same young face that flouts me with its youth so meaningless, when all within is aged, palsied cold. How I envy the calm and restful dead. Pass on, ye happy peasants. Here is one who hovers on the outskirts of your joy, in which he dare not mingle. Press your red grapes—if you could sprinkle on your fields my blood, ye'd do a service richer than all the vintages of Thrace—and loose from me this haggard load of years. I love ye, happy peasants, a love that needs must ripen and decay within, like fruitage in a desert. Laugh on! Laugh on!

[*Enter* HERA]

HERA Sir, be good to me.

CLAUDIAN What want you?

HERA Upon the road my aged mother lies way-worn and helpless. My child, too, sick and parched with trouble. A small piece of silver would buy some room in a passing wagon, and we could reach the village.

CLAUDIAN The villagers are yonder—go to them!

HERA Sir, they will give me food, not money.

CLAUDIAN I must refuse. I cannot help you.

HERA My child may perish on the road. But a small piece of silver.

CLAUDIAN I cannot help you.

HERA Then I must return to them. Perhaps help may reach us there.

[*Exit* HERA]

CLAUDIAN Poor girl. I could have filled her two pale hands with gold. My gold! 'Twould leave the plague spot where should have fallen the touch of mercy and love.

[*Confused noise heard off, 'Shame', 'Let him go', 'Injustice'. Then a crowd of peasants rush across the stage.* CLAUDIAN *stops one of them*]

CLAUDIAN Maiden, what has happened?

PEASANT O sir. Agazil, the betrothed of our Almida, has been arrested by the Tetrarch's orders. We go to warn his friends. [*rushes off*]

CLAUDIAN I have come amongst them, and at once their sunshine is obscured.

[*Enter* ALMIDA, *crying. She has a bunch of flowers in her breast*]

CLAUDIAN Maiden, wouldst thou sell those flowers in thy breast?

ALMIDA [*wiping her tears*] These, sir, if it doth please you, I will give them.

CLAUDIAN Nay, I must buy them. Here is a gold piece.

ALMIDA Sir, the flowers are not worth an obolus, and I do not need money.

CLAUDIAN There is one who needs it sorely. See you yon poor girl? Her mother and her babe lay way-worn and weary on the unsheltered road. I offer thee a joy denied to me. Give this gold piece to her.

ALMIDA Sir, with all my heart!

CLAUDIAN But not from me! 'Tis thine, you give it, maid. E'en while we talk the child may die.

[*Hurries her off*]

CLAUDIAN A gentle, pensive face! Made double sweet by tears— grief's jewellery. What is her grief? Why should I seek to know, whose balms can only blister? What have I to do with woman's beauty, and what is woman's love or grief to me? She returns. I'll go—no—I must stay. O, for this torturing, meddling pity which compels my will to question her, to comfort, and perhaps to kill.

[ALMIDA *re-enters*]

ALMIDA I have given her the money. See, she still waves her thanks.

[ALMIDA *gestures to the supposed* HERA *in the distance*]

CLAUDIAN From thyself?

ALMIDA Well, it passed for so.

CLAUDIAN Thou, who hast ministered to others, I think thou hast some trouble of thine own. Is it not so? Come, tell me.

ALMIDA I am so troubled, sir, and in need of counsel. Sir, you are young. Perhaps you know how sweet it is to love and to be loved.

I am betrothed today to Agazil, our village smith. I was so happy,
I almost cried, and we wished well to all in the world. What think
you, sir? Our cruel Tetrarch waits till our happiness is at the full
and then arrests my lover, Agazil.

CLAUDIAN Upon what charge?

ALMIDA How could a man who works all the day and thinks of
nothing but his love do wrong?

CLAUDIAN The Tetrarch had some unworthy motive. What was it?

ALMIDA My father says he honoured me too much.

CLAUDIAN I can guess. What is your name?

ALMIDA Almida.

CLAUDIAN I have indeed some powers vested in me might curb this
man's injustice, no matter how I hold it or of whom.

ALMIDA Then some good angel led me to you, sir.

CLAUDIAN Pray that it was not some evil angel. I do not know this
Agazil of thine. And if I bid this tyrant to release him, I show in
this no favour to you or to your lover.

ALMIDA But, sir, you do.

CLAUDIAN I can claim no gratitude. My act is but cold justice—
neutral in the law. Is not that the Tetrarch walking yonder?

ALMIDA Yes, sir.

CLAUDIAN Bid him come hither.

ALMIDA He is proud, sir.

CLAUDIAN Then he needs humbling. Bid him hither, and wait apart.
        [*Exit* ALMIDA]

CLAUDIAN In this, then, there is no sophistry with heaven. 'Tis not I
who do release her lover, but this false steward and at my first
command. I do not know this man. How can any say I do him
kindness? The curse can never touch him.
        [*Enter* THARIOGALUS. CLAUDIAN *starts*]

THARIOGALUS Sir, how presume you to use such a phrase to me as
'Bid him come hither'. Know you who I am?
        [CLAUDIAN *remains silent with his eyes fixed on him*]

THARIOGALUS Beware, sir, I may bid you come to me in the tribunal.

CLAUDIAN Sir, I was silent to measure for a moment the height to
which your arrogance has grown. Know you that signature?

THARIOGALUS The imperial signature—'tis Claudian of Charydos.
Most illustrious sir—your pleasure?

CLAUDIAN You recognize my power to call you to account?

THARIOGALUS Most humbly, most obediently. What is your most
condescending will? The Emperor, I hope, is well.

CLAUDIAN Why hast thou cast this youth in prison?

THARIOGALUS Your servant would not think of troubling thee, Illustrious, with the petty details of his office.

CLAUDIAN I am not so punctilious, sir. If this youth is not released at once, thyself shall fill his cell tonight.

THARIOGALUS He shall be released at once, at once.

CLAUDIAN Why was he arrested?

THARIOGALUS Ahem! Illustrious one, you see, ahem! I've since found 'twas an error.

CLAUDIAN What a stammerer is falsehood. Enough! Release him— go!

THARIOGALUS [going out] I'll turn the knave of a smith out. I'll seize his land.

CLAUDIAN Return. What dost thou mutter?

THARIOGALUS Most illustrious, I said I would atone for my injustice.

CLAUDIAN Thou shalt be watched, so pick thy steps and cringe to others, not to me. Begone!

[Exit THARIOGALUS]

CLAUDIAN No harm can come to this young lover. 'Tis this man's unwilling act, not mine.

[Re-enter ALMIDA]

CLAUDIAN Thy lover will immediately be freed. That beaming face of thanks! Remember [with cautioning finger].

ALMIDA Sir, I do not thank you—you have done us no favour. You have been cruel, savage, unjust. I am obedient. Still, might I kiss your hand and drop my happy tears on it?

CLAUDIAN Give that kiss to thy lover. He will meet thee here. He'll be released at once.

[Enter HERA hastily]

CLAUDIAN How is the child?

HERA Oh, he is dead—dead.

[Exit HERA]

ALMIDA Sir—do not grieve, for you have done your best. She is grateful.

CLAUDIAN [with vehemence] Grateful! You must not breathe the word to me. If he, thy lover, should talk of thanks, freeze thou his gratitude upon his lips, or ill will come of it. Give me the chance of but one passing thought that to a creature on this earth some act of mine has brought no ill. Deny me not the pleasures of that thought. Say his release has come from the false Tetrarch, but not from me, not from me. Promise! Promise!

ALMIDA I promise.

[*Exit* CLAUDIAN]

ALMIDA What a sigh was that? A lead of misery! A pale and noble
face! What change hath come upon me. He said my lover is
released. I had almost asked him, who is released? My heart ne'er
leaped to welcome such news. 'Tis like some sorcery such as our
nurse told me of—the potion that cures love or conjures. It cannot
be—one meeting with a stranger—a look, a few kind words—could
wipe out all the love which hath grown in me these two long years.
Agazil! Agazil! The name used to call up the blood to my cheek,
and now my tongue repeats it carelessly. How can I rid me of this
fascination? I am infected by it. Where is it? In my heart, my blood,
my brain? Oh, how could I wring it out from hair or garment.
[AGAZIL *laughs outside*] O wretched me, he comes, and I feel as
though I could fly from him.

[*Enter* AGAZIL]

AGAZIL I am free again, free as the wind. My love—welcome. They
thought to part us. None could drive a ploughshare thro' my love
and pride in thee. It's welded to thee.

ALMIDA [*faintly, with an effort*] Welcome, Agazil!

AGAZIL That knave of a Tetrarch! We have triumphed over him—not
that I blame him for loving thee, for when I hold thee and look
at—why, what is it? Thy hand rests coldly in mine. Thine eye that
laughed into mine is downcast.

ALMIDA Oh, I've been frightened—in suspense.

AGAZIL Take heart. You've not seen the pretty home. I've worked
for't as if I had four arms and twenty hammers—clang, clang at ten
anvils, clang, clang. You would hear it at the church when those
beautiful eyes were asleep, and the money came in, and the roses
got thick in the garden, and they—now maid, may God so deal
with me if there not be some change in thee, Almida. Thou hast
never loved me.

ALMIDA I have—I have—as true as thou lovest me. Dost thou believe
in evil enchantment?

AGAZIL Aye, but I have another name for it. I call it woman's infidelity.

ALMIDA Be gentle with me. Dost thou remember when we walked
together last Lord's Day? I lost from my brooch—thy gift—a little
agate heart? We searched for it—it was lost. You said it would bring
ill luck.

AGAZIL I but jested. [*Stands out before her*] I am a simple man. If I must
suffer, I like to take trouble by the armful. Say what you mean.

ALMIDA Even as that little heart was lost—I cannot help it—my love is gone—gone—gone.

AGAZIL Never say thy love is gone. You never loved me.

ALMIDA Indeed, I vow I loved thee as if I had loved some song and suddenly gone deaf, some perfumed flower and lost the sense of smell. Shall I say I love thee? Still, I will say it. Make me thy wife, and I will be thy handmaiden—toil for thee. Give me thy kind, honest hand, Agazil—I cannot help it—I cannot help it.

AGAZIL [*flinging away her hand*] I can't string pretty words together when I am tangled in a doubt. I kick through it. You love another. I will find out who wronged me—and now I remember—a young and comely noble, a cunning sadness in his face, and I have heard he had some hand in my release. Better he had barred the door with triple bolts. I'll find him—he is rich and powerful, but the poor man's law when he is crushed and ruined, robbed of his last treasure, is in his strong right arm. Shame! Shame! I'll not mourn for thee. I'll find him. [*Rushes away*]

ALMIDA Agazil! Hurt not that stranger.

[*Savage laugh without*]

ALMIDA O give me back my love for this good man. [*Exit*]

Scene 2

[SCENE:[40] *Room in* ALCARES's *house, partly open to the sky, opening to serve as a door and leading to the fields at the back. Another opening leading to an inner apartment R. Another door, if required, L. Furniture to move with scene consists of a couch and two stools with arms. Enter* BELOS, *followed by* EDESSA]

EDESSA Now, Belos. Make a bigger fool of yourself than you are. The soldiers were only laughing at you.

BELOS Were they though? I know better. They were admiring me. Look at that thumb. Do you know what its shape means?

EDESSA Conceit, dear.

BELOS Conceit, woman. It means valour—it means manhood. You should have seen me: 'Friend soldier,' I said, 'lend me your sword.' 'Why?' he asked, 'I'll show why,' said I.

EDESSA I hope you didn't hurt yourself.

[40] As staged by Wilson Barrett at the Princess's Theatre, this scene-change was eliminated, and the action continued in the setting of the previous scene.

BELOS Hurt myself! You're a nice maid, Edessa, but you mustn't talk of such things that you don't understand. I took the sword. I stood on guard—so. I fenced—I lunged—I parried—so—
[*Enter* OFFICER]

OFFICER Bravo! Well done, my man. Why, you were born to be a soldier.

BELOS That's what I say, good sir, that's what I'm always saying. [*To* EDESSA] You see, I was right.

OFFICER Are you quite sure, my fellow?

BELOS Look at that thumb. Nature moulded me to be a soldier.

OFFICER Then we won't baulk nature. A soldier you shall be. I'm come by the Tetrarch's orders to levy soldiers here, and you shall be the Wrst.

BELOS Oh, I—I—I—

OFFICER Why, what ails you? Your teeth chatter—your face . . .

BELOS O, sir, 'tis for joy—'tis my great happiness. [*Aside to* EDESSA] Do beg of him to let me go.

EDESSA Oh, good sir, don't take away my poor Belos—my betrothed lover. He's a poor harmless creature who—

BELOS Never handled a sword in all his unhappy life.

EDESSA Timid by nature.

BELOS As harmless as a lamb.

EDESSA He only talks big.

BELOS But he doesn't mean it, good sir.

OFFICER I don't believe a word of it—you're too modest. You're my man. Come, it's your fate to be a hero.

BELOS [*to* EDESSA] You don't want to be a heroine do you? [*To* OFFICER] Let me say farewell to my poor Edessa.

OFFICER O certainly, say farewell. Be brief.

BELOS This is what comes of getting the beautiful cottage through the strange lord.

EDESSA It's brought us ill luck. He released poor Agazil.

BELOS And brought poor Agazil misfortune, too. And here am I—a respectable farmer who paid his rates and taxes and was as harmless as a lamb—as a lamb [*howls*].

EDESSA Somebody told him you wanted to be a soldier.

BELOS But I don't want—I don't want—I don't want to hurt any-body. I want—

EDESSA There—there. Take heart.

BELOS Who'll keep the house warm? Who'll reap my barley? Who'll milk my cows?

EDESSA Father'll look after it as well as he can, and I'll go with you, if they'll let me.

OFFICER What, tears? We'll soon set that right. Come—you've had time enough to say goodbye.

[BELOS *embraces* EDESSA]

OFFICER Come! Come! We'll change all that. Thou shalt have a chance to prove thy valour.

BELOS Valour!

OFFICER Come! March!

[*Exit* BELOS, *roaring, followed by soldiers and* EDESSA. *Enter* ALCARES *and* CLAUDIAN]

ALCARES Sir, having learned of your kindness to my friend, the honest smith—

CLAUDIAN No kindness, friend, to him. I know him not. My motive was to punish wrong—no more. Ill chance attends my gifts even as the shadow on the floor doth follow me.

ALCARES And there's such a thing, good sir, as this ill chance. And also there's bewitchment. Now, sir, who'd think it? There's my child, Almida. The girl was always constant in her nature—sure, she is bewitched.

CLAUDIAN How mean you?

ALCARES This morning I would be sworn that she loved Agazil, for the Governor Thariogalus asked her to be his lady, and, for this Agazil, steadfastly did she refuse him.

CLAUDIAN Happily she repents.

ALCARES You'll pardon me, good sir, there's no depending on women.

CLAUDIAN Hath she found another love in a few hours?

ALCARES Ah, that's it! Edessa tells me since the child has seen thee, she talks of the pale, melancholy stranger—so noble, gentle, kind.

CLAUDIAN This cannot be the truth.

ALCARES It is the truth. Not that I blame thee.

CLAUDIAN In all my brain of misery, this is the bitterest pang—these two young lives cankered by me. If I may not excise this fatal craze e'er it take root, she is lost.

ALCARES You were saying, sir—

CLAUDIAN [*still aside and walking up and down*] Love me! Whose kisses would be poison—whose embraces would be death. [*To* ALCARES] Sir, I would see your daughter instantly. I hope all may be well. It shall be well.

ALCARES I thought so. I will send her hither. Mock at her, sir. Shame her! There's no cure for love like ridicule.

[*Exit* ALCARES]

CLAUDIAN Now shall I see if there be pity in heaven. She is too
good—too sweet to share my curse. O God, may it be so.
    [*Enter* ALMIDA. CLAUDIAN *stands looking silently at her for a
moment. She stands with downcast eyes*]

CLAUDIAN Maiden, how long has thou loved Agazil?

ALMIDA In secret, these two vintages.

CLAUDIAN And how long ceased to love him? [ALMIDA *is silent*] The
Governor Thariogalus offered thee his hand this morning, and thou
art dazzled, tempted, is it not so?

ALMIDA O sir, believe me, I am not so base.

CLAUDIAN This morning, then, you loved poor Agazil. You pleaded
with me full of tearful zeal, with eyes that brimmed with love's own
gentle lustre, with lips that burned with love's own eloquence. You
pictured him to me as simple, brave, and loyal.

ALMIDA He was all that and more.

CLAUDIAN And is much angered.

ALMIDA He is much angered. [*Sobs*]

CLAUDIAN Thy youth and his are brief. [*With feeling*] Some happy
hours, and then the blossom drops. [*More excitedly*] I have seen lovers
bright and young as you—their light quarrels like summer frost
which the sun smiles away. I have watched their beauty fade, seen
them grow old and grey—and die—but ne'er again hath come the
love blossom.

ALMIDA [*puzzled*] You, sir—you are as young as Agazil.

CLAUDIAN Take care. It is a brave, large heart that you trifle with.
You cannot mend it like a shattered bauble when once you break
it. [*Softening*] Oh, I implore, school thy young fancy which now
plays the truant. Love will come back to thee.

ALMIDA I can't love him. I know not why I cannot. And every word
you say but parts us farther. What spell is over me? I tumble to hear
you speak, and my ears hearken as one who waits the word of life.
[*Quite abashed*] what have I said? I utter words I should lock in my
heart. I know it is a wrong—a foolish fancy. Forgive me. Do not
scorn me.

CLAUDIAN [*with suppressed agitation*] By all your reverence, simple girl,
beware what part I have with thee, or thou with me. Think.
Remember, until this morn the summer of your happiness seemed
without one cloud—now all is overshadowed with black misery,
and I—I—am the cause. The child is dead who had my charity.
Even the poor peasant found my aid his ruin. The beggar has his

mate who shares his crust, but I am as a leper, crouched aloof, without the walls—feared—hated—abhorred—alone! The people look askance when they come by, and yet this bosom swells with love for them.

ALMIDA What is this curse? Why do they hate thee?

CLAUDIAN Look on me. Dost thou see upon this head the curse which sits there for ever and for ever. I could send forth pity that would fill the world—dry the tears of sorrow, feed the starving, and be like daylight shared by all my brothers—but for this curse which makes my love a poison—my pity a wingèd pestilence.

ALMIDA This is too terrible!

CLAUDIAN See yon calm evening sky. If I should pray for rain in parched fields, the bounteous clouds might come, but in their bosom the blessed rain would turn to rattling hail and kill what it should nourish. The very skylark singing o'er my head his matin song to teach me how to worship—methinks would drop stone dead should I but mutter 'Sing on small heart of music, I too love thee'. O God! How long? How long? How long?

ALMIDA Why hast thou told me of thy piteous lot? Why dost thou break my heart with grief for thee?

CLAUDIAN Thou darest pity one whom heaven will not pity. Thou darest to cool this hell-parched tongue with water. The coil around my heart loosens its fastening pressure. Thou angel. Thou hast brought the tears at last. Pray for me—say even in thy prayer, 'Lift, lift his punishment from his doomed head. 'Tis greater than he can bear.'

[*Enter* AGAZIL *and* ALCARES]

AGAZIL And is it thus I find thee? It is not that thy love for me is dead, but that you love another? [*To* CLAUDIAN] Traitor. Compared to thee our tyrant governor is merciful and just. But wert thou the Eastern Emperor, I'll have it out with thee even to the death. [*Makes a rush at* CLAUDIAN. ALCARES *holds him back*] Aye, as I strike my anvil, I will kill thee.

[ALMIDA *attempts to throw herself between them.* CLAUDIAN *puts her aside softly and stands before her*]

CLAUDIAN Let him. I am unarmed. Kill me—thou coulds't not do for me a better service. [*To* ALCARES] Loose him. [AGAZIL *makes a rush at him with a dagger but stops short*]

AGAZIL [*throws down the dagger*] I cannot strike! Ye heavens! I cannot strike! There's something numbs my will—there's something stays my hand. [*Furiously to* CLAUDIAN, *then breaking down*] Why not let me rot within the prison cell, where I could think of her, could fancy I saw her, a sunbeam in my darkness. Now, in full daylight, all is black for me.

CLAUDIAN Thy words, poor fellow, cut far deeper than could thy dagger. Thou art sorely avenged. Plead with her. There she stands.

AGAZIL [*bitterly*] Aye, with her gaze on thee. All's over with me. Never again, when the day's toil is done, shall I wipe my wet brow and say, 'She waits for me—I've earned her kiss.' O false! false! false! Ah, cur that I am. Like a weak woman, I but talk and weep, when my wrongs call on me to strike and kill. How is it with me? What is it binds my hands? Am I possessed, and is this man the devil?

[*Enter* GALENA *and the* TRAMP, *an ill-clad old woman, leaning on a staff. She is followed by* BELOS, ALCARES, EDESSA, *and villagers*]

GALENA Aye, thou hast said—I know him, the curse of Byzantium. Kill him before he injures you! Kill him!

[ALCARES *takes* ALMIDA *aside. Villagers assume threatening attitudes*]

ALCARES Stand away from him, Almida.

ALMIDA No! No!

CLAUDIAN [*calmly*] Well, what would you?

GALENA What? He asks—out on him! Disaster follows disaster where he comes—fire, famine, fever follow him. The poor babe is dead from a cursed piece of money from his hand. Hunt him without! Stone him!

[*Some of the men rush at* CLAUDIAN. *He simply puts up his hand. They stagger back*]

CLAUDIAN Poor fools! Would you could do it!

OMNES Out with him! Kill him!

[*He stands looking at them calmly*]

ALCARES There's witchcraft in the man. Thou hast brought misfortune to this happy village.

OMNES Out with him!

PEASANT He's a sorcerer! Down with him.

CLAUDIAN I cannot blame you. Denounce me all. Sadly familiar to my woe-worn ear are the shouts—the howls of hatred. Could the blow follow the menace, then your execrations would come like greeting. I'll go. But there is one here whom I have not injured. To her I'll say farewell—she out of all the world hath pitied me.

ALMIDA [*breaking away wildly*] She out of all the world shall cling to thee.

ALCARES Shame, daughter!

GALENA 'Tis sorcery! Hold her back!

ALMIDA [*to* CLAUDIAN] Cleave thou thy bitterness in twain. Dearer than half a kingdom, I'll follow thee.

ALCARES Shame! This man is accurst, accurst!

ALMIDA For that I hold him dearer. Loosen me! Heart of my heart, let thy anguish be mine. I would lift from thy soul the fever and pain. If thou wert a leper, I would cling to thee. Raise me to bear the half of thy sorrow, for I would think it bliss to die at thy feet. [*She raises herself to him*] O I love thee so! [*Suddenly she gropes*] Oh, what is this? All is dark—all is dark!

    [ALMIDA *sinks on her knees*]

CLAUDIAN For mercy! Speak! Look!

ALMIDA [*feeling her way*] What is it? I cannot see you. All is black night before me—but I love thee, I love thee [*clings to* CLAUDIAN].

CLAUDIAN O merciful heaven. Is the measure full? She too! She is blind! She is blind!

    [*Curtain*]

ACT II

Scene 1

[SCENE: *The city of Charydos in Bithynia. On the O.P. side, the postern gate, with a pair of gates to close—practical—is opened outwards, showing a bridge over the mountain river which forms the city moat and the country beyond. Crossing from the gate, almost at right angles across the stage, are the turreted battlements, practical and solid. Next to the gate, a turret forms the guardhouse of the Goths, with a door leading into the turret, and another door on the first storey leading out of the same on to the battlements. On the prompt side, another turret flanks the stage. This also has a practical door leading from the battlements, and is supposed to be a passageway through to the battlements and the buildings beyond. Between the two turrets— and projecting from the battlements—a smithy is built into the solid rock wall of the battlements. The forge is on the prompt-side corner in full blaze, and on the same side an arched door is supposed to lead to an inner room. At the back, a barred opening shows the river outside and the country beyond. In the smithy, all around, are hung and stacked the usual implements of a smith's trade. A heavy table and two wooden stools L. On the table, on a wooden service, is laid a frugal meal, and a leather bottle contains wine. At the rising of the curtain, AGAZIL, BELOS, and EDESSA are discovered in the smithy. AGAZIL is at work on a set of chains. BELOS, in the dress of a soldier of the legion of Herculeans, is eating his meal. EDESSA busies about the place. Outside the smithy, the whole scene is full of movement. It is supposed to be the time just preceding the nightly closing of the gates, and streams of townspeople are entering the city. The gate is guarded by the soldiers of the legion of the Goths of the Danube. Some of these are loitering. Two are playing dice on the wall between the turrets. One is standing as sentry. The sentry alone is fully accoutred. BELOS is a little unsteady with wine, but not intoxicated]*

EDESSA [*seated, back of table*] Agazil, you have laboured long enough. Rest awhile.

AGAZIL [*L.*] Labour is all my solace. It stops me thinking. My poor lost girl. Where is she? Is she in trouble? Danger? Want? And I rooted here, in all but name a slave. I feel if I had not something to strike, I should go mad.

BELOS [*R. of table, eating and drinking*] Nothing inflames sorrow like hunger. Share my trencher, old neighbour.

AGAZIL [*L.*] Nay, nay. I must work, work, work.

EDESSA [*C.*] This persecution comes from the Tetrarch's spite. You stood between him and the poor Almida, and so he vents his savage spirit on us all. You, he puts to forging chains. Belos is a soldier, I am a drudge. Poor Belos. His crime is he loves me.

BELOS [*pathetically*] Ah! Poor Belos—that crime is his joy.

[*Drinks, comes forward and, with skin bottle, mildly intoxicated and with maudlin affection*]

BELOS Why, if I lost Edessa, I'd—I'd . . . [*affectionately offering bottle to* AGAZIL] Have a drop?

AGAZIL Nay, friend, your comfort is not mine. I thank you.

EDESSA [*to* BELOS] Hold your tongue and sit down.

[BELOS *retires subdued and drinks*]

EDESSA 'Tis like that tyrant Tetrarch knows where Almida is.

AGAZIL Who stole her love from me? 'Tis like that he broke the coffer, stole the treasure.

EDESSA You think the good Prefect Claudian knows?

AGAZIL Who hath had good from him?

EDESSA [*despairingly*] I don't know how to cheer you.

BELOS [*advancing, bottle in hand, unsteadily*] O my pigeon, you make me cry. Your goodness to our friend the smith lifts you in my love above rubies! Try a drop [*offers the bottle*].

EDESSA Fool! Here comes the Tetrarch.

[BELOS *retires*]

EDESSA [*to* AGAZIL] Now work away. Don't let him see you idle.

AGAZIL I'll not drag through the mire all that's left to me—the pride of a man. I'll not lift a hammer.

[*Shuts up forge, fire is put out. Enter* RHAMANTES *from L. He is a civil officer of* CLAUDIAN'S *court, followed by a few retainers and soldiers, different in costume from that worn by* BELOS, *and with* THARIOGALUS, *also with guard. They go straight to the gate. The guard of Goths turn out in full accoutrements*]

RHAMANTES [*R.C.*] The town is well ordered, Tetrarch. Your soldiers only have been guilty of excesses.

THARIOGALUS [*L.C.*] Sir, you take too much on you. I was Tetrarch of this province before your Claudian came.

RHAMANTES There is no need to talk of this great good man whom you and I both serve—I willingly, and you reluctantly. I am his deputed officer in this city of Charydos which he built.

THARIOGALUS Yes, verily. A town of vile construction. Built upon the rocks beside a river cataract which troubles my sleep with its roar. Pah! A vile town. None dare look over yon wall.

RHAMANTES Remember, I have given you warning, and thus I leave you.

[*Exit R. with train*]

THARIOGALUS And a fig for your warning [*stamping his foot, turns suddenly on* AGAZIL, EDESSA, BELOS]. What are you staring at? You, sir, why don't you work?

AGAZIL You have chains enough, Tetrarch. I've forged my last link today.

THARIOGALUS Then it's for yourself. [AGAZIL *throws down his hammer*] Oh! You sulk do you?

EDESSA We want to know, illustrious sir. What does it mean—a free village smith toiling here like a poor slave?

THARIOGALUS It means, wench, that whoso crosses my path, I treat him as they treat vermin, kites, and weasels. I nail him to my door, him and his tribe all in a row.

EDESSA [*aside*] My temper is getting up.

BELOS [*aside*] I shall punch that man directly.

EDESSA [*aloud*] The Prefect Claudian does not treat men as vermin, kites, and weasels! How would he treat you if he saw you as you really are, little ugly man?

BELOS Beautiful! He got that in the wind!

THARIOGALUS What? 'Little ugly'? Hark you. There's a ship in the harbour trafficking for young females. I'll see you, saucy wench, and at a bargain, at a bargain.

BELOS [*advancing, not valiantly*] I say, if you dare sell my pigeon for a queen's ransom, I'd—

EDESSA Hush! Fool!

BELOS [*feeble falsetto*] Save a drop! [*Offers the bottle hesitatingly,* EDESSA *pushes him back*]

THARIOGALUS [*savagely*] Oh, my man—[*to* BELOS] you're saucy. We'll cure you—you shall have stripes! [BELOS *groans*] Your wine shall be cut off—[BELOS *groans fearfully*] And you—[*to* EDESSA] wild cat, you'd scratch. Make complaints! Ha! Two sisters both alike! Coarse, lying jades.

AGAZIL [*pushes at him*] Revile me. I bear it. But say another slanderous word [about] Almida, and I'll stifle it in your throat.

[*Strikes him. Soldiers seize him and drag him away and hold him*]

THARIOGALUS [*brushing down his ruffled garments*] Oh, it's time. Chain this fellow. Chain him with the heaviest chains he has forged! Threaten me! Attack me!

> [*Soldiers chain* AGAZIL. BELOS, *not valiantly, tries to interfere, but is dragged away by* EDESSA, *who, taking a pitcher in her hand, goes towards him*]

BELOS But I will—I shall.

EDESSA Fool! What can you do now? They'll chain you as well if you stay, and flog you perhaps. Come, we shall return presently, when that man is gone.

BELOS Oh! I shall never be a hero.

THARIOGALUS That's right. Chain him! We'll flog him presently.

> [CLAUDIAN, RHAMANTES *and suite enter*]

CLAUDIAN Stay! Another outrage! Unhand this man.

> [*Soldiers retire*]

THARIOGALUS But, Illustrious—

CLAUDIAN Why is this man in chains?

THARIOGALUS This caitiff! Why, Illustrious, this is the wretch who insulted and threatened you! I've even heard he dared to raise his hand against thy god-like person.

CLAUDIAN I have not ordered his punishment. Why is he in chains?

THARIOGALUS You remember not, perhaps. He is the man who collected the village rabble, and led them on to insult and assault your Excellence.

CLAUDIAN I ordered not his punishment. Retire! I would speak with this man alone.

THARIOGALUS But, most illustrious—

CLAUDIAN Retire. I require not your presence. [THARIOGALUS *and his soldiers retire R.I.E*] Close the gate!

> [*The gates are closed. The Goths retire into the guardhouse. All exeunt except* CLAUDIAN *and* AGAZIL]

CLAUDIAN Friend, I have heard that you believe I know, and yet conceal, news of Almida. Hath trouble bred ungenerous suspicion? Indeed, I know not where she is.

AGAZIL 'Tis easily said. I say as easily, I do believe you know of her.

CLAUDIAN But thou wast in the village after me and knowest at my departure she was with her father.

AGAZIL If I see a hand upraised against me, I can guess who struck the blow.

CLAUDIAN How is my hand upraised against thee?

AGAZIL You are the Prefect. Why am I in chains?

CLAUDIAN Once have I freed thee—hast thou prospered since?

AGAZIL Since then I have been so beaten down with trouble that I've not heart even to speak a curse on thee.

CLAUDIAN A mightier voice than thine has spoken it. I left your village all alone. I left her blind. I thought her very helplessness would knit her heart to thee again—join the rent tissues. Since then I have not seen her.

AGAZIL She was bewitched from me by you. Your grandeur, or your wealth. I do her wrong! It was some power of hell!

CLAUDIAN It is a power that circles her and thee and me, and clips us in with heartbreak, pain, and death. Her blindness is a shadow from that power. As after the doomed ship the petrel skims, so has it followed me. Ask not how long.

AGAZIL I would I could believe thee.

CLAUDIAN [smiling] I know not what is at my heart, but I would pray, and deem it a high boon, if you would strike your honest hand in mine and frank by say[ing] 'I do believe thee'. [outstretches his hand]

AGAZIL [hesitating, at last frankly] Yes, there's truth in thy look and in thy face. Ah, if I dared! If one so humble—

CLAUDIAN Two honest, suffering men, even smith and prince, have in this kindred hour equality, and may as such clasp hearty hand in hand.

AGAZIL I do believe thee. [They grip hands]

CLAUDIAN Rhamantes!

[RHAMANTES and suite enter]

CLAUDIAN You see this man? Do justice.

RHAMANTES Shall I release him?

CLAUDIAN Ask me nothing, but do justice.

[Exit CLAUDIAN]

RHAMANTES [to soldiers] Release him! Chains of thine own forging, too! The Tetrarch is cruel—but justice has been done this time at least [while the soldiers unchain AGAZIL]. Now thou art free. Be careful you offend not again the Tetrarch. Help may not be so near.

[Exeunt RHAMANTES and suite. Two Goths are placed on guard at the gate]

AGAZIL My poor Almida! Where is she now? Where? Heaven will send her to me again. These many nights I have lain awake and thought of her. There's a strange peace at my heart. I'll sleep tonight. I'll rest.

[Exits into inner room of smithy. Stage is clear. Only the two Goths are left on guard at the gate]

1ST GOTH The Tetrarch has been humbled tonight. The old wolf will
    show his teeth for it.

2ND GOTH Yes, on the first poor lamb that bleats.

1ST GOTH I wish I were out of his service.

    [ALMIDA *is heard singing without. The soldiers stop to listen*]

ALMIDA [singing]

    There was night in my heart when my love lay asleeping,
    With its rosy gilt furrions tied close to its side.
    There was night in the fields, and the flowers were weeping
    For the sunshine of love to come shine in its pride.

1ST GOTH Hark! A woman's voice or a sprite's.

2ND GOTH It's a woman's, a young one, too, I swear. Let's open the
    gates.

    [*They open the gates.* ALMIDA *enters, led in by* HERA. *The Goths
    close the gate again*]

HERA You are inside the gates.

ALMIDA At last! At last! His city. I am near him at last! My master
    and my king.

1ST GOTH Well, songster. What want you?

ALMIDA Who is that?

HERA One of the guards at the gate.

ALMIDA [*eagerly*] Go ask where we may find him.

    [HERA *crosses to gate*]

HERA Pray tell me, soldier, where dwells your Prefect Claudian?

1ST GOTH Why, what want you with him?

HERA We are strangers here, but not to him.

2ND GOTH [to ALMIDA] I will show you where the Prefect lives.

ALMIDA Show it to my companion. I am blind.

1ST GOTH Blind? Oh, you've been blinded like the bullfinch to make
    you sing sweetly.

2ND GOTH Yonder marble palace, my girl, that overlooks the second
    gate, there lives our Prefect [*gets to gate*].

HERA Thank you, sir.

ALMIDA [*eagerly, drawing* HERA *aside*] Go to him, Hera. [HERA *crosses
    S.L.*] I wait here his commands. Say that I fear to come unless he
    bid me. Tell him how I have journeyed day and night like a poor
    loving dog that seeks his master.

HERA 'Tis the last service, if it be a service, which I can render you
    [*crosses as she speaks*].

ALMIDA And be not long, not long.

    [*Exit* HERA]

1ST GOTH Now tell us, what wouldst thou with the Prefect?

ALMIDA I wouldst speak with him. You are his soldiers?

> [*The soldiers laugh*]

1ST GOTH We are the guard of the Tetrarch Thariogalus.

2ND GOTH And thou art like to speak with him before the Prefect. I see him coming.

ALMIDA [*terrified*] The Tetrarch coming here! For pity sake, kind soldiers, guide me—is there no lurking place? I will crouch in the shadow of the wall—I dare not meet him.

2ND GOTH Hide the poor girl for a moment. You know our Tetrarch.

1ST GOTH Come, I'll hide thee. [*Takes her hand and leads* ALMIDA *to corner of smithy*]. There, I'll warrant he'll not notice thee.

ALMIDA Am I hidden here? O good soldier, be secret.

1ST GOTH Hush! Lie close!

> [*Enter Tetrarch and four soldiers*]

THARIOGALUS Where is the soldier Belos?

2ND GOTH Off duty, sir, till the fourth hour.

THARIOGALUS When he returns, arrest him strictly.

> [*Soldier salutes.* THARIOGALUS *crosses to R., passing* ALMIDA *without seeing her. Suddenly returns*]

THARIOGALUS And if Rhamantes should—[*sees* ALMIDA] My, what have we here? Daisies and buttercups! Milk and honey! My saucy peasant maiden who went blind all of a sudden. Very well met! What meanest thou following me hither? Eh?

ALMIDA Sir, I have come to see the great Claudian.

THARIOGALUS Ah! Is that it. I will lead thee to him.

ALMIDA I have sent a messenger—if I leave this, I may miss him.

THARIOGALUS I'll lead thee on the way. [*Loosens his cloak*]

ALMIDA I'll tarry here, sir, if it please you.

THARIOGALUS You do not trust me?

ALMIDA No, sir—I dare not.

THARIOGALUS Why, in this poor garment, you are cold—I'll muffle thee. [*Throws his cloak around her head*] That'll stifle her cries. Quick, some of you, take her up. Bring this vagabond maid to my chamber. Grave matter against her. I follow you. Let her not scream. Hah! That's the way to catch nightingales.

> [*The soldiers drag* ALMIDA *towards the turret. Re-enter* EDESSA *followed by* BELOS]

EDESSA Whom are they bearing away?

> [ALMIDA *frees her head for a moment and shrieks 'Help! Help!' The cloak is again put round her and she is dragged along*]

EDESSA Why, it is Almida's voice, Belos.

BELOS [*running forward*] Let her alone. Let her go. I know her well.

THARIOGALUS [*turning on him*] Dost thou? Here! Gag this meddling fool. Bind him.

    [BELOS *is seized, bound, and flung into smithy*]

EDESSA My poor sister! My poor sister!

    [*Exits into inner room after* AGAZIL]

EDESSA Help, Agazil! Almida, thy Almida, they are dragging her away. Come! Help!

THARIOGALUS [*during gagging of* BELOS] We'll cut his tongue out— food for dogs. Tighter! Tighter! That's right. Now follow me.

    [*Exit into tower after soldiers.* AGAZIL *enters from room, with* EDESSA]

AGAZIL Almida, you say! Where? Where?

EDESSA Through that tower.

AGAZIL [*rushes to door*] Locked, but that shall not hinder me.

    [*Climbs up side of smithy on to battlements, and reaches them just as* THARIOGALUS *emerges above, followed by soldiers.* ALMIDA *is being taken across first*]

AGAZIL [*as he is climbing*] You cowardly ruffians—you'll have me amongst ye.

EDESSA What have I done? What have I done? He'll be lost.

AGAZIL Coward, would you kidnap a free woman?

THARIOGALUS Who hath unchained thee? Back knave. Respect the law.

AGAZIL This is villainy, not law. Thou the chief villain.—Out of my way.

    [*Strikes him. Soldiers come between and seize* AGAZIL]

THARIOGALUS Seize the vile traitor. Strike the Tetrarch? Hold him! Drag him hither! Now—over the battlements with the knave. Over with him! Over with him!

    [*Soldiers throw* AGAZIL *over. Shout of despair and splash*]

EDESSA [*shrieks*] They've murdered Agazil. He will drown. Help! Help! [*Rushes out R.*]

THARIOGALUS Ah! There you go. Swept in the stream! One struggle. There's the knave! Up go his hands! Gone! Good-night.

    [*Exits after soldiers L.* CLAUDIAN, HERA, *and retinue enter L.*]

CLAUDIAN The place is deserted.

HERA I left her here.

CLAUDIAN Her blindness should have kept her near the gate. Something is wrong. [BELOS *groans*] Who is here?

HERA Alas! I feared! I feared!

CLAUDIAN Belos, gagged and bound. [*Soldiers unbind* BELOS] Hast thou seen Almida?

BELOS O sir! Robbery, knavery! Oh, my jaw's broke.

CLAUDIAN What's the matter, man?

BELOS Yonder, sir, yonder. The Tetrarch has had Almida dragged away.

CLAUDIAN That man—always that man. Through that door, my men. Quick, after him. [*They find door is bolted, try to force it*] No, waste not your time. We'll follow him through the tower postern. We'll find him there. Quick, my men, quick! You, Rhamantes, provide for this poor woman—[*points to* HERA] and thou canst tell me thy tale on the way.

BELOS But the Tetrarch—he said he would cut my tongue out.

CLAUDIAN Thou art with me—if I cannot bless, I can punish.

[*Exit. Change of scene*]

Scene 2

[SCENE: *A stone chamber within the walls of Charydos. A rough bench, a small window, open, admitting light R. in flat, high up. Doors opening R. and L.* ALMIDA *brought in by two soldiers, followed by* THARIOGALUS]

THARIOGALUS Place her here, and leave us. [*Exits to R.*] Keep good watch.

[*Exeunt soldiers*]

ALMIDA [C.] Where am I? Oh, where am I?

THARIOGALUS [R.] You know me?

ALMIDA I know your voice, sir. 'Tis with sad amazement I find the man whose office 'tis to punish the wrongdoer do cruel outrage towards a helpless woman. Sir, I demand instant release.

THARIOGALUS 'Demand' it? 'Tis a pretty sweet petition. The dove, caged, coos to its charmed master, 'Release me!' Pretty! [ALMIDA *feels for the door*] Your cage is quite secure. Caught. Can't get out. I owed you, saucy one, a grudge. You'll not find the door.

ALMIDA Is there no honest soldier in the room, or is there none that calls himself a man, to aid or bring relief?

THARIOGALUS We are alone. To see thee feel the way with thy white hands enflames my admiration. Sweet peasant, once I condescended to thee. Now 'tis marvel to myself I find I love thee! [*He approaches, she retreats with outstretched hands*] How sweet is helplessness! Here! Take my hand.

[*She suddenly throws herself on her knees before him*]

ALMIDA O sir! I kneel to you. Take pity on my weakness. Heaven has afflicted me with helpless blindness. Open your door to me.

THARIOGALUS After I have dressed in a silken robe which, tho' you cannot see, you'll hear it rustle. [*She sobs*] You melt in tears. Turn to your Thariogalus. I must chastise that pout upon thy lips by a sweet kiss.

ALMIDA [*with a cry of horror, she pushes him back and fronts him defiantly*] O give me power to tell this man how I do loathe him. What words! What figure! What comparison! Sir, in our garden was a weedy pool, and I have noticed, squat upon a stone, a toad who stares at me; the shiny venom oozed from its wrinkled mouth. I'd sooner make that thing my playfellow than have thee for mine husband.

THARIOGALUS Once, wench, I might have been your husband. No, you're my chattel, to do with that which I list. Think you I would wed an eyeless, saucy beggar girl. No, all is changed.

ALMIDA Help! Help!

THARIOGALUS Sweet dove, I am thy hawk. [*She struggles*] Don't flutter thy white plumage in my talons.

ALMIDA Help! Help!

[*Enter soldier quickly*]

SOLDIER Excellence! The Lord Prefect comes. Claudian!

ALMIDA Thank heaven! [*Breaks from* THARIOGALUS]

THARIOGALUS None have told him? He knows not? Answer on thy peril.

SOLDIER I know nothing, Excellence. I kept guard without.

THARIOGALUS Haste! Bear this girl to the secret chamber. Haste, haste, haste!

[*In trying to avoid* THARIOGALUS, ALMIDA *goes right into the grip of the soldier. He seizes her, and drags her to the L. door*]

THARIOGALUS Make sure the door. Haste! Haste! Haste!

ALMIDA O come, master. Save me! Save me! [*Dragged out by soldier*]

THARIOGALUS He's here.

[*Enter* CLAUDIAN, *followed by* RHAMANTES *and escort*]

CLAUDIAN Where is Almida?

THARIOGALUS Eh? Oh! You mean that maid who lived in the—in the—

CLAUDIAN Where is Almida?

THARIOGALUS Illustrious, it is my duty to fulfil my public functions. I do not inform myself of maidens wandering about the town.

CLAUDIAN How knowest thou she is wandering about?

THARIOGALUS [*taken aback*] Oh! Well! I might perchance have casually heard. Ahem! I now remember, most illustrious, I heard some woman singing and, coming up, I saw this Almida insulted by the soldiers. I gave her gold and, with all gentle courtesy, I bade her go in peace.

CLAUDIAN Liar! Thou hast dared to lie to me and cans't not even mask thy lies with cunning. There! Belos! Stand forth!

[BELOS *advances, almost tottering with fright*]

BELOS [*to* THARIOGALUS] Tetrarch—I—I—your pardon.

THARIOGALUS [*to* BELOS] If thou liest of me, vile peasant, I'll have you flogged—whips, boiling oil, eyes pulled out. Beware.

CLAUDIAN [*C.*] Stand back. How darest thou threaten a better man than thou.

THARIOGALUS Better? I, the Tetrarch?

CLAUDIAN I'll pluck the chain of office from thy shoulders, and then what shall remain? Lies and corruption. Have no fear, Belos. Speak— [*with impatience*] and quickly man. What hast thou seen?

BELOS [*R.*] I—I saw—saw—[*catches* THARIOGALUS's *frown*] saw . . . He's looking at me.

CLAUDIAN Drop thine eyes, sir. Proceed.

BELOS I saw Almida who—who—who—

CLAUDIAN Rhamantes, stand between them!

BELOS [*with great effort*] I saw Almida at the gate. She tried to escape and—he's looking at me [*dodges behind soldier*]. Oh, you did—you know it. You held her arms and—yes, frown away—you had the poor maiden dragged away. Hah! I don't fear thee, bull Tetrarch!

[BELOS *exits*]

CLAUDIAN [*to Tetrarch*] Inhuman wretch, finish the tale thyself. Where hast thou concealed her?

THARIOGALUS Illustrious one, she—she—she is safe—safe—

CLAUDIAN Where?

THARIOGALUS I will confess. Knowing the interest you take—

CLAUDIAN Interest? I value one golden hair of hers more than thy whole life and office. Must I wring an answer from thee?

THARIOGALUS I confess—I confess—

CLAUDIAN Out with it! Out with it!

THARIOGALUS Almida—

CLAUDIAN Well? Well?

THARIOGALUS Almida is in the secret chamber known to my guard.

CLAUDIAN Bring her here at once.

[*Exit* RHAMANTES]

CLAUDIAN [*to* THARIOGALUS] She was thy prisoner there? She has had insult from thee? [*He grips him*]

THARIOGALUS Loosen me, Illustrious!

CLAUDIAN Hound! She has had insult?

THARIOGALUS Not the slightest. No—no—no—

CLAUDIAN I see the falsehood on thy ashy lips. Aye, thou hast cause to tremble. If thou hast dared to crawl upon the hem of her pure vesture with one loathsome approach, better be an imprisoned toad in yonder rocks than meet me face to face.

[*Enter* EDESSA, *wildly pushing her way through R.*]

EDESSA I must see him! I must speak with him.

CLAUDIAN What brings you here? Quick!

EDESSA I have a charge to make against that tyrant. Such a cruel deed will set our village weeping. Poor Agazil.

CLAUDIAN What of him?

EDESSA Death! Frightful murder at the hands of that man.

THARIOGALUS [*chattering with terror*] A wicked, wicked invention.

CLAUDIAN [*to* THARIOGALUS] Another word! Thou shalt be gagged. (*To* EDESSA) What is this news of horror!

EDESSA I saw poor Agazil seized by his orders—hurled over the battlements into the deep foaming river—I heard his drowning cry.

THARIOGALUS Hear me. I gave an order—it was—it was—it was an accident. [*Soldiers seize him*] I'll leave the town for ever—I'll atone—unhand me.

CLAUDIAN Hear thy sentence. Anger hath left me now. Men are not angry with a trapped wolf—they slay him. Thou shalt be dragged to the battlements, even to the spot where thou hast murdered this good man, and there thyself shall die his death. Bind him without and hurl him into the river [*throws* THARIOGALUS *round to the soldiers*].

THARIOGALUS [*breaks from soldiers, kneels*] Not from there! Be merciful to me—not in the roaring torrent! Imprison me, starve me, flog me—but not that death.

CLAUDIAN Away with the vermin.

THARIOGALUS O mercy! I hear his scream! The splash his body made! Do not murder me.

[*Enter* ALMIDA, *with soldier*]

CLAUDIAN At last—thou'rt safe. I'll protect thee. Come!

THARIOGALUS [*attempts to cling to her*] Intercede with—beg my life.

CLAUDIAN Leave him! Come.

THARIOGALUS Spare me! Spare me! I'll do penance. Spare me.
  [*The soldiers drag him out*]
CLAUDIAN The victim of this murderous wretch loved thee. Come.
  I will guide thee into safety. Frightened? My arm protects thee.
  [*Exit with* ALMIDA. *Scene changes*]

Scene 3

[SCENE: CLAUDIAN's *palace by moonlight. Vast marble columns,
court and garden showing terraces after terraces of the city beyond and,
across a valley extending at the back, the sea, with its shores strewn
with villas and houses. Lighted lamps are swinging from the arched
colonnades, and brass standards with unlighted lamps are standing on
each side of the stage. Huge bronze pots are filled with flowers. Marble
statues are seen here and there, and the whole has the appearance of
grandeur.* GRATIA, *a slave girl in the service of* CLAUDIAN, *and*
CLORIS, *a lad in the same service, are discovered. Other servants cross
the stage.* GRATIA *and* CLORIS *are lighting the lamps at the standards*]
CLORIS How hot and faint the air is. 'Tis like some coming tempest.
  [*Enter* SABELLA]
SABELLA Have you heard the news?
CLORIS Nay, nothing of harm.
SABELLA There is a little craft just entered harbour. The sailors say
  that, not a league from land, an island is upheaved, known to no
  chart. An island verdured with sea greenery of weeds and bleached
  coral, and strange things which crawl on deep sea shoals lie dead—
  dead upon its clefts.
GRATIA Strange! Now I do remember at the third hour I heard a peal
  of thunder.
SABELLA That was no thunder, or else thunder of the earth.
CLORIS You mean an—
GRATIA You frighten us.
CLORIS How know you of such horrors?
SABELLA My mother witnessed the ruin of the town of Issa.
GIRLS O tell us, tell us.
GRATIA Nay, I'll not hear it, [*rising*]. Three times I dreamed last night
  that I was falling down some fearful cave. I'll go. [*Comes back
  fascinated*]
SABELLA You know where stood the thriving town of Issa—its ruins
  are the haunt of owl and jackal. My father perished there. And by

good hap, or by God's aid, my mother just escaped with her only child.

GRATIA Go on.

SABELLA My mother, who was drawing at the well outside the walls, had brought me on her arm, an infant of two years. The well was touched with sulphurous odours—a small misty cloud hung in the air above it. As 'tis now, all nature seemed to listen for some dread secret pausing to be told. Sounds that the ear of superstition knows— so ghostly deep and undefinable—broke on the ear, moans as the distant roar of herding lions. [*Rises*] And the earth shuddered as in mortal awe. Suddenly, as by gigantic ploughshare, in flaming furrows rifled street and court, earth seemed an ocean, and the toppling houses, like desperate wrecks, foundered with crash on crash. Whilst you could lift your hand three times, it lasted. But in that span temple and battlements, and people, and their wealth, and homes, and babes were like a fleeting show, sunken and gone. The living town, a ghastly skeleton.

CLORIS Hunph, 'tis nothing! One of Sabella's ghostly tales. Come, let us look without.

SABELLA Hush! The Prefect comes!

[*Exeunt* SABELLA, GRATIA, CLORIS, *and others. Enter* CLAUDIAN *and* ALMIDA]

CLAUDIAN Almida, seat thee and rest. [ALMIDA *is mute*] Almida, you have sought me—you have found me—only to part again.

ALMIDA Then lead me to thy portals, and I will sit upon the lower step and rest all day to catch a little footfall within, where thou dost dwell. Happy within! And sometime I will catch a little waft of thy kind voice addressed to another, more blest than I.

CLAUDIAN [*affected*] You have somewhat to tell me. What is it?

ALMIDA Sir, I have thought and reasoned with myself, and I am full of a most glad conclusion which came to me, and—shall I tell you master?

CLAUDIAN Tell me briefly—for I must look, Almida, to your safety, find you some escort, some retreat, where you and I can never meet again.

ALMIDA [*rising*] Do not drive me away.

CLAUDIAN Not till I have heard you.

ALMIDA You see, dear master—may I call you master? It is a humble and a loving word—

CLAUDIAN Go on! Go on!

ALMIDA [*mysteriously*] Well, I have thought, since 'tis I who bear the penalty of blindness, and not thou, that if I be for ever by thy side, those other pains and troubles of thy doom might light on me.

CLAUDIAN Heaven forbid! That would be terrible!

ALMIDA That would be triumph! Thrice-told happiness. [*Sits*]

CLAUDIAN Then heaven hath found for me its sharpest pang. 'Twill be to see that hour when thou shalt bear an added pain for me. Listen, my child, I do not need thy pity. Of late my doom sits lighter on my life. I know not but that heaven doth lift its hand. The poor are eased, and secret charity doth fill the city, and the good that's done is not for this man, or for that, but for all. 'Tis like the sunshine of which the veriest beggar hath his share. Therefore, grieve not for me. Already thou hast had disaster, blindness, from me. The flowers, the woods, and all the pomp of clouds, the sight of which are fairy gifts to youth, are black for thee. Is't enough?

ALMIDA [*with simplicity*] Ah, but I thought my blindness was a blessing as we came hither, because it gave me thine encircling arm. Thou wert mine eyes. This helplessness, it is the only bond betwixt my humbleness and thy sad splendour.

CLAUDIAN [*aside*] That poor blind look o'ermasters me. My heart goes out to her. Let her bide awhile. Her Agazil is dead. I do not wrong him by gentleness to her. Why should I put this precious solace from me for a short day—one short day?

[*Thunder*]

ALMIDA [*plantively*] Hark, was that thunder? I may tarry here!

CLAUDIAN I dare not look at her whilst I repel her. [*Aloud*] Why hast thou come to me? Why hast thou followed me?

ALMIDA You will let me rest. I cannot tell why I followed thee. [*Caressingly*] Master, I am come.

CLAUDIAN [*mildly*] If thou dost love, canst thou not hide it from me? In woman's mercy, take thy blind gaze from me. I cannot bear it. Think of me as a demon. Hie thee home!

ALMIDA [*shaking her head*] I never can return. I am so changed. I could almost believe the Almida that was sits smiling there in her small chamber with her past love, past pleasures, and lost sight, and that I am some pale and wandering spirit, blest with this mission, to mingle all my utmost thoughts with thine, to draw my very life and breath from thee—thou art my sight, my hope, my very life.

CLAUDIAN [*aside, overcome with suppressed joy*] Has my sun set for ever in the storm? Here comes a great glad down again for me. Joy that I had forgot comes shyly back. Her love may be the talisman long sought. Haply the curse may lift and fly from me. [*Restrains him-*

self] Merciful heaven, whither am I borne? O let me pause, let me pause!

ALMIDA [*with simplicity*] I may stay! I know I may. Your voice is soft. The air is strangely lulled, stifling and breezeless—some storm about to break. You will not send me hence. If I should leave you, I should pine and die. You would not kill me.

CLAUDIAN [*with outburst*] I know not if this be a way of peace, or the swift smoothness of the swollen torrent. I care not if all nature bade me stop. I'd still go on. Almida, turn thy sweet blind face to me. Outstretch thy hands, white tendrils of the heart, to cling to me. Thy very touch doth send a luxury of light and hope and balm through every pulse. Thy presence fills my heart so long vacant. Be thou as close and linked a companion as was my sorrow, never leaving me. Claudian, of late a spectre of the past, now man again and filled with passionate rapture, spreads out his arms to thee. Come! Come! Fill them! I love thee! I love thee!

[*At that moment, with a sudden roar, the stage is upheaved—the columns topple over, the arches fall with a crash.* ALMIDA *is swept away. Flash after flash of lightning only increases the darkness, which grows every moment. Between the flashes, the audience can see the increasing destruction. The palace has disappeared in heaps of crumbled ruins—the city all around has suffered the same fate.* CLAUDIAN *alone is left standing where he was*]

CLAUDIAN [*with despairing cry*] And I alone cannot die! I alone cannot die!

[*Curtain*]

ACT III

[SCENE: *Same as Scene 3 of ACT II was left, but quiet, calm moonlight.* CLAUDIAN *heard without, calling*]

CLAUDIAN Almida! Almida! Almida! [*Enters*] Almida! Almida! Where art thou? 'Twas here I stood, and she was at my side upon this spot. O spot of earth most desolate of all, because most happy then. O that these stones had tongues to tell me of her. I have searched the caves and rifts, shouted her name down ruined colonnades—no voice replied, but fearful echoes from the dead. Almida, thou one last link to earth, gone from me with the rest—all, all, is ruin. The last link of life is shattered. [*Sinks into shuddering horror, sobs*] E'en the city that I loved—a hecatomb of dead. I saw amid—[*then, in horror, recounts*] the glare and thunderous dust wild, fleeting masses of poor fugitives clutch at the yawning lip of the abyss, and there, with stifled shriek, drop writhing down into the sulphurous depths. Wild eyes did cast on me speechless reproach. And all was death. [*Pauses a moment, the ruin catches his eye*] Peace! Peace to them. What blessed memory flits across my brain? The rocks have rent. The gulf hath opened. So said the hermit, 'When the rocks rend'. Ah, there is peace for me. Now I may choose. Oh, happy memory. A sunburst in the tempest. Now shall I sleep in dreamless rest for ever, and grass and flowers shall sprout above my grave, sown by the birds, and they shall be uncursed. Meek daffodils shall not transform to nightshade and to hemlock. Above these ruins shall the forests grow. They shall drink deep of the dew from morn to even, and not give forth the pestilence at noon. [*Pause*] Where art thou, thou old prophet, thou whose blood so long hath been upon my guilty head. I call upon thee for thy promise, give me that best boon, that heart balm—death. Give it to me here. I beg for it. Thou hast given the choice, I hold thee to thy pledge, dread visitant. Where art thou? Where art thou? Where art thou?

[*Spectre of hermit* [CLEMENT] *appears*]

HERMIT Here!

CLAUDIAN My brain reels, and the chill again around my heart, as on the fatal day. The dead! Stains of decay upon his shroudy garment. His spectral eyes hold mine in frozen awe. I know thee. Thy dying look is branded on my memory. Speak!

HERMIT Thou hast summoned me. Thy hour of choice is come. Choose life or death.

CLAUDIAN I fear not death, but thee. My mind is steadfast. I'll meet death as a babe its mother's bosom. But that past sin, thy murder, withers me—and that wan, reverend face! O hence! O hence!

HERMIT Again a woman's fate rests in thy hands. Thy curse is shared by her while thou dost live. With thy death, drops from her the evil spell cast on her heart by thee. The love she owes to him, like a fresh bride shall return to him. O forfeit not thine heavenly crown. Choose life or death.

CLAUDIAN But she is dead. Beneath these ruins she lieth crushed and buried.

HERMIT She lives! Choose life or death.

CLAUDIAN [mildly] She lives. Why hast thou told me that she lives? Was it to shake my choice, to sap my manhood—she loves me, loves me—no. I cannot die. Leave me but her—and forfeit be my heavenly crown. Her love, her pity, be my crown on earth. Whilst she is living, I choose life! Life! Life!

HERMIT Again thou darest impiously to thrust thyself between a good loving man and her whom heaven hath given him.

CLAUDIAN Have I not done a long, soul-crushing penance? May I not now be trusted? Have I not learned the bitter lesson of the wage of sin, until my heart was aching sore with yearning to atone—atonement that was never granted me? Have I not earned the respite, the relief?

HERMIT Thy old crime rises again to wither—against thee and this relief—but means another ruin.

CLAUDIAN But he is dead—drowned in the rushing torrent. The sea holds his remains.

HERMIT He lives. The providence which laid its hand on thee hath saved this good man from the raging waters. A cedar tree, torn by the sapping torrent from its banked roots, lay prone across the stream within his grasp. He is saved—whether for weal or woe does rest with thee. His fate and happiness doth hang in the same balance as thy life or death, and still unpurified by thy long penance. Thy hard and selfish will outlives the trial. Thrice have I offered thee thy prayer. Choose life or death before the moon.

[Spectre begins to fade]

CLAUDIAN [wildly] O tarry! I did not tempt her. I thought that heaven in pity sent me her—because I patiently endured so long. Let me live only while she lives—then let me die, clasped in her arms. O hear me! Give me clinging diseases and pain and poverty until another man would pray for death. But my great love—no love like

it hath been—will make me smiling blest. Gone, all is dark. O life,
life, life! How precious thou art now!

[AGAZIL *and* ALMIDA *enter R.*]

They come, and hand in hand, whom I would part. Aye, put a
world between. [*To* AGAZIL *and* ALMIDA] Do not approach me. I
have a struggle in my riven heart. Thy presence fights against me.
I would conquer. [*Aside*] How softly both of them do gaze at me.
I will not let them see my agony.

ALMIDA Master, how is it with thee? Agazil, my betrothed, and I have
sought thee in thy great trouble to be near thee, master, and offer
thee our loving, faithful service. I almost see thee.

CLAUDIAN And they both thought of me in my despair, and bring their
gentle sympathy to me. My jealous heart be secret—hide thine
anguish. If I must love her, love her to the death. She shall not know.
[*Aloud, wildly, almost harshly*] Why come ye to me, poor injured
ones. Look around—I am the cause of all these ruins. If ye have
tears, give them to the dead, not me. Learn to forget me. If ye can't
forget me, then learn to hate me. Shudder at my name, tell over all
the ills ye had from me—blindness and beggary and fatal passion—
and thou, good fellow, aid her in the task. Thy ruin, peril—lonely,
broken-hearted. Repeat the tale, and thank thy guardian saint that
Claudian the accurst has passed away. [*Faltering*] My hour is come.
Why should ye see my death or waste your tears on such a wretch
as I?

ALMIDA A light seems faintly breaking through my tears. [*To* CLAU-
DIAN] You must not die. You must not teach me how to think of
you. My heart shall be recorder—I'll remember.

CLAUDIAN [*with contrast of overwhelming emotions*] What have I said? To
hate—to forget. I ask thee to remember me with tears. With pardon. With thine own sweet woman's pity. Mid all the curses heaped
on my memory, be thy gentle voice upraised for me. Say of me
with a sigh, 'He wished for good that every harm he wrought. He
suffered more, ten times, than the dear one whom he had harmed.'
Join sometimes in a prayer for one who prayed even in vain—who
would have stretched out hands of blessing to you, ample as heaven,
yet died with empty hands. This hour your trouble shall be lifted
from you. Farewell is bitter without full forgiveness. You owe me
nothing. It is I who beg. [*Crosses to* AGAZIL]

AGAZIL I pardon thee with all my heart, with all my heart.

ALMIDA I have no right to pardon and can never forget. [*Aside*]
Methinks I see him smile.

CLAUDIAN [*aside, making his choice of death*] Great spirit, for her sake I
die. My choice is death.

[*Thunder. Flash of lightning.* ALMIDA *clutches* AGAZIL. *A change
comes over* CLAUDIAN. *He slowly sinks*]

CLAUDIAN I bless you—'tis the first time I dare say these words—I
bless you. Be happy—true to your life's end, and think of me. On
the grey threshold of eternity, I say farewell. Ah, darker, darker!
This is death.

ALMIDA [*with enthusiasm*] I see a light upon his face forbidding us to
weep. Master, I am no longer blind! It is the first scene that greets
my sight—thy death!

[CLAUDIAN *rouses himself*]

CLAUDIAN My curse is lifted from me. I thank God. Farewell—I bless
you, and you shall be blessed. Ah, the moment's come! What peace!
What peace! Farewell!

[*Dies with radiance. Curtain*]

THE LAST DAYS OF POMPEII

James Pain

Whilst toga drama was drawing audiences to theatres, a wholly distinct form of toga play, performed to audiences of more than 10,000 persons at a time, began to reach spectators in Britain, America, Europe, South America, and throughout the British Empire. Conflicts—between Christian and pagan, between civilizing white and black, oriental, or red-skinned heathen, between good imperialists and bad imperialists— were being staged in pyrodramas. *The Last Days of Pompeii* was the most popular and longest-enduring of these outdoor melodramas staged on a grand scale.

'Outdoor pictures with fireworks', or 'set-piece fireworks', had come into existence by the late 1840s. It was not unusual for the semi-rural pleasure-grounds which edged British cities to offer late-evening firework displays before large scenic backcloths painted to represent a named locale and illuminated from behind by bonfires. A favoured subject for these static displays was the destruction of Pompeii in AD 79. By the early 1850s, George Jennison, the proprietor of Belle Vue Gardens in Manchester,[41] had added live performers to the scenic display. The practice spread. In 1879 Alexandra Palace in North London opened to pyrodramas staged by the South London firework manufacturer, James Pain.[42] The 'Ally Pally' pyrodrama was the show-piece of Pain's British operation, but business with a single annual set piece was so successful—as many as 25,000 spectators may have seen one bank holiday performance[43]—that he was not obliged to enlarge his repertoire or to offer multiple attractions. The very nature of Pain's attractions—outdoor dramas which ended with a known historical city

---

[41] See my 'The World on Fire: Pyrodramas at Belle Vue Gardens, Manchester, c.1850–1950 in John MacKenzie (ed.), *Popular Imperialism and the Military* (Manchester, 1991), 179–97.

[42] See my 'Romans in Britain 1886–1910: Pain's *The Last Days of Pompeii*, *Theatrephile*, 2 5 (Winter, 1984–5), 41–50.

[43] See my 'A Wet Bank Holiday at the "Ally Pally" ', *Nineteenth Century Theatre*, 12 1–2 (1984), 75–92.

destroyed by cataclysm (sometimes a natural disaster, as at Pompeii, but, more frequently, by siege and war)—alerted audiences to the factual aspect of the drama. The heroine Ione, the hero Glaucus, and the villain Arbaces may have been fictional inhabitants of Pompeii, but Pompeii was historically real. Romans persecuted Christians and, at their whim, fed them to lions. The power of Rome and the weaknesses of Rome were there to be seen. Pyrodramas had become international entertainment when Pain opened a New York office in 1882. His first objective was the five mile expanse of sandy seashore that met the Atlantic at the southern end of Brooklyn on Coney Island.

The geography and amusements of Coney Island are of significance because they constitute a link between toga drama and the earliest surviving toga film, and because they demonstrate the transatlantic traffic in toga dramas. Coney Island was developing as New York's semi-rural summer resort. At the eastern end were the working-class pleasure-grounds—crowded, carnival-like attractions—shows, swing-boats, lodging-houses, and beer gardens. Midway along the sea front to the west was the resort community of Brighton Beach, with small cottages, a three-storey hotel in the shape of an elephant, and a racecourse. Still further west was Manhattan Beach, dominated by a few exclusive and more expensive hotels. The Long Island Rail-road from New York and the boroughs served all three areas, carrying day-trippers from the city and horses to the racecourse.[44] The sand-spit was narrower here, because Sheepshead Bay lies behind Manhattan Beach to the south, and in between there is an irregular marsh.

Pain secured a piece of land approximately 300 feet to the rear of the Manhattan Beach Hotel, and erected a rectangular enclosure 345 feet wide and 495 feet deep.[45] At the southern end of the enclosure, he built a narrow grandstand 300 feet across, with seating for several rows of spectators. From the grandstand ran a sloped ramp 30 feet deep to accommodate standing spectators. For each performance—nightly in July and August—as many as 10,000 spectators stood or sat with their backs to the Atlantic to face the stage to the north. At the lower

[44] John F. Kasson, *Amusing the Million: Coney Island at the Turn of the Century* (New York, 1978).

[45] The location and precise dimensions of Pain's enclosure, and its handiness to Brighton Beach racecourse for the 1907 filming of *Ben-Hur*, can be read on large-scale maps: *Insurance Maps of the Borough of Brooklyn, City of New York*, xiv (New York, 1904), pls. 123–6. The two Coney Island maps in this volume are derived from these fire insurance maps (see page 98).

end of the slope, Pain erected a platform for an orchestra,[46] and dug a lake 260 feet wide and about 70 feet across, in front of a stage that was as wide as the enclosure and 120 feet deep. The lake, filled by water seeping in from the marsh at Sheepshead Bay, may have been no more than a few feet deep; it needed only to be navigable by skiffs seen to be fleeing from a burning Pompeii. The lake was intended as a safety barrier, protecting spectators from falling firework debris and sparks, but it served also as a reflector, mirroring the fireworks, and as a surface over which a crosswind was likely to blow, thus preventing smoke from hanging between spectators and the stage. The lake, moreover, placed an unbridgeable distance between spectator and the pyrodrama. Dramatic actions were at once immediate and remote. Illuminated by fire and pyrotechnics and arc lamps from the stage, and unevenly reflected in the broken surface of the lake, the double illusion accentuated the exoticism and otherness of the setting and the drama within it.

Although no details of the stage survive, it is likely that it was constructed like other pyrodrama stages, built upon ramped earth, with a slope that, from the upstage end, descended sharply down stage to the water's edge. The stage would have been slightly 'dished', that is, rising at the sides. The overall effect would have been to intensify perspective and to distance effects created by graduated rows of flat and profile stage scenery. The scenery itself—in this instance for *The Last Days of Pompeii*—was made to resemble the façades of domestic, civic, and recreational Pompeian buildings. Most were of canvas, painted in oil pigments and stretched over iron-rimmed frames. The backs of some of these were 'opaqued' in places so that bonfires— added for further effect—burning behind the scenes would not show through, whereas others were treated with an oil solution that made the canvas glow as if the building were burning from within. Often, upper segments of flats were hinged along irregular horizontal cuts and then propped with stage-braces. When, during the conflagration of the city, stage-hands removed the braces, the upper storeys of the buildings appeared to collapse, sometimes revealing behind them twisted skeletal frames seen as wreckage of the fallen structures. Al-

[46] The theatre's orchestra, led by Patrick Sarsfield Gilmore, occasionally did double duty, moving between the fireworks enclosure and a nearby 'music amphitheatre' for afternoon and evening concerts. At such times the pyrodrama was sandwiched between Gilmore's concerts, one concert scheduled for 3.30 p.m., another at 7.15 p.m., and a late one at approximately 9.15 p.m. The timetabling of concerts and the length of musical programme suggest that the pyrodrama required about 45 minutes to perform.

though these sets were treated with fireproofing compounds, it was a practice to douse the entire set and the stage with water before each performance. None the less, small fires would break out.

Pain's theatrical skill lay in bringing to life a Pompeii inhabited by no fewer than 300 meticulously costumed actors, mostly supernumeraries hired locally and a few trained performers. It was the travelling stage-director's responsibility to drill his supers in individual and crowd movements and to arrange the tableaux which realized a number of paintings known to audiences as popular engravings. In *The Last Days of Pompeii*, at least two pictures, both inspired by Bulwer-Lytton's novel, are realized: Edward Poynter's *Faithful unto Death*, and Lawrence Alma-Tadema's *The Flower Girl*. Given the abbreviated text and the obligation to mime most of the action, characterization was necessarily minimal. Male roles are normally differentiated between hero and villain, and the female roles, both virtuous, are distinguished by being sighted and passive or blind and active.

Pain's *The Last Days of Pompeii* enacts the troubled courtship of two Pompeians, Glaucus and Ione. Although Ione is promised to Glaucus, his suit is vexed by her guardian Arbaces, the corrupt priest of the cult of Isis. Glaucus is beloved secretly, distantly, by the blind flower-girl Nydia. The drama's conflict is slight. It involves little more than short mimed episodes in which Arbaces hampers and restricts Ione's access to Glaucus, and eventually has Ione imprisoned in his house. He accuses Glaucus of being a secret Christian, and persuades the Pompeian mob to deliver the young man to the arena to face the lions. However, before the lions are loosed, there are processions and Roman games to be held. At the last moment, as Glaucus is cast into the arena, Vesuvius, ominously puffing smoke at the rear of the set, erupts. Pompeians flee in all directions, taking to the boats, falling under toppling buildings, looting before dying. Arbaces dies beneath a falling column. Glaucus frees Ione, but, in the dark of the volcanic smoke, they become dependent upon Nydia for their salvation. Only when the lovers are safely in a boat can the rejected blind girl take her life and Glaucus and Ione safely acknowledge their conversion to Christianity.

Whereas Bulwer-Lytton's novel interrogates the class and political issues of the 1830s, Pain's adaptation, straightforward in its narrative and anxious to avoid offence, eliminates such nuances, in particular leaving out the characters of a parvenu middle-class merchant and his daughter, a rival to Ione. Thus the Pompeians caught in the apocalyptic volcanic eruption are not categorized by class, but by moral qualities. Roman and Egyptian decadence and corruption are spectacularly terminated in a finale that provided audiences at Alexandra Palace or Coney Island with a rich mixture of historical education, Christian morality, and fiery entertainment, a combination that satisfied and justified the quest for pleasure.

The cataclysm is, of course, dependent upon pyrotechnics. Victorian pyrotechnics, unrestricted by modern safety regulations, could be far more varied and exciting, and used at closer range, than today's Bonfire Night and 4 July fireworks. Pain's Vesuvius was seen with cascades of lava descending its sides—in actuality, raft-born fireworks bobbing down in transparent glass water-troughs. Vesuvius was lit by coloured 'lances' of burning chemicals, and similar effects were seen thoughout Pompeii. Indeed, the success of Pain's *The Last Days of Pompeii* and of the other pyrodramas which were to occupy his Manhattan Beach site and to travel across America to other cities—Buffalo, St Louis, Peoria, Chicago, Cincinnati, Cleveland, and others—lay in his skill in industrializing the pyrodrama. In any one tour, Pain or his associates packaged a number of settings for pyrodramas on a wide variety of historical or topical subjects, excavated lakes and built stages and grandstands identical in dimension to the Manhattan Beach enclosure, trained and costumed casts of 300 actors and extras, and then transported some of the cast to new sites, where the process began again. He developed the technology of firework-making so that, daily, several hundredweights of pyrotechnics could be manufactured and stored on site. He marketed a tour that induced local businessmen to venture into a profit-sharing arrangement, assured that Pain would provide promotional material, seating, a director to hire and train extras and to incorporate local performers, and a bandmaster to conduct local musicians.

Citing spectacle as the element common to both media, Nicholas Vardac[47] has identified pyrodramas as one of the Victorian dramatic entertainments that influenced the development of cinema. Vardac might have taken his comparison further. Pyrodramas such as James Pain's *The Last Days of Pompeii* conditioned audiences to observe and understand extended narrative intelligible only through action, minimal facial expression, and gesture performed with the emotion-informing assistance of accompanying orchestral music. With both media, the eye and the ear collaborated, between them inferring all meaning apart from what might be gathered from either a few shouted words or brief inter-titles.

[47] Vardac, *Stage to Screen*, 44–5.

The text of the scenario of *The Last Days of Pompeii* is taken from *Prospectus: James Pain and Sons, Pyrotechnicians, America, England, Australia—Producers of Pain's Gorgeous Spectacles*, printed for H. B. Thearle & Co., New York and Chicago, 1891.

Poster for *The Last Days of Pompeii. c.*1890 (Courtesy of the Pain Archive)

Pain's *The Last Days of Pompeii* at Manhattan Beach, Coney Island, 1885. From *Harper's Weekly*. (Courtesy of the Pain Archive)

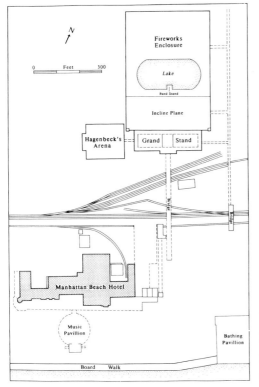

Plan of the fireworks enclosure
at Manhattan Beach and nearby
buildings as depicted in the
Sanborn Map Company's fire
insurance maps, 1904.

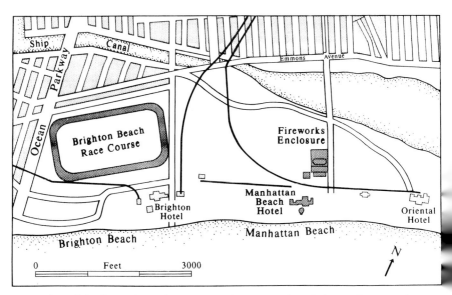

Plan of the fireworks enclosure at Manhattan Beach and the Brighton Beach
Racecourse, 1904. (See Kalem film of *Ben Hur*, 1909)

Frame from the chariot race sequence in the 1907 Kalem film version of *Ben Hur*. The sequence was filmed at the Brighton Beach Racecourse on Coney Island. The set in the background is a section of the setting for James Pain's pyrodrama, *The Last Days of Pompeii*.

PAIN'S GREAT SPECTACLE
The Last Days of Pompeii
The Most Realistic Spectacle Ever Produced in Any Country

This gorgeous representation shows the ancient city with its streets, bath houses, temples, amphitheaters, etc., and Vesuvius in the distance. Covering over ten thousand square yards of oil painting, upon wood, iron and canvas, produced in a marvelously artistic manner by Joseph Harker, from special designs taken on the spot, the great subject containing real buildings from twenty feet to forty feet high, while Vesuvius towers above in the distance, nearly one hundred feet, the entire work being three hundred feet long, with an immense lake of real water, two hundred and seventy-five feet long and seventy feet wide, the whole covering an area of nearly five acres, with a grand stand to accommodate ten thousand persons. The dramatized work is from Lord Lytton's immortal novel, 'The Last Days of Pompeii' and depicts, as accurately as possible, one of the greatest events recorded in history. The streets are filled with citizens, soldiers, priests and priestesses, while on the lake are numerous gondolas filled with citizens. Several hundred people in correct and picturesque costumes, made in and imported from Italy, take part in this wonderful and never-to-be-forgotten entertainment. All the sports of the Roman Amphitheater, including races, boxing, wrestling, fencing, gladiatorial combats, etc., vividly reproduced with the solemn procession of priests and choir boys, grand march and drill of the Roman guards, etc., concluding with the marvelous eruption of Vesuvius and total destruction of the city—the burning lava running in torrents into the lake, spreading desolation and destruction in its course. Each representation will terminate with a brilliant display of Pain's celebrated Manhattan Beach fireworks, including novel set pieces, fire portraits, aerial and aquatic wonders. The music is composed and arranged by P. S. Gilmore, and performed by a full military band.

Synopsis of Events

I. Nydia at the Altar (Prayer). II. Pompeian Games by the Citizens. III. Body of Roman Guards, Body Guard to escort Senators to Palace.

IV. Grand Procession of Guards, Priest, Priestess, Flower Girls and Attendants, with the great Arbaces, who comes to meet Ione, who is seen in company with Nydia and Glaucus on the Water. Approaching in their Gondolas. V. The Departure of Arbaces with Ione to his Palace.

The Sport Now Begins

VI. Racing by the Boys of Pompeii. VII. Grand Brother Act. VIII. Boxing by Roman Athletes. IX. Bicycle Performance. X. Grand Wrestling Bout between Roman and Greek. XI. Dance of Flower Girls. XII. Trident Fight by Roman Gladiators. XIII. Procession of Arbaces to the Temple. XIV. Death of Arbaces and Destruction of the City by the Awful Eruption of Vesuvius.

After the eruption of the mountain, and while everything is in darkness, commences—

The Fireworks

Every night being a special night, a complete change of programme in the pyrotechnical features will be made with new, novel and appropriate designs and devices, startling effects, etc.

As the performance begins, the streets fill up with 'the people', the populace, who arrive singly and in groups in order to secure seats to witness the procession and festivities. Husbands and wives and little children mingle with flower girls, refreshment venders and priests, while lads and lasses eagerly press about in search of places which command the best views of the pageant.

Presently a trumpet is heard, and at the same time small flower-decked barges pass across the ornamental lake, and the prows of the galleys make their appearance, as from under the triumphal arches a group of soldiers, with standards and musical instruments, emerge, and announce the coming of Arbaces. The soldiers are followed by a dozen negro slaves, holding up inscriptions and bannerets in honor of the powerful Egyptian. Then come priests in white robes, next a number of dancing girls and a senator or 'member for Pompeii', with his attendants; next some ladies, and lastly a guard of honour, two and two, in front of Arbaces, who, clad in purple and gold, walks under a canopy. This procession crosses the stage and bows to the officials of the city, who sit under a canopy to the right, in a building

overlooking the water. The procession then turns to the left, and part
of it, including Arbaces, passes down the steps to the water's edge to
await the arrival of the galleys, which now enter in full view. They
advance gradually, and from the first alight soldiers and slaves, from
the second, Ione and her affianced bridegroom, the Greek, Glaucus.
Arbaces receives Ione with profound obeisance, but barely conde-
scends to notice Glaucus, thereby indicating his jealousy and dislike.
The procession reforms, and the guests take positions under the portico of Arbaces' house. By this time it is dark, and the beautiful city,
with its villas and temples, appears brightly lighted with divers kinds
of lights and lamps. Music strikes up, and, upon the signal of a blast
of trumpets, the doors of the temple of Isis are thrown open, and the
temple's illuminated interior is discovered. The priests in white garments, and the priestesses in white and dark blue robes, issue solemnly
bearing aloft the golden image of the Egyptian goddess, which they
place in the center of the stage. All kneel for a moment, and then the
dancing girls begin a slow movement, and Nydia, the blind girl, appears
and dances gracefully. Suddenly Arbaces cries out, '*If there be Christians
present, and known to any of you, let them be denounced and brought forward
to adore the great goddess, Isis.*' The people in return cry out, '*Glaucus is
a Christian; let him worship the goddess, or death be unto him!*'

Ione, upon hearing these cries, and knowing her affianced husband
to be secretly a Christian, rises in terror, but Glaucus boldly descends,
and, sword in hand, advances toward the idol, which now appears to
glow with internal fire. Vesuvius also begins to show signs of an
approaching eruption. Glaucus is about to strike the goddess, when
the blind Nydia, guessing his intention, and guided by his voice,
prevents him, and, rushing toward the goddess, herself overthrows the
tripod which stands at the idol's feet.

All rise in confusion, the earth quakes, the dread mountain vomits
forth flames and clouds of smoke; the temple columns totter, and the
people, forgetting Isis and her priests, remember only their danger.
Glaucus seizes Ione, and with Nydia clinging to them, they manage
to enter a boat, and are seen, amid the flashes of lightning and the
glow from the torrents of flaming lava, escaping across the water from
the doomed city. Arbaces is killed by a falling column, while the
people, screaming and shouting for aid, rush in wild confusion in every
direction, realizing Lord Lytton's magnificent and graphic description
of the appalling catastrophe:

The sudden illumination, the bursts of the floods of lava, and the earthquake,
which we have already described, chanced when Sallust and his party had just

gained the direct path leading from the city to the port: and here they were arrested by an immense crowd, more than half the population of the city. They spread along the fields without the walls, thousands upon thousands, uncertain whither to fly. The sea had retired far from the shore; and they who had fled to it had been so terrified by the agitation and preternatural shrinking of the element, the gasping forms of the uncouth sea things which the waves had left upon the sand, and by the sound of the huge stones, cast from the mountain into the deep, that they had returned again to the land, as presenting the less frightful aspect of the two. Thus the two streams of human beings, the one seaward, the other from the sea, had met together, feeling a sad comfort in numbers arrested in despair and doubt. 'The world is to be destroyed by fire', said an old man in long loose robes, a philosopher of the Stoic school. Stoic and Epicurean wisdom have alike agreed in this prediction: and 'the hour is come!' As he spake, there came that sudden illumination which had heralded the death of Arbaces, and glowing over that mighty multitude, awed, crouching, breathless—never on earth had the faces of men seemed so haggard;—never had the meeting of mortal beings been so stamped with the horror and sublimity of dread;—never, till the last trumpet sounds, shall such meeting be seen again: And above rose the form of Olinthus, with outstretched arm and prophet brow, girt with the living fires. And the crowd knew the face of him they had doomed to the fangs of the beast, then their victim, now their warner; and through the stillness again came his ominous voice; 'The hour is come!' The Christian repeated the cry. It was caught up—it was echoed from side to side—woman and man—childhood and old age—repeated, not aloud, but in a smothered and dreary murmur—'the hour is come!'

THE SIGN OF THE CROSS

Wilson Barrett

Whatever merit may be assigned to previous toga pieces, without *The Sign of the Cross* and its attendant success there would be conspicuously fewer toga plays, and Chance Newton's double-edged term of disparagement and acknowledgement might have passed unremarked. The play still attracts hostility—now from critics who have neither read nor seen it—much as it did when it toured the North of England in late 1895 and began its London run early in 1896. Critics favouring the 'New Drama', William Archer and Bernard Shaw especially, were both aggressive and playful, and Shaw continued to worry the play and Barrett's less successful adaptation of *Quo Vadis?* (1900) until 1913, when he bundled both dramas into *Androcles and the Lion*. *Androcles* demonstrates that Shaw, even as he mocked the genre's tendency to primitive theology, had absorbed the conventions of toga drama and that, even at that date, the power of toga plays was not lost on theatre audiences.

The Sign of the Cross is effective drama both by the standard of earlier and subsequent toga plays and by the broader standard of melodrama. As well as benefiting from the virtues of melodrama, *The Sign of the Cross* also suffers from the excesses of melodramatic characterization, even if these excesses are an intentional element of Barrett's strategy. Barrett's Christians, if occasionally weak in the face of persecution and torture, are infallibly good; Romans, pagans all, are, with the exception of Marcus, wicked or corrupt or, at best, spoilt, superficial, and cynical. Those who do not hold political power are drawn as boring socialites; one of Marcus's orgies would be tedium itself.

As much as *The Sign of the Cross* meets the configurations of popular melodrama, it also invades the territory of the New Drama and what moral censors were stigmatizing as 'the drama of the divorce court' or 'Mayfair divorce comedy'. G. W. Foote, Barrett's antagonist, senses something of this invasion and Barrett's appropriation of dialogue and costuming techniques from 'Society' comedy when he sneers: 'A red-faced paunchy devotee of Bacchus [Glabrio] amuses the audience with his hackneyed jocosity, while a few ladies expose naked arms and indulge in frivolous conversation about marriage—which immensely tickled the listeners and brought a curious leer on some sedate faces.'[48] Dacia's party (Act I), which Marcus never manages to attend, Glabrio's bemused fascination with Mercia, both in the street and at Marcus's home (Act III, scene iii), and Berenis's meetings with Dacia (Act III, scene i) and Poppaea (Act IV, scene i) are similar in dialogue and characterization to episodes from contemporary West End Society plays which weigh the values of worldliness, sophistication, and dissimulation against innocence, virtue, and duty. A leading term of abuse—wielded by moralists and by such morally orientated New Dramatists as Henry Arthur Jones and Arthur Pinero—is 'cynicism'. To be cynical is to reject all values, and Barrett's Romans, Marcus no less than the others, are cynics. To the religious person of the late nineteenth century, cynicism was but a step short of scepticism, and beyond scepticism lay doubt and atheism. One thread of *The Sign of the Cross* is the redemption of Marcus from *fin de siècle* cynicism, and his grasping at cynicism's antithesis, faith. It is the possession of faith that in part distinguishes Mercia. Their courtship confounds Marcus's cynicism and expectations of easily won satisfactions. In the novel that Barrett produced from his playscript to create a popular souvenir of *The Sign of the Cross*, he describes Marcus's early view of marriage:

He had grown weary of the wiles of the women he had constantly to meet. He knew their weaknesses, their vices, their allurements by heart. The flesh alone had been moved—never his soul. The brightest, wittiest, and most clever among them he had found some pleasure in, but there was always a something wanting in them that usually drove him with impatience away. They were not all vicious actually, but vice was not abhorrent to them. All who dared hope for the honour (and there were few who did not) schemed and plotted to become his wife. 'Marriage! faugh! a mere licence for profligacy, immunity from shame; the husband a shield that protected but did not hide the wife's laxity. No, he would have none of it.'[49]

Thus, at the play's beginning Marcus is a rake with no respect for marriage:

GLABRIO . . . Marcus. You should take unto yourself a wife.
MARCUS With pleasure, Glabrio. Whose wife would you recommend?
GLABRIO Ha! Ha! That's good, by Venus.
DACIA Why don't you marry, Marcus?

[48] Foote, '*The Sign of the Cross*', 28.
[49] Wilson Barrett, *The Sign of the Cross* [novel] (Preston, 1896), 59–60.

MARCUS Because I hate the tedious formalities of divorce, and nowadays in
Rome it is thought more honourable to support your friend's wife than
your own, while women of fashion reckon their lives not by their years
but by the number of their husbands.

DACIA Do no noble ladies keep their husbands?

MARCUS Yes, those who wish to pique their lovers.

DACIA Rumour saith—

MARCUS Rumour hath many tongues—mostly lying ones, lady. I may commit many acts of folly, but not matrimony. (Act I)

Marriage to Berenis would do nothing to remove him from the
corruption of Nero's court, but marriage, even a spiritual marriage, to
Mercia promises the recovery of faith:

MERCIA My crown is not of earth, Marcus—it awaits me there, [*points
upward*].

MARCUS Mercia—in pity—by thy love for me—and by my love for thee—
live—Live for me and for my love. I pray thee, do not leave me.

MERCIA I love thee, Marcus—but I leave thee to go to Him.

MARCUS I cannot part from thee and live, Mercia—I have, to save thy
precious life—argued and spoken against thy faith—thy god—but, to speak
truth to thee, I have been sorely troubled since first I saw thee—Strange
yearnings of the spirit come in the silent watches of the night—I battle with
them—but they will not yield. I tremble with strange fears—strange
thoughts—strange hopes. If thy faith be true—what is this world—a little
tarrying place—a tiny bridge between two great eternities—that we have
travelled from—that towards which we go. How can I know, Mercia?
Teach me—and teach me how to keep thee ever by my side.

MERCIA Look to the cross and pray—'Help, thou, my unbelief—'

MARCUS But to keep thee by my side—

MERCIA Give up all that thou hast and follow me?

MARCUS Follow thee—whither?

MERCIA To the better land—There, where He waits for us with outstretched
arms ready to pardon—eager to welcome.

MARCUS Would He welcome even me?

MERCIA Even thee, Marcus—(IV. iii)

Within Barrett's melodrama/Society-play strategy, the play offers
compelling scenes: Berenis's attempts to attract Marcus and her subsequent refusal to help Mercia are as well written as any rival Society-
play scene by Jones or Pinero. There are several *coups de théâtre*, most
notably the orgy scene in which the orgiasts' bacchanal is drowned
out by Christians singing a hymn from an adjoining prison. The secret
to that *coup* lies partly in Edward Jones's music—the hymn 'Shepherd
of Souls' and the rival bacchanal constructed on the same harmonic

principles so that one song can blend with and then dominate the other without dissonance. A second *coup*, Mercia preventing Marcus's lustful assault by holding a cross before her—one of the 'miracles' that so impressed Barrett's new audiences—is more problematic in its effectiveness and demands. Audiences, more than critics, praised two further episodes: the massacre of the Christians at the Cestian Bridge, and the torture of the boy-Christian Stephanus. This latter scene proved so popular that torture scenes, each more lurid and explicit than its predecessor, became obligatory episodes in the spin-off toga dramas which followed the successful *The Sign of the Cross*. Above all, there is a line of action to this play that is irreducibly essential. When *The Sign of the Cross* was filmed, first by Frederick Thomson in 1914 for Famous Players/Lasky and again by Cecil B. DeMille in 1932, the directors might embellish the action with further incidents and episodes, but they were unable to cut or alter Barrett's plot.

The dialogue, often stilted and frequently mawkish to modern ears, sounded excessive to those Victorians who claimed educated tastes, but the speeches rang with truth and sufficient verisimilitude for the new audiences encouraged by sermons and sermonizing pamphlets to attend Barrett's performances. However, the very qualities of moral truthfulness that encouraged late Victorian chapel-goers may pose problems for us in approaching this play. There is such an air of forced sanctity imposed upon this drama, that modern readers may be embarrassed. Nowhere is this problem more evident than in Scene 3 of Act II, where Favius preaches a sermon to his band of Christians which paraphrases the sermon on the Mount. The language and tenor of this scene are somewhat justified by the very ruthlessness of the Roman legionnaires and their leaders who break in upon the worshippers to slaughter and capture.

Where *The Sign of the Cross* represents an advance over its predecessors is in the development of comic roles. The earlier roles of Belos and Edessa in *Claudian* typify the frequently low expectations of the melodramatic comic couple. But Barrett's comic Romans, especially Dacia and Glabrio, function with some skill. Dacia enacts the vacuity and obliging promiscuity of the Roman aristocracy. She has some wit, some social graces, good manners, and few morals. Glabrio and Philodemus, male counterparts to Dacia, remind us of what Marcus might in time become, were he to succumb wholeheartedly to the cynical Roman morality.

The Sign of the Cross, in many respects the archetypal toga play, falls short of archetype in failing to find a means to permit Roman and

Christian to coexist in Nero's Empire. Marcus, still ignorant of Christianity other than that Mercia is a Christian and that Mercia is desirable, will become a Christian and so defy Nero. But there is no reprieve. The lions are to dine. Reconciliation and coexistence were not in Wilson Barrett's mind as he described the play and its characters. He first confided to Jerome K. Jerome—and, through Jerome, to the world at large—his design for the drama:

My heroine is emblematic of Christianity; my hero stands for the worn-out Paganism of decadent Rome. She is strong with the faith of a woman; he, strong with the self-reliance of a man. As I see her, she is beautiful with a half-divine loveliness, and an exquisite soul looks out through a beautiful face. She has given up the world for the sake of her new-found faith, in which and for which she lives, and is resolved, if need be, to die. Nero is on the throne, and has decreed the extermination of the Christians. The execution of this decree is entrusted to my Pagan patrician, and thus he is brought in contact with the Christian girl. In her, he at once recognises an almost sacred beauty, a beauty of holiness; and, voluptuary that he is, he sets out to win her. Twice he stands between her and death, and she is consequently moved to regard him with tender interest. But his persuasive pleadings and soft arts are of no avail. Steadfast in her faith she resists all temptation, and he is driven, in spite of himself, to seek a reason for her sovereign power and his own crushing defeat. He finds it in the uplifting and ennobling influence of her creed, and his soul is quickened by the breath of her spirit, and kindled into something of a likeness to itself, he flings honours, wealth, all to the winds, and hand in hand with her goes willingly to share the martyr's doom.[50]

Because Barrett insisted that he had conceived *The Sign of the Cross* as a riposte to 'the drama of the divorce court', he responded to questions about a season that had seen the premières of two of Pinero's serious Society plays, *The Profligate* and *The Second Mrs Tanqueray*. Continuing in Jerome's article, Barrett confided his views on the morbidity and potentially baleful influence of *The Second Mrs Tanqueray*:

If Tanquerays are to be the fashion in drama—before we know where we are, we shall be in the swamp at the bottom. Pinero, philosopher as well as playwright, probes to heal. Success makes imitation quite inevitable. And

---

[50] These thoughts have a curious and unsatisfactory chronology. Barrett may have written this schema in 1894, when he first took *The Sign of the Cross* to America. He subsequently gave the statement to Jerome, who incorporated it in 'The History of *The Sign of the Cross*' (*Idler*, Mar. 1896: 264–73). Barrett then placed segments of Jerome's article in the illustrated *Souvenir to The Sign of the Cross* (Lyric Theatre, 1896). Barrett's remarks about the baleful influence of *The Second Mrs Tanqueray* and the dichotomy between the 'woman with a past' and 'a woman with a future' appear in the article, but are not passed on.

Pinero's imitators will—to go one better—first seek out his uglier wounds, and then, lacking his philosophy if not his stagecraft, proceed to probe simply for probing's sake.

Reviewing recent stage events, Barrett argues that he has opposed Paula Tanqueray, Pinero's adventuress, 'a woman with a past', with Mercia, 'a woman with a future'. The play is also Barrett's answer to *fin de siècle* pessimism about the nation and the Empire in decline. What is corrupt and decadent can be redeemed by a new infusion of Christian values and morality. Mercia, Barrett's New Woman, is his imagined agent of this change.

What neither the play nor Barrett's summary prepare us for is the response to this drama. James Thomas confirms that, by the time of Barrett's death, *The Sign of the Cross* had been performed by Barrett or by one of his touring companies more than 10,000 times, and that during its London run (1896–7) it was attracting audiences at the rate of 70,000 per week.[51] Critics' opinions were divided, with the popular press and religious and family journals siding with Barrett. Sermons were given in praise of the play. The *Theatre* reported that the Bishop of Norwich had granted dispensation from Lenten obligation to the congregation of St Clement's Church in his diocese provided that they witnessed *The Sign of the Cross*.[52] The Revd Sydney Fleming, vicar of St James's, Croydon, gave a sermon urging his congregation to attend the play. The sermon was published in the *Croydon Guardian*, then republished and sold as a twopenny pamphlet. Fleming spoke on the history of the stage and the traditional antagonism between the Church and the theatre, but concluded that Barrett had purified the stage and that Christians of all sects might attend without misgiving or shame. It was precisely this appeal which gathered Barrett's new audiences into theatres. Jerome K. Jerome, travelling with Barrett's pre-London tour in the North of England, described the reverential behaviour of these spectators: 'At Rochdale I myself was witness of surely an unparalleled tribute to the power of the stage. I saw the rough cotton-factory workers slip off their clattering wooden shoes, and between acts steal softly about the pit and gallery in stockinged feet, as though, with *The Sign of the Cross* in the theatre, they trod upon sacred ground.'[53]

These audiences bought and carried home Barrett's souvenirs. Edward Jones's Act III hymn, 'Shepherd of Souls', the one that stopped

---

[51] Thomas, *The Art of the Actor Manager*, 134.

[52] *Theatre*, 27, (June 1896), 310. See also the advice of the Capuchin monk cited in n. 7.

[53] Jerome, 'The History of *The Sign of the Cross*', 264–73.

Marcus's house guests in mid-orgy, was published in versions for piano, organ, violin and piano, and guitar and piano, and was sold in theatre foyers. The same foyers sold a large coloured photolithograph of the first Mercia, Maud Jeffries, holding a small wooden cross. The picture, called simply *The Sign of the Cross*, was intended to double as a devotional picture. A souvenir album carried statements by Barrett and photographs of the performers. There were, alas, no cast recordings and no T-shirts. The play also elicited attacks against its content and against Barrett himself. G. W. Foote, a Humanist, lectured at St James's Hall, sharply criticizing Barrett's moralizing; he ridiculed the play for its absurdities. When Jerome K. Jerome wrote slightingly of this lecture, Foote responded with a weighty 47-page sixpenny pamphlet.[54] Foote's criticism, an analysis of the shortcomings of melodrama and Barrett's techniques of characterization, is apt and generally well written. Finally, there were theatrical repercussions—plays written in imitation of *The Sign of the Cross*, and, later, two motion pictures.

Unfortunately, Frederick Thomson's 1914 motion-picture adaptation of *The Sign of the Cross*[55] is incomplete. All of the play up to Scene 3 of Act III—the orgy at Marcus's house—has been lost, but the remainder largely follows Barrett's script. There is, overall, the sense that Thomson reveres Barrett's performance and production, and that he is attempting to use the medium of motion pictures to accomplish what silent film cannot do. There is also a sense that Thomson is attempting to make a film which, if not reverential, takes seriously the conflict between Roman and Christian. There are, however, some filmic additions. When Marcus, rebuffed by Mercia but admiring her principles, queries her faith, he asks: 'Unfold to me the story of the Cross.' As Mercia speaks, there are intercut shots of Christ's infancy and childhood, healing the sick and raising the dead, the Last Supper, and the Crucifixion. Poppaea is more active in seconding Berenis's appeal to Nero to persecute Mercia: 'If she would live, let her renounce her faith. Caesar hath spoken.' And when Berenis is convinced that she has been forsaken for Mercia, she kills herself. Barrett's play ends in the prisoners' cell at the Coliseum, but Thomson follows Mercia and Marcus into the arena and the presence of the lions. When the lovers have embraced (inter-title: 'Mercia, my bride', 'My bridegroom'), the camera returns to the cell, where a little girl wanders among the empty shackles abandoned on the floor. A cross, in silhouette, precedes the end-titles.

[54] Foote, '*The Sign of the Cross*'.
[55] American Film Institute Collection, FEA 4192, 4193.

DeMille's *The Sign of the Cross*, made in 1932, is an altogether different sort of film. The play is there only to provide a plot. DeMille is preoccupied with the overpowering luxury of Rome, and appears to envy—or to excite envy at—the Roman appetite and ingenuity for vice. DeMille wants his audience to see everything: Roman games, captive animals, banquets, an Empress in her bath. The film is strikingly visual and restless, as if the camera were a participant in Roman high society and low life. The film was shot before the advent of the motion-picture industry had instigated a policy of self-censorship, and some of the episodes of orgy and intimacy—especially as there were Christians imprisoned in the adjoining room—invited the ire of the Roman Catholic Legion of Decency when the film was prepared for re-release in 1944. In response, a filmic foreword had to be added: an American bomber, heading for a German target in Northern Italy, contains two Army chaplains, a Roman Catholic and a Protestant. As the plane flies over Rome, the chaplains muse on the plight of Christians down below. They recall that persecution of the weak is not new; it happened before, under the decadent tyrant Nero. With the licentious and blasphemous Romans firmly condemned, *The Sign of the Cross* begins.

Wilson Barrett began planning *The Sign of the Cross* as early as 1893, and was writing and performing it in America as he and his company toured there from 1894. The play was first performed in St Louis on 25 March 1895. Within weeks it was evident that the play was a success, and *The Sign of the Cross* was added to the repertoire. Returning to Britain, Wilson Barrett submitted the script for licensing by the Lord Chamberlain. However, between the first British performance of the play at the Grand Theatre in Leeds on 26 August 1895 and its first London performance at the Lyric Theatre on 4 January, 1896, Barrett made further revisions to the text.

Moreover, even as he toured from Leeds to Manchester, Cardiff, Bristol, Sheffield, Nottingham, Hull, and Newcastle and settled into his London run, Barrett began to construct a novel from his play. His plan, direct and simple, is easily inferred: after an introductory chapter to present his characters and their backgrounds, he would describe his play, including all of the play's dialogue, but enriching his characters' speech and the bare stage directions with accounts of stage action— right down to inflections and small gestures. Barrett devised additional chapters to describe actions between scenes. Throughout, he provided elaborate descriptions of hand-properties and settings and costumes.

He seems particularly concerned that his readers should experience the production's range of colours and varied textures. The novel was published for the Christmas market in December 1896, and allowed readers who had seen the stage play to revisit the rich spectacle of *The Sign of the Cross*. As well, the novel doubtless attracted new audiences for his drama. In my view, confirmed through comparisons of passages in the novel with extant photographs of the actors, sets, and costumes, the novel is a remarkably precise and vivid account of the production in its late, if not final, state, as well as a record of Barrett's theatrical practices.

My editorial strategy has been an unorthodox one, justified, I hope, by the availability of Wilson Barrett's novel and by the certainty that this was published after the play was an established success and is therefore a reliable supplement to the script. There is no definitive script of the play, but I have endeavoured to provide an acting text (based on the Library of Congress copy, the British licensing copy, Add. MS 53568-N, and subsequent revisions) of *The Sign of the Cross*. However, in order to recapture the full spectacle of this drama and to register its impact on late Victorian audiences, I have supplemented Barrett's meagre stage directions, enclosed, as usual, in square brackets and set in italic type, with additional descriptive material from the novel, also enclosed in brackets, but set in a smaller typeface. In the novel these descriptions of action, settings, costumes, and properties are furnished in the past tense. Here I have altered them to the present tense to conform to theatrical practice. I have intentionally preserved the idiosyncratic punctuation of Barrett's typescripts, especially his use of the omnipresent dash between words and phrases, because I believe that this punctuation offers some insight into stage readings. I have turned to the novel only where word order or punctuation in the scripts has been hopelessly garbled. Occasionally, where I found it useful to indicate substantial variants in the text or other points of information, I have added footnotes.

The programme for the first production in London at the Lyric Theatre on 4 January 1896 acknowledged the following: the music (conducted and composed) by Edward Jones; the costumes by Miss D. Bernstein; the wigs by W. Clarkson; the armour and jewellery by R. White and Sons; the dances arranged by Miss E. Goss; the solos by Miss Wetherall and Miss Desmond (together with the boys of Mr Steadman's choir); the business management of A. E. Field; and the stage-management of Charles Cathcart.

The cast and settings (with designers) were as follows:

Pagans

Marcus, Prefect of Rome	Mr WILSON BARRETT
Nero,[56] Roman Emperor	Mr FRANKLIN McLEAY
Tigellinus,[57] counsellor to Nero	Mr AUSTIN MELFORD
Licinius, Aedile	Mr EDWIN IRWIN
Glabrio and Philodemus,	Mr AMBROSE MANNING and,
patricians	Mr GEORGE HOWARD
Metullus, a general	Mr G. BERNAGE
Signinus[58]	Mr NELSON BARRY
Servillius and Strabo, spies and	Mr HORACE HODGES and,
informers	Mr MARCUS ST JOHN
Viturius, Captain of the Guard	
to Marcus	Mr C. DERWOOD
Slave to Nero	Mr HENRY LUDLOW
Berenis and Dacia, wealthy	Miss ALIDA CORTELYOU and,
patricians	Miss D. BELLMORE
Poppaea,[59] Empress of Rome	Miss GRACE WARNER
Ancaria	Miss CONSTANCE COLLIER
Daones	Miss E. LAWRENCE
Julia	Miss CECILIA WILMAN
Cyrene	Miss GERTIE BOSWELL
Edoni	Miss ALICE GAMBIER
Zona and Catia, slaves	Miss BESSIE ELMA and,
	Miss CONSTANCE McGRATH
Mytelene	Miss M. BRIERLY

Christians

Favius	Mr ALFRED BRYDONE
Titus	Mr STAFFORD SMITH
Melos	Mr PERCY FOSTER
Stephanus, a boy	Miss HAIDEE WRIGHT
Mercia	Miss MAUDE JEFFRIES

Guards, nobles, slaves, christians, etc., etc.

---

[56] Lucius Domitius Ahenobarbus Nero (AD 37–68, Emperor, AD 54–68).

[57] Gaius Sofonius Tigellinus, prefect to Nero (d. AD 68). According to Tacitus, Tigellinus, pandering to and encouraging Nero's lower tastes, wooed him from his tutor Seneca and became one of the Emperor's most powerful advisers.

[58] Programmes for the London and provincial runs list the role of Signinus and identify actors in the role. However, there are no lines for this role, nor is any action indicated in either the playscript or the novel.

[59] Poppaea Sabina (Empress AD 62–5), initially Nero's mistress, later his wife. According to Tacitus, 'she possessed every quality she might want—except virtue'. Pregnant, she died when kicked in the abdomen by Nero.

Act I: A Street in Rome (Stafford Hall).

Act II, Scene 1: Favius's House (Stafford Hall).

Scene 2: Prison of the District (Stafford Hall).

Scene 3: The Grove by the Cestian Bridge (Stafford Hall).

Act III, Scene 1: The House of Berenis (Walter Hann).

Scene 2: Atrium of Nero's Palace (Walter Hann).

Scene 3: Marcus's Palace (Walter Hann).

Act IV, Scene 1: Hall in Nero's Palace (Stafford Hall).

Scene 2: Street in Rome (Walter Hann).

Scene 3: A Dungeon of the Amphitheatre (Walter Hann).

Time: AD 64.

Poster for *The Sign of the Cross*, *c.*1900.

SHEPHERD OF SOULS.

Song from

THE SIGN OF THE CROSS.

Written by

Wilson Barrett.

Composed by

EDWARD JONES.

The above arranged as an Anthem, PRICE 6p. NET.
Ditto   ditto   Tonic Sol-fa, PRICE 2p. NET.

Price   4/=

METZLER & Co. LIMITED.
42, Great Marlborough Street, LONDON, w:

By the same Composer:
"HYMN OF DEPARTURE." Price 6d.

TELEGRAMS: "LERMETZ, LONDON."	CODE.	25 Copies.	50	100	250	500	1,000
		131	02130	05130	06130	08130	09130

Edward Jones's hymn "Shepherd of Souls" as sold in theatre foyers at performances of *The Sign of the Cross*.

Act II, scene 2. Stephanus is interrogated by Tigellinus. Photograph made for a touring production of *The Sign of the Cross*.

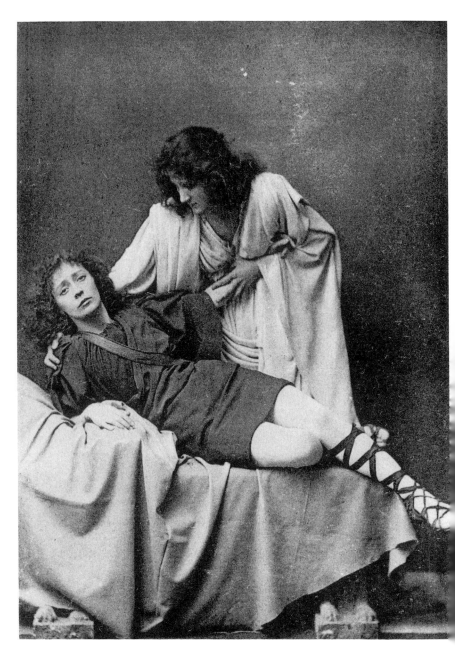

Act II, scene 2. Mercia finds Stephanus after he has been tortured by Tigellinus. From the London (principal) production.

Act III, scene 1. Berenis awaiting morning visitors.

Act IV, scene 1. Berenis and Poppæa influence Nero's decision to continue the persecution of Mercia.

The orgy scene, Act III, sc. 3. Marcus displays Mercia to Glabrio.

Act III, sc. 3. Mercia's virtue causes Marcus to halt in his rape attempt and to fall at her feet in awe and wonder.

Act IV, scene 3. In a dungeon of the amphitheatre Mercia explains the virtue
of self-sacrifice to Marcus.

Act IV, scene 3. Wedded in death, Mercia and Marcus enter the amphitheatre
to face the lions.

ACT I

[SCENE: *A street in Rome.* [*Afternoon, shortly before sunset*] *Arch C.,
through which can be seen the Tiber. House L. Steps leading up to
balcony and entrance. This house should be handsome. Garlands of
roses hang round the doorway. Citizens, pedlars, etc. grouped about
the stage.* STRABO *and* SERVILLIUS, *two spies, seated on ground
under balcony L.* [*The two men of the poorest class, dirty, ragged and
unkempt. Servillius almost wolf-like in appearance—a resemblance height-
ened by a badly cured skin of one of those animals, which he wears as a
half-shoulder-cloak. Strabo taller than his companion, with a more stupidly
brutal expression on his face. They are apparently intent upon a game of
dice, but, as they rattle them in their hands and throw them with loud
comments upon the marble steps, each is casting furtive glances on all that
passes around him. . . . The street, though not thronged, is busy. Porters bear
burdens from the landings; women of the middle class on their road to
purchase provisions; flower-sellers; a swarm of beggars; men hurrying from
business*] *Soldiers cross from R.U.E. to L.I.E., guarding two men in
chains and poor garments* [*One man somewhat advanced in years. The
prisoner's hands are bound to a heavy triangle of wood passed over his head
and fastened there by an iron lock. The man ill, worn, and feeble. A woman
following the party holds the hand of a little girl of five or six years of age,
loudly sobbing*] *They seem faint and weak, one totters for a moment.
A soldier strikes him with the butt of his spear. He staggers, and the
crowd laugh and jeer at the men—he struggles on and exits with
soldiers*]

STRABO That was a hard knock, Servillius.

SERVILLIUS Well, what matters? It was only a dog of a Christian.

STRABO Oh—

SERVILLIUS I know that fellow. I've been watching him for weeks,
but Vinius got him, and so I lost Nero's reward of two hundred
sesterces.

STRABO Christian-hunting pays well—eh?

SERVILLIUS It pays well and is good sport too. It is as exciting as
wolf-hunting and has none of its dangers. For all their child-killing
and secret murders, they are a poor-spirited lot. They never strike
back. Ha! Ha! Ha! They are a cowardly crew.

     [VITURIUS [*richly clad*] *crosses with a guard of* [*handsomely dressed and
     equipped*] *soldiers from L.U.E. to R.I.E.*]

SERVILLIUS That is Viturius, Captain of the guards to Marcus Superbus.

STRABO Marcus Superbus—ah—I'd like to be that fellow.

SERVILLIUS O Jupiter—O Apollo—eh? As well wish to be a god as to be Marcus Superbus. Next to the Emperor—he is the richest man in Rome.

STRABO And the luckiest. It's an accursed shame that one man should have much and another nothing.

SERVILLIUS Aye, Strabo—we're goodly men, but we haven't a copper coin between us—while Marcus has his horse shod with gold, and, on a banquet he gave to Nero, he spent four million sesterces.

STRABO Whew—is there so much money in all this hungry world?

SERVILLIUS Yea, is there, and some of it may be ours if we can but trap a Christian or two.

> [*Enter* FAVIUS *R. and* TITUS *L.*] [*Though dressed in the ordinary costume of the citizen of the time, there is about them, their faces and their bearing that which would have attracted the attention of a much less alert observer than the spy. The elder man is Favius, who looks as the prophet Moses might, so dignified and majestic is his carriage and bearing. His mantle partly covers his long snowy locks; he holds a staff in his hand, but scarcely uses it as a support. He sees and notices with a look of keen interest the stranger, Titus, who is approaching him. The man is evidently a traveller, his garments soiled with the dust of country roads. He is some fifty-five years of age, sturdily built, and capable of enduring much fatigue*]

SERVILLIUS Hush—here's a stranger—keep your ears and eyes open, my Strabo.

> [*They seem to sleep—but are watching keenly.* FAVIUS *and* TITUS *meet in the C., regard each other curiously—*TITUS*, with his staff, draws the sign of the Cross* [*two simple marks in the dust in the road*] *upon the stage. Music of the Christians' Hymn is played.* FAVIUS *looks at the sign*]

FAVIUS The sign of the Cross—what art thou?

TITUS A fisherman from Galilee.

FAVIUS How know you me?

TITUS By my Master's badge.

FAVIUS What is that?

> [TITUS *takes* FAVIUS's *sleeve, bares his right wrist, and points to a tattoo of a cross thereon and shows a like sign upon his own*] [*The men's hands meet in a warm and fervent clasp*]

FAVIUS Who sent thee hither?

TITUS Paulus of Tarsus, apostle of Him they crucified.

FAVIUS Speak lower—even the stones of Rome have ears. Dost thou tarry long in Rome?

TITUS Only long enough to give Paulus's message to the brethren. Where meet they tomorrow?

FAVIUS [*whispering*] At the Grove, next the Cestine Bridge.

TITUS At what hour?

FAVIUS The tenth.

TITUS How many?

FAVIUS [*seeing* STRABO *and* SERVILLIUS *nearing them*] Hush, the stones have ears.

STRABO In the name of Caesar, hail.

FAVIUS Hail, friend [*He takes his friend's arm*] [*going with* TITUS].

SERVILLIUS [*half in good fellowship, half in threat*] Whither so fast?

FAVIUS About mine own business.

SERVILLIUS Where dwellest thou?

FAVIUS What is that to thee?

SERVILLIUS Thy friend seems way-worn and weary—hath he come from afar?

TITUS I have travelled some days.

SERVILLIUS And art athirst I'll wager. Come with me; a cup of good wine from yonder wine shop will wash the dust of the roads from thy throat.

TITUS So will a cup of good water from yonder fountain. I thank thee for thy courtesy, but have no time to tarry with thee.

SERVILLIUS Strangers tarry in Rome longer than they plan to do at times. Especially strangers who come from Galilee.

[TITUS *starts, but controls himself*]

SERVILLIUS Nero looks not with favour on Galileans nor Nazarenes. He finds rest for them, however [*points to the earth as to a grave*].

TITUS I have heard as much.

SERVILLIUS Nero may send rest for thee.

TITUS When my day's work is done—I shall welcome rest and peace, whoever sends them.

SERVILLIUS What is thy work?

TITUS My Master's.

SERVILLIUS Who dost thou serve?

TITUS The Son of Man.

[*With a slight but courteous inclination of the head, Titus lays his hand on Favius's arm and walks away*] [*Exit L. with* FAVIUS]

STRABO The son of Man—what means he?

SERVILLIUS My Strabo, I smell money here—Christians these—didst mark their secret signs? Ha! Ha! Ha! Here's sport and money both. Follow, dear Strabo, follow.

[*They sneak off after* FAVIUS *and* TITUS. *Music of song heard off R.U.E. Night approaches. Citizens and others cross the stage. A band of singers* [*richly dressed and garlanded in roses*] *precede* PHILODE-MUS *and* GLABRIO, R. [*They are accompanied by musicians with lutes, citharas, and pipes*] *They stop at* [*Dacia's*[60]] *house L.2.E. Singing*] [*While this song is being sung, an exquisitely graceful girl, lightly clad in rich sky-blue silk, dances airily in front of the steps of the house, scattering roses over them. Philodemus is robed in a pale yellow silk tunic and toga, trimmed heavily with gold and jewels. His face is worn, his frame slight, his manner effeminate in the extreme. He has a slight lisp, rolling, vacant eyes, and a languid, listless air. Glabrio is a man of fifty, rotund of body, rubicund of face, beaming with humour and good temper, a rich unctuous voice and a continuous chuckle, as if life was one huge joke. Not for him mere existence, but life. The vine leaves and roses are never out of his hair. His dress is symbolical, being of the colour of his favourite red wine, trimmed with vine leaves worked in gold. On his head is a fillet which, in sympathy with his drooping eyelid, has slid over his brow. His gait is not too steady, and he seems cautiously to feel his way with his gouty toes. Both men carry fans of feathers, after the effeminate custom of the time*]

SOLO

What is life where love is not?

CHORUS

A sunless world.

SOLO

Life itself is love begot.

CHORUS

Then love and live.

SOLO

Love is light—and love is fire—
Those who love not live in vain—
Life is but one long desire—
Either love or die in pain.

CHORUS

Then love and live.

[*As L. door opens, slaves line the entrance to the house.* DACIA *appears, attended by two beautiful girls*] [*The sound of music brings Dacia out of*

---

[60] In the manuscript submitted to the Lord Chamberlain, the house is Cytherea's and is obviously a brothel. It was subsequently changed to the home of Dacia, a young married woman with a complaisant husband.

the portico. With her come two richly robed slave girls, who spread cushions upon the seats and embroidered draperies upon the balcony. Dacia is laughing merrily at some jest with her attendants]

DACIA Well sung. Who are your masters? Ah, I see Philodemus and Glabrio. What want ye, gentlemen?

PHILODEMUS Leave to worship.

DACIA Leave to worship, Nero grants to all—save the Nazarenes. At whose shrine wouldst thou bend the knee?

PHILODEMUS Venus, I.

GLABRIO And Bacchus, I.

DACIA Hast not worshipped the ruby wine god enough already, good Glabrio?

GLABRIO Never can I worship him enough. The sacred fire of Bacchus is in my veins—my heart—my blood—my brain—and to some extent in my legs, as you may see. They are a trifle at variance with each other—while my right leg would fain go East—my left struggles to convey me West.

DACIA At variance this early in the day?

GLABRIO Faith, yes—they've never been otherwise since the last banquet Marcus gave. When—but he spares nothing, the good Marcus. What wine—what women; he's a rare taste in both.

DACIA And remains unmoved by either.

PHILODEMUS True—he's a head of iron for wine—and a heart of stone for women.

GLABRIO Iron melts and stone breaks. He'll get caught some day.

PHILODEMUS Marcus? Never.

GLABRIO My son, let an older and a wiser and a more sober man advise thee—I have lived in this [*staggers*] somewhat unsteady world for two score years and ten—I have visited many lands—but never yet found I a young and high-mettled man who did not sooner or later—usually sooner—succumb to fair woman.

PHILODEMUS Never Marcus—Woman? He values woman a little more than his dogs—a little less than his horses.

GLABRIO To all of which I answer, 'Wait'—my Philodemus—'wait'.

[A sudden howl of execration and a rush of idlers to the corner of the street. The patricians rise and peer over the balcony to discover the cause of the uproar. A dense crowd, composed chiefly of the rabble and the lower orders, but some are of the better class, have surrounded Favius and are hustling and otherwise ill-treating him, aiming blows with fists and sticks. Favius's garments are torn, and a deep cut on his forehead testifies to the savagery of the attacks upon him] [Uproar L.I.E. Rabble shouting 'Death to the Christians'.

Enter FAVIUS, *followed by* SERVILLIUS *and* STRABO *leading other citizens*] [*As the mob reaches the centre of the street, opposite Dacia's house, Favius is hurled violently to the ground by the rabble*]

CROWD Death—death to the Christians.

SERVILLIUS Nay—nay, I found him—he is mine—I claim the reward. Let's take him to the aedile.

CROWD Nay—Death—death.

GLABRIO What hath the old man done?

SERVILLIUS Bowed down to the God Anokoites. He's a Christian—he worships the God of the ass's head.

GLABRIO Hath he bowed down to thee?

SERVILLIUS Nay—He is a Christian, I tell thee, and is worth two hundred sesterces—and Nero will make a torch of him.

GLABRIO He'd never burn, friend—he is but skin and bone.

CROWD Death—death—death.

[*As they again hustle him,* MERCIA *enters and stands between* FA-VIUS *and the crowd. She is in pure white. She stands calmly with outstretched hands—the crowd fall back and gaze with awe at her, as if at some spirit*] [*Mercia is tall beyond the common for her sixteen years; of beautiful but exquisitely fragile figure; with the face of a Madonna, clear-cut as a cameo. It is no marvel that she should compel earthly love in the hearts of men who are privileged to meet her. Of this, Mercia knows little and heeds less*]

MERCIA Are ye men or wolves? Are ye blind? Are white hairs no longer reverenced in Rome? Are you hurt, my father?

[*Mercia wipes the blood from Favius's face*]

FAVIUS I feel no pain, my daughter.

MERCIA But there is blood upon thee—look, men of Rome—are ye not ashamed?

GLABRIO By Bacchus, what a beauty.[61]

PHILODEMUS She's worth her weight in gold.

DACIA The girl is pretty, in good sooth.

MERCIA Let me lead thee home—good father.

[*Going up stage towards R., leading* FAVIUS. *Crowd gather round and block the way*]

SERVILLIUS Not so fast. What say ye, citizens—shall a pair of pretty eyes and a baby face rule Rome and Romans?

CROWD No! No! No!

---

[61] In the Lord Chamberlain's text, the line, addressed to Cytherea, continues: 'What an attraction she'd be for thee, good Cytherea.'

GLABRIO They have done until now. There's fun in this, Philodemus. I'll bet thee a thousand sesterces that beauty defeats the brute.

PHILODEMUS Done.

MERCIA I beg of thee to let this old man go. There is no harm in him—I know him well—he hath wronged no one—unless it be a wrong to nurse the sick—comfort the weary—help the helpless— All these things hath he done—would you slay him for that?

CROWD He is a Christian—Death—death—death.

[*The crowd surround him.* [*Mercia is clinging to him vainly, trying to shield him from the rabble. A dozen strong hands are upon her, tearing her from Favius*] *A trumpet is heard. Enter soldiers with* MARCUS. MAR- CUS *and soldiers break up the crowd and rescue* FAVIUS *and* MERCIA. *Crowd shouts 'Marcus—Marcus'*] [*Marcus is dressed in military costume; a short, white linen tunic, barely reaching to the knee, is covered by a coat of mail, heavily studded with bosses and plates of brass, and jewelled with emeralds and rubies; from under this, fall lambrequins of white leather, heavily trimmed with gold and jewels and edged with gold fringe. A helmet of polished brass glistens on his head, and a short mantle of old-gold-coloured silk hangs from his shoulders. His sandals are topped with flat rings of gold, and over the centre of each is the head of a lion, wrought in the same precious metal*]

MARCUS What means this brawl? Stand away there. What hath this old man done?

SERVILLIUS He is a Christian.

MARCUS [*pausing and looking at* SERVILLIUS *quietly*] Buffet that fellow over the mouth, Viturius.

[VITURIUS *strikes* SERVILLIUS *and throws him R.*]

SERVILLIUS Nay, great Marcus—I have done no wrong.

MARCUS [*in a deep, rich, yet gentle tone*] What is thy name, girl?

MERCIA [*her voice trembles as she answers*] Mercia.

MARCUS [*aside*] By Venus, what a beauty. [*Aloud*] Thy name, friend?

FAVIUS Favius Fontelus.

MARCUS Is this maid thy daughter?

FAVIUS Nay, sir.

MARCUS Nor any kin of thine?

FAVIUS No.

MARCUS How comes it then that she is with thee?

FAVIUS She came between the rabble when they did set upon me—to protect me.

MARCUS Protect thee? The lily protect the tottering oak. [*Aside*] What a lovely face. [*Aloud*] What is this man to thee?

MERCIA He is my teacher.

MARCUS So? Teach you in the public schools?

FAVIUS No.

[MARCUS *is puzzled and doubtful*]

MARCUS Of what sect are you?

FAVIUS I am a philosopher.

MARCUS Humph. Clear the street, Viturius.

[*Soldiers drive off the crowd, who exit shouting 'Long live Marcus—Marcus'*] [*and 'Death to the Christians'*]

GLABRIO Philodemus—I have won—beauty hath defeated the brute.

[MARCUS *steadily watches* MERCIA]

MARCUS If ever thou shouldst be in need of a friend, girl, come to me.

MERCIA Sir.

[*Mercia shrinks a little from Marcus. Favius comes between them and addresses Marcus*]

FAVIUS Shall the dove seek the hawk for friendship?

MARCUS Well, not if the hawk be hungry—but am I the hawk?

FAVIUS Thou art Marcus Superbus.

MARCUS Well?

FAVIUS One woman more or less is naught to thee—this child is purity—innocence itself—

MARCUS [*laughingly*] Canst thou vouch for that, old man?

FAVIUS With my life.

MARCUS [*with a slight sneer*] Innocence is a rare jewel in Rome and, for its rarity, much desired.

FAVIUS Thou hast done a good action in saving her from the rabble—it will be recorded in thy favour—Do not stain that record with evil—let this maiden go her way unharmed.

MARCUS I do not hinder her or thee—Prithee, go thy ways.

FAVIUS [*imploringly*] O promise—Excellence—

MARCUS [*impatiently*] Enough—I have saved thee both—let that suffice. Go.

[*Leads* MERCIA *off R.I.E.*] [*To the last, her eyes are fixed on Marcus*]

MARCUS [*quickly*] Viturius—follow them—learn who they are, where they reside—of what family the girl is—Quick, bring me news of her.

VITURIUS Yes, Excellence.

[*Exit R.I.E.*]

MARCUS [*watching* MERCIA] The newest—freshest—most enticing piece of womanhood I've seen for many a day.

DACIA Most noble Marcus—

MARCUS What would you with me, fair Dacia? Ah, Glabrio and Philodemus.

GLABRIO Hail, Marcus. That was a pretty piece of flesh—eh?

MARCUS I was just thinking as much—but what wantst, Dacia?

DACIA Thy company, most noble Marcus. Join those gentlemen—Come, honour my poor dwelling with thy presence.

MARCUS Nay, good Dacia, Duty—stern, inexorable duty—calls me elsewhere.

DACIA Art afraid?

MARCUS Of what?

DACIA Of the sharp tongue of Berenis.

MARCUS Neither of her tongue nor of thy sweet lips. Why should I fear Berenis?

DACIA Rome doth link thy name with hers.

MARCUS How?

DACIA 'Tis said thou art betrothed to Berenis.

[MARCUS *laughs*]

GLABRIO Hope that is true, Marcus. You should take unto yourself a wife.

MARCUS With pleasure, Glabrio. Whose wife would you recommend?

GLABRIO Ha! Ha! That's good, by Venus.

DACIA Why don't you marry, Marcus?

MARCUS Because I hate the tedious formalities of divorce, and nowadays in Rome it is thought more honourable to support your friend's wife than your own, while women of fashion reckon their lives not by their years but by the number of their husbands.

DACIA Do no noble ladies keep their husbands?

MARCUS Yes, those who wish to pique their lovers.

DACIA Rumour saith—

MARCUS Rumour hath many tongues—mostly lying ones, lady. I may commit many acts of folly, but not matrimony.

DACIA Berenis will make thee change thy resolve. Come within, gentlemen. Farewell, Marcus.

MARCUS Farewell. Remember, gentlemen, you sup with me tomorrow.

PHILODEMUS I will not fail thee Marcus.

[*Exit into house*] [*escorting Dacia*]

GLABRIO Nor I—if my legs do not fail me.

[*Exit into house*]

MARCUS Marriage—no, by the gods—but this girl—how her face haunts me—what innocence! What grace! Is it possible that such

purity can dwell in the heart of one of these despised Christians?—
Ah, Viturius.

[*Enter* VITURIUS]

MARCUS Well, Viturius—where dwellest the girl?

VITURIUS In a small house, the fourth on the right from the statue of
Hermes, Excellence.

MARCUS Know you aught of the inhabitants of that house?

VITURIUS The house is suspected, Excellence.

MARCUS Suspected of what?

VITURIUS Of being a rendezvous of Christians.

MARCUS Ah—Is this gossip?

VITURIUS No, Excellence—I know that the aedile of the district hath
set a special watch upon the house.

MARCUS A secret watch?

VITURIUS Yes, Excellence.

MARCUS Who is the aedile of the district?

VITURIUS Licinius.

MARCUS Licinius, the tool of Tigellinus—my bitterest enemy and the
most sycophantic—unmerciful—bloodthirsty officer in Rome. The
gods help those people if he suspects them. If there be no evidence
against them, he will make it. Viturius, return at once to the
house—learn from the spies what they know and what is to be
done—Come at once to me if any arrest is ordered or contemplated.
Let me be instantly advised of all, you understand.

VITURIUS Perfectly, Excellence.

MARCUS Then go.

VITURIUS Will you go unattended, Excellence?

MARCUS Yes, go.

VITURIUS I obey, Excellence.

[*Exit*]

MARCUS Licinius—a wolf—The gods help that poor white lamb unless I play the shepherd—and—umph—I think I will.

[*Goes to R.I.E.* [*The reverie of Marcus is broken by a musical, cultivated
voice*] *Enter* METULLUS, *a Roman general, with* BERENIS, *a beautiful
and richly dressed patrician lady.* [*Berenis is above the average height of
a woman. She has dark hair and blue eyes. Berenis is seated in a gold and
ivory bedecked* lectica *chair, carried on the shoulders of two gigantic negroes.
At her side walks Metellus, a bluff and heavy-moving man of middle age, in
the dress of a Roman general. At a little distance behind her are two elegantly
attired and handsome female slaves*] *She is attended by slaves*]

BERENIS Marcus—

METULLUS Marcus.

MARCUS Ah—Hail, Berenis—Hail, Metullus. Ah, fine lady—

BERENIS What is the latest gossip?

MARCUS That Berenis is still Berenis.

BERENIS Is that a compliment?

MARCUS If I say the sun is still the sun—can I pay its light a higher
compliment—If I say the rose is still the rose, can I praise its
sweetness more? What say you, Metullus?

METULLUS [glaring at MARCUS] Nay, Marcus, I am but a rough soldier,
and the tricks of tongue are not for me. I can give an order or obey
one—I can fight for a woman with my sword—but not with my wit.

MARCUS A man who would carve his way to a woman's heart is like
to find love butchered there.

METULLUS [glaring at MARCUS] So, Well, being butchered, it could
not be another's.

BERENIS You make me tremble, terrible Metullus—what, woman that
I am—only think if that thy love were given to me.

METULLUS If?—If—Why I—I—

BERENIS I did not say if—let it stand at that for the present. If thou dids't
love me, thou woulds't woo me thus—Berenis, I love thee—then,
with thy right hand flourishing thy sword and thy left hand entwined
in my hair, thou woulds't thunder forth—thy love or thy life.

METULLUS Nay, I would say—

BERENIS Not here—not in the public streets of Rome. Wait a more
fitting time. Good Marcus, shall I be honoured?

MARCUS How, gracious lady?

BERENIS With thy escort home.

MARCUS Why—thou hast thy escort, lady.

BERENIS Wilt visit me today?

MARCUS I am busy on State affairs—alas, I must deny myself that joy.

BERENIS Tomorrow then?

MARCUS I dine some friends—and shall be glad to welcome Metullus
with the rest.

METULLUS [about to decline] I—I—

BERENIS [aside] Say 'yes'—I wish it.

METULLUS Yes—I wish it.

MARCUS [smiling] You honour me too much.

BERENIS You invite not me—that's scarcely kind or flattering.

MARCUS It is a man's feast, fair lady.

BERENIS Will there be no ladies present?

MARCUS I think I may safely say there will be no ladies present.

BERENIS   No women either?

MARCUS   Ahem—well, some players or some singers—perhaps—

BERENIS   Marcus at least is frank. He does not hide his vices.

MARCUS   Is it a vice to love?

BERENIS   Love? Does the word apply in such cases?

MARCUS   It serves.

> [Enter GLABRIO] [*Glabrio, charged with Dacia's hospitality, staggers on to the balcony, and sinks rather suddenly on to the seat at the top of the steps*]

BERENIS   Have you no heart, Marcus?

GLABRIO   Yes, I'll wager he hath—I thought not until a moment ago, but beauty vanquished, and I won—[*on balcony*]

BERENIS   I hardly understand—

GLABRIO   No? Why, pretty Christian—black eyes—Marcus rescue—lovely girl—

BERENIS   Christian? Lovely girl?—What is this, Marcus?

MARCUS   A mental hallucination of Glabrio's, consequent upon too early devotion to the God of wine.

GLABRIO   Eh? What—what's that? Early 'lucination?—not at all—won my wager—Ask Philodemus—Philodemus—

> [Enter PHILODEMUS]

PHILODEMUS   Why have you left the table, Glabrio?

GLABRIO   To taste the air. Didn't I win my wager? Eh? Beauty vanquished brute—eh?

PHILODEMUS   Certainly.

BERENIS   Who was the beauty, Philodemus? This Christian?

MARCUS   This has gone far enough, Glabrio. Wine is a grateful servant but a tyrannical master—Philodemus, give thy friend thine arm. Conduct him within.

PHILODEMUS   Thou hast better follow me, Glabrio.

GLABRIO   But—beauty—black eyes—Christian—

PHILODEMUS   Yes—yes—of course, within—

GLABRIO   Within? Eh—

PHILODEMUS   Of course, within.

> [Exit with GLABRIO]

BERENIS   Did you fear he should speak too much?

MARCUS   He hath spoken too much already.

BERENIS   This strange girl—this Christian—

MARCUS   She is no Christian—a young girl and old man were attacked by a rabble—my guards protected them and dispersed the crowd. Glabrio saw too much—or heard too little—not an uncommon failing with men in his condition.

BERENIS Men in wine speak the truth—

MARCUS Another saying, fair lady—when the wine is in, the wit goes wandering.

[*Enter* SOPHENIUS TIGELLINUS *with* [*a file of*] *guards*]

TIGELLINUS [*coldly*] Well met, Prefect.

MARCUS [*coldly*] Hail, Tigellinus.

TIGELLINUS Hail, gentle lady—Hail, Metullus—Prefect, I was on my way to seek thee. The Emperor greets thee and sends thee this [*hands him roll of paper or parchment*].

MARCUS Is it urgent?

TIGELLINUS Most urgent.

MARCUS Pardon me.

[*Walks aside and breaks seal and reads*]

BERENIS Your news seems to trouble the noble Marcus.

TIGELLINUS It should not do so—'tis but a fresh edict from Nero to exterminate at any cost these accursed Christians. To Marcus is alloted this special duty.

BERENIS To exterminate at any cost the Christians.

TIGELLINUS Aye, gentle lady. The Emperor has been informed by traitors in their sect that they plot against his life. His edict condemns to torture and death all who are proved to worship with them—or help them in any way.

BERENIS Torture and death?

MARCUS I kiss the mandate of the Emperor, Tigellinus.

TIGELLINUS [*sternly*] And will obey it.

MARCUS [*haughtily*] Can you doubt it?

TIGELLINUS Go you, honoured lady—let me add to your escort.

BERENIS Gladly. Farewell, Marcus. The Emperor hath chosen wisely. Torture and death to all Christians—without distinction of sex—a wise decree and a timely one—Farewell, Marcus.

MARCUS Farewell, lady.

[*Exit all L.I.E.*] [*As they leave him, Marcus again unrolls the scroll he holds in his hand, and rereads the command.*]

MARCUS [*reading scroll*] A goodly command, indeed. Let me read it once again. [*Reads*] 'To my well-beloved servant, Marcus Superbus, greeting. I learn that the accursed sect of the Christians, so far from being exterminated, is increasing, and that they plot together to destroy my throne and life. They will not bow down to me nor call me king nor pay tribute unto me. They are murderers and fanatics, venomous and bloodthirsty. Arrest all suspects—put them to the torture until they confess—spare neither man, woman nor

child. If you prove any guilty, slay instantly those who are dangerous. The others I will send to the beasts in the arena. Show mercy
to none. On thy life I charge thee. On thee, Marcus my prefect,
be the whole responsibility to purge Rome of these pests. Caesar,
Emperor.'

[*Enter* VITURIUS]

VITURIUS Excellence.

MARCUS Well, Viturius.

VITURIUS The young girl—

MARCUS Mercia—

VITURIUS Yes, Excellence. I was watching the house as you did
command me—when I saw the door cautiously opened—a boy
came out and looked carefully up and down the street. Not observing me, he beckoned the girl. Mercia, with a mantle over her head,
came softly forth—I doubled upon them to tell thee—see, here they
come.

MARCUS Stand aside, Viturius.

[*They retire L.U.E. Enter* MERCIA *and* STEPHANUS, *a youth*] [*of
twelve.*[62] *He is dressed in a short brown tunic girded by a buff leather belt.
His face is handsome and ingenuous; his long light-brown hair falls in clusters
over his forehead, which is broad and well shaped; the eyes are frank and
affectionate; his mouth and lips are curved; his chin rather too sensitive and
pointed for the rest of his face and head. Mercia wears a mantle of a delicate
puce colour over her white robes. Stephanus holds Mercia by the hand and
chats gaily as he strolls by her side*]

MERCIA Indeed, I am safe now—Stephanus—Return to Favius.

STEPHANUS Nay, I will not leave thee, Mercia, until I see thee within
thine own doors. The streets are not safe for thee.

MARCUS [*stepping from the shelter that has concealed him*] [*coming down*] Indeed, they are not—nor for thee either, boy. Take heed.

STEPHANUS I care not for myself—but for her.

MERCIA Come—come, Stephanus.

MARCUS Let me attend thee, lady. This boy is no protection to
thee.

MERCIA I thank thee, sir—but do not need thy help.

MARCUS Dost thou fear me, lady?

MERCIA I have been told to avoid thee.

MARCUS By the old man Favius?

[62] The role of Stephanus was performed by an actress in Barrett's company and in all
touring productions mounted or licensed by Barrett.

MERCIA He and others.

MARCUS Ah—I bear a bad reputation, I fear.

MERCIA [*frankly*] Yes.

MARCUS Delightfully frank, at least. Perhaps I am better than my reputation.

[*Enter* SERVILLIUS, *followed by* TIGELLINUS]

SERVILLIUS [*to* TIGELLINUS] That is the very woman, Excellence.

[*As Servillius speaks, he slinks, wolf-like, round the base of a statue of Nero*]

TIGELLINUS Who is this woman, Prefect?

MARCUS Her name is Mercia.

TIGELLINUS [*angrily*] This man denounces her as a Christian. If it be so, 'tis thy duty to arrest her.

MERCIA Arrest me.

MARCUS [*coldly*] Be sure I know my duty, Tigellinus, both to the Emperor and this lady. Viturius.

[*Enter* VITURIUS]

MARCUS Viturius—attend this lady—see her safely home.

TIGELLINUS [*scornfully*] Have a care, Marcus—if thou dost neglect thy duty—

[*Marcus's hand moves quickly to the handle of his sword, a movement that startles the spy and makes Tigellinus blench. Marcus looks at Mercia and, with some effort, controls himself*]

MARCUS Enough, Tigellinus. I command here. Viturius, obey me— I hold thee responsible for that lady's safety. Go. [*With a bow in which reverence and admiration are curiously blended*] Lady, farewell.

[MERCIA *and* STEPHANUS, *with* VITURIUS, *are moving up stage.* TIGELLINUS *makes a movement to follow but is met by* MARCUS— *the two men are face to face*—MERCIA *turns and looks at* MARCUS *at the upper entrance. Curtain*]

ACT II

Scene 1

[SCENE: *Interior of wooden hut. Doors R. and L. Discover at table* TITUS *and* FAVIUS, STEPHANUS *at the side of* FAVIUS] [*The house of Favius is simple and plain even to barrenness. It is but a rude hut of wood and rubble, with a slight foundation of brick, and consists of only two small rooms. The living-room has in it but one rough deal table, two stools, and a small trunk, which holds some books and writings. The other room contains a small pallet bed-couch and his few household necessaries. The room is dimly lit by an oil lamp, placed on the table by which Favius is seated. Titus stands beside it. Both are deeply interested in the answers the boy, Stephanus, who is on his knees by the side of Favius, is making to their questions*]

FAVIUS And Marcus ordered his soldiers to accompany thee?

STEPHANUS Yes.

FAVIUS Did he have speech with Mercia?

STEPHANUS But a few words.

FAVIUS What thou hast already told us?

STEPHANUS Yes.

FAVIUS You did not again see either Tigellinus or the spy?

STEPHANUS No.

FAVIUS Stephanus, thou art but a child, but thou knowest evil from good—

STEPHANUS Yes, my father.

FAVIUS And thou lovest Mercia.

STEPHANUS I love Mercia.

FAVIUS She is in deadly peril, Stephanus. This Marcus seeks her destruction. He is bold, unscrupulous and powerful. As yet he knows not Mercia is a Christian, but she is suspected—Thou hast been in her company. It may be that thou wilt be arrested—they will think that, being young, thou may'st be induced to betray us and Mercia.

STEPHANUS I, betray thee and Mercia?—Never, father.

FAVIUS You know what the Master did for thee?

STEPHANUS He died for me.

TITUS And if thou betrayest the smallest of His children—thou betrayest Him.

STEPHANUS I know it, father.

TITUS So that thou wilt be faithful?

STEPHANUS Until death, my father.

FAVIUS Now speed thee to our brother, Melos. Tell him the brethren are gathering at the Grove next the Cestine Bridge at the tenth hour, and we desire his presence. Be faithful and vigilant, my son. Keep to the byways. See that thou art not followed or watched. Go. The Spirit of Him we serve be with thee—now and forever.

STEPHANUS Amen, my father.

[*Goes out quickly L.* FAVIUS *bars the door*]

FAVIUS A brave child, and faithful.

TITUS But still a child. Why choose a child for such an errand?

FAVIUS Because he is less likely to be suspected and followed. Until he was seen with Mercia, none have met him with the brethren.

TITUS Now that he has been seen—take my counsel brother—choose another messenger.

FAVIUS After tonight I will.

[*Three peculiar knocks*] [MERCIA *without*]

MERCIA Father—Open—open quickly.

[FAVIUS *unbars door. Enter* MERCIA] [*She is excited and trembling. Her drapery partly conceals her face*]

FAVIUS What is it daughter?

[*She sinks into a seat beside the table*]

MERCIA I have been followed, father.

FAVIUS By whom?

MERCIA I know not. As I left my home, I saw a man with his mantle o'er his face start up from behind a pillar—I tried to elude him by turning back but could not—I hid in a doorway, and he passed me. When he was out of sight, I ran on.

FAVIUS He did not see thee enter here?

MERCIA I think not.

FAVIUS Thou seest, Titus, how the brethren fare in Rome. Hunted like beasts—neither age nor sex are regarded. At the last performances in the amphitheatre, Nero threw young maidens into the arena, where hungry tigers leapt out upon them and lapped up their blood, and they died, glorifying the Shepherd. The aged brethren he ordered to fight with his trained gladiators, and when they threw down their weapons and refused to defend themselves, Nero commanded the gladiators to cut them to pieces, and they died praying for their persecutors. Others who would not abjure the

Master, he coated with pitch, set them on high poles, and burned them as torches to light up his infamous orgies, and as they burned they sang the song of the Redeemer. Were they not faithful unto him?

TITUS Yes, brother—even as thou art—and thou wilt be, my daughter, when thy turn comes. So, in the blood of the saints, the message shall be written to the whole of the earth and to the millions yet unborn—the glad tidings shall be given that He died that they might live.

  [*Loud knocks at door*]

FAVIUS Hush—[*Favius goes to the door*]—Who knocks?

VOICE [*without*] Open and see.

FAVIUS What want ye?

VOICE Speech with Favius.

FAVIUS Do I know thee?

VOICE Open and see.

TITUS Dost know the voice?

MERCIA It reminds me of—

  [*Knocking again*]

TITUS Better open the door.

FAVIUS Go thou within, Mercia.

MERCIA Yes, father.

  [*Exit door R. [Mercia leaves her cloak on the table*] FAVIUS *unbars the door. Enter* MARCUS, *disguised* [*as an old man in a cloak and hood, well drawn over his face*]—*plain brown dress, with hood and beard. He looks round furtively*]

MARCUS Hail, Favius.

TITUS Who art thou?

MARCUS My name is Tyros—I am a boatman on the Tiber, but I wax old apace, and my arms grow too feeble for my work.

  [*Favius points to the stool and courteously motions Marcus to be seated. Marcus gives a slight start as he touches the cloak Mercia has left*]

MARCUS Who is with thee?

FAVIUS A friend.

MARCUS Is he of Rome?

TITUS No.

FAVIUS What is thy errand, Tyros?

MARCUS May I speak before him?

FAVIUS Why not?

MARCUS May I?

FAVIUS You may.

MARCUS Well, thou wert accused yesterday of being a Christian.

FAVIUS I was.

MARCUS Art thou?

FAVIUS What gives thee the right to question?

MARCUS The wish to serve thee.

FAVIUS How canst thou serve me?

MARCUS I know men who have influence with those who sit in high places. Those who have the power over life and death. Some there be who hate the Christians as men hate the plague.

FAVIUS That all men know.

MARCUS Others who care little one way or the other—but must obey those who command them.

FAVIUS Well?

MARCUS And still others who would fain spare, even if guilty, some who may be misguided—or, in their innoncence, misled.

FAVIUS Of what speak you now?

MARCUS Of this strange worship—this foreign superstition.

FAVIUS Know you of what you speak?

MARCUS I know but little. It is sure, though, that they worship strange gods and work in secret to effect the downfall of the Emperor.

FAVIUS I have heard no such tale, sir. It has been told me they worship but one God—and He the everlasting—that they seek the downfall of no man, even be he such a thing of evil as Nero—the monster ye call your king—whose mouth is full of bitterness and curses—whose feet are swift to shed blood—under whose reign Rome hath become as a wanton—filled with lust and drunkenness. Woe unto him and Rome—Woe—woe—woe. For the Kingdom of Heaven is at hand.

TITUS [stopping him] Brother—

MARCUS That speech, heard by other ears than mine, would cost thee thy life, old man, and the lives of all who consort with thee. Have a care.

FAVIUS Thy errand here?

MARCUS I come as a friend to warn you. You are watched. Beware of Tigellinus—beware of Licinius. They seek thy life, and the life of the maiden thou dost call Mercia. If that thou be what men do call the followers of this Christos—for the sake of the maiden, cast her from thee. Thou art old, and thy time is near. She is young, with all youth's warm blood in her veins. Let her live her little life in happiness.

FAVIUS Happiness? Dost thou know what the word means? [*Favius crosses to the door of the inner room*] [*Calls*] Mercia, come hither.

[*Enter* MERCIA]

MERCIA Yes, my father.

FAVIUS This stranger desires me to cast thee from me.

MERCIA Why, my father?

FAVIUS That thou may'st live in the world—for the world—as others live who know not the truth—Wouldst thou so live?

MERCIA No.

FAVIUS He saith that there is happiness.

MERCIA He knoweth not of what he speaks. The Kingdom of Heaven is not meat and drink—but righteousness and peace and joy— [*With an arresting gesture*] But why say I this unto thee? Father, this is the man who followed me.

FAVIUS Ah—Why didst thou dog this maiden's footsteps, Tyros of Tiber?

MERCIA He is not Tyros of Tiber—but Marcus Superbus.

FAVIUS } Marcus—the Prefect?
TITUS }

MERCIA Dost thou deny it?

MARCUS [*laughing*] [*he brushes away his disguise with a sweep of his hand*] Nay, not I—Maiden, thine eyes are as keen as they are beautiful.

[*Mercia moves instinctively towards Favius*]

FAVIUS I should have thought Marcus would pay others to spy for him.

MARCUS By the gods, old man, and so I might—but there was something here I wished to see for myself and would go far and through much to behold [*looking at* MERCIA]. Well, I am unmasked. Tyros hath left the stage, and here stands Marcus and would fain befriend thee, but he holds Caesar's command to exterminate all Christians—men, women and children—to shew mercy unto none. There is at present no proof against thee—let there be none—for, as the King liveth—I will obey him. For thy sweet sake, maiden, I would do much—but my duty I must do. So, again, be warned in time.

[*Three knocks at the door. The Christians look at each other understandingly,* MARCUS *enquiringly*]

FAVIUS Who's there?

MELOS [*without*] Melos—thy friend—Haste! I bring bad tidings.

[*Favius unlocks the door and Melos, a young Christian of about twenty-five enters*]

MELOS Licinius hath arrested Stephanus. Ah [*starts at seeing* MARCUS].

FAVIUS ⎫ Arrested Stephanus?
TITUS ⎬
MERCIA ⎭

MELOS Who is this?

MARCUS Marcus Superbus, Prefect of Rome.

MELOS What doth he here?

MARCUS Let that rest. Who is this Stephanus? The boy I saw with thee?

MERCIA Alas—yes—

MARCUS When was he arrested?

MELOS But now—

MARCUS By Licinius himself?

MELOS I—I—

MARCUS Speak, and speak quickly.

MELOS Yes—

MARCUS Whither have they taken him?

MELOS To the prison of the district, and he—

MARCUS Tell me no more. If that the boy knows aught against thee— fly the city, for he will be made to speak by torture. Be warned in time. I go to Licinius—I cannot prevent him doing his duty—I may stay him from doing more. Heed my words—Farewell—[*a low bow to Mercia*] Lady, we shall meet again.
     [*Exit L. door*]

FAVIUS I pray not.

MERCIA O my father, poor Stephanus—Can we not aid and succour him?

FAVIUS We cannot—but there is One who will.

MERCIA The poor boy—O father, it is hard to think he is in prison— Would that I could be with him to share his pain.

FAVIUS There is other work for thee, my daughter. We cannot stay our march because one falleth by the way. The night is far spent— the day is at hand—we will cast off the work of darkness and put on the armour of light. Art thou afraid, daughter?

MERCIA Nay, my father. That which my Master calleth me to do, I will do. Let the task be what it may, I have put my hand to the ploughshare, and I will not look back.

FAVIUS Even though death and the grave lie before thee?

MERCIA Even though death and the grave lie before me.

FAVIUS Let us hence. We cannot stay the brethren—they are by this time on their several ways to the trysting place by the waters of the Tiber. We will go to them to pray or to suffer with them as He willeth. He will be with us, though the wicked encompass us around and, though we go down into the depths, He will uplift us.

[*Exit all. Change of Scene*]

Scene 2

[SCENE: *The prison. Rude table C. Chair at back, in which sits* TIGELLINUS. *Soldiers on guard.* SERVILLIUS *cringing and fawning L. Doors R. and L.* LICINIUS *seated L.*] [*The two officers, richly dressed, grim, grizzled, fierce, and relentless, are seated at a table; the spy cringeing and fawning at their feet; guards, heavily armed, at the doors, silent and immovable as statues. The room is ill-lit by a lamp, which throws distorted and monstrous shadows crawling up the walls and on to the ceiling and back again. The voices of the officers are subdued, but firm and authoritative*]

TIGELLINUS Go on.

SERVILLIUS I followed him to the house of one Melos—I heard him say 'the brethren meet at'—then he saw me and stopped. I then denounced him to Licinius.

TIGELLINUS [*to* LICINIUS] Hath he said aught to thee?

LICINIUS Not a word.

TIGELLINUS Bring him before us. We must terrify the boy into confession. This girl, Mercia, may be useful to us, can we but get her into our hands.

[STEPHANUS [*dragged by the guards*] *is brought in in chains*] [*At his heels follows a gaoler—a big, burly brute of a man, with a bushy black beard, who holds a whip of several knotted cords in his hand. The guards roughly thrust Stephanus into the room*]

TIGELLINUS Thy name, boy.

STEPHANUS Stephanus.

TIGELLINUS Art thou a Christian?

STEPHANUS [*hesitating*] I serve my Master.

TIGELLINUS Where dwelleth he?

STEPHANUS By the right hand of the Father.

LICINIUS Answer directly, you cub of darkness—Drop this jargon—or the gaoler's whip shall let it out with thy blood. Art thou a Christian? Answer.

STEPHANUS I have answered.

TIGELLINUS Answer again. Are ye a worshipper of the strange God Anokoites?

STEPHANUS No, I worship the living God. No brazen image of any kind.

LICINIUS Are you a follower of the Nazarene? This Chrystos?

[STEPHANUS *is silent*] [*He looks around searchingly for some means of escape*]

LICINIUS Answer, you spawn of evil.

[STEPHANUS *is silent*. LICINIUS *gives a sign to the gaoler, who lashes the boy with his whip*. STEPHANUS *gives an involuntary cry*]

LICINIUS Ah, that will open thy mouth. Follow ye this Chrystos. Eh?

STEPHANUS I will not deny my Master—I do.

LICINIUS Ah—

TIGELLINUS This man heard thee tell Melos that the brethren meet tonight. Who are the brethren?

STEPHANUS That I will not tell.

LICINIUS Where is the place of meeting?

STEPHANUS I will not say.

TIGELLINUS Thou dost know it.

STEPHANUS I do know it.

LICINIUS Then tell it.

STEPHANUS I will not tell it.

LICINIUS Let him taste that whip once more.

[*The gaoler lashes him.* STEPHANUS *falls on the ground*]

LICINIUS Thou shalt answer, or I will slay thee.

STEPHANUS [*faintly*] Thou canst slay my body—thou canst not kill my soul.

TIGELLINUS Answer, and save thyself further pain.

STEPHANUS He who suffered for me will help me.

TIGELLINUS [*aside to* LICINIUS] The calmness of the fanatics passes my understanding.

LICINIUS Give him a turn on the rack—that will shake his calmness.

TIGELLINUS Once more boy—give us the name of the brethren and their place of meeting, and we may pardon thee.

STEPHANUS Thou mayst pardon me, but not my conscience.

LICINIUS Thou dost refuse then?

STEPHANUS I do.

LICINIUS Enough. Put him to the rack.

[*They take* STEPHANUS *up the stage*] [*He is dragged into an adjoining apartment*]

TIGELLINUS If we could but drag Marcus into this—

LICINIUS [*with a bitter sneer*] Nero would believe no evil of his paragon.

TIGELLINUS Excite his fear—he will believe anything. He starts at shadows—anything. Shudders at the fall of a leaf. Each bush to him doth hide an assassin—poison lurks in every dish. The very air to him is peopled with the ghosts of those he hath slaughtered. He dare not go on, yet dare not stay. Once rouse his fear—let him once believe Marcus favours these Christians—Marcus's death is certain, and his wealth Nero would seize and share with us.

[*A piercing scream is heard from* STEPHANUS,[63]]

LICINIUS [*at door*] Ah, the rack hath found his tongue. Wilt thou answer now?

STEPHANUS I cannot bear it—Mercy—mercy.

LICINIUS Answer then.

STEPHANUS I dare not—

[LICINIUS *signals again. There is another scream*]

LICINIUS He hath fainted—Bring him hither—some wine there—

[*They bring in* STEPHANUS *and lay him on the ground. One of the guards brings wine, which* LICINIUS *pours down* STEPHANUS's *throat. He gradually recovers*]

TIGELLINUS He recovers—

STEPHANUS [*faintly*] Spare me—

LICINIUS Answer—

STEPHANUS The Grove—

TIGELLINUS Where?

STEPHANUS By the Cestine Bridge—

LICINIUS The hour—

STEPHANUS Ten—

LICINIUS Aha—We have them, my Tigellinus, we have them—Their names—

STEPHANUS I cannot—

LICINIUS You shall—

STEPHANUS I will not—Kill me—kill me—

LICINIUS Ah no—the dead speak not—Thou shalt answer—

STEPHANUS No—

LICINIUS The rack again then—

[*Soldiers lift up* STEPHANUS. *Enter* MARCUS]

---

[63] This moment was a favourite with the play's audiences. Spectators, arriving late, would query theatre ushers, 'Has he screamed yet?'

MARCUS The rack for whom? For this child? [*To soldiers*] Set him down.

LICINIUS Obey me, soldiers.

MARCUS Obey me.

> [*The soldiers hesitate, looking from one to the other*]

TIGELLINUS How darest thou presume?—

MARCUS Presume? Set down that boy—I, the Prefect, command you. Disobey me—and, as Caesar liveth, thou shalt take his place.

TIGELLINUS This is treason against Caesar—and, as Caesar liveth, thou shalt answer it to Caesar.

MARCUS I will answer it, Tigellinus. I have Caesar's orders. I execute them as I think fit.

LICINIUS Thou dost not execute them, Marcus—Thou art shielding these Christians—and thou art a traitor.

MARCUS Recall that word—Recall it, and that quickly, or, aedile or no aedile, I'll cleave thee from thy head to thy heart. Recall it—

TIGELLINUS Licinius was hasty—he did not mean—

MARCUS I desire not thy apology, Tigellinus, but his. I want the yelp of the wolf—not the whine of the fox. Recall that word 'traitor', I say.

TIGELLINUS [*aside*] We shall let them slip. Give way.

LICINIUS I was too hasty—I regret—

MARCUS Enough—

TIGELLINUS Captain, get me ten good men and follow me. Guards, see to that boy. Come, Licinius. Time flies—we shall be late.

> [*Exit with Captain*]

LICINIUS [*looking back*] My turn is coming.

> [*Exit*]

MARCUS Is that wine there?—Give it to me. Have they had him on the rack?

SOLDIER [*holding up* STEPHANUS] Yes, Prefect.

MARCUS The cowards. The wolves.

> [*He goes to the fainting boy and lifts his head from the ground*]

MARCUS Come boy—come take this—

STEPHANUS [*bursting into tears*] Ah, the pain—the pain—

MARCUS Drink—'twill revive thee.

STEPHANUS Nay, let me die—Kill me—in mercy, kill me—I have betrayed my Master.

MARCUS What mean you?

STEPHANUS 'Twas not my heart—but my tongue that spoke—I told them where the brethren meet tonight.

MARCUS Who are the brethren?

STEPHANUS I dare not tell—but, if you would save Mercia—

MARCUS [*starting in surprise and alarm*] Mercia—What of her?

STEPHANUS She will be there—

MARCUS Where?

STEPHANUS In the Grove by the Cestine Bridge.

MARCUS Didst thou tell this to Tigellinus?

STEPHANUS Not the names—but the meeting-place—

MARCUS And she is to be there?

STEPHANUS Yes—Kill me—but save her. She is an angel—Save her and let me die—save her—

MARCUS Viturius—quick—Viturius. [*To soldiers*] Take care of this child. Have him taken to my palace. Bear him gently.

[*Soldiers take up* STEPHANUS]

STEPHANUS Kill me—I am not fit to live—I have betrayed them—Kill me—kill me.

[*They bear him off R. Enter* VITURIUS]

VITURIUS You called me, Excellence.

MARCUS Yes—How many men hast thou at hand?

VITURIUS But four, Excellence.

MARCUS And he asked for ten—but what of that? Thou and I and four good men are more than a match for fifty of Tigellinus's gang. On, good Viturius—as thou dost love me, on—I'll save this girl from Tigellinus—even though Nero himself should bar the way. On, good Viturius, on—

[*Exit. Change of Scene*]

Scene 3

[SCENE: *Grove by the Tiber by moonlight. Crescent moon and ripple of cloth and stars twinkling. Cut woods. A band of Christians dis-covered, worshipping. One or two have lanterns*] [*On a slight eminence stands Favius; a little lower down is Titus; a little lower down kneels Mercia. In her right hand she holds a horn lantern; in her left a large cross, made of two branches, broken from trees before the meeting began, and lashed together with a leathern thong. It has been hurriedly made on the spot. The band of Christians are kneeling facing Favius. Nearest are the children, then the women, and, on the outer rings, the men. All are quietly and soberly attired, and the white robes and drapery in which Mercia is wrapped makes her figure stand out against the background of green foliage. All are singing a hymn*]

Shepherd of souls that stumble by the way—
Pilot of vessels storm-tossed in the night—
Healer of wounds—for help to thee we pray—
Guide, thou, our footsteps—send the morning's light—
    O lead us home.

All we like sheep have strayed—where is the fold—
That shelters all who seek its loving breast—
There, where the cross doth shine like heavenly gold—
Emblem of pain—giving eternal rest—
    O lead us home.

[*At the end of the hymn Mercia rises, raising the lantern in her left hand, to enable Favius to read the Epistle, which he has unrolled, while, with her right, she still grasps the cross*]

FAVIUS [*reading from scroll,* MERCIA *holding lantern*] And now, brethren, be faithful—Love them that hate you—Pray for them that despitefully use you—Love one another. Be patient in sorrow—Rejoice with them that do rejoice. Weep with those that are in grief. If the enemy hunger, feed him—if he thirst, give him drink. Do unto others as you would they should do unto you. Love thy neighbour as thyself. For to teach this came the Master into this world. Now, may peace that passes all understanding be with you now and forever.

ALL (*chanting*) Amen.

    [*All rise*]

TITUS Brethren. Too long hath the nation wandered in darkness. The dawn is at hand, but the splendour of the morning gold will be streaked with blood—the blood of the saints. Treachery is around you—and lies in wait to snare your feet. But, though the wicked pursue thee even unto death, death is but the gate to life eternal. Be patient and endure.

    [MELOS *rushes on* [*down the bank of the dell*], *pale and terror-stricken*]

MELOS Father—Favius—Mercia—brethren, we are betrayed—

ALL Betrayed—

MELOS Tigellinus and his soldiers are upon us—Fly—fly, and save yourselves.

    [*Some people are about to fly. The children are clinging to their mother's garments, frightened and helpless. The men are endeavouring to calm them and assist the women to escape. Mercia, seeing that flight is impossible, raises the cross on high*]

MERCIA Stay, brethren, by the cross, I implore you. Ye cannot escape. Meet your enemies like Christians. Be not afraid.

[*All are calm and reverent once more. Sinking down on their knees, they recommence their hymn*] [*Enter* TIGELLINUS *and* LICINIUS *with soldiers, L.U.E. and R.U.E.*]

TIGELLINUS [*L.C. with* LICINIUS] Fall upon them—Spare none of the dogs.

[*The soldiers surround the Christians and cut them down and stab them.* [*When a woman is aimed at, a man will step forward and calmly receive the thrust; mothers throw themselves upon the sword to save their little ones. Children, who have been spared for the moment, pray silently over their parents. Servillius finds the child of the man he had seen struck to the earth in the street by Dacia's house.*[64] *The bereaved woman lifts her hands in passionate entreaty. Licinius seizes Titus and runs his sword through his heart. Tigellinus rushes at Favius*] MERCIA *rushes in front of* FAVIUS, *who is struck down* [*by Tigellinus*], *and stands over him, protecting him. The soldiers hesitate to touch her*]

MERCIA Kill me, but spare this aged man.

LICINIUS Kill the jade with the rest—Kill her—

[*He seizes* MERCIA, *swings her round with his left hand and, with his right, he takes sword from soldier.* MERCIA *falls to her knees. He is about to strike her when* MARCUS *enters with his soldiers. He takes sword from* LICINIUS *and hurls him to the ground*]

MARCUS Hold, in the name of the Emperor. Slay no more—take them all prisoners. No, leave this girl to me.

[*The soldiers sheath their swords. Tigellinus calls his troops to fall in, and they march off*] [*Picture*]

[*Mercia has gone to Favius and has lifted his head to her knees. Marcus kneels by her and takes his hand. Mercia holds his other hand. Favius, to the last, has his eyes fixed on Mercia*] [*Curtain*]

[64] See Act I.

ACT III

Scene 1

[SCENE: *Room in* BERENIS'S *house. All in exquisite taste and refinement. Sweet incense burning.* BERENIS *discovered* [*reclining*] *on couch by table L., attended by* ZONA, *her slave girl, who* [*kneeling*] *is touching her eyebrows with a black pencil.* BERENIS *takes a* [*small steel*] *hand-mirror and is looking at herself. She is exquisitely dressed*] [*in creamy white silk, her bust outlined by a massive band of many-coloured gems. A belt of the same rich character draws the robe together at the waist, while the hem of this garment is wrought so closely with jewels that the material is entirely hidden. A drapery of the most delicate shade of heliotrope, bordered with gold and caught at the side with an immense jewelled clasp, seems to display rather than hide her figure. On her arms are bracelets; in her hair are entwined gems*]

BERENIS Give me the pencil, Zona—you're careless this morning.

ZONA Nay, lady, I—

[*Berenis slaps her face. Zona sinks back on the floor and ruefully rubs her stinging cheek*]

BERENIS Don't answer me—This eyebrow is all askew—What ails you, girl? Art sick or in love? Or both. Why don't you speak, fool?

ZONA Lady, you told me not to answer, and—

BERENIS Well, answer now—How do I look this morning?

ZONA Radiantly beautiful, lady. The noble Marcus must love you—or he is but a marble man, not one of flesh and blood.

BERENIS Why speak of Marcus? There are scores of others who would give their lives for me.

ZONA That they would indeed, lady—There's Metullus.

BERENIS Metullus—I despise him—he's a fool.

ZONA He's rich—and a rich husband, who is a fool to boot, is not a thing to be despised—Then there's Tigellinus.

BERENIS He's a brute.

ZONA Brutes can be tamed, lady.

BERENIS Pah—they all weary me unto death—Marcus is worth a score of such. He must love me—he shall—he—

[*As she speaks, she tries the effect of a red rose over an ear. Zona stretches herself out on a tiger's skin beside the couch, her head upon the beast's head, and prepares to doze*] [*A gong is heard outside R.*]

BERENIS That may be Marcus—Put those things away, quick—
        [*Berenis puts the rose into a small vase*] [ZONA *hides articles of toilet*]
BERENIS Now take thy lute and sing.
        [ZONA *sits at the feet of* BERENIS *and takes her lute*] [*striking a few*
        chords. Berenis falls back upon the couch in a tempting attitude]
BERENIS Enter—enter—
        [*Enter slave girl* CATIA]
CATIA The lady Dacia would have speech with thee.
BERENIS [*disappointed*] Oh, Dacia—admit her—There, get up, girl, I
        thought it was Marcus—you need not sing for Dacia.
        [*Enter* DACIA, *gorgeously dressed*] [*in pale rose-pink silk. Her draperies,*
        broidered with heavy gold fringe, are crossed over her bosom with bands of
        rubies and other precious stones. A string of rubies is entwined in her golden
        hair, and a pale blush rose fastened on either side of her head]
DACIA Ah, my Berenis.
BERENIS Well, my Dacia—what brings thee hither?
DACIA A fit of depression—
BERENIS Have you been gambling and losing again?
DACIA Worse—I would not mind the losing—but that stupid Philo-
        demus tells me he cannot pay my losses.
BERENIS Ask your husband to do so.
DACIA I asked, but he laughed and told me that, if Philodemus could
        not afford to pay my debts, to get another lover who could. That's
        the disadvantage of being frank enough to let your husband know
        you have a lover—As for him, he was sore pressed himself—You
        know what that means, my Berenis—that hook-nosed wife of Vi-
        nius is ruining him. That woman's a perfect vulture. All is meat that
        comes to her now. What the men see in her I can never understand.
        Vinius is the fourth husband she has had in two years.
BERENIS The third—
DACIA Third—I thought it was four she had had.
BERENIS No, only three.
        [*Dacia drops a plate of grapes. Berenis again takes the rose from its vase and*
        tries its effect, gazing at it in the steel hand-mirror. Dacia picks up the vase]
DACIA Well, one cannot be particular to one or two, when a woman
        changes her husband as often as that.
BERENIS There are others as bad as she—
DACIA Worse, Berenis, worse—There's Adrostia—How that woman
        dares to show her face is beyond me. She got her husband Helladi-
        nus to divorce her that she might marry his friend Adoncus, and,
        when she had ruined him, divorced him to marry Scymnus—[*drops*

the vase] ruined him and divorced him, remarried her first husband, Helladius—and invited all the divorced ones to the wedding supper.

[*Dacia begins to handle a gold-mounted cup of coloured glass, studded with gems. Berenis quietly but firmly takes it and puts it safely from her*]

DACIA What do you think of that?

BERENIS That she is a very liberal woman. What has become of your friend Ambascius?

DACIA Oh, don't speak to me of Ambascius.

BERENIS Why not speak of him—I thought he really loved you.

DACIA So he does—the mean-spirited creature, but he calls it a sin to have a love affair with a married woman. Pah—such men are only fit for servant girls—Ah, that reminds me—Marcus—

BERENIS What of Marcus?

DACIA Have you not heard?

BERENIS Heard—what?

DACIA About this Christian girl he is so infatuated with.

BERENIS What?

DACIA Oh, all Rome is talking of it.

BERENIS Of what—of what—

DACIA Strange you should not have heard—but then, thank the gods, lovers and husbands are always the last to hear what pranks their dear ones are practising.

BERENIS What of the Christian girl and Marcus?

DACIA Tigellinus will tell you.

BERENIS I haven't seen Tigellinus for two days—What is it?

DACIA Tigellinus swept down on a nest of these vipers—these Christians—and would have exterminated them—but, if it please you, the noble Marcus steps in and protected one of the wretched females and has her taken to his house.

BERENIS What!

DACIA And Tigellinus swears that Nero shall know of it—but then all Rome knows the state Nero is in—always drunk. Moreover, there's Poppaea—She rules the Emperor, and, as she's half in love with Marcus herself—

BERENIS But this Christian girl—what is her name?

DACIA Mercia—I think the creature's called—

BERENIS The same—

DACIA What do you mean?

BERENIS I've heard of her before—What is she like?

[*Dacia begins to study herself in the steel mirror*]

DACIA They say she's beautiful—Philodemus told me Marcus was quite foolish over her—but she, forsooth, gives herself virtuous airs and repulses him.

BERENIS Ah these men—these men—

DACIA That's exactly what I say.

[*Gong rings*]

BERENIS Enter—

[*Enter* CATIA]

CATIA Tigellinus and Licinius would have speech with thee lady.

BERENIS Ah—good—they come in time—Admit them—

[*Exit* CATIA]

DACIA Now you can hear the whole story.

[*Enter* TIGELLINUS *and* LICINIUS]

TIGELLINUS The gods be with thee, ladies.

DACIA Some of them are, Tigellinus, and they could well be spared.

BERENIS Welcome, gentlemen. What's the news in Rome?

TIGELLINUS Marcus has a new toy.

BERENIS You mean the Christian girl. It is true then?

TIGELLINUS It is, and Rome pities Berenis.

BERENIS Why?

TIGELLINUS 'Tis said she mourns a faithless lover.

BERENIS Marcus has never been my lover, Tigellinus.

LICINIUS Therefore Rome pities thee the more. It is horrible, but tongues will wag and the gossip is that, although you woo Marcus, he does not respond.

BERENIS Do they dare say that of me?

DACIA Indeed they do, and laugh at you for your devotion.

BERENIS Dids't thou come here to tell me this?

TIGELLINUS No, but to serve you.

BERENIS How cans't thou serve me?

TIGELLINUS By helping thee to revenge thyself.

BERENIS On this girl, Mercia?

LICINIUS And on Marcus.

BERENIS How?

TIGELLINUS Marcus has full power to judge and condemn these Christians. He has chosen to spare this girl Mercia, and keeps her a prisoner in his own palace.

BERENIS Repeat this to Nero—not to me.

TIGELLINUS ⎫ Ah—
LICINIUS ⎭

BERENIS Well, why not?

TIGELLINUS And Poppaea? If she should learn that I had tried to injure Marcus—the gods be with me—for Nero would not.

BERENIS What, then, do you propose?

TIGELLINUS That you do visit Poppaea and tell her of Marcus's infatuation, and induce her to influence Nero and persuade him to send this Mercia to the lions.

BERENIS A contemptible piece of work.

TIGELLINUS Then let Mercia live, and let Rome still pity Berenis.

[BERENIS *walks up and down in a conflict of emotion*]

DACIA Berenis—have more spirit—I should like to see the man who would fling me aside for any Christian creature.

BERENIS What to do?—What to do?

TIGELLINUS Revenge yourself for the slight that has been put upon you. This man, Marcus—

[*Enter* MARCUS. *There is a dead silence*] [*Dacia sits at one of the couches and munches grapes that she takes from a nearby table*]

MARCUS Hail, ladies. Am I in the way? Was my character under discussion? Were Tigellinus and Licinius wearying you with praising me, fair Berenis? I know how dearly they do love me—Silent still?— Ah, my Licinius—hast thou not yet recovered the breath I knocked out of thy most precious body in that little accident in the Grove.

LICINIUS I've breath enough to keep me alive, Marcus.

MARCUS Provided thou dost not attack anything stronger than a weak boy or a frail girl—eh, Licinius?

LICINIUS The boy and the girl were traitors both—I did but my duty.

MARCUS Duty? Ah—how many crimes are committed under the cloak of duty. But do I intrude?

BERENIS No—no—pray stay, Marcus—I wish to speak with thee.

DACIA I was just about to go, Marcus. Adieu, Berenis—Gentlemen, will you be my escort—it will be better I think that you accompany me—verily, you look so fierce—both of you—that I fear for Marcus should he be left alone with them.

MARCUS Pray have no fear for me now, lady. The harm they may do to me will be done when my back is turned. It is not the soldier's sword—but the assassin's knife and slanderer's tongue that Marcus need fear from Tigellinus and Licinius.

TIGELLINUS [*furiously*] [*stung, he partly draws his sword*] By the gods, Marcus—

MARCUS [*coolly*] Yes?

TIGELLINUS Have a care—or else—

MARCUS Yes?

BERENIS Stop this, Tigellinus—this is my house—I will have no brawling here—Please go.

TIGELLINUS I obey, lady—

MARCUS How glad is Tigellinus to be obedient.

DACIA Come—come—I am in haste—do you accompany me—or not? See that my chariot is at the door, Licinius.

LICINIUS Yes, lady—Farewell, Berenis.

[Exit]

DACIA Your arm, Tigellinus. Berenis, adieu—Marcus—be sure you take good care of your fair Christian, Mercia—but do not run into danger of Nero's anger. A few hours gazing on a pretty face is but scant reward for disgrace and a dungeon. Be prudent.

[Exit with TIGELLINUS]

MARCUS I will, fair Dacia. Most prudent. Well, my Berenis—you sent for me, lady[65]—

BERENIS I did.

MARCUS You honour me.

BERENIS I degrade myself.

MARCUS How, fair lady?

BERENIS In so far forgetting my womanhood. That I, Berenis—should send for any man—how I hate myself—

MARCUS [lightly] You are singular in this regard. If Berenis really hates Berenis—she is the only mortal who does.

BERENIS [impatiently] I want no compliments from Marcus.

MARCUS [more softly] What dost thou need of Marcus? Anything he has to give is thine for the asking.

BERENIS I want that that I gave thee unasked—

MARCUS [as if to stop her avowal] Berenis—Berenis—

BERENIS I know—I know—it is unwomanly, but it is true—O Marcus, why do you hate me?

MARCUS I do not hate thee, Berenis.

BERENIS I am young—rich—not hideous to gaze upon—and—and I[66] love thee, Marcus—as no other woman could love thee—

MARCUS I must not listen, Berenis—

BERENIS You shall listen—Unless I speak, my heart will break—This is no mere fancy. It is the love of years—it has been kept pent up so long that it chokes my life—unless it is unbound, its bonds will strangle me—I love you so—I love you so.

---

[65] There is a substantial variant addition/emendation to this scene in later versions of the text. It is included as an appendix at the end of the play.

[66] The variant version ends here.

[*Flings her arms round his neck. He disengages himself*]

MARCUS With all the respect that man can feel for woman, I—If devotion—if friendship—

BERENIS 'Friendship'—I ask for bread. You offer me a stone—

MARCUS I offer all I have—

BERENIS Marcus—have you never loved?

MARCUS Never—that is—I do not know—

BERENIS [*fiercely*] There is a doubt then—

MARCUS I do not think there is—I am not sure.

BERENIS Is the doubt about this girl, Mercia?

MARCUS Pardon me, Berenis—my secrets are my own—

BERENIS [*furiously*] There is no doubt—I feel it—you love Mercia.

MARCUS Had we not better speak of something else?

BERENIS Do you love Mercia?

MARCUS Was it for this that you sent for me?

BERENIS No—I longed for the sight of thee—the sound of thy voice— to be near thee—anything—After I had sent for thee, I heard of this girl.

MARCUS Ah, my dear friends Tigellinus and Licinius have been busy, I find.

BERENIS Is it true—dost thou love her?

MARCUS Really, Berenis, I am not bound to answer thee.

BERENIS I will answer myself then—Thou dost love her, Marcus, caught at last by the baby face of a miserable Christian girl—whose life is forfeit to the law—a wretched, nameless Christian—a thing despised and loathed—the companion of thieves and murderers— the scum of Rome—a degraded schemer—an outcast—a—

MARCUS Stop—I will not hear you.

BERENIS You shall hear me—

MARCUS Pardon me, lady—I will not. I take my leave [*going*].

BERENIS You shall not go until you have heard me—Love is so near to hate—that one step—one hair's breadth past the boundary line, and love is merged in loathing. Have a care, Marcus—Berenis will not be scorned and bear it.

MARCUS Does Berenis stoop to threaten?

BERENIS Stoop?—Yes, gods—can I stoop lower than I have done?

MARCUS Yes—true love is no dishonour—treachery is.

BERENIS I care not—I will love or hate—Dost thou think all Rome does not know this girl is in thy house?

MARCUS I care not.

BERENIS Rome laughs, and swears you plead to her in vain.

MARCUS I care not.

BERENIS Is it true?

MARCUS Really, Berenis—To be just to the girl—it is.

BERENIS [*laughing hysterically*] Poor Marcus—refused by a Christian baggage—who—

MARCUS Stop again, Berenis, and understand. What Rome may say of me troubles me nothing—what Rome or even Berenis may say of Mercia—may trouble me much—She is no schemer—no degraded woman—she is the purest—sweetest and most crystal soul that lives in Rome today. I know women fairly well—their wiles—their arts—their tricks. I am not to be gulled or fooled by acted innocence. I have seen too much of it—What this Christianity is, I know not—but this I know: if it makes many such woman as Mercia, Rome—nay, the whole world—will be the better for it.

BERENIS You dare speak thus of her to me.

MARCUS Why not?

BERENIS How, if I repeat your words?

MARCUS Repeat them, if thou wilt.

BERENIS To Nero?

MARCUS To Nero.

BERENIS Yes—what then?

MARCUS [*quietly*] It is hard to say—what then. I can only hope that Berenis will never play the part of an informer against Marcus.

BERENIS Will you give up this girl?

MARCUS No.

BERENIS You shall—I will force you—Take care—measure my determination with your own, and add to my advantage the hate I bear her and Nero's power to injure you.

MARCUS Berenis—neither your love—nor hate—nor Nero's power, backed by all his legions, can turn me from my purpose—I will have Mercia—though degradation and death follow the possession. There's not a nerve in my body that does not call for her—not a thought in my brain that does not embrace her. Now, the truth is told—I leave you—no good can come of further talk. Farewell [*going*].

BERENIS Stay—Marcus—stay—

MARCUS No, lady. I have stayed too long. I cannot fight a woman, even with words. Adieu.

[*Exit*]

BERENIS Fool—fool—besotted—lovesick fool. O but he shall dearly pay for his folly. Reject me for this wretched, tawdry, mock-modest piece of low-bred trumpery—Insult me for her—Scorn Berenis for a Mercia—O for the power to humble him as he has humbled me—To Nero, that is—yes, that's it—I'll do it—I'll do it—I'll do it—

[*Exit. Change of Scene*]

Scene 2

[SCENE: *Atrium of Nero's palace. Enter* TIGELLINUS *and* LICINIUS *preceded by a slave*] [*A crowd of courtiers, who are already in attendance, fawn obsequiously upon them*]

SLAVE His Sacred Majesty, the Emperor Nero, will give thee audience here at once.

[*Exit slave R.*]

TIGELLINUS Good. If Berenis do but win the Emperor, Marcus's sun will quickly set.

LICINIUS Would it were quenched in everlasting midnight. His arrogance is past all bearing.

[*Music and buzz of voices heard off R.*]

TIGELLINUS Hush, Nero.

[*A file of Ethiopian*] [*Guards*] [*clad in particoloured skirts, reaching from the waist to within an inch of the knee, wearing across their bare breasts and shoulders the skins of leopards (the heads thereof being brought over their own foreheads, thus lending them an appearance of savage ferocity); with brawny arms and legs unclothed; carrying in their right hands long spears, with heads of polished bronze, and bearing over their left arms shields of tanned lion-hide[67]*] *cross the stage.* [*They are followed by splendidly dressed heralds with long trumpets of gold, upon which they blow a rude blare of harmonized chords as a signal of the approach of Nero*] *Then enter* GLABRIO, PHILODEMUS, METULLUS *and other courtiers. Then* NERO. *The courtiers bend almost to the floor, and walk backwards, keeping their faces towards* NERO. [*He leans on the necks of two feminine-looking boys. They are garbed in short white tunics, their golden hair bound with fillets of gold; their legs are bared to the sandals, and they mince and smirk with all the airs and graces of girlhood. Nero is gorgeously dressed, but there is a suggestion of effeminacy in his attire, the outcome of deliberate design, which robs it of all dignity. The underdress is soft, cream-coloured silk, richly embroidered with gold,*

[67] Queen Victoria's Jubilee celebrations in 1897 had placed African, Indian, and oriental troops in the Queen's escort, thereby signalling the vastness of the Crown's dominions and the loyalty of these troops to a white sovereign.

scarcely reaching to the knee. The toga was of Tyrian purple, studded with amethysts and emeralds] He is fat, lame, and half-drunk. His manner nervous and shifty—he has the aspect of a man who is constantly on the verge of delirium tremens. He is pompous and inflated—his eyes always shifting here and there, as if expecting some terrible apparition or fearing assassination]

ALL Hail, mighty Caesar.

NERO Ah, Tigellinus and Licinius—wert whispering. [*His quick, furtive, frightened gaze shifts uneasily from one to the other*] Eh? Eh? Eh? Plotting—eh? What treason is toward?

TIGELLINUS Our treason is toward High Olympus. We would dethrone the gods and make them slaves to Nero.

NERO Good—Ah—good. There is at least one god whose place I could fill. Canst guess who 'tis?

TIGELLINUS Nay but one? Your Majesty is too modest—but, in sooth, Apollo must lay aside his lyre when Nero sings.

NERO Ah—right—right—A statue of myself as Apollo—shall I have it done—Eh?—Eh?

TIGELLINUS Nay, Caesar—I dare not advise—but be careful what part of Olympus thou dost choose for thy future residence, lest the burden of thy greatness disturb the equilibrium of the world.

NERO Well thought—well said, Tigellinus—but Apollo, eh? I can sing—eh? An artist—eh?

TIGELLINUS A great poet too, Caesar. Dost remember thy lines on the sheen of a dove's neck wherein Cythrea's name appears?

NERO [*glowing with vanity*] Nay, I write rapidly and forget as quickly— but a thousand sesterces I'll wager that neither thou nor any present can repeat the lines.

TIGELLINUS 'Fair Cythrea's frightened doves illume—With sheeny lustre every glancing plume.'

NERO Wrong—wrong—Not 'frightened'—'startled' is the word. [*He declaims*]

    'Fair Cythrea's startled doves illume—
    With sheeny lustre every glancing plume.'

[*The courtiers applaud sycophantically*]

TIGELLINUS I confess I was wrong, Caesar.

NERO 'Startled' is so much more euphonius. Remember when next you quote those lines—'startled', not 'frightened'. I was just saying we want new games in the circus.

GLABRIO Wilt thou race the next games, Caesar?

NERO I have not decided—but we'll have sport, be sure. How fares this Christian conspiracy?

TIGELLINUS They still plot against thy life, Caesar.

NERO [*frightened*] How—What?—What?—Thou knowest this—and yet they live? What means this? Have I not ordered their extermination?—Eh?

TIGELLINUS Indeed thou hast, Caesar.

NERO Well? Well?

TIGELLINUS Licinius and thy servant have done all that was in their power—but—

NERO But what?—What?—Our sacred person in danger, and our orders not obeyed. Who dares hesitate when Caesar commands?—

TIGELLINUS Not thy servant Tigellinus.

LICINIUS Nor Licinius.

NERO Who then? Who then?—Eh?—Eh?—

TIGELLINUS We would rather not betray—

NERO Ho—ho—Then Caesar's life must be in peril because thou woulds't rather not betray some cowardly associate. Thou wouldst betray me—eh?—Eh? Who is it? I command thee—

TIGELLINUS Since thou dost command, Caesar, thy servant must obey—thy prefect, Marcus—

NERO Marcus? No—no—not Marcus. Have a care, if thou dost belie our Marcus—the best officer we have—

TIGELLINUS Licinius knows I speak the truth—He did stay my hand when—for the sake of thy sacred life—I did put one of these Christians—a boy—to the torture to force him to reveal the meeting-place of the conspirators, and, again, when I set upon them, he did bid me spare them—and—and—

> [*Enter* POPPAEA *and* BERENIS. TIGELLINUS *hesitates, stammers and ceases speaking, bowing to* POPPAEA. POPPAEA *is gorgeously dressed. She is a beautiful blonde—and moves and speaks with great authority.* NERO *is evidently afraid of her*]

NERO Ah—my Poppaea—thou dost come in time—Here's treason, foul treason, towards our sacred selves—Ah, Lady Berenis—

POPPAEA Treason—Who says this?

NERO Tigellinus and Licinius both do accuse Marcus—

POPPAEA [*scornfully*] Of treason?

TIGELLINUS Nay, Emperor—but—but—

NERO What else than treason to Caesar, if he protects those who plot against Caesar's life.

POPPAEA There's been some exaggeration here—I know the whole truth, Caesar—Berenis hath confided it to me, and I was

even now about to seek thee and ask for thy authority to set
the matter right. Possibly zeal for thy safety hath induced Tigellinus and Licinius to overestimate the importance of Marcus's
error.

NERO What is it—eh?—What hath he done? Eh?—Eh?

POPPAEA Marcus is a man and, lacking thy constancy, great Caesar,
is too easily caught by a pretty face—Of all these hordes of Christians that we hear of—he hath but spared one—and that a mere girl
who, for the moment, hath caught his wayward fancy—

NERO Is that all?—Only one girl, eh?

POPPAEA [warningly] I do not think Tigellinus can name another, eh?
How say you, Tigellinus?

TIGELLINUS No, Emperor—no—

NERO Only one girl—that matters but little—yet even a girl—

POPPAEA May be dangerous, and so it were in thee, my love, to give
power to Tigellinus to take this girl out of the hands of Marcus and
leave thee to deal with her thyself.

NERO Yes—yes, of course—deal with her myself. Thou shalt have
power.—Accursed be the whole race of Christians—Seek our sacred
life? I'll throw them to the beasts—I'll dress them in skins of wolves
and set the bloodhounds on them. Ha—ha—ha—that would be
sport—I'll soak them in oil and tallow, as I did before, and set them
blazing—all Rome shall be aflame with them. Come, I'll write the
mandate—come—Seek my life—eh? I'll exterminate the vermin—
I'll blot them off the earth. Come—come—

[Exit all, save POPPAEA and BERENIS]

POPPAEA Now thou hast thy desire, Berenis.

BERENIS I thank thee, Poppaea—but—but—

POPPAEA What now? Dost regret—

BERENIS Not for the wretched girl, but for Marcus—Should any evil
come to him—

POPPAEA I will see that no evil come to him through Caesar—but
keep me ever informed of all. Tigellinus and Licinius hate him, and,
were I absent, might bring about his ruin. Poor Berenis.—I verily
believe thou art already sorry for thine action—have courage—Marcus will soon forget the girl—once she is out of his sight—and then
Berenis will have her wish. Nero shall command that Marcus wed
thee—

BERENIS O lady, how I thank thee—

POPPAEA Reserve thy thanks until thou hast tried Marcus as a husband. After all, it may be a cruelty, not a kindness, that I am doing

thee—we weak women never know these men until we have married them.

[*Exit R. Change of Scene*]

Scene 3

[SCENE: *Atrium in the palace of* MARCUS. *Song of love, with full chorus, heard off L.U.E. Enter* MARCUS]

MARCUS How they weary me! Men lie and flatter—women fawn and leer, and all are false as water and as transparent. Friends? All friends for what I have—not one for what I am. I'd freely give them all for one sweet look from Mercia. What is it possesses me? These people were well enough until she came—she, Mercia, and now—how loathsome their drunken antics seem to me. What is it in the girl that so uplifts her beyond the rest? Her beauty? No—yet, yes—but not the beauty of her face or form—some inward light there is that glows through the windows of her soul and dims the lustre of her body's loveliness. What is it? Virtue? I have seen other virtuous women. Is it this faith of hers? What is their faith? Certainly, not the foul idolatry, the ignorant superstition, men do say it is—one look of hers and the ribald jest that is on my tongue dies there, and yet I'm sick with longing for her—is this love or what?

[*Enter* GLABRIO *L.U.E.*]

GLABRIO Well, my Marcus—why hast thou left the table?

MARCUS I—well—the heat stifled me—

GLABRIO I have been sent to beg thee to return—The fun lags without you—the wine cheers not—the song enlivens not—the jest falls flat—Ancaria sighs like the bellows of a smithy—Return to her.

MARCUS Ancaria—

GLABRIO Aye, Ancaria—By Venus, she is fair—doth she not content thee?—

MARCUS Contentment is for the gods—nay, even they seek for that pearl in vain.

GLABRIO But Ancaria—a flower—a rose—the very rose of roses.

MARCUS Plucked some days ago and fading—with just the touch of decomposing that coming death sprinkles o'er roses and o'er other flowers—as mortal, if less frail.

GLABRIO Marcus, thou art in a parlous way. Something is out of order with thee. Is it the heart or stomach?—If 'tis the latter, send for the

leech—if 'tis the former send for the woman—leeches and women
resemble each other in this—'tis kill or cure with both.
MARCUS Send for the woman—Glabrio, thou art a fool—but thy folly
hath ever a something of wisdom—I will send for the woman.
[*Strikes gong. Enter a slave*]
MARCUS Bring the prisoner, Mercia, to me.
[*Christians' Hymn is* [*faintly*] *heard off R.*]

Shepherd of souls that stumble by the way—
Pilot of vessels storm-tossed in the night—
Healer of wounds—for help to thee we pray—
Guide thou our footsteps—send the morning's light—
O lead us home.

GLABRIO Ah, ho—then 'tis thy heart that is out of gear—the woman
is sent for—Hearken to my folly—That which a man has—he
seldom longs for—longing makes a man sick. If thou wouldst be
well—long no longer—thou art hungry with longing—a good full
meal, my Marcus, is what my folly counsels.
MARCUS [*hastily*] She comes—Go back to my guests, Glabrio.
GLABRIO No—let me see this beauty—have one embrace—
MARCUS Ah, no—your very look would pollute her—Go—
GLABRIO Come—come, Marcus—I'm fairly good tempered—drunk
or sober—but 'pollute' is a harsh word—Faith, I'm not the plague.
MARCUS Go back—say nothing of Mercia—make some excuse for me
to the others.
GLABRIO But 'pollute'—
MARCUS Well, I was wrong—but go—
GLABRIO [*listening to hymn*] How those prisoners sing—night and day—
are they always at worship, these Christians?
MARCUS Go—she's here—
GLABRIO Well—I go—I'm no spoilsport—[*Going*] Remember, friend—
a good full meal—the surest cure for hunger is a good full meal.
[*Exit R.*]
MARCUS She comes—the very air grows purer for her presence.
[*Enter* MERCIA, *guarded by two soldiers. She is in chains*]
MARCUS [*angrily*] Take off those chains—Who dared to place them
on this lady?
SOLDIER The gaoler Excellence [*taking off chains*].
[*The hymn ceases*]
MARCUS Send him to Viturius—he shall repent his officiousness. Go—
[*Exit soldiers*]

MARCUS Believe me, lady—I regret this—'Twas done without my orders—

MERCIA I do not wish for favours, sir—What my companions suffer, I wish to share.

MARCUS But they are different.

MERCIA Indeed, yes—and some of them less able to bear the chains than I. Take off their chains, and give me back mine.

MARCUS That lovely form—those tender wrists were made for other chains, sweet Mercia—the chains of love.

MERCIA Why didst thou send for me?

MARCUS To feast upon thy beauty—to hear the music of thy voice— to watch the light that beams from those bright eyes—and see the warm young blood in maiden blushes come and go upon thy velvet cheek.

MERCIA Wouldst thou do me a service?

MARCUS Gladly—Command—I obey—you have but to name your wish.

MERCIA Send me back to my fellow prisoners.

MARCUS Ask anything but that—

MERCIA That and their freedom is all I wish.

MARCUS I cannot grant thee either—

MERCIA Why? Thou art all powerful—

MARCUS I cannot give them freedom because the law is stronger than its officer—I cannot send thee back to them—because my love is stronger than my desire to please thee.

MERCIA Sir, I am the prisoner of the law. [*With great dignity*] if I have transgressed that law, punish me—I have been taught to suffer without murmuring—

MARCUS Suffer—nay, I would not have thee suffer a single pang. Come, let us be friends—

[*Marcus endeavours to take her hand. Mercia avoids him*]

MERCIA Friendship with the good cannot exist without respect.

MARCUS And thou hast no respect for me—is that it?

MERCIA How can I respect unrighteousness.

MARCUS Am I unrighteous?

MERCIA In what art thou righteous?

MARCUS To be honest—I do not know—I have little praise for my-self, and, if thou art to judge of me—my own estimate of myself—I fear I shall be condemned.

MERCIA I am not thy judge—but I know thou art not good—

MARCUS I give freely—

MERCIA And easily—Thou hast so much that giving with thee is nothing—in giving there is no self-denial.

MARCUS Why should I deny myself that which I have and want? Happiness is rare if it comes my way—why should I reject it?

MERCIA Pleasure is not happiness—True happiness is indeed rare—it is the choicest gift of God.

MARCUS What god, lady?

MERCIA The only God—the Everlasting—

MARCUS So we consider all gods. Are they not all immortal?

MERCIA There are no gods save One.

MARCUS To avow that, is to admit thyself a Christian. [*Mercia is silent*] You are a Christian. Have no fear. I promise thee I will not use thy confession to thy detriment. But is it true or is it not? Thou art a Christian?

MERCIA I will not deny it.

MARCUS Why didst thou become one?

MERCIA Why does the sun shine? The flowers bloom? The birds sing? Because He willed it.

MARCUS Are thy parents living?

MERCIA They both died for their faith.

MARCUS Hast kin of any kind?

MERCIA None. A brother I had—he too was killed for his belief.

MARCUS Art thou rich or poor?

MERCIA Rich in the inheritance of my Father's Kingdom—poor in worldly goods—for I gave up all to the poor of my own faith—It is written: 'It is easier for a camel to go through the eye of a needle than for a rich man to enter the Kingdom of Heaven!'

MARCUS [*aside*] How divine she looks—To make her love me—as I love her—I'd freely give—But she shall love me—am I a cur—a coward—that I let this girl so master me? She's in the clouds, and if I do not exercise my will, she'll drag me after her—I'll bring her back to earth. [*Aloud*] Lady, we stand arguing like two parchment-dried philosophers—we who are young and feel youth's hot blood galloping through full veins—we who are not musty pedants—but warm, passionate children on the threshold of life—Leave philosophy and doctrine to grizzled grey beards, and let us love—

MERCIA Let me go hence—I fear thee—

MARCUS Nay, I will not harm thee—love is kind and soft and gentle. What hast thou to fear?

MERCIA Let me go—even unto death—

MARCUS Death? Let tomorrow welcome grisly death.

[*He goes to the table and pours out a full goblet of wine*]

MARCUS Nay, today thou shalt taste first some of the joys of living.

[*Strikes gong. Slave enters*]

MARCUS [*to slave*] Bid my friends come hither. [*He empties the cup*] By all the gods, my blood must be half-frozen that I have let thy beauty waste itself in solitude so long.

[*Enter all guests. Dancers, singers, slaves bearing wine cups and garlands. They are laughing, singing and shouting*]

MARCUS Wine, there—Ah, friends, you come in time—

[*Ancaria enters the room quickly. Not observing Mercia, she goes straight to Marcus and throws her arms about his neck*]

ANCARIA Ah, thou truant, I have found thee at last.

GLABRIO In time for what—the feast—Eh Marcus? Ah, but we were merry yonder. And there's no one sober but myself—Philodemus is in his second drunk—look at him—

PHILODEMUS Nay—nay—let uth be honeth—my third—Eh, sweet Aphro—Aphro—du—Aphro—dusia—[*Sees* MERCIA] Eh—there's the pretty Christian.

ANCARIA Why has thou forsaken us? Come, return to thy friends. The wine lacks flavour, and the feast its zest, while thou art absent.

[*Marcus fiercely disengages himself from Ancaria's embrace*]

GLABRIO Ha—ha—Marcus said I should pollute—

ANCARIA What means this sudden change in thee? Dost thou no longer love Ancaria?

MARCUS Enough—enough—This is the Lady Mercia—these are my friends, fair Mercia—merry souls who eat and drink today, for tomorrow they die—Wine, there. [*They serve the wine*] More—more—I thirst—I'm frozen—

GLABRIO Still hungry and athirst. By the gods, she's fair. Eh, my Ancaria?

ANCARIA Is that the beauty that hath bewitched Marcus?

GLABRIO Aye—and little wonder—she's lovely—Dost not think so?

ANCARIA I care not for that style of loveliness—if loveliness it be—

MARCUS Pass round the cup—Come, a song—a song of love—Here's a young vestal here that would congeal the blood of Venus herself—She is not yet awake—let us arouse her. A song—a song of love—

[*The men and women group themselves in attitudes of abandon. The musicians seated on the floor—the singers standing L.* MARCUS, *on a divan, is drinking furiously.* MERCIA *stands in quiet dignity alone R.*]

What though tomorrow cometh grizzly death—
Today the roses bloom—the wine runs red—
Red wine to red lips, hot breath to hot breath—
Love's lips would waken me—ee'n were I dead—
Elysium is but fulfil'd desire—
And Hades but desire still unfulfil'd.

[*The hymn of the Christians rises above the love song. The singers hesitate, break down, and stop.* MERCIA *stands wrapped in religious ecstasy*]

Shepherds of souls that stumble by the way—
Pilot of vessels storm-tossed in the night—
Healer of wounds—for help to thee we pray—
Guide, thou, our footsteps—send the morning's light—
    O lead us home.

ANCARIA What is that?

GLABRIO Those Christians prisoned in the cells yonder. They are like caged linnets. They sing better in bondage.

MARCUS Strike up—sing—drown the voices of those crazy fanatics.
    [*Singers commence again*]

    Elysium is but fulfil'd desire—
    And Hades but desire still unfulfil'd—

[*Again the singers break down—the hymn rises triumphantly*]

All we like sheep have strayed—where is the fold—
That shelters all who seek its loving breast—
There, where the cross doth shine like heavenly gold—
Emblem of pain—giving eternal rest—
    Leading us home.

[*A change comes upon the revellers—they are quiet and dull*]

MERCIA The Master is with them—even though the prison walls encompass them—still are they free.

GLABRIO What ails us all, Marcus? I feel like—like—a woman. I almost want to cry—

ANCARIA I shiver as with cold, Marcus—Art thou dazed? Give us more wine—

MARCUS Some wine here—

ANCARIA That girl is a witch—she's no true woman—Let her join us or go—Glabrio, give that girl some wine—she's freezing us.

GLABRIO Ah do, my pretty one—do, drink—Drink and be merry, for tomorrow we die.

MERCIA No—tomorrow we live—today thou art dead in unrighteousness.

GLABRIO Drink—

MERCIA [*speaking as one inspired*] I will not—and woe to you who would tempt me, for ye are lost—Hark to the voice of the Shepherd—Turn from the ways of darkness—Seek the light—'tis shining there to guide thee—Woe unto those who reject its gleams—woe unto this nation—its fall is near—The Kingdom of man is tottering—the Kingdom of Heaven is at hand.

ANCARIA Stop the witch's mouth—Give her some wine—

GLABRIO Yes, drink—drink—thou shalt—

MERCIA I have said I will not—

GLABRIO By the gods, thou shalt—

> [*Seizes her.* MARCUS *dashes him on one side and throws the wine cup to the floor*]

MARCUS No—let any man touch her if he dare.

ANCARIA A pretty host, forsooth—insult his guests thus for this wretched imposter. He must be mad.

MARCUS Perhaps I am—my brain is reeling, and my veins are fire. Hence, all of you—ye are not fit to breathe the same air with her—for your breath reeks of wine, and your gold-bought kisses blister the lips of those you prey upon and fool—Hence, all of you—I hate and loathe you and all your kind—Hence—

> [*All are going L.*]

GLABRIO Come—he's not himself—she hath bewitched him—If she be no Christian, she should be burned for sorcery—Come friends—come—

> [*All exit, crying 'Shame', 'The sorceress', 'Hospitality is outraged', etc., etc. Some are singing the love song*]

MARCUS Now, art thou content—I have driven them hence—

MERCIA Now, I pray thee, let me go—

MARCUS No, sorceress or witch, no—You beautiful statue—you cold, glittering star—you have driven my guests from my house—but you must stay. Your icy chastity burns into my very heart's core and fires my every nerve—I never knew desire until I knew you—If your touch were poison, I would possess you. [*He rushes to her, seizing her in his arms*] If death lurked in your kisses, I would feast upon them—Come to me—come—come.

MERCIA For shame—do not touch me—Are you a man or a brute?

MARCUS Both—all the brute in the man is roused by your disdain—all
the man in the brute is enthralled by your glorious beauty. [*Mercia
slips from his arms*] Ho there—quench those lamps—
    [*Slaves do so quickly*]
MARCUS Fasten the doors—Let no one enter, either man or woman,
unless I order them—Haste, you laggards—haste—
MERCIA Do not leave me—Men—if you be men—if ye have sisters—
wives—stay with me—by the love your mothers bore you—
MARCUS Hence, you slaves—I rule here—
    [*Exit slaves*]
MARCUS I am your master—
MERCIA No—
MARCUS You are my slave—
MERCIA No—no—
    [*She runs to the window and attempts to throw herself from it*]
MARCUS There is no escape. We are alone, and you are mine, body
and soul—
MERCIA No—you cannot defile my soul—that is inviolate—He who
gave me that soul will keep it pure—unsmirched, and unto His
mercy and into His hands I commit it.
MARCUS No—no—no—into mine—mine—mine—It is not enough
that your body should be mine, I must have your soul—Mercia,
give me your love, and you shall be worshipped as never woman
was—See here how I grovel at your feet [*he falls to the floor and
clutches at her robes*]. Your master is your slave—I kiss the hem of
your garment—Love me. I'll load you with gold—but love me—
I'll cover your delicious beauty with the rarest gems—but love
me—
    [*Seizes her and covers her with kisses*]
MERCIA Ah, mercy—mercy—have mercy—
MARCUS Have thou mercy—yield to me—yield—I love thee—love
thou me—love me.
    [*She breaks from him [and runs to the door, beating on its brazen panels*]
    He catches her again]
MARCUS No—no, the doors are locked—We are alone—you cannot
escape me—Love me—
MERCIA Art thou man or devil?
MARCUS Devil or man—love me—[*kissing her passionately*]
MERCIA I faint—I—
MARCUS Ah, you yield—

[*The Christians' Hymn is heard*] [*The darkened room is illumined by a soft white light*][68]

MERCIA [*transfigured*] A sign—the Master has spoken—He is here— [*She throws Marcus from her*]

MARCUS You are alone—

MERCIA No—He is with me—He has saved me—[*Holding up cross*] All fear has fled—you cannot harm me now.

MARCUS I will—I will—[*Marcus falls to his knees, burying his face in his, hands. A loud knocking. Tigellinus, off-stage, calling 'Open in the name of Caesar! Make way, slaves. Open the door.' Sound of bolts being drawn back*] [*Enter* TIGELLINUS *and* LICINIUS *and soldiers*] [*bearing torches*]

MARCUS How darest thou intrude?—

TIGELLINUS A mandate from Caesar that you do instantly surrender the Christian girl, Mercia, into his keeping.

MARCUS Ah, Mercia—thou goest to thy death—

MERCIA Ah—no—I go to life everlasting—I am ready.

[*Stands as if transfigured as soldiers come down to arrest her. The Christians' Hymn is heard until the curtain falls*]

---

[68] This moment, commemorated in numerous photographs, usually shows Mercia backlit by a shaft of light that forms a halo about her head. Holding aloft in her right hand a small wooden cross, she stands amid overturned vessels and other debris of Marcus's feast. Marcus is usually depicted fallen back upon one knee, his hands folded close to his abdomen, gazing at Mercia's face.

ACT IV

Scene 1

[SCENE: *Atrium [one of the smaller rooms] in* CAESAR's *Palace [thronged with courtiers and officers of state].* NERO *discovered [reclining on a throne raised upon a marble platform, approached by marble steps. Over the steps and platform are flung magnificent draperies; cushions, skins of tigers, leopards, and wolves strewn everywhere. Heavily armed negro guards stand behind him. His cup-bearer and taster kneels at his feet. At his right hand sits Poppaea and, at her feet, Berenis],* POPPAEA *by him. Courtiers present grouped R. and L.* NERO *is reading parchment scroll] [listing perfomances in the circus for that day. Berenis and Poppaea are at work, embroidering a silk scarf]*

NERO The games in the circus for today, Poppaea. Here's goodly sport indeed. The Chariot and the Foot Races—The Gladiators—The Masque of Venus—and, last sport of all—the lions, tigers, and two hundred Christians. Ha, ha—eh—eh—The beasts have been well starved, Metullus?

METULLUS Aye, Caesar.

NERO And they are strong and fierce?

METULLUS Rome hath never seen such beasts, Caesar.

NERO Good—good sport. And when the sun goes down, we'll have the living torches all round the amphitheatre at a distance of twenty paces—Let those Christians be bound, soaked with pitch and oil, and at my signal let the vermin burn—ha—ha—ha—And see that the stakes are placed beneath their chins, that they do not too easily suffocate and so die too soon. Moreover, that way I can better see their faces as they roast, eh?

    [*Enter* TIGELLINUS *L.*]

NERO Well, Tigellinus? Well?—

TIGELLINUS The girl is arrested as thou didst command.

NERO Good—good—Make a torch of her—and place her near to Marcus's seat—They say she was cold to him—we'll see her afire tonight—ha—ha—What said he, eh? What said Marcus?

TIGELLINUS He raved against Rome—the laws and thee, great Caesar.

NERO Ah—did he dare?

POPPAEA Forgive him that, Caesar. This choice morsel of his—has been snatched from his lips—He may rave, but he will be faithful.

NERO Dost thou think so, eh—Eh?

POPPAEA I do know it.

NERO Well—well—I'm glad—We cannot well afford to part with Marcus—But the girl—eh—did she scream and faint—and plead for mercy?

TIGELLINUS No, Caesar—she was calm and said that she was ready.

NERO Strange—eh—the obstinacy of these fanatics—They die so calmly—it robs the killing of them of half the fun. Perhaps some of the rats may squeak today. Eh? Eh—ha—ha—ha—

  [Enter slave [prostrates himself on the ground before Nero], announcing MARCUS]

SLAVE The Prefect Marcus would have audience with Caesar.

NERO Eh—Eh—[Looks at POPPAEA, who nods assent] Yes, admit him. [Exit slave]

NERO What wants he now?

  [Enter MARCUS] [Marcus kneels before Nero. After greeting Nero, he bows to Poppaea]

MARCUS Hail, Caesar—Hail, lady.

NERO [simulating interest in the programme of the circus and speaking coldly] What wouldst thou, Marcus—Eh?

MARCUS Mercy, great Caesar.

NERO For whom—eh?

MARCUS An innocent girl.

NERO Dost thou mean Mercia, the Christian?

MARCUS Yes, Caesar.

NERO She is not innocent.

MARCUS Of what is she guilty?

NERO Eh? Thou knowest well—she is accused of being a Christian.

MARCUS By whom?

NERO Well—[deflected from naming Berenis by a warning look from Poppaea] by Tigellinus and others.

MARCUS The others being Berenis and—[looking at POPPAEA]

NERO Berenis?

MARCUS A jealous woman, Emperor, is not always a reliable witness. Berenis is angry unto madness with me, and to glut her fury hath accused this girl.

TIGELLINUS There is other proof. Thou knowest, Marcus, she was captured at one of their secret meetings—caught in the very act of—

MARCUS Act of what, Tigellinus?—Act of worship?—Prayer and praise? What harm is there in that? I am firm convinced Caesar has no more virtuous subjects than these Christians.

POPPAEA [*with a smile of contempt*] And thou hadst to fall in love with a Christian to gain that conviction, eh Marcus?

NERO Even if true, their virtue is hardly a recommendation to my mercy—Virtue—virtue is one part vanity—the rest hypocrisy—virtue would smother half the joys and pleasures of this world.

MARCUS Vice hath already smothered the other half—

NERO Eh—well—well—But these Christians are, Marcus, gloomy—austere fanatics who worship a wretched Jew whom Pontius Pilate crucified between two thieves. Eh—

MARCUS And testified he could find no sin in him.

NERO There Pontius was wrong—I would be King of the East, and they set up this Nazarene as king.

MARCUS Not as temporal king, Caesar.

NERO [*looking at* POPPAEA] Eh—Come, enough of this—I am Caesar—I have power over life and death—eh—I have decided—this Mercia dies with the others this very day.

MARCUS Hear me, Caesar—Thou dost know me to be faithful—thou hast many flatterers—few friends.

NERO How—how—Eh?

MARCUS I dare to tell thee truths—around thy throne are many who serve for greed—for fear—but scarcely one for love. The people groan beneath taxation—the army is restless—discontented. The families of those whom thou hast punished hate thee.

NERO By Jupiter, thou art going too far, Marcus—Have a care.

MARCUS Of what, Caesar—thy anger?—Has it come to this, then, that to be faithful to thee is to incur thy displeasure—thy resentment?

NERO Nay, but to insult me thus.

MARCUS Poppaea—I appeal to you—Dost thou believe me faithful to Caesar?

POPPAEA I know that thou art faithful, Marcus.

MARCUS The hour of darkness looms close to thee and Rome. In that hour at least one faithful hand to guide thee and protect thee, even unto death, will be thine, if thou wilt but grant me this maiden's life—Caesar, I never asked of thee a boon before—wilt thou refuse this little thing?—The life of one weak girl?

NERO [*aside*] Eh—what, Poppaea?

POPPAEA No.

NERO It cannot be, Marcus. The whole of the vile horde are not only enemies to Caesar, but enemies to the public as well. She is a Christian, and she must die with the rest.

MARCUS Ah—no—no, Caesar, mercy—[*looking with hatred at Poppaea*] Christianity is not a crime.

POPPAEA Marcus pleads strongly—Can it be possible that he is to turn Christian too?

MARCUS Lady, I am almost persuaded to follow where I see such angels lead.

POPPAEA [*laughs*] Ha—ha—Marcus, thou art very much in love indeed.

MARCUS With all my heart and soul, lady.

POPPAEA These Christians must be sorcerers in truth, so easily to enmesh thee, Marcus.

MARCUS Mercia's sorceries are the most potent—her spells the most powerful, weaved by magician since the world began—the charm of innocent and virtuous womanhood.

NERO But she is a Christian.

MARCUS Even if she be—give me her life, Caesar—it is so small a thing for thee to give—'Twill cost thee but one little word, and that one little word gives me a world. I will serve thee as never man has served thee yet—Give me her life—

NERO [*aside*] Really, Poppaea—I—

POPPAEA No.

NERO I cannot, Marcus.

MARCUS Thou cans't, Caesar. Think—Have I ever hesitated to risk life and treasure in thy service? To me the wish of Caesar has been law—To obey that law, scores of these Christians have suffered— wives have been torn from their husbands—children from fathers— and the arena has been swamped with their blood. Until now all this hast seemed just and necessary—even if harsh and cruel—but now this simple girl hath opened mine eyes. I see that, even if sedition and rebellion do exist in the Christian ranks, they are not Christian. Christianity is not murder—lust—treason, or sin of any kind. It is love and peace—self-sacrifice and charity. Caesar, for the sake of thine own welfare—for the sake of Rome—give me this girl's life.

[*With clasped hands and bowed head, Marcus throws himself in supplication at Nero's feet*]

MARCUS Only her life!

NERO [*aside*] Poppaea—

POPPAEA [*aside*] No—[*Aloud*] Marcus, you of all men know that these Christians are alike condemned—To spare one—and destroy another is not justice. No man or woman can profess Christianity in Rome and live. The decree of Caesar hath gone forth.

MARCUS Then must she die?

POPPAEA Let her renounce publicly—renounce her faith. Then she
may live.

NERO Eh—yes—yes—then she may live.

MARCUS And if she will not?

NERO Then let her die—and die this day—Caesar hath spoken. Come,
friends, come—the games await our presence—Let us to the arena,
we'll have rare sport today.

[*Exit all, save* MARCUS, *R.*]

MARCUS Renounce her faith? Mercia, renounce her faith? Never—
And yet to die: Mercia to die—today. She shall not, but how to
save her? She knows no fear and will be constant unto death. Mercia
and death—horrible—Curse these woman who have done this thing.
Curse them—curse them.

[*Enter* BERENIS *L.*]

BERENIS Marcus.

MARCUS [*bitterly*] Ah, you are here—Are you content?

BERENIS With what?

MARCUS Mercia is to die—and to die this day.

BERENIS 'Tis well—

MARCUS With whom is it well?

BERENIS With thee—at least, it should be well. When she is dead, thy
senses may return to thee.

MARCUS When she is dead? When Mercia is dead—then Marcus will
die too.

BERENIS What—

MARCUS When Mercia is dead—methinks the world will lose its light.
The flowers will bloom no more—no more the birds will sing—the
stars and moon will veil their beams in sorrow—the glorious dawn
will never come again—the sun will set in darkness everlasting—
when Mercia is dead.

BERENIS Others will live, though Mercia be dead.

MARCUS 'Others will live, though Mercia be dead'—Hearken, woman—
Not one of those who have sought her death shall live when Mercia
be dead—neither thou nor Tigellinus—Licinius—Poppaea or Nero
shall live when Mercia be dead. Dost hear—dost hear?

BERENIS Marcus thou art mad—She was no mate for thee.

MARCUS She was my mate—the gods did plan it so in the beginning
of all time—My very mate—the better part of me—that killed the
worser moiety—lifted my soul from filth and degradation—made
me abhor evil and strive for good. Opened mine eyes to light and

truth, woman. Mercia is so much my mate—so much the soul and breath of me that, when she dies, she will take with her the breath and soul whereby I live.

BERENIS Then let her die—and die you too—I'd sooner see thee dead than be alive with Mercia.

MARCUS She shall not die—I will pluck her from her cell—There are no guards—no bars—no laws—no power that can keep Mercia from me. Tell that to Nero, and tell it now.

    [*Exit*]

BERENIS I will—I will—

    [*Exit. Change of Scene*]

Scene 2

[SCENE: *A street in Rome. (Front scene) Citizens cross and recross. Enter L.* DACIA *and* PHILODEMUS, *meeting* GLABRIO *L.*]

GLABRIO Hail, Dacia—whither goest thou?

DACIA To the circus, of course—[*Dacia drops her fan. It is immediately recovered by Philodemus*] Dost not thou come with us?

GLABRIO I do not know—I doubt it.

DACIA Why?

GLABRIO Well—[*gravely shaking his head*] I am ever tender-hearted, and this slaughtering of Christians pleaseth me but little.

DACIA Art growing effeminate in thine old age, Glabrio?

GLABRIO Effeminate—by Vulcan, no. It is no longer feminine to pity or to be tender. The sexes are changing—women do all the wooing nowadays. Men are no longer the hunters—they are the hunted. The wounded gladiators look up to the circles for mercy, and 'tis the woman's thumbs that are turned down for his death. Bah—there is nothing left for us poor men but the wine cup—and even at that game some of the weaker sex are our masters.

DACIA All the better for thee—men are only fit to be women's slaves.

GLABRIO Ah—umph—and pretty tame kittens they become when enslaved, do they not? Look at poor Philodemus—he is thy slave—there's a nice playful little pussy for thee—I had hopes of him until he met thee—and now—well—I have done—Get thee a silken cord, and tie it round his willing neck, and make him caper as thou wilt—I have done—

PHILODEMUS Nay, friend Glabrio—one must humour the weaker sex.

GLABRIO Weaker—If there exists aught weaker than a tame man, it is the spider's slender thread that a puff of the west wind shatters.

DACIA So sour, Glabrio—Canst get no woman to love thee?

GLABRIO I can get scores to say they do, while my purse hangs out. Women are cheap enough in Rome—Which doth remind me that that pretty Christian, Mercia, on whom Marcus hath lost his wits, is to die tonight. You had some hand in her arrest, I hear.

DACIA Why not?—She was in the way.

GLABRIO Whose way?

DACIA That of Berenis—and we women do sometimes help each other.

GLABRIO Willingly to pull some frail woman down. Poor Marcus— poor Mercia.

DACIA Oh, thy head is sore from last night's drinking. Come, Philodemus—let us leave him.

[*She allows a rose to fall from her hair*] [*Exit R.*]

PHILODEMUS [*recovering the rose*] Farewell, friend Glabrio.

[*Exit R.*]

GLABRIO Farewell, friend pussy—mieu—mieu—mieu—Well, the gods keep me in love with wine. He who loves wine may have his senses sometimes—he who loves woman, never.

[*Noise and tumult L.U.E.*]

GLABRIO What have we here?

[*Enter* VITURIUS, *with soldiers dragging in* SERVILLIUS, *pale and disordered* [*his clothing torn*], *the guards following him.* STRABO *follows after the guards*]

VITURIUS Come on, thou coward.

SERVILLIUS I beg of thee to let me go—I am no Christian—I swear by all the gods.

VITURIUS This man doth swear he hath seen thee at a score of their meetings.

SERVILLIUS But as a spy—I went to denounce them—I am well known as an informer—Let me go—I have sent scores of Christians to their deaths. I have denounced hundreds.

VITURIUS Ah, well—now comes thy turn—Thou wilt feel what it is to be denounced thyself.

SERVILLIUS Ah, no—no—Spare me, good Viturius—This man is a liar— he hath denounced me because he wanted more of the rewards than I could give him—he is forsworn—Release me, and I will denounce a dozen Christians ere the sun goes down—Have mercy—

VITURIUS Bah—You sicken me, you crawling thing—you wolf without its courage—I would pay myself to see thee in the circus meet the lions.

SERVILLIUS Spare me—Mercy—mercy—

VITURIUS On with him—

SERVILLIUS Ah, good Glabrio—Thou knowest me—thou didst see me denounce Mercia and Favius—when thou wert with the Lady Dacia at her house.

GLABRIO Did I? Well, and I did, eh? What then?

SERVILLIUS Plead for me—I am a good Roman.

GLABRIO An thou art, I forswear my country. Now hearken, good Viturius—And thou wouldst serve Rome—Caesar—Marcus—and help to cleanse this somewhat dirty world—take that carrion to the beasts—I'll thank thee for the deed. Farewell.

[*Exit*]

SERVILLIUS Strabo—good, Strabo—re-call thy accusation—I have money—thou shalt have it all.

STRABO Nay, I'll not go back on my word.

VITURIUS On with him. We've lingered long enough.

SERVILLIUS Mercy—rescue me, friends—Mercy—do not let them take me—

[*He is dragged off screaming. Change of Scene*]

Scene 3

[SCENE: *A dungeon under the amphitheatre. Heavy brick and stone arches.* [*Gloomy, destitute of furniture of any kind, save a wooden bier to serve as a couch for the suffering Stephanus. At each end of the cell are*] Doors R. *and* L. [*leading to the corridors. In the centre, approached by a few stone steps, are*] Large sliding double doors, R.C., [*of iron which run in oiled grooves*] *which, when opened, show the circus arena beyond, bathed in sunshine.* [*The arena can be seen and, with it, a section of the first maenianum and its occupants. The roars of hungry beasts can be faintly heard, even when the doors are closed; so can the equally merciless howls of the bloodthirsty populace. At intervals, trumpet calls, summoning different performers, ring round the arena*] *Grouped round the stage are men and women of all ages on their knees, singing the following hymn*] [*Mercia comforts Stephanus*]

Glory—Glory—Glory—Hail to thee, the father—
We, thy children, crave thy hand to guide our steps aright—

Glory—Glory—Glory—Thou who sent the Saviour—
Lead me through darkness to eternal light.

Glory—Glory—Glory—Thou, who died to save us—
By thy cross of Calvary—we kneel in trust this night—
Glory—Glory—Glory—Thou wilt walk beside us—
Through death's dark valley to eternal light.

[*At the end of the hymn* [*a sudden blare of trumpets and a roar of delight from multitudes in amphitheatre. A file of armoured guards lines either side of the steps and passage*] *Enter* TIGELLINUS, LICINIUS *and guards R.*]

TIGELLINUS Stand up there—up, you vermin—up. [*Pointing R. to the younger men*] Stand on this side, you—[*To* LICINIUS] These are for the gladiators.

LICINIUS They'll not give the gladiators much trouble—they're a puny lot.

TIGELLINUS Stand here, you—[*the older men range L.*] These old rats we'll give to the tigers to toy with—these women to the lions with the boy, there. [*Sees* MERCIA] Ah—he—thou, here? This is the wench Marcus made so much ado about. Where's thy lover, girl—is he not here to save thee? Answer.

MERCIA I have no lover—

TIGELLINUS Marcus Superbus—

MERCIA I do nothing know of him.

[TIGELLINUS, *with guards, asks the names of the men and writes them down on his tablets*]

LICINIUS Ah, that is like Marcus—Little he cares what befalls his cast-off strumpets.

MELOS [*springing forward*] You lie—you tyrant—Unsay those words.

MERCIA Hush, Melos—answer not—His words move not me.

LICINIUS No? Well, perhaps the flames—or the lions—will shake thy obstinacy. Dost know't will be either the beasts or the fire for thee tonight?

MERCIA The Master will be with me.

LICINIUS [*to* STEPHANUS] And you—you young scorpion—call on thy god to help thee—thy sun sets this night, too.

[STEPHANUS *trembles*]

LICINIUS Ah—you tremble—eh?

MERCIA [*enfolding Stephanus in her arms*] He will not tremble when the hour doth come.

[*Trumpets sound*]

TIGELLINUS The gladiators are ready. Open the doors.

[*The doors are thrown open R.C., and the arena is seen beyond, flooded with light*]

TIGELLINUS Now then—March.

[*For a moment there is a pause. Then Mercia begins the hymn. All, save Stephanus, join in*] *The men, two and two, holding each other's hands, are marched out. They go out calmly and quietly*]

MERCIA Courage, brethren—have no fear—the Master will be with thee.

[*As the men exit, those on the stage repeat*]

Glory—Glory—Glory—Thou, who died to save us—
By the cross of Calvary—we kneel in trust this night—
Glory—Glory—Glory—Thou wilt walk beside us—
Through death's dark valley to eternal light.

[MELOS *is the last to go—he turns and looks at* MERCIA, *who points to Heaven. He smiles—bows his head and exits. With him,* TIGELLINUS *and* LICINIUS]

MERCIA O Father, give them stength to endure. [MERCIA *sinks to her knees by the couch*] Stephanus, what is this?

STEPHANUS I am sore afraid, Mercia. I am so young to die—Think, to die—to die tonight—to leave this bright and beautiful world tonight.

MERCIA For one more bright—more beautiful. Where pain and sorrow is not—nor persecution nor parting—where happiness is, and purity and holiness evermore.

STEPHANUS But the pain—Mercia—the pain—

MERCIA Think of His agony who died for thee—thou wilt not faint again—Fix thine eyes on the cross—when the hour doth come.

STEPHANUS Shall I dare?—Have I not betrayed thee all?

MERCIA Thy soul was true—the weak body, only, was false.

STEPHANUS Yes—yes—but, Mercia—I am a coward—I have not thy courage—

MERCIA [*Mercia takes Stephanus in her arms*] My courage is not my own—it comes from Him—the Master—Look to Him. He will give thee strength.

[*Great shouts are heard from the arena. Trumpets sound. The doors are again thrown open. Enter guards L.C.*] [*With a gesture, the leader signifies that Stephanus is to accompany him. Stephanus stands half-dazed in terror, but Mercia, by a look and a caress, urges him to be calm*]

GUARD Come you all—save the girl, Mercia—Come, hasten, you vermin.

[*He strikes one of the prisoners with the butt of his spear*]

2ND GUARD Gently, comrade—gently—in a little while they will be with the beasts—punishment enough, I trow—Keep thy blows for those who are to live—not for those about to die. Forward, all— March.

[*As Stephanus passes the threshold, the scene of horror in the arena terrifies him beyond control and, with a piercing shriek, he dashes back into the cell, falls on his knees, and buries his face in Mercia's garments*]

STEPHANUS Mercia—Mercia—the time is come—I cannot, I cannot! Save me! Save me!

MERCIA Stephanus—Stephanus—thou wilt not falter? [STEPHANUS *is half-swooning*] Stephanus, thou didst ever say that thou didst love me. [*She holds him to her*] If that is true—by all the love thou bearest me—by all the love I bear thee—by all the love the Master bears to all—be true—Promise that thou wilt not shrink—promise.

STEPHANUS [*with a great effort of self-control*] [*clenching his hands and crossing them rigidly across his breast*] I promise, Mercia. Ah, the dread—the fear, hath gone—Feel my heart, Mercia, 'tis all calm now—He hath come to guide me—He doth walk beside me. I see the cross. I am no longer afraid.

[*Goes slowly out—his eyes upraised. The doors are closed—* MERCIA *is alone.* [*Mercia sinks to her knees, with her face pressed against the iron doors, sobbing quietly*] *Shouts are heard—then the hymn in the distance.* MERCIA *remains motionless, with her arms crossed on her breast. A bright light falls on her—all the rest is in shadow. After a pause, there is a clanking of chains and bolts at the L. door. The door opens and two guards enter and stand either side of the door—pause—then enter* MARCUS—*he is cloaked.* MERCIA *at first does not see who it is, but stands calmly, waiting.* MARCUS *dismisses the guards—they go, closing and barring the door.* MARCUS *stands for a moment watching* MERCIA]

MARCUS [*he stretches his arms over her*] [*softly*] Mercia—

[MERCIA *gives a little start at the sound of his voice and trembles slightly, but does not answer*]

MARCUS Mercia—

MERCIA What would you with me?

MARCUS I come to save thee.

MERCIA To save me—from what?

MARCUS From death.

MERCIA How?

MARCUS I have knelt to Nero for thy pardon.

MERCIA [*calmly*] And did he grant it?

MARCUS He will grant it on one condition.

MERCIA What is that?

MARCUS That—that—[*tremblingly*]

MERCIA Well—

MARCUS That thou dost renounce this false worship.

MERCIA It is not false—it is true and everlasting.

MARCUS Everlasting—nothing is everlasting. There is no afterlife. The end is here. Men come and go—drink their little cup of woe or happiness—and then to sleep—the sleep that knows no awakening.

MERCIA Art thou so sure of that? Ask thyself, are there no inward monitors that, in thy more thoughtful moments, silently teach thee there is a life to come?

MARCUS All men have wishes—for a life to come—if it could better this.

MERCIA It will better this—if this life be well lived. Hast thou lived well?

MARCUS My love for thee is love indeed—Forgive me that I did so mistake thee and myself. The brute is dead in me—the man is living—thy purity, that I would have smirched, hath cleansed me— Live, Mercia, live [*kneels*]—and be my wife.

MERCIA Thy wife?—[*With a sob of joy*] Thy wife, in very truth?

MARCUS In very truth—my wife—my honoured wife—

MERCIA O Marcus—Marcus—

MARCUS Wilt thou be my wife?

MERCIA And renounce my faith?

MARCUS That must be.

MERCIA That can never be.

MARCUS It must be—Think, Mercia—think—

MERCIA There is no need to think—we do not need to think—to breath, while we have life—the heart beats—the blood flows through our veins—without our thought—God hath made us so. So I, without thought, worship him. I need no thought to make me true to Him. He hath made me so—I cannot be otherwise—would not be otherwise.

MARCUS If thou didst love me—

MERCIA Hear me, Marcus—I know not how or whence it came—but love came for thee when first I saw thee.

MARCUS [*springing towards her*] Mercia—

MERCIA Nay, stay where thou art, Marcus, and hear me. This love I speak of came—I know not whence—nor how, then—Now I know it came from Him who gave me life—I receive it joyfully because He gave it. Think you He gave it to tempt me to betray Him?—Nay, Marcus—He gave it to me to uphold and strengthen me, Marcus. The world is passed away for me, and, as on the threshold of the other life all worldly things are left behind and all worldly thoughts—I have no shame in telling thee I love thee next to Him.

MARCUS And thou wilt live—

MERCIA I will be true unto Him.

MARCUS Thou wilt live.

MERCIA I will not deny Him who died for me.

MARCUS Mercia—if thy God exists—he made us both—one for the other. Hearken—I am rich beyond riches—I have power—skill—strength. With these the world would be my slave—my vassal. Nero is hated—loathed—is tottering on his throne—I have friends in plenty—who would help me—The throne of Caesar might be mine, and thou shalt share it with me—if thou wilt but live—The crown of an Empress shall deck that lovely head—only consent to live—

MERCIA My crown is not of earth, Marcus—it awaits me there [*points upward*].

MARCUS Mercia—in pity—by thy love for me—and by my love for thee—live—Live for me and for my love. I pray thee, do not leave me.

MERCIA I love thee, Marcus—but I leave thee to go to Him.

MARCUS I cannot part from thee and live, Mercia—I have, to save thy precious life—argued and spoken against thy faith—thy god—but to speak truth to thee, I have been sorely troubled since first I saw thee—Strange yearnings of the spirit come in the silent watches of the night—I battle with them—but they will not yield. I tremble with stange fears—strange thoughts—strange hopes. If thy faith be truc—what is this world—a little tarrying place—a tiny bridge between two great eternities—that we have travelled from—that towards which we go. How can I know, Mercia? Teach me—and teach me how to keep thee ever by my side.

MERCIA Look to the cross and pray—'Help, thou, my unbelief—'

MARCUS But to keep thee by my side—

MERCIA Give up all that thou hast and follow me?

MARCUS Follow thee—whither?

MERCIA To the better land—There, where He waits for us with outstretched ams ready to pardon—eager to welcome.

MARCUS Would he welcome even me?

MERCIA Even thee, Marcus—

[*Trumpet sounds. Doors open and* TIGELLINUS *and guards enter*]

TIGELLINUS Prefect—Caesar would know this girl's decision. The hour has come. Doth she renounce Chrystos and live—or cling to him and die?

MARCUS Mercia—

TIGELLINUS Answer, girl.

MARCUS Mercia—

MERCIA I cling to Him and die—I am ready—

TIGELLINUS Guards, take her.

MERCIA Farewell—Marcus.

MARCUS No, not farewell—death cannot part us—I, too, am ready. The light hath come—I know it now—Thou hast shown me the way—my lingering doubts are dead [*he takes Mercia's hand*]. Return to Caesar—Tell him Chrystos hath triumphed—Marcus, too, is a Christian—[*Drawing her closer to him*] Come, my bride—

MERCIA My bridegroom—

MARCUS Thus, hand in hand, we go to our bridal [*they ascend the steps*]—There is no death for us, for Chrystos hath triumphed over death. The light hath come. Come, my bride. Come—to the light beyond.

[*Exit, hand in hand, into the arena*] [*Curtain*]

Appendix

Variant of Act III, Scene 1

MARCUS You sent for me, lady?

BERENIS I did, and most unwillingly thou hast come.

MARCUS Unwillingly? Nay, Berenis doth not know Berenis. How can I serve thee, lady?

BERENIS Now Marcus is himself. The purse is open. How much will serve?

MARCUS Nay, Berenis can need no gold of mine.

BERENIS But if I did?

MARCUS If thou didst, then I should say not, 'How much will serve?', but, 'All that I have is thine'—knowing full well that it would be returned.

BERENIS Ah, so in my heart said I, 'All that *I* have is thine'—*not* knowing it would be returned.

MARCUS I do not understand thee, lady.

BERENIS Thou wilt not understand.

MARCUS Perhaps it is better that I do not try.

BERENIS Am I so very repulsive? Others do not think so.

MARCUS Others? Nay, all are agreed, patrician Rome can boast no fairer daughter than Berenis.

BERENIS *Patrician* Rome. Marcus could scarce look lower. We are both rich; indeed, our wealth united might buy an empire.

MARCUS Berenis—

BERENIS Marcus, Marcus, canst thou not see what is in my heart? Dost thou not know it is no girlish fancy, but the deep, strong love of a woman who has never loved before—whose whole nature has held back so long that, unless the floodgates are unbarred, the pent-up tide will burst all bounds and engulf her.

MARCUS Berenis, thou dost pain and shame me! Thou art so prodigal of love, and I so miserly.

BERENIS Marcus—

MARCUS Believe me, I am honoured, grateful; and if all the respect that man can show for a woman, if devotion, friendship—

BEN-HUR
As adapted for the stage by

William Young

People who have never read the novel or the play or seen the film of
Ben-Hur know that it contains a chariot-race. It deserves to be remembered and enjoyed for more than that.

Ben-Hur is different from other toga plays in several particulars. It
is a stage adaptation from General Lew Wallace's original novel,[69]
made nearly twenty years after the novel had appeared and had
gathered a world readership unequalled, at that date, by any publication apart from the Bible. The play, therefore, reached audiences
whose expectations had long been coloured by familiarity with the
story, among them people who were apprehensive that the play might
be blasphemous or, at the very least, over familiar with sacred text.
William Young's 1899 theatrical adaptation of *Ben-Hur* is different in
another particular. It is a play by an American dramatist, initially
performed for American audiences, taken from a novel by an American author. Thus, whilst *Ben-Hur* uses and develops many of the
conventions of toga drama—which, by the end of the 1890s, had
become international—these conventions are used to address American perceptions and problems.

The novel's author, General Lew Wallace, had left military service
(he fought, first in the Mexican War of 1847 and again in the American Civil War) to serve briefly as emissary to Bolivia and then as
Governor of the territory of New Mexico. New Mexico, annexed
after the Mexican War, had a mixed population of native Americans,
Mexicans, and Anglo-Whites nearing 120,000 in the late 1870s. By
comparison to life in more settled parts of the nation, creature comforts were minimal; a railroad did not reach the largest settlement,
Albuquerque, until 1880. Competing ethnic cultures continued to
dispute title to areas of the territory. It was during the period of his
governorship that Wallace began *Ben-Hur*. The arid and mountainous
New Mexican landscape, where people of different races and lan-

---

[69] Lew Wallace, *Ben-Hur: A Tale of the Christ*, (New York, 1880).

guages jostled for priority and position, may have evoked thoughts of Judaea and Syria in the first century BC. It is not altogether surprising that the author's descriptions of the Holy Land mirror the topography and politics of New Mexico,[70] and his occasional anachronisms remind readers that, in part, he may be writing about American encounters with 'other' cultures in the late 1870s.

Similarly, the Roman Empire of *Ben-Hur* is not the empire of the British toga drama. In Wallace's Roman Empire, Romans, Hebrews, Arabs, Egyptians, Cypriots, Cretans, and Greeks meet in market-places, on wharves, and in stadia. All cultures, even the Judaeans, are 'other' cultures. The Romans may be the dominant culture, as the British had been in America, but their hegemonic influence is merely political and military. Wallace perceives the Romans as a temporary phenomenon before the rise of Christianity, which is to arrive 'without following, without armies, without cities or castles; a kingdom to set up, and Rome reduced and blotted out'.[71] The Romans, meanwhile, cannot halt the local rites of Eros and Daphne; they cannot contain the exuberant naturalness of Sheikh Ilderim. *Ben-Hur*, play and novel, may therefore be, unintentionally, a further representation of America—as well as of the New Mexican territory—as a land where disparate cultures rub shoulders; it is a new Holy Land where the solution to harmony is not contention and rebellion (another civil war), but tolerance, democracy, or Christianity.

Ben-Hur meets the configurations of the second archetypal toga drama—a quest for self and intimations of salvation in an alien world. Novel and play begin in Jerusalem, Judah Ben-Hur's home, and follow the arduous life of a wealthy Jewish man maliciously and falsely accused of attempted murder by Messala, his former boyhood companion, now wholly Roman, arrogant, and cruel. Sent to be a slave in the galleys, to row until death, he is freed, becomes wealthy and, by adoption, a Roman. However, Judah uses his wealth, skill, and strength to re-establish his position in Judaea and Syria, extract revenge against Messala in a chariot-race, avoid seduction and choose a good wife, and rescue his long-lost mother and sister.

As the novel's subtitle, *A Tale of the Christ*, informs, it is a journey through the Mediterranean world of the Roman Empire, beginning with the birth of Christ and ending with the Crucifixion (except for

---

[70] Wallace prided himself on his historic and geographic research for *Ben-Hur*, but he was strongly susceptible to the character of the places that he lived in and visited. Cf. *Lew Wallace: An Autobiography*, 2 vols. (New York and London, 1906).

[71] Wallace, *Ben-Hur*, 262.

a postscript that reports Judah and Esther, now Christians, endowing
and building the church of St Calixto within the catacombs). In the
novel, Judah's life periodically intersects with the life of Jesus. Sometimes Judah is the beneficiary of Jesus's kindness; sometimes Judah is
a witness or a bystander, but the effect of Christ's examples and the
teachings of Balthasar, one of the Magi, turn Judah towards Christianity—or to the non-specific, non-sectarian goodness that is toga
Christianity.

The play, however, proceeds without the presence of Christ, apart
from one key incident. Although there was no official censorship in
New York (as there was in Britain) which forbade the representation
of Jesus or deity on the stage, Lew Wallace was aware that the play
would offend public taste if Christ were portrayed. That awareness lay
behind his refusal to permit the novel to be adapted for the stage. He
declined separate offers from Imre and Bolossy Kiralfy, each a producer of large-scale stage entertainments and environmental exhibi-
tions, to adapt *Ben-Hur* for theatrical performance. According to
Wallace, 'The Kiralfys . . . proposed leasing thirty acres of ground on
Staten Island, of which two acres were to have been fitted up for that
[*Ben-Hur*] exhibition. I need not speak of their reputation, but not
withstanding it, I gave them a refusal.'[72] It was not until Marc Klaw
and Abraham Erlanger, owners and managers of a large theatrical
circuit, approached Wallace and in 1889 persuaded him to allow
William Young to attempt a stage adaptation that would not bring the
character of Jesus on to the stage, that Wallace agreed to a production.

Young produced a script in which characters acknowledge that a
man who can work miracles is, and has been, among them: no
problem there. But it is necessary to the plot of the novel and the play
that Judah's mother, Miriam, and sister, Tirzah, should at last be healed
of the leprosy that they contracted when heartlessly and cynically
imprisoned by Messala. Young's solution is to stage the healing in a
vision that Judah dreams and awakens from to find true, and the Jesus
of the dream is not an actor, but a beam of limelight. Both the effect
and Young's solution, the *Playgoer* informs us, are successful:

Finally, there is the reconciliation of Ben-Hur with his mother and sister, who
haggard and worn, are lepers, and hiding in the dreary vale of Hinnom.
Ben-Hur, wandering in search of them, has come to this place and, falling
asleep, he has a vision. The scene changes to the slopes of Mount Olivet; a
vast crowd await the passing of the Saviour. The mother and daughter kneel

[72] Wallace, *Autobiography*, 1001.

in their midst. Suddenly they are enveloped in a blinding shaft of light. The
miracle has happened; the lepers are made whole. 'Hosannah!' is the cry, and
to the singing of an anthem, and the gentle waving of palm branches, the
curtain falls on this impressive and very beautiful picture.[73]

Conventional melodrama ends with the defeat of the villain. In
William Young's *Ben-Hur* the villain is disposed of in the Antioch
arena at the close of Act V, but a further, final, act remains. What had
been a race against Messala and Roman injustice now becomes a race
against disease and obscure death in the vale of Hinnom. Whereas
Mercia and Marcus—without hope of rescue—give up their struggle
and go docilely to the lions, Judah has other obstacles to face. The
removal of Messala thus focuses concern not merely on the recovery
of Miriam and Tirzah, but also on how Judah is to conduct his future
life. A new leader to his people, will he now lead the Zealots in
rebellion, or will he find in precept and divine example the means to
bring about change peaceably, to choose evolution rather than revolution? The impetus to violent rebellion having been calmed by Christian precept, the audience may observe a more thoughtful young man
exchange the tempting adventuress Iras for the Hebrew *ingénue* Esther,
and rejoice in the recovery of sister and mother. It is a weak ending
for a melodrama, but—perhaps—satisfactory for the parable-seeking
spectator: not only have female counterparts to Lazarus been healed
and raised up, but Dives has entered Heaven—a rich man has passed
through the needle's eye—an action that could not have disappointed
newly prosperous Americans.

The seriousness of the subject-matter of *Ben-Hur* appears to have
imposed upon Wallace—and subsequently upon Young—its own law
of gravity, because neither novel nor play offers much in the way of
comedy or humour. A melodrama without some comedy, even some
ironic undercutting of the leading characters' intellectual immobility,[74]
is almost a novelty, and *Ben-Hur* is nearly in this class. What small
amount of comedy there is helps to define Iras as a woman of intel-
ligence and perception. Here is a further variant of the dangerous New
Woman: Iras has the understanding—indeed, the wisdom—of the
ancient world. She is travelled and experienced and educated—as
Esther is not. And she alone has a penetrating and perceptive humour
joined to great physical allure. These qualities, in Wallace's and
Young's plans, fail to make Iras a suitable mate for Judah. She is

---

[73] *Playgoer*, 2 (Apr.–Dec. 1902), 121.
[74] Manabu Noda, 'The Role of the Comic Man in the 19th Century Melodrama',
British Film Institute conference paper, 1992.

cynical, and the proof of her cynicism is her loyalty and attachment
to the drama's other cynic, Messala. It is therefore an essential of the
final act that Judah, as a sign of his discovery of faith, should choose
Esther and reject Iras.

It was generally held by New York critics in 1899 and by London
critics in 1902 that the drama's intellectual and dramatic content were
both less effective and less significant than its spectacle, and that, as a
consequence, *Ben-Hur* was deeply dependent upon the technical resources deployed in the production. Klaw and Erlanger, who mounted
both productions, seem to have shared that opinion. Their manner
with the press was to hint at secret new technology, to deny press
access, and then to allow favoured reporters views of the play in
preparation. About the mechanism of the star guiding the Magi, less
an innovation than the application of electric light and electric motors
to earlier backstage technology, they were open. The effect, however,
was critically dismissed:

Men may come and men may go, as the poet Tennyson has comprehensively
remarked, but the atmosphere of that weird, mysterious, and sublime night,
when shepherds were watching their flocks and the awful portent of revealed
Divinity flamed in the wintry sky, can never be expressed by canvas and
calciums. A glorified circular buzz-saw, in a mist of paint and gauze, is no
adequate representation of the Star of Bethlehem.[75]

The episode aboard the Roman galley and the apparent sinking of
the vessel by pirates were contrived by skilled use of traditional
scene-building and painting techniques. The design of the chariot-
race was another matter. Again, there was no new technology: moving
scenic backcloths or dioramas set as 'endless belts' had been used in
theatres since the 1820s. Treadmills that enabled horses to gallop in
place and that moved forwards or backwards at the touch of off-stage
controls had been in theatrical use for a decade. It was the combination
of these techniques, and the overall design, that gave the scene its
apparent uniqueness and originality. Klaw and Erlanger secured pro-
tective international patents for the design and machinery, but, when
it was clear that *Ben-Hur* would be opened at Drury Lane and that
'the Lane's' scenic artisans and painters would share the building of sets
for the London and United Kingdom run, Klaw and Erlanger insisted
that only their American artists should build and paint the effects.

The chariot-race in *Ben-Hur* is based on the concept of 'realizing'
a recent painting—a known painting, but not so well known that

[75] *New York Daily Tribune*, 30 Nov. 1899.

viewers of the vividly coloured lithographic poster for *Ben-Hur*, or the spectators in the theatre would detect subtle alterations. The picture, Alexander von Wagner's *The Chariot-Race* (1893), which had become popular in Britain and America through inexpensive lithographic and engraved copies, depicts a chariot-race in Rome's Circus Maximus. Some chariots have crashed, and now two unidentified charioteers, one in the lead by a length, are driving their violently straining horses into the final laps. Klaw and Erlanger's poster for *Ben-Hur* reveals how von Wagner's painting was exploited: Edgar Albert, the designer of the stage effect, changed von Wagner's layout to show the leading teams racing nearly neck to neck, and—as specified by the novel—altered the drivers' colours to identify one driver, in scarlet and gold, as Messala, behind a team of two black and two white horses. The second driver, in white, driving a team of bays, is recognizably Judah.

In the theatre the background and sides to the painting were broken into three moving backcloths, synchronized so as to create the illusion of the racecourse and spectators retreating behind the rapidly advancing chariots. The chariots and horses—one chariot and a four-horse team each to Judah and Messala—were mounted on treadmills facing down stage. According to one enthusiastic reporter,

The stage has been propped underneath by enormous cross-beams and great uprights until it is impossible for the eight horses that pound away for dear life to break through. The great treadmill, large enough for eight horses and two chariots, is neatly fitted into the floor and seems to be part of the stage, so that you don't notice that it is any different from the roadway of the circus. By a most ingenious contrivance of rubber and felt covering . . . the affair is practically noiseless, or at least such noise as it makes is drowned in the furious gallop of the horses and the whirring of the chariot wheels . . . The great panorama of the crowds in the circus seats move semi-circularly around the stage, and when the horse are tearing along, as though in a contest for life and death, the illusion . . . is all but perfect and thrillingly effective . . . The horses have been rehearsed daily . . . off they go at a killing pace. As the chariots alternately draw ahead . . . the horses plunge and rear and gallop . . . Powerful electric fans in the wings raise a wind that blows the loose trappings of the horses into the air . . . and the cloaks and skirts of the drivers flutter in the wind as they lean out over in front of the chariots. A powerful blast of air from under the horses hooves and under the chariot wheels raises what seem to be great clouds of dust, that are caught up and whirled away behind the charioteers . . . And the 'smash-up' when Ben-Hur drives against Messala's wheel and brings about the catastrophe is so realistic that even the wheel that is knocked off the chariot goes spinning off the stage . . . Just as the catastrophe occurs, every light in the house goes out for a second leaving the theatre black as night; a scene 'drop' is suddenly let down between Ben-Hur's chariot, which is nearest the footlights, and Messala's wrecked affair. The panorama stops [it is up stage of the drop], a crowd of one hundred and fifty run on the stage in the darkness, up go the lights—and you see Ben-Hur and his panting, foaming steeds, victors . . . and the crowds yelling their hurrahs . . .[76]

The drop is a reverse angle of the original background to von Wagner's *Chariot-Race*.

Klaw and Erlanger, the producers of *Ben-Hur*, guarded their property jealously. They authorized a printing of the script by Harper and Brothers of New York and London in 1899, and in the same year they allowed a printing of Edgar Stillman Kelley's vocal score. The script may have been available from booksellers, but the small number of copies to survive suggests that circulation was restricted to those who had some legitimate reason for requiring it. This is the only version of the playscript to exist, and may have been intended less for recreational reading than for rehearsing touring productions and individual cast replacements. The Harper and Brothers script was eventually deposited as the British licensing copy. The text in this volume is from the New York (1899) printing, with spellings and punctuation regularized for clarity. The printed vocal score, which substantially abridges Kelley's manuscript orchestral and vocal score held by the Library of Congress and discussed in Katherine Preston's essay, may have seen use only on the parlour piano.

The programme for the American production at the Broadway Theater in New York, 'beginning Wednesday Evening, November 29th, 1899' acknowledged the contribution of Klaw and Erlanger as well as Wallace's original novel, and went on to mention the direction of Joseph Brooks; the music of Edgar Stillman Kelley; the scenery by Ernest Albert and Ernest Gros; the costumes by F. Richard Anderson, Simpson, Crawford and Simpson, and Dazian; the 'mechanical construction' by McDonald and Hager; and the electrical effects by H. Harndin and George Enright. The programme stated that 'the entire production [was] staged under the direction of Ben Teal', and goes on to list stage-managers, ballet mistresses, etc.

The cast and settings (with designers) were as follows:

In the Prelude
Balthasar, the Egyptian   FRANK MORDAUNT

[76] *New York Herald*, 5 Nov. 1899.

Gaspar, the Greek	F. S. THORPE
Melchior, the Hindu	CHARLES J. WILSON

In the Drama

Ben-Hur, Judah, the son of Ithamar	EDWARD MORGAN
Simonides, steward to the House of Hur	HENRY LEE
Ilderim, a Sheik	EMMETT CORRIGAN
Messala, a young Roman noble	WILLIAM S. HART
Balthasar, the Egyptian	FRANK MORDAUNT
Arrius, the Tribune	EDMOND COLLIER
Malluch, attendant of Simonides	FREDERICK TRUESDELL
Hortator, Captain of the Galley	CHARLES J. WILSON
Khaled, servant of Ilderim	CHARLES CRAIG
Sanballat, merchant friend of Simonides	ROBERT MANSFIELD
Drusus and Cecilius, young Romans	PAUL GERSON and HENRY DEVERE
Metellus, Roman officer	WILLIAM FREDERIC
Centurion	HENRY MONTROSE
Officer of the Galley	WILLIAM FORD
Iras, daughter of Balthasar	CORONA RICCARDO
Mother of Ben-Hur	MABEL BERT
Esther, daughter of Simonides	GRETCHEN LYONS
Amrah, nurse to the family of Hur	MABEL SHAW
Tirzah, sister of Hur	ADELINE ADLER

Prelude: The Desert: (Albert) Meeting of the three Wise Men (Ernest Albert).

'In the morning arise, and go and meet them. And when ye have all come to the holy city, Jerusalem, ask of the people, "Where is He that is born King of the Jews?—for we have seen His star in the East, and are sent to worship Him."

Suddenly in the air before them, not further up than a low hilltop, flared a lambent flame. As they looked at it the apparition contracted into a focus of dazzling lustre. And they shouted as with one voice, "The Star! The Star!" ' (*Ben-Hur*, book I, ch. 5)

Act I: The Housetop of the Palace of Hur, Jerusalem: The Power of Rome (Ernest Albert).

Act II, Scene 1: Interior of Cabin of the Roman Galley *Astraea*: The Galley Slaves (Ernest Albert).

Scene 2: The Open Sea: The Rescue (Ernest Albert).

Act III, Scene 1: Apartment of the House of Simonides in Antioch: The Wise Servant and his Daughter (Ernest Gros).

Scene 2: The Grove of Daphne, Temple of Apollo: The Masque of Eros (Ernest Gros).

'The Grove of Daphne! Nobody can describe it—only beware! It was begun by Apollo and completed by him. He prefers it to Olympus. People go there for one look—just one—and never come away. They have a saying which tells it all: "Better be a worm and feed on the mulberries of Daphne than a king's guest." ' (*Ben-Hur*, book IV, ch. 2)

Scene 3: The Fountain of Castalia: The Revels of Daphne in the Spider's web (Ernest Gros).

Act IV, Scene 1: The Dowar[77] in the Orchard of Palms: Preparing for the Race (Ernest Gros).

Scene 2: By the Lake: The Arts of Cleopatra (Ernest Gros).

Act V, Scene 1: Exterior of the Great Gateway of the Circus, Antioch: Making the Wagers (Ernest Albert).

Scene 2: The Arena: The Race (Ernest Albert).

Act VI, Scene 1: Apartment in the Palace of Hur, Jerusalem: Tidings of the Lost Ones (Ernest Albert).

Scene 2: The Vale of Hinnom: The vision (Ernest Albert).

Scene 3: Mount Olivet: The Miracle (Ernest Albert).

'Now, however, about the commencement of the fourth hour a great crowd appeared over the crest of Olivet, and, as it filed down the road, thousands in number, the watchers noticed with wonder that every one in it carried a palm-branch, freshly cut.' (*Ben-Hur*, book VIII, ch. 4,)

Grand Chorus:

'Hosanna! Hosanna! Hosanna! in the Highest,'

The programme for the production at Drury Lane, London, continues to acknowledge both Klaw and Erlanger and General Lew Wallace, and, if anything, has more to say about the contributions from other individuals. Arthur Collins (managing director), Sidney Smith (business manager), Edgar Stillman Kelley (music), Ben Teal (stage direction), and Joseph Brooks all rate a mention at the top of the

---

[77] '[Ilderim] had there a really respectable *dowar*, that is to say, he had there three large tents—one for himself, one for visitors, one for his favourite wife and her women; and six or eight lesser ones, occupied by his servants and such tribal retainers as he had chosen to bring with him as a body-guard.' (*Ben-Hur*, book IV, ch. 12)

programme, and, following an announcement that 'The Management
would esteem it a favour if all Ladies would remove their hats, as it
is obvious that the enjoyment of many is entirely spoilt by the view
being obstructed by Ladies Hats', there are the usual notices about
costumes (Alias, Auguste, Simmons), armour (Nestore), electrical
effects (M. Bissing and Bretherton), dances (E. D' Auban), and wigs
(Clarkson), together with the announcement: 'Panoramic Effects in
the Chariot Race Scene Invented and Patented July 10th, 1900'.

The cast and settings (with designers) for the London production
were as follows:

In the Prelude

Balthasar, the Egyptian	Mr CHARLES ALLAN
Gaspar, the Greek	Mr H. WATERS
Melchior, the Hindu	Mr M. BATES

In the Drama

Ben-Hur, Judah, the son of Ithamar	Mr ROBERT TABER
Simonides, steward to the House of Hur	Mr J. E. DODSON
Ilderim, a Sheikh	Mr SIDNEY VALENTINE
Messala, a young Roman noble	Mr BASIL GILL
Balthasar, the Egyptian	Mr CHARLES ALLEN
Arrius, the Tribune	Mr ALFRED BUCKLAW
Malluch, attendant of Simonides	Mr JULIAN CROSS
Hortator, Captain of the Galley	Mr A. CLIFTON ALDERSON
Khaled, servant of Ilderim	Mr A. FORREST
Sanballat, merchant friend of Simonides	Mr W. E. PAYNE
Drusus and Cecilius, Young Romans	Mr FRANK COLLINS and Mr A. BENNETT
Metellus, Roman officer	Mr ERNEST MAYNE
Centurion	Mr F. LLEWELLYN
Officer of the Galley	Mr W. WOOD
Iras, daughter of Balthasar	Miss CONSTANCE COLLIER
Mother of Ben-Hur	Miss MAUD MILTON
Esther, daughter of Simonides	Miss NORA KERIN
Amrah, nurse to the family of Hur	Miss BEVERLY SITGREAVES
Tirzah, sister of Hur	Miss FLOSSIE WILKINSON

Prelude, Scene 1: Curtain, Symbolic of Rome and Jerusalem (T. E.
Ryan).

Scene 2: The Desert: Meeting of the Three Wise Men (T. E. Ryan).

'In the morning arise, and go and meet them. And when ye have all come to the holy city, Jerusalem, ask of the people, "Where is He that is born King of the Jews?—for we have seen His star in the East, and are sent to worship Him."

Suddenly in the air before them, not further up than a low hilltop, flared a lambent flame. As they looked at it the apparition contracted into a focus of dazzling lustre. And they shouted as with one voice, "The Star! The Star!" ' (*Ben-Hur*, book I, ch. 5)

Act I: The Housetop of the Palace of Hur, Jerusalem: The Power of Rome, (T. E. Ryan). *Interval of Seven Minutes.*

Act II, Scene 1: 'Tween Decks of the Roman Galley *Astraea*: The Galley Slaves (Bruce Smith).

Scene 2: The Open Sea: The Rescue (Bruce Smith). *Interval of Five Minutes.*

Act III, Scene 1: Apartment of the House of Simonides in Antioch: The Wise Servant and his Daughter, (R. and C. Caney).

Scene 2: The Grove of Daphne, Temple of Apollo: The Masque of Eros (T. E. Ryan).

'The Grove of Daphne! Nobody can describe it—only beware! it was begun by Apollo and completed by him. He prefers it to Olympus. People go there for one look—just one—and never come away. They have a saying which tells it all: "Better be a worm and feed on the mulberries of Daphne than a king's guest." ' (*Ben-Hur*, book IV, ch. 2)

Scene 3: The Fountain of Castalia: The Revels of Daphne (T. E. Ryan). *Interval of Five Minutes*

Act IV, Scene 1: The Dowar[78] In the Grove of Palms: Preparing for the Race (R. and C. Caney).

Scene 2: By the Lake: The Arts of Cleopatra (T. E. Ryan). *Interval of Eight Minutes*

Act V, Scene 1: Exterior of the Great Gateway of the Amphitheatre in Antioch: Making the Wagers.

Scene 2: The Race (Ernest Albert).

Scene 3: The Arena: Triumph of Ben-Hur (McCleery). *Interval of Ten Minutes*

[78] See n. 77.

Act VI, Scene 1: Apartment in the Palace of Hur, Jerusalem: Tidings of the Lost Ones (E. and C. Caney).

Scene 2: The Vale of Hinnom: The Vision (T. E. Ryan).

Scene 3: Mount Olivet: The Miracle, (T. E. Ryan).

'Now, however, about the commencement of the fourth hour a great crowd appeared over the crest of Olivet, and, as it filed down the road, thousands in number, the watchers noticed with wonder that every one in it carried a palm-branch, freshly cut. (*Ben-Hur*, book VIII, ch. 4)

Grand Chorus: 'Hosanna! Hosanna! Hosanna! in the Highest'

Leopold von Wagner, *The Chariot Race*, c. 1893 (Manchester City Art Galleries)

Klaw and Erlanger's poster, 1901, for the American production of *Ben-Hur* which informs would-be spectators that the chariot race sequence "realises" von Wagner's well-known painting. (Tracy Keenan Wynn)

Reverse angle of the chariot race sequence as seen in the final drop scene, Act V of *Ben-Hur*, 1899. From the souvenir programme to *Ben-Hur*. (New York Public Library for the Performing Arts)

PRELUDE

[*The music composed for the meeting of the Three Wise Men in the desert will take the place of the conventional orchestral prelude. The first bars of this will be played before the house drop is lifted. Not more than two or three minutes should thus be consumed. The house drop will then ascend, showing gauze drop, with backing. Then the chorus is heard behind the curtain. Another interval, of not more than a minute, filled with music. The backing to gauze drop will then ascend, showing view of desert.* DISCOVERED: BALTHASAR *and* MELCHIOR, *the latter a Hindu in appropriate costume. They stand gazing, and one of them pointing off, R. or L. Two camels, with howdahs and other fitting equipments, kneeling, R. or L. Enter, R. or L., third camel, equipped like the others, bearing* GASPAR, *a Greek.* GASPAR *descends from his camel, and the three exchange salutations in pantomime. They turn towards back—the star appears—they fall upon their knees. The star becomes more brilliant—it is surrounded by a corona, and the entire sky becomes illuminated. The music reaches its culmination—the backing to gauze drop descends. The music continues till curtain rises on Act I*]

ACT I

[SCENE: *Roof of the palace of Hur, with view of Jerusalem. The back line of roof is defined by a low parapet, beyond which a gap, between the housetops, indicates a street—a bower or summer-house, at edge of roof, R.C.—entrance from below by stairway, L.—seats in bower and elsewhere about the roof.* DISCOVERED: TIRZAH *and* AMRAH, *seated in bower, up R.C.* TIRZAH *rests her head on* AMRAH's *lap. The latter looks out, frequently and anxiously, into street below. The* MOTHER *of* BEN-HUR *and* SIMONIDES *stand L.C.* SIMONIDES *gazes off L., and, slowly turning, sweeps with his eyes the panorama of the city*]

MOTHER And how many years since thou hast looked upon it?

SIMONIDES A full score.

MOTHER So many? But it is no less fair to thee than of old?

SIMONIDES [*with emotion*] Where is there a city like to Zion? Who would not prefer it 'above his chief joy'?

MOTHER And some day thou wilt return. Here, where the youth was passed, thou wilt spend the quiet evening of thy life.

SIMONIDES It is still my prayer. But now I must wean my eyes from it. The day beginneth to wane, and by dusk I should be far beyond the gates.

MOTHER And thou wilt not tarry, even for a night, after so long a journey?

SIMONIDES My visit was only to thee. My affairs in Antioch are many and weighty. And if thou wilt not review mine accounts—[*producing papers*]

MOTHER Must I tell thee again, good Simonides, as my husband trusted thee, so do I trust thee. It is enough for me to know that the Lord hath prospered thee.

SIMONIDES But how greatly He hath prospered me—or rather thee and thine—thou mayst not fully estimate. The sum that thy husband—my master—entrusted to me hath grown beyond all foreseeing. It hath multiplied ten—yea, twenty fold. There are those that call me the 'miser of Antioch', and I am looked upon with envy for the wealth that is in my hands. But thou knowest for whom I keep it. It all belongeth to the House of Hur, whose servant I am.

MOTHER Not so!

SIMONIDES [*offering papers*] At least, I may leave this reckoning with thee?

MOTHER I beg thou wilt not. Whatever thou mayst have gained with the means which my husband provided, continue to guard it as thy wisdom may direct; and let it be, for the present, as it hath been, a secret between us two. Here we have more than our needs require; and Judah is still young. If, indeed, there is such wealth in store for him, I would not have him know it now. Never was mother blessed with a better son; but in riches, great riches, there is such temptation!

SIMONIDES If thou wilt have it so!

MOTHER I pray thee, so let it be. Later, when he hath looked upon life, and learned its pitfalls and perils, it may prove to him a blessing, not a curse, as now I fear it might.

SIMONIDES It shall be as thou sayest.

MOTHER But I would thou mightst see him before thou goest; for at thy last visit he was but a babe.

SIMONIDES Would that it were permitted me!

MOTHER Shall I not send for him? He is at the Temple with his teachers.

SIMONIDES Gladly would I see again my master's son, but reason upon reason might I give thee why I should not delay.

[*A trumpet sounds at a distance*]

SIMONIDES And hark! Another!

[*At the sound of the trumpet* AMRAH *and* TIRZAH *rise, and, betraying alarm, look over the housetops*]

MOTHER The Roman trumpet.

SIMONIDES Where doth it not sound? Today you expect the Procurator?

MOTHER Gratus? It is true. Today he will arrive. He cometh in person to rule Jerusalem.

SIMONIDES And it were well if, before he cometh, I were gone.

MOTHER Why, what dost thou know of him? Should we fear him more than the governors he hath sent us?

SIMONIDES All underlings of Rome are birds of prey, and the nearer to the eagle in size and power, the greater the maw that must be filled. I would not affright you—I trust you may be undisturbed. The fame of the Prince of Hur, and the favour in which he was held by Caesar, should be for you a safeguard; but no such protection have I. In Antioch I am robbed; I live but by submission to robbery. And to feed the harpies of two provinces—that were over-much.

MOTHER Then, if thou must go, peace go with thee! Come, Tirzah! Bid our guest farewell; for he must leave us.

[*She summons servant by means of a bell-cord which hangs from a post of the entrance-way, L.C. A bell is heard to ring below. Meanwhile,* TIRZAH *approaches*]

SIMONIDES [*laying his hand on* TIRZAH's *head*] The Lord bless thee, my child!

MOTHER [*to* TIRZAH] He knew thy father, and was his friend.

TIRZAH My father? Oh, didst thou know him?

SIMONIDES And never knew I a man more noble. I, too, have a daughter—not unlike to thee, but her lot hath been cast in a land of strangers.

TIRZAH I pray thee, give her my love.

MOTHER And mine.

[*Enter servant, L.C.*]

MOTHER Where hast thou left thy attendants? The servant will go with thee, and see thee safely forth on thy journey.

SIMONIDES It is not required. Yet one thing more—Heaven shield you from all misfortune, but should your enemies afflict you here, forget not that in Antioch—

MOTHER I shall remember.

SIMONIDES [*concluding his speech*] . . . you have a refuge. The peace of the Lord be with you all! [*He turns, gazes again upon the city, and lifts his hands*] And with thee, O thou city of my fathers!

[*Exit* SIMONIDES, *L.C., followed by servant*]

AMRAH [*anxiously approaching*] O mistress! Mistress!

MOTHER Well?

AMRAH Judah hath not returned! Shall I not go in search of him?

MOTHER 'In search of him'? Thou speakest as if he were lost.

AMRAH It is past his hour. Surely he hath left the Temple; and the streets are thronging fast.

MOTHER Thou art foolish, Amrah. What harm can come to him? He is no longer a child. Dost think because thou wast his nurse that he must never stray from thy sight or mine?

AMRAH Well, well, I am foolish then, mistress.

MOTHER [*aside*] Yet I would he were here!

[AMRAH *returns to parapet and continues to watch street below*]

TIRZAH [*pointing off R.*] Mother, hast thou seen the Tower of Antonia—how it is bedecked with banners? And now, above the palace of the High Priest—what is it that they hoist?

MOTHER [*looking*] The great standard of Rome. [*Again aside*] Never before hath it been displayed there. [*To* TIRZAH] Through an angry city will Gratus pass today. Save for the plaudits of his own minions, a city silent and sullen. [*She glances over the housetops as she speaks*] Pray Heaven there be no blow struck, for Jerusalem is powerless!

AMRAH [*at parapet*] O mistress, he cometh!

MOTHER Judah?

AMRAH And he is not alone.

[TIRZAH *hurries to parapet and looks over with* AMRAH]

MOTHER Who is with him?

AMRAH A Roman—a youth.

MOTHER [*startled*] A Roman? What Roman doth he know?

TIRZAH [*turning to her mother*] Messala!

MOTHER It cannot be.

TIRZAH It is he, mother.

MOTHER Amrah, go thou and meet them.

[*Exit* AMRAH, *hurriedly. The* MOTHER *turns again to* TIRZAH]

MOTHER But how shouldst thou remember Messala? He hath been gone for years.

TIRZAH And why should I not remember Judah's friend?

MOTHER [*turning away, displeased and concerned*] I had thought their intimacy was broken, and could have wished that Rome had kept him. Why doth he return?

[*Enter* BEN-HUR, *followed closely by* MESSALA. MESSALA *is in Roman military dress. Enter, immediately following the two,* AMRAH]

BEN-HUR [*running to his mother*] Mother, I am late. But thou has not been alarmed? And see whom I brought with me! Messala!

[*He speaks joyously.* MESSALA *bows with a mixture of condescension and haughty indifference*]

MOTHER [*acknowledging* MESSALA's *salutation*] Thou art indeed a stranger. [*She speaks courteously but with constraint*]

BEN-HUR Five years since he left us! Five years, mother! He hath been in Rome, as thou knowest. And now he is a soldier.

MOTHER Indeed?

BEN-HUR He is with Gratus, and hath a place in his command.

MOTHER [*to* MESSALA] I am pleased to hear of thy good fortune; thou hast my best wishes for thine advancement.

MESSALA [*again bowing*] I doubt neither thy good wishes nor mine advancement.

[BEN-HUR *turns to* TIRZAH, *who stands timidly beside her mother,*
half-concealed by her]

BEN-HUR [*drawing her forward*] Tirzah, why dost thou hide thyself?

MESSALA Tirzah! Perpol![79] Thou hast grown. A beauty, too! Judah,
thou shouldst take her to Rome. But I see she hath not forgotten
to blush. In Rome that would not commend her.

MOTHER Come, my daughter!

[*She takes* TIRZAH's *hand and addresses* MESSALA, *her displeasure*
scarcely concealed under a formal politeness]

MOTHER Thou wilt hold us excused. Judah will entertain thee—and
the house is thine while thou art pleased to remain. Amrah will
serve you with refreshments, my son.

[MESSALA *bows. The* MOTHER *and* TIRZAH *go towards entrance,*
L.C.]

BEN-HUR [*seizing his mother's hand and kissing it*] Thank thee, good
mother!

[*Exeunt* MOTHER *and* TIRZAH. BEN-HUR *turns to* MESSALA]

BEN-HUR We will have our table spread here, as in the old days. What
sayest thou?

MESSALA And what wilt thou give me? A turbot? A collop of wild
boar from the Rhine? Larks' tongues? Honey of Hymettus? And,
for libation to the gods, a draught of Falernian?

BEN-HUR Thou knowest we have no such fare.

MESSALA Then give me nothing. I dine at the palace, good Judah;
and, craving thy pardon, I would not pall mine appetite with wine
of Judaea and unleavened bread. I have but a moment to spare. Let
us talk. [*He throws himself into seat*]

BEN-HUR [*hurt and saddened*] Go then, good Amrah.

AMRAH But, Judah! Thou wilt be served? Thou hast not eaten since
the morning.

BEN-HUR I wish for nothing.

[AMRAH, *with look and gesture indicative of distress and dislike of*
MESSALA, *turns and exits*]

MESSALA Doth thy nurse still pamper and weep over thee, as of
old?

BEN-HUR Amrah is faithful.

MESSALA And thy mother and sister—thou art still their idol?

BEN-HUR Their love for me is beyond my deserts.

---

[79] Perpol! An exclamation, 'By Pollux', probably dog-Latin and probably one of
Wallace's anachronisms. The more usual expression is 'Edepol' (e + deus + Pollux), 'By
the god Pollux'.

MESSALA [*with light and mocking laugh*] 'Love'! And I dare say this is thy only experience of the passion. But, in truth, there is no such thing. In Rome, marriage is but the first step to divorce. Virtue is a tradesman's jewel. My master, in his last lecture, thus phrased it: 'Go, make your lives great. Remember, Mars reigns—Eros hath found his eyes.' Love is nothing—war everything.

BEN-HUR But is it so?

MESSALA By the Fates, Judah, I pity thee. A life without opportunites. From the college to the synagogue! Then to the Temple! And then— O crowning glory—a seat in the Sanhedrin! The gods help thee!

BEN-HUR And thou hast come back from Rome to tell me this?

MESSALA Now I have offended thee?

BEN-HUR Thou art in jest, I know. But the Messala I once knew would not, even in jest, have hurt the feelings of a friend.

MESSALA O tragic Judah! But why think me in jest? In sober earnest, I pity thee.

BEN-HUR And to what dost thou look forward?

MESSALA I? Ah! The world is not all conquered. A campaign in Africa, another against the Scythian; then, a legion! Most careers end there, but I—by Jupiter, what a conception! I will give up my legion for a prefecture. Think of life in Rome with money—money, wine, women, games; poets at the banquet; intrigues in the court; dice all the year round! Or here is Syria! Judaea is rich. Antioch, a capital for the gods! I will succeed Cyrenius—and thou shalt share my fortune.

BEN-HUR At thy going away I wept—yes, I confess it—for I loved thee. And today when I met thee, I was glad, for I thought—[*He breaks off*]

MESSALA Well? And what didst thou think?

BEN-HUR A foolish thing, perhaps. I thought our old-time friendship might be renewed. I knew I should find thee changed in many things. I saw thee princely, accomplished; but I did not suspect— how could I?—that thy heart—

MESSALA 'Heart'! [*He rises, again laughing lightly*] Oh, my simple-minded Judah! But with all the heart I have, I—like thee. Will not that suffice? And I would be of service to thee. I would, by—how shall I swear it? By the shades of Damon and Pythias—who probably never existed—I would and I can. I have the ear of Gratus, and can all but promise thee place and preferment. Only get rid of thine antiquated notions—the teachings of women and priests—and for-get thou art a Jew.

BEN-HUR Forget I am a Jew?

MESSALA Why remember what can bring thee neither pride nor profit?

BEN-HUR In 'sober earnest' thou sayest this? Thou canst propose to
me a thing so infamous? Thou art here, my guest; I cannot answer
thee as I should; but I were meaner, viler, than a Samaritan did I
not let thee know the contempt in which I hold thine offer. Forget
thou that thou art a Roman, before the day cometh when the
remembrance will bring neither pride nor profit to *thee!*
   [*He confronts* MESSALA, *aflame with indignation.* MESSALA *gazes on
   him, speechless, for a moment*]

MESSALA Dost thou know, thou speakest now rank treason? And it is
well that no one heareth thee—but a friend.

BEN-HUR [*in a tone in which anger contends with affection*] Messala!
   [*A trumpet sounds at a distance—a prolonged call*]

MESSALA I am called. And for thee, too, that should have a note of
warning. But I will not waste further advice upon thee. Thou hast
rejected my friendship. [*He turns towards entrance*]

BEN-HUR [*In a conciliatory, almost appealing tone*] Messala! [*As he speaks,
he steps to* MESSALA's *side*]

MESSALA No, I thank thee. I can find mine own way.

BEN-HUR Do not go! Let us not part so! Say that I have mistaken
thee—that thy words were meant in pleasantry, and I will forget—

MESSALA Thou forget? But that is what a Roman never doth. Down
Eros! Up Mars!
   [*Exit* MESSALA]

BEN-HUR [*solus*] Oh! And from him! My more than friend! As I had
thought, my brother! Scorned! Reviled! And here, in the house of
my fathers! But I, too, will learn wisdom. Love—friendship—I will
forget them. For all but mine own people, hate for hate. And for
the Roman, above all, evil for evil!
   [*Enter, L.,* MOTHER]

MOTHER Judah!

BEN-HUR [*running to her and embracing her*] O my mother! [*He hides his
face upon her shoulder*]

MOTHER He is gone, and in anger. And thou art almost in tears.

BEN-HUR [*passionately*] Tell me, my mother, wherein am I inferior
to a Roman? Why, even before Caesar, should I cringe like a
slave?

MOTHER It hath come. I feared it. He hath revealed himself. He hath
taunted thee with the condition of thy race?

BEN-HUR [*again giving way to his emotion*] Mother! Mother!

MOTHER Yet it may be thou art the gainer, for now thou wilt no longer be deceived in him. But oh, the pride, the arrogance of the Roman! [*She sinks into seat*] Ruthless robbers! Under their trampling the earth trembles, like a floor beaten with flails.

BEN-HUR And shall it ever be so?

MOTHER Heaven forbid it!

BEN-HUR Why, if there be the blood of warriors in our veins, as our books tell, why submit we to be trodden upon, crushed, ground into the dust? And how fell we to such an estate [*casting himself down beside her*]?

MOTHER And dost thou ask of me, my son? For our sins have we been chastened, and oh, how heavily! Yet we know that it is not for ever. The yoke shall be lifted.

BEN-HUR Ah! But when?

MOTHER When the King cometh. We have the promise; thou hast heard it from thy teachers.

BEN-HUR But, mother, the time is long! Shall I see the coming?

MOTHER Thou mayest.

BEN-HUR Then should I not be prepared?

MOTHER What dost thou mean?

BEN-HUR Mother, thus far my life hath belonged to thee. And how sweet, how gentle hath been thy control Would it might last for ever! But thou knowest by the law every man of us must have some occupation. What calling hast thou chosen for me.

MOTHER [*troubled*] What hath brought this to thy mind?

BEN-HUR It is no new thought, mother.

MOTHER Then, hast thou already made choice?

BEN-HUR Till today I had not, but now—yes. I would be a soldier.

MOTHER O my son!

BEN-HUR How else can I serve so well the King when He cometh, or my people? There have been soldiers of my family. Fought they not as bravely as the Roman?

MOTHER It is true. But Judah! My Judah!

BEN-HUR How often hast thou told me of their deeds! And how often praised them for their valour and their victories!

MOTHER And was I but kindling a flame in thy breast?

BEN-HUR But why may not that flame burn? Mayhap it may kindle others; till, in time, our shackles be melted, and even Rome be consumed.

MOTHER [*with burst of feeling, embracing him*] My hero! For such wouldst thou be! But how, even if I were willing, couldst thou realize thy wish? In what school couldst thou gain thy training? Thou wouldst not serve in the ranks of Rome?

BEN-HUR [*rising and pacing, R.*] Yes, if through her teaching I might one day turn my arms against her.

MOTHER Thou wouldst war against thine own?

BEN-HUR Mother! Canst thou so misjudge me? But there are other fields—Africa—Parthia—Scythia—

MOTHER O my son! I will not say thy dream is vain. Maybe it is Heaven-born. And thou art right to look to the future. Too long have I closed mine eyes to it, through dread of the day of separation, which yet I knew must come. I see now mine error. And listen, for this will I now promise thee. There is in Antioch one whom we may trust, and of whom, perhaps, I should have spoken to thee sooner—a merchant, Simonides, who was thy father's friend. He hath wisdom, and great wealth and influence. With him will I consult, and it may be he can advise thee and serve thee.

BEN-HUR [*kissing her hand*] Thou art good, thou art kind, my mother.

MOTHER And yet one thing more have I neglected; and now I tell it thee. The times are rife with chance and change, and should sudden misfortune divide us—

BEN-HUR My mother!

MOTHER But hear me. I would have thee remember that, in this Simonides, thou mayest hope to find not merely a wise counsellor in the matter of thy present wish, but in all things a friend, faithful and true, as thy father found him—and help in the hour of need. Thou wilt not forget?

BEN-HUR I promise. But far distant be the day, my mother, when I shall have need to recall it!

[*Enter* TIRZAH, *timidly. She pauses at entrance*]

MOTHER Tirzah!

TIRZAH Mother, may I come?

[*The* MOTHER, *her right arm about the kneeling* BEN-HUR, *extends her left towards* TIRZAH. TIRZAH *rushes to her mother's side, L. Kneels, and is clasped in a close embrace*]

MOTHER My child! Thou art troubled—thou art trembling. But it is all past! The angry tones that so frightened thee shall be heard no more. Messala is gone, and Judah hath lost a friend. But what if the world forsake us, so this little circle remains unbroken?

BEN-HUR Mother!

TIRZAH Dear Mother!

MOTHER My heart's treasures!

[*A trumpet sounds in the distance. It is instantly answered by another, nearer, and this, in turn, by a third, shrill and near.* BEN-HUR, MOTHER *and* TIRZAH *rise as with one accord*]

MOTHER Gratus, the Procurator, in march!

[BEN-HUR *hastens to parapet, and looks off R.*]

BEN-HUR And with many cohorts! He comes this way. [*He runs back to his mother*] May I see him pass?

MOTHER Look, but say nothing, do nothing. In presence of the conqueror, nothing so becomes the conquered as silence.

BEN-HUR Fear not; I would see this power of Rome.

[*Exit* MOTHER. BEN-HUR *and* TIRZAH *go towards parapet. Citizens, men and women, appear on roofs of houses across street. Trumpets near and far answer each other, producing an almost continuous fanfare*]

TIRZAH Oh, hark! Hark!

BEN-HUR [*looking down into the street, comments*] The legion! Rank upon rank. They step as one man. And look! That must be Gratus. How proudly he rides.

TIRZAH [*with startled look and gesture*] And near him—there, at his right hand!

BEN-HUR [*looking*] Messala! Stand back, Tirzah, back, out of sight. [*He recoils, drawing back* TIRZAH] Did he look towards us?

TIRZAH Yes. And waved his hand.

BEN-HUR For the old love, would I see him once more.

[*He leans upon the parapet, looking over. A portion of the wall on which he leans crumbles and falls outward, a tile amongst the debris. Instantly, a yell rises from the street*]

TIRZAH [*with a cry of terror*] Judah! Judah! [*She clutches him as he recoils*]

BEN-HUR [*motionless, stricken with horror*] It fell upon him! I saw it strike—and now he is down!

TIRZAH What fell?

BEN-HUR A tile.

TIRZAH And who is down?

BEN-HUR The Procurator, Gratus!

A VOICE [*from the street, shouting*] Help! Help! Treason! The Procurator hath been murdered!

[*Commotion in the street, which continues and rapidly increases. The people on the adjacent housetops disappear*]

BEN-HUR [*again looking over the parapet*] Tirzah! Tirzah! I have killed Gratus.

TIRZAH Oh! What will befall us? But thou art not to blame.

[*A sound of heavy blows upon a door below*]

BEN-HUR Listen!

A VOICE [*from the street, shouting*] To the housetop!

BEN-HUR They are beating in the door.

  [*He turns towards entrance*]

TIRZAH [*clinging to him*] O brother! It is for thee they come. What will they do to thee?

BEN-HUR Our mother! I must go to her.

TIRZAH [*still clinging*] Thou wilt tell them it was but a mischance. They cannot harm thee? Or is it too late to fly?

BEN-HUR [*disengaging himself*] Tirzah!

  [*Enter, hurriedly and in terror, the* MOTHER, *followed by servants.* BEN-HUR *rushes to her and clasps her in his arms*]

BEN-HUR Oh, mother!

MOTHER Judah, my son! What hath happened?

BEN-HUR Misfortune! Ruin! I have brought them upon thee. [*He points to wall*] The wall—I leaned upon it, and a tile fell upon Gratus.

MOTHER Heaven have mercy!

BEN-HUR O mother, mother! As God lives, I did not aim to hurt him, Roman and tyrant though he be.

MOTHER Thou art innocent. But oh, will they believe it?

  [*Commotion without increases. Trampling on stairway*]

MOTHER They come!

A VOICE [*without, from stairway*] Up! Up!

  [*Enter* CENTURION, *followed closely by* MESSALA. MESSALA, *in turn, followed by soldiers. Behind these, enters* AMRAH. *The* CENTURION, *as he gains the roof, casts one glance on* BEN-HUR *and the women, then turns inquiringly to* MESSALA]

MESSALA [*speaking as he enters, and pointing to* BEN-HUR] That is he.

CENTURION What? That the assassin? He is but a boy.

MESSALA His was the hand that did it. I saw him throw the tile.

BEN-HUR [*stepping towards* MESSALA] Oh, thou—[*Turning suddenly, he appeals to the* CENTURION] But hear me—

CENTURION [*interrupting*] Seize—bind him!

  [*Soldiers spring forward to seize* BEN-HUR]

MOTHER [*frantically interposing*] No! No! Ye shall not. He is guiltless. It was an accident—accident, I say! Will ye not hear his defence?

CENTURION The women, too! Bind them all!

  [*Soldiers lay hands on the* MOTHER *and* TIRZAH. *Servants shriek in terror. At the same instant,* BEN-HUR *is seized*]

BEN-HUR [*shaking off the grasp of the soldiers*] God! Hast thou forsaken us? Messala, by the memory of our childhood! If, indeed, thou wast witness, thou knowest how guiltless I am. Speak the word of truth. [MESSALA *averts his face*] Thou wilt not? Then acquit these [*pointing to his mother and* TIRZAH], and save them! For thou canst. They, at least, have never offended thee! Oh, in the name of thine own mother—

MESSALA [*to* CENTURION] I can be of no more service to thee. There is better entertainment in the street.

> [*He turns and exits. With a cry of rage,* BEN-HUR *springs towards the retreating* MESSALA]

CENTURION Secure him! To the Tower with the women!

> [*Soldiers throw themselves upon* BEN-HUR. *Others drag* MOTHER *and* TIRZAH *towards entrance*]

TIRZAH [*crying in terror*] Judah! Judah! My brother! Help!

BEN-HUR [*struggling with soldiers*] Tirzah! My mother!

AMRAH [*clinging alternately to* TIRZAH *and the* MOTHER] Mistress! Mistress!

CENTURION [*to soldiers with whom* BEN-HUR *struggles*] Haste! Overpower him! Make him fast! What! A stripling, and he playeth with you!

> [*During the struggle the* MOTHER *and* TIRZAH *are dragged off. Servants, shrieking, exeunt.* AMRAH, *attempting to follow her mistress, is thrust back. She turns to the struggling group*]

AMRAH Oh, ye monsters! Ye beasts! [*She attacks the soldiers*]

CENTURION Off, thou hag.

> [*He hurls* AMRAH *to the floor, R., where she lies motionless. Meanwhile,* BEN-HUR's *assailants have forced him down upon one knee, and then tie his hands behind his back. The* CENTURION *continues*]

CENTURION Now! To the street!

BEN-HUR [*still in kneeling posture*] O Lord, in the hour of thy vengeance [*he struggles to his feet as he speaks—his head lifted, his eyes raised*], mine be the hand to put it upon him!

> [*He sinks back exhausted, but is supported in an upright position by the soldiers. The* CENTURION *points towards entrance. A trumpet sounds without. Curtain*]

ACT II

Scene 1

[SCENE: *Interior of cabin of galley, looking towards bow—rowers' benches on either side. Cabin closed in at back by set piece, in which are doors, R.C. and L.C.—between the doors, a platform, on which is the seat of the Tribune, backed by mast. On either side of platform, racks containing armour and arms. Immediately in front of the Tribune's seat, and a little below it, the seat and sounding-board of the* HORTATOR. *Time: night—lanterns lighted.* DISCOVERED: ARRIUS, *in Tribune's seat, helmet on head and otherwise partially armed. The* HORTATOR *in his seat. Slaves on the benches on either side—on the bench L. front,* BEN-HUR. *Soldiers scattered about playing dice etc. At curtain, the slaves are rowing a steady but not rapid stroke; the* HORTATOR *beating time on the sounding-board.* ARRIUS, *leaning forward, watches intently the scene below*]

ARRIUS [*to* HORTATOR] Slacken! Thy slowest stroke!

[*The* HORTATOR *strikes on the sounding-board two strokes in rapid succession. The slaves cease rowing, holding their oars poised. He strikes again, a single stroke, and they dip oars and resume rowing, but very slowly, timed by the* HORTATOR. *Enter, door R. C., officer.* ARRIUS *turns his head quickly and addresses him*]

ARRIUS Officer!

METELLUS [*saluting*] Noble Tribune, the fog thickens. There is neither sight nor sound upon the waters. Hast thou any orders to give?

ARRIUS [*to* HORTATOR] Cease rowing!

[*Again the* HORTATOR *signals with two strokes on the sounding-board, and again the slaves rest on their oars.* ARRIUS, *rising from his seat, addresses officer*]

ARRIUS The calm still holds?

OFFICER There is a breath from the south, scarce enough to give us headway.

ARRIUS So much the better. Thy signals are burning?

OFFICER As thou didst order.

ARRIUS Keep them so.

[*Officer salutes and exits, door R.C.* ARRIUS *descends to floor of cabin*]

ARRIUS Hortator, a question. [*The* HORTATOR *leaves his seat and joins him*] That youth among thy rowers—the foremost in the left rank—

HORTATOR Bench sixty?

ARRIUS Tell me his name, and for what crime he is here.

HORTATOR The ship is but a month from the maker's, and the men
are as new to me as the ship.

ARRIUS He is very young.

HORTATOR But our best rower.

ARRIUS Of what disposition is he?

HORTATOR He is obedient. Once he made a request of me.

ARRIUS For what?

HORTATOR That I would change him alternately from the right to the
left.

ARRIUS Did he give a reason?

HORTATOR He said, if confined to one side, his body would become
misshapen; and that, on some day of storm or battle, there might
be need to change him, and he would then be found unserviceable.

ARRIUS Strange forethought in a slave!

　　　　[*He goes forward, stands in front of* BEN-HUR, *and regards him for
　　　　a moment*]

ARRIUS So, thou are still concerned for the future? Thou hast ambition?

　　　　[BEN-HUR, *holding his oar, looks in the face of* ARRIUS. *Enter, door
　　　　R.C.,* METELLUS. ARRIUS *turns to him*]

ARRIUS Metellus!

METELLUS Tribune!

ARRIUS Is there change in the wind or weather?

METELLUS None.

ARRIUS Nor signs of the fleet?

METELLUS I sometimes catch lights from the other galleys. The fleet
must be near.

ARRIUS [*speaking in a low voice*] Metellus, hast thou noticed the rower
yonder?

METELLUS Number sixty?

ARRIUS Hath he not a right noble bearing? And amidst his cutthroat
fellows, caitiffs and brutes, shines not his face in another light than
hangs over them?

METELLUS Such interest in a slave, O Tribune?

ARRIUS I confess it. These many days I have been observing him. A
mere boy. 'Tis pity.

METELLUS And how, with so soft a heart, hast thou won thine honours?

ARRIUS By doing my duty. And of that, now a word. We left Naxos,
thou knowest, after dividing the fleet, fifty sail remaining with me,

the other fifty passing north of the island of Euboea and descending
the channel between the island and Hellas, so to catch the Tunisian
pirates between us and sink them. By this time the other division
should be in the channel, coming down. Where now, by the
reckoning, are we?

METELLUS Well within the channel at its south end.

ARRIUS The gods permit! The enemy is lapped in security. When the
fog lifts, I propose to engage them.

METELLUS Alone, O Tribune?

ARRIUS Some of my fifty galleys are near. Thou sawest their lights?

METELLUS I saw them.

ARRIUS I am bid sweep this pirate horde from the Aegean, and will
attack at sight.

METELLUS I see, O Tribune, thy heart is not all so soft.

ARRIUS Go now, Metellus. Look to the preparations. Thou knowest
what is to be done. And while thou lookest after it, I will to the
deck and sacrifice to the gods. Jove first, Fortune next.

  [METELLUS *salutes and exits*]

ARRIUS Well is it, whatever befalls, that there is none to mourn for
me. But he—that youth—Hortator! Thy number sixty. Bring him
here.

  [HORTATOR *goes and speaks to* BEN-HUR, *who is on his bench,
  rowing.* BEN-HUR *leaves his oar in its sling, and stands before*
  ARRIUS]

BEN-HUR Thou hast sent for me?

ARRIUS The Hortator tells me thou art his best rower. How long hast
thou been at the oars?

BEN-HUR 'How long?'

ARRIUS Thou hast kept account of time?

BEN-HUR In my calendar, three centuries; in thine, mayhap, three
years.

ARRIUS Three years! The labour is hard. Few men survive it a year;
and thou—thou art but a boy.

BEN-HUR I have had cause to live.

ARRIUS What cause? [BEN-HUR *stands silent, casting down his eyes*] If I
mistake not, thou art a Jew.

BEN-HUR [*lifting his head*] My ancestors, further back than the first
Roman, were Hebrews.

ARRIUS The stubborn pride of thy race is not lost in thee. I once knew
one who was not unlike to thee. But he was a prince. Of what
degree art thou?

BEN-HUR Answering thee from the bench of a galley, I am of the degree of slaves. My father was a Prince of Jerusalem, known and honoured in the guest-chamber of Augustus.

ARRIUS And his name?

BEN-HUR Ithamar, of the House of Hur.

ARRIUS [*recoiling*] A son of Hur? Thou? What brought thee here? Hold! I remember. It was by one of thy name that Valerius Gratus was stricken down in the streets of Jerusalem. Art thou that assassin?

BEN-HUR 'Assassin'?

ARRIUS Well was it for thy father that he died before this shame came upon him! And thy mother—if she yet liveth—

BEN-HUR Mother! My mother! Tirzah! [*Breaking down and falling upon his knees*] O noble Tribune! Think of me what thou wilt; but if thou knowest aught of my mother or sister, tell me—I beseech thee, tell me! The horrible day is three years gone—three years, O Tribune!— and every hour a lifetime, in a bottomless pit, with never a word, a whisper to tell me of their fate. Oh, if I could but shut it from mine eyes! That sight—my sister torn from me—my mother's last look. I have heard the tempest lashing the seas; I have felt the plague's breath, and the shock of ships in battle; but that horror hath quelled all others—their shrieks have rung the loudest. Oh, if thou canst give me no better comfort, tell me they are dead, and I will bless thee—dead, and at peace from the woes I brought upon them.

ARRIUS Then, dost thou admit thy guilt?

BEN-HUR [*springing erect*] Thou hast heard of the God of my fathers? By His truth and almightiness, I swear that I am innocent.

ARRIUS Yet thou wast condemned.

BEN-HUR Unheard! Upon the testimony of one lying voice—that but an hour before had called me 'friend'.

ARRIUS Didst thou not have a trial?

BEN-HUR No.

ARRIUS No trial? No witnesses? Who passed judgment upon thee?

BEN-HUR They bound me, and thrust me into a vault in the Tower. I saw no one. No one spoke to me. Next day, still without a word, they dragged me in chains to the seaside. Even my countrymen, as we passed, shrank from me as from something accursed. One only— a boy, by a well, blessed me, and gave me a draught of water. How beautiful his face! With what light of heaven his eyes shone. His voice trembled with infinite mercy. All that, O Tribune, do I remember, because it hath been, through all these years, my one measure of human kindness.

ARRIUS What couldst thou have proven, hadst thou had a trial?

BEN-HUR I was a boy, too young to be a conspirator. Gratus was a stranger to me. If I had meant to kill him, that was not the time or the place. He was riding in the midst of a legion, and it was broad day. I could not have escaped. I was of a class most friendly to Rome. My father had been distinguished for his services to the Emperor. We had a great estate to lose. Ruin was certain to myself, my mother, my sister. I had no cause for malice, while every consideration—property, family, life, conscience, the law—to me, as the breath of my nostrils—would have stayed my hand, although the foul intent had been ever so strong. I was not mad. Death was preferable to shame; and, believe me, I pray, it is so yet.

ARRIUS Who was with thee when the blow was struck?

BEN-HUR I was on the housetop—my father's house. Tirzah was with me, my sister, the soul of gentleness. To see the legion as it passed by, I leaned upon the parapet. It crumbled—it fell. Thou knowest the rest.

ARRIUS And this is the truth?

BEN-HUR [*proudly*] My word is but the word of a slave. Yet, O Tribune, I speak as if in the ear of God.

ARRIUS It seems not improbable. But now, get thee back to thy place. Cherish no hope. I promise thee nothing.

BEN-HUR Thou canst not deny me hope.

ARRIUS I would not have thee build upon what I have said, yet one favour I think I may grant thee. Metellus! [METELLUS *comes forward*] If we go into action this morning, do not iron this man.

  [METELLUS *retires.* BEN-HUR *would speak again, but* ARRIUS *stops him*]

ARRIUS Thank me not. Back to thy bench.

  [BEN-HUR *is retiring, his head upon his breast. A sudden cry from the deck is heard. Enter officer hastily*]

OFFICER Tribune! Tribune!

ARRIUS What now?

OFFICER There are strange lights dimly seen ahead of us. I have counted forty of them. Galleys of the pirates, I think.

ARRIUS And ours—where are they?

OFFICER Coming—some are here. I heard the beating of their oars.

ARRIUS Be ready to sound to arms.

  [*Officer runs through door, R.C. The* HORTATOR *descends to the deck of the galley. Enter by door, R.C., four soldiers, fully armed.* ARRIUS *puts on his armour*]

HORTATOR [*to the four*] Ho, guards! The irons! Make fast!

[*The four soldiers, two on a side, pass down and lock the shackles attached to the benches about the ankles of the rowers, some of whom submit with furious cries. A soldier approaches* BEN-HUR, *and is about to iron him. The* HORTATOR *interposes*]

HORTATOR Do not shackle that man!

[*The soldier passes on.* BEN-HUR *lifts his eyes to heaven, as in thanks, and renews his grasp upon the oar*]

OFFICER [*heard without*] On deck! On deck! Everyone to quarters!

[*Exeunt soldiers by doors, R.C. and L.C.* ARRIUS, *now in full armour, and with helmet, shield and sword*]

ARRIUS [*to* HORTATOR] After the sacrifice, at sound of the trumpet, do thou drive the galley—every oar with a man's soul in it.

[ARRIUS *passes out by door, L.C. The* HORTATOR *takes his seat. There is a brief lull of noise, as if the sacrifice was in progress. Suddenly, a trumpet is heard without. The* HORTATOR *strikes once with his gavel. The slaves hold their oars poised. An officer appears in door, R.C., and, standing there, repeats orders from without*]

OFFICER [*to* HORTATOR] Hold fast! Steady!

[*Again the trumpet sounds a call, shrill and spirit-stirring*]

OFFICER Now, Hortator, it is time! Full speed!

HORTATOR [*seizing a second gavel, beats with both hands hard and fast, shouting at the same time*] Full speed now!

[*The slaves, catching time from the gavels, row with all their strength at utmost speed*]

HORTATOR Bend to it, everyone! Drive! Cut them down! Pull! Life or death! Let them have it!

[*The crash of a collision is heard, and its effect simulated. The officer in the door staggers, the* HORTATOR *lurches backwards, the slaves lose stroke and reel on their benches; a number fall off*]

HORTATOR Up! Up! To your oars again! For your lives, pull! We ride them down and over them! Pull!

[*A second shock of collison, accompanied by the sound of rending timbers. The slaves, hurled off, struggle to regain their benches. Shrieks and yells for help are added to the uproar. On deck, fierce shouting and the clash of steel.* METELLUS *staggers in by door, R.C.*]

OFFICER [*at door*] Ho, Metellus!

METELLUS We are boarded—sinking—I am done for. [*He falls and dies*]

OFFICER Sinking! All is lost.

[*Exit through door*]

HORTATOR Your benches, dogs—back to your benches!

[*Through all the confusion, he keeps the gavels going*]

ARRIUS [*without, shouting*] Jove with us! Jove with us!

BEN-HUR The Tribune!

[*Enter* TRIBUNE *by door, R.C.* ARRIUS, *retreating backwards, fights desperately with pirates, who finally press him to the floor of the galley*]

ARRIUS Metellus! Romans! Ah, they are not—the sea hath swallowed them. Be it so. No surrender. Fortune hath deserted me, and at last I have found my death.

BEN-HUR Stand fast, brave Tribune! Thou shalt not die alone. I come!

[*Pulling in his oar, he breaks the blade, and, wielding the handle as a weapon, springs to the assistance of* ARRIUS. ARRIUS, *reeling from a blow upon his helmet, falls back into* BEN-HUR'*s arms.* BEN-HUR, *supporting* ARRIUS, *swings the fragment of the oar above his head, and confronts the pirates, who recoil before him. A third shock of collision. Darkness covers the stage. Change of Scene*]

Scene 2

[SCENE: *The open sea. Time: early morning—sunrise effects. The sea strewn with wreckage.* DISCOVERED: BEN-HUR *and* ARRIUS *on a floating plank (or spar).* BEN-HUR'*s left arm is closely clasped about* ARRIUS, *who lies prone, swaying helplessly as the fragment of wreck rolls in the waves*]

ARRIUS Leave go thy hold! Leave go, and let me drown! Thou canst not save me.

BEN-HUR By God's help, I will.

ARRIUS Let the waves take me! I have had my day. A Roman should never survive defeat.

[BEN-HUR, *his left arm still about* ARRIUS, *shades his eyes with his right hand, and peers across the water*]

BEN-HUR But art thou yet defeated? Did I not hear the speak of help at hand? I see fresh sails.

ARRIUS [*eagerly, striving to lift his head*] Where? In what quarter?

BEN-HUR [*pointing off R.*] Yonder! Towards the open sea.

ARRIUS Thou art sure?

BEN-HUR Sail upon sail! And one that beareth down upon us.

ARRIUS What signal doth it show?

BEN-HUR I cannot tell. I see no signal.

ARRIUS Look to the mast-head.

BEN-HUR Nothing.

ARRIUS Then it is no Roman.

BEN-HUR It neareth fast. Its decks are thick with people. Its hull is black.

ARRIUS Enough. Look no more.

BEN-HUR [*turning his head and gazing off L.*] But those to landward fly. They surely fly.

ARRIUS Thine eyes deceive thee. Enemies—all. Seest thou this ring upon my finger? Take it off. [*He lifts his hand, displaying ring to* BEN-HUR. BEN-HUR *hesitates*] Take it, and swear to do my bidding.

BEN-HUR [*still hesitating*] What shall I swear?

ARRIUS Obey me. [BEN-HUR *takes the ring from his finger*] My course is run; but thou mayest be saved, for now thy slave's garb will protect thee. With that ring thou mayest purchase thy freedom—or, shouldst thou live to see Rome again, it will insure thee both freedom and reward.

BEN-HUR And what of thee?

ARRIUS Thou shalt report of me that I died as a Roman should.

BEN-HUR [*renewing his grasp upon* ARRIUS] But if I live, thou shalt not die; and if thou diest, how shall I report thee, for I shall be with thee.

ARRIUS Foolish boy! Wouldst thou hold me in life against my will? My mind is fixed. To a Roman, honour is all in all. Swear that, if yonder galley be a pirate, thou wilt release me to the death I crave.

BEN-HUR Then should I be thy slayer. I will not.

ARRIUS I command thee.

BEN-HUR And yet will I not. One other oath have I sworn, O Tribune—to repay the debt of kindness that I owe thee; and that will I keep, or perish with thee. Take back thy ring.

ARRIUS Art thou mad?

BEN-HUR Then to the seas do I give it.

[*He casts away the ring, and, as he does so, his eyes, following the sweep of his hand towards R., suddenly become fixed. He starts— cries*]

BEN-HUR And look! Look! Here! Close upon us! A galley! A trireme!

ARRIUS [*excitedly*] Lift me up!

BEN-HUR And now, at the mast-head—

ARRIUS What?

BEN-HUR A helmet!

ARRIUS A helmet?

BEN-HUR Golden—

ARRIUS And the crest?

BEN-HUR An eagle! I see it glisten in the sun.

ARRIUS [all his spirit returning] Jove with us! A Roman! We are saved.
Thank thy god! And call to them!

BEN-HUR [hailing] Help! Help!

ARRIUS Wave thy hand! Fortune hath not deserted me. The victory
shall yet be mine. And thou—I knew thy father—thou shalt be my
son. Call to them! Shout!

BEN-HUR [hailing and waving his hand] Help! Help! Ho!

> [An answering hail is heard at a distance. On from R., in middle
> distance, sweeps a Roman galley. Curtain]

ACT III

Scene 1

[SCENE: *Apartment in the house of* SIMONIDES *at Antioch. Door C., door, L. Other arrangements, as in the artist's design.* DIS-COVERED: SIMONIDES, *being wheeled in, in great chair, by a slave, door C. He is attended by* MALLUCH. SANBALLAT *closely follows*]

SIMONIDES [*to bearers*] Gently! Gently, my children! [*His chair is placed R.C.*] How ill did mine enemies reckon when they mangled these poor limbs of mine! For on feet that are both swift and faithful still may I go abroad. Now, Sanballat, I will hear thee.

[SANBALLAT *approaches. Exit slave, door C.*]

SIMONIDES Thy search was thorough?

SANBALLAT As my best wit could make it.

SIMONIDES Thou didst not spare gold?

SANBALLAT There is scarce in all Judaea an officer of Caesar's who is not the richer for my fee.

SIMONIDES And all in vain!

SANBALLAT Good master, the family of Hur have vanished from the earth. The youth, as thou knowest, was consigned to the galleys.

SIMONIDES [*sadly*] Of him I expected no tidings.

SANBALLAT And of the women there is even less trace. On the day of their arrest—now eight years past—they were cast into the Tower of Antonia, but he who was then governor of the Tower was that day removed. The governor today hath never seen their faces. So doth he avow, and I believe with truth. Nor is there record of knowledge of them there or elsewhere that I, by search or bribery, could discover. May not their fate be guessed?

SIMONIDES [*with sad conviction*] Murdered?

SANBALLAT Can it be doubted?

SIMONIDES And Gratus—the monster!—survived his hurt?

SANBALLAT He survived.

SIMONIDES And not content with their blood, he hath fated himself upon their treasure?

SANBALLAT In that matter Heaven hath favoured thee, and wonder-fully granted thy wish.

SIMONIDES Ah!

SANBALLAT [*producing papers*] In the division of the spoil, the palace was claimed by the master robber, Caesar, and from him have I purchased it.

SIMONIDES [*eagerly seizing the paper which* SANBALLAT *extends to him*] Thou hast it?

SANBALLAT Look! The imperial seal.

SIMONIDES [*inspecting paper*] Thou hast done well—well.

SANBALLAT As for the price—thou wilt find it in my account, which I leave with Malluch. [*He gives second paper to* MALLUCH]

SIMONIDES [*aside*] That it should pass, at last, into my hands—the house I first entered as a slave!

SANBALLAT And now have I a curious thing to tell thee. The doors were sealed, yet within I found a tenant.

SIMONIDES A tenant?

SANBALLAT A woman—an Egyptian—who had once been nurse in the family of the Hurs; and who, through all these years, had dwelt there undiscovered, keeping the place against their return.

SIMONIDES Marvellous! She could tell thee nothing?

SANBALLAT On the contrary, she begged me for knowledge. And, seeing her so faithful, I left her in charge.

SIMONIDES In that, too, thou didst well. Yet one thing more. I bade thee inquire concerning a certain Messala.

SANBALLAT Thy reports of him were correct. He was high in favour with Gratus; he shared in his leader's spoil, and, it may be, was privy to his vengeance. But nothing more could I learn of him, save that he is now, with his legion, in this quarter of the world.

SIMONIDES In this quarter?

MALLUCH Master, may I speak a word? There is even now in Antioch a Roman called Messala.

SIMONIDES [*surprised*] How knowest thou?

MALLUCH In the chariot-race next week, he will be the champion of Rome. It is so announced.

SIMONIDES [*aside*] If it should be he!

MALLUCH Shall I make sure?

SIMONIDES Without fail—yet stay! I will think of it. Enough for the present! Good Sanballat, thou hast discharged thy whole duty. And mark—not a word of this to living soul!

[SANBALLAT *bows and exits, door C.*]

SIMONIDES Malluch, go say to my daughter I would see her. And I expect the Sheik-Ilderim. Him, too, will I see. But no other this day.

[MALLUCH *bows, and exits, door C.* SIMONIDES *continues, solus*]

SIMONIDES Why should I seek further? Have I not done what man may do? To amass this wealth for others, have I not racked my brain without mercy—yea, from the morn of life till the even? To preserve it, for others, have I not suffered my body to be racked, even to the dividing of the joints and the marrow? Now, what more doth duty require? What hope that from this Messala, I could learn aught that would now avail? Or gain aught but renewal of strife? May I not now think of mine own?

[*Enter* ESTHER, *door L.*]

ESTHER [*running to him and embracing him*] My father!

SIMONIDES [*caressing her*] My one delight! Balm for mine eyes! My star of the morning! Thou hast slept well?

ESTHER [*kissing him*] And thou?

SIMONIDES Care and pain are but sorry bedfellows.

ESTHER [*sitting on hassock at his side*] And already thou hast been at thy labours? [*She picks up the paper left by* SANBALLAT, *which lies on the arm of* SIMONIDES' *chair*] When wilt thou have done with this toiling and scheming?

SIMONIDES Dost thou think I may find rest on earth?

ESTHER If only thou wilt. But who hath been with thee so early? And what strange parchment is this?

SIMONIDES [*unfolding the paper in her hand*] Dost thou know the seal?

ESTHER [*awed*] It is Caesar's. He hath not revoked his promise?

SIMONIDES Fear not. So long as I pay, I shall have his favour. And see—he hath granted me a palace.

ESTHER A palace? Where?

SIMONIDES In Jerusalem. [ESTHER *shows emotion*] Doth that name move thee? The city of thy fathers; but what saith the Psalmist? 'By the rivers of Babylon, there we sat down and wept when we remembered Zion'—[*With deep feeling, he breaks off, his hands clasped, his eyes upraised*]

ESTHER [*excitedly*] Father! Of the palace—what hast thou to tell me?

[*Enter* MALLUCH, *door C.*]

SIMONIDES [*turning his head*] Well?

MALLUCH The Sheik-Ilderim.

SIMONIDES Let him come in.

[*Exit* MALLUCH, *door C.* SIMONIDES *turns to* ESTHER, *and lays his hand upon her head*]

SIMONIDES Patience. Our talk will wait. Sit here.

[*Enter* ILDERIM, *door C.*]

ILDERIM Peace be with thee—and with thine!

SIMONIDES Good Ilderim, thou art always welcome. And what bringeth thee to Antioch at such a time?

ILDERIM [*laughing*] What bringeth all the world, my friend?

SIMONIDES Thou hast not come for the sports in the circus?

ILDERIM [*half-banteringly, stroking his beard*] And why not?

SIMONIDES Thou?

ILDERIM Canst thou tell me where I may find a charioteer? For the honour of the desert!

SIMONIDES And such thine errand?

ILDERIM It is announced that in the chariot-race the best blood of the earth will compete. To make the promise good, I have brought with me four horses which have never been yoked to car. And now, if I may but find one to break and drive them—

SIMONIDES And thou! In thine old age!

ILDERIM [*smiling, and stroking his beard*] Age is not all a matter of years. Howbeit, I have another and better excuse for troubling thee.

SIMONIDES As I judged. Yet, now that thou hast spoken of it, who are to be thy competitors in the race?

ILDERIM I take account of but one.

SIMONIDES And he?

ILDERIM A Roman.

SIMONIDES Dost thou know his name?

ILDERIM [*with negative shake of his head*] He is a Roman. That sufficeth.

SIMONIDES For thee—and me. Well, to the greater matter.

ILDERIM Listen then. It may not have escaped thy memory that I once gave thee an account of how there came to be, in my tents in the desert, now nearly thirty years since, three strangers—wise men from three different countries, fleeing for their lives from Herod, and seeking protection.

SIMONIDES I remember.

ILDERIM They had been led by a wondrous star in the East, one from Egypt, one from the land of the Greeks, and one from farthest Ind; and, guided by the star, they had found, in a village of Judaea, a child who was born King of the Jews. Such, at least, their tale.

SIMONIDES I remember.

ILDERIM Well, one of them hath again appeared.

SIMONIDES So?

ILDERIM The Egyptian—Balthasar by name—is now, with his daughter, my guest in my orchard of palms.

SIMONIDES And what saith he now?

ILDERIM His beard is like the hoar-frost, but still holdeth he to his story. And more, he will have it that soon—mayhap within the year—this king will appear and establish his kingdom. Now, what thinkest thou? [SIMONIDES *by his manner displays his doubt*] Ah, I see—thine old-time caution and distrust of man!

SIMONIDES Have I not had cause for caution?

ILDERIM But this would I know. Is there not, in thy holy books, a prophecy concerning the coming of such a king?

SIMONIDES Not one alone, but many. And here is one who will quote them to thee [*laying his hand on* ESTHER*'s*].

ILDERIM Is it so?

SIMONIDES Esther, this is a subject dear to thy heart.

ESTHER [*to* ILDERIM] And where didst thou say this child that is King of the Jews was found?

ILDERIM In a village of Judaea. By name—[*He pauses, calling upon his memory*]

ESTHER [*suggesting*] Bethlehem?

ILDERIM The same! How didst thou know?

[ESTHER *looks at her father, who returns her gaze*]

ESTHER [*gazing into her father's eyes, quoting*] 'But thou, Bethlehem Ephrath, though thou be little among the thousands of Judah, yet out of thee shall he come forth that is to be Ruler is Israel.'

ILDERIM What? It is so written?

SIMONIDES Even so.

ILDERIM [*exultantly*] Then hath the Egyptian confirmation?

SIMONIDES But may not this Balthasar have seen the writing?

ILDERIM Simonides, let me tell thee: I am but an Ishmaelite; but were I of *thy* race, had I suffered thy wrongs, and had I thy gold—

SIMONIDES Well, what then?

ILDERIM By the splendour of God! I would wait for no king, I would equip, not caravans, but armies.

SIMONIDES Wouldst thou? And who would lead them? No, no, good Ilderim, mistake me not. Think not my zeal is less than thine. When the King cometh, when I may see and know Him, all I have is His. But till then, hadst thou suffered what I have suffered, and didst thou sit where I sit, thou wouldst oppose force with craft, biding thy time in patience, and purchase thy peace with Caesar, as I have purchased mine.

[ILDERIM *makes the gesture of one silenced but not convinced. Enter, door C.,* MALLUCH, *followed by servant*]

MALLUCH Good master, I crave thy pardon: there is a Roman at the door.

ILDERIM A Roman?

MALLUCH A soldier who will give no name, and yet will not be denied.

SIMONIDES Hast thou talked with him?

MALLUCH Not yet. The door-keeper hath reported him. Thou wilt not see him?

SIMONIDES I like not to leave a mystery unsolved. I will see him. Thou, Malluch, remain.

[*At a sign from* SIMONIDES, *exit servant, door C.* SIMONIDES *extends his hand to* ILDERIM]

SIMONIDES Good Ilderim—

ILDERIM [*taking his hand*] Should I leave thee?

SIMONIDES [*smiling*] Not all thy spears, trusty friend, could serve me so well as doth the safeguard of Caesar. I thank thee for thy visit.

ILDERIM But thou wilt see this Balthasar?

SIMONIDES If occasion serve. Peace go with thee!

ILDERIM [*going*] I will have a look at thy visitor as I pass.

[ILDERIM *salutes, and exits, door C.*]

SIMONIDES Malluch, place thyself there [*pointing towards hangings, L.*].

[MALLUCH *conceals himself behind hangings, L.* SIMONIDES *turns to* ESTHER]

SIMONIDES My daughter—

ESTHER I pray thee, let me bide.

SIMONIDES Thou? But wherefore? Would it be wise.

ESTHER [*entreatingly*] I pray thee—

SIMONIDES [*fondly*] Well, have thy will.

[*Enter, door C.,* BEN-HUR, *in Roman military dress, shown in by slave. Exit servant, door C.*]

BEN-HUR Peace to the master of this house. Peace to all that is his.

SIMONIDES [*politely but coldly*] Peace to thee.

BEN-HUR I speak to the merchant Simonides?

SIMONIDES Thou dost.

BEN-HUR I am called Arrius.

SIMONIDES I have not the honour of knowing thee.

BEN-HUR That could I hardly expect. [*Half-aside*] And yet had I hoped—

ESTHER [*timidly, passing behind her father's chair, from his R. to his L., and addressing* BEN-HUR] I pray thee, be seated—and welcome!

BEN-HUR [*regarding* ESTHER] Thou art kind. But before I accept thy kindness, let me make known mine errand. Noble Simonides, I am told thou wast once a dweller in Jerusalem.

SIMONIDES [*in half-whisper to* ESTHER, *his eyes fixed on his visitor*] Esther!
  [ESTHER *returns to her place at* SIMONIDES *side, R.* SIMONIDES
  grasps her hand and speaks to BEN-HUR]

SIMONIDES Well?

BEN-HUR And that thou hadst for friend there, in days gone by, one
  called the Prince of Hur.

SIMONIDES [*his voice sinking and his gaze increasing in intensity*] I knew
  him. Well?

BEN-HUR And he was thy friend?

SIMONIDES In days long past.

BEN-HUR Long past! But his family—thou hadst knowledge also of
  them? And some trace of them thou mayest have kept? May I not
  hope—

SIMONIDES [*interrupting*] What wouldst thou know?

BEN-HUR I would know if there be one of them who is yet among
  the living.

  [SIMONIDES, *without relaxing his gaze, slowly shakes his head*]

BEN-HUR Thou canst not tell me? Or wilt not? I pray thee, think
  again. There was a son—

SIMONIDES There was a son. He was accused of a crime and condemned to the galleys. Hardly can it be—

BEN-HUR [*interrupting*] That he yet liveth? Strange would it be, I grant
  thee. But the mother and sister of this hapless wretch—canst thou
  tell me nothing of them?

SIMONIDES [*leaning forward imperatively*] Who art thou?

BEN-HUR [*removing his helmet*] I am Judah, son of that Ithamar, Prince
  of Hur, whom thou knewest; and I beg of thee, now, open thy lips,
  and tell me if I have come from the dead in vain.

SIMONIDES [*recoiling, holding and patting* ESTHER'*s hand*] Esther! Peace!
  Peace!

BEN-HUR O look not upon me with such unbelieving eyes!

SIMONIDES But how am I to know that thou art he? And who hath
  told thee—

BEN-HUR Listen. On that last day of our happiness—a day of which
  thou hast surely heard—my mother, oppressed with a dread of ill
  all too soon to be realized, told me of thee.

SIMONIDES And what did she tell thee?

BEN-HUR That if disaster should ever befall, I should find in thee a
  friend—even such a friend as my father found. And look upon me
  now, I pray thee, and see if in my face thou canst read no likeness
  to his. For if thou canst not, no proof have I to give thee.

SIMONIDES But mere resemblances are not uncommon. And how—if thou art he—comest thou here in Roman dress?

BEN-HUR My story is quickly told. That I was falsely accused of the crime for which I suffered, I will not trouble to affirm—

SIMONIDES That needst thou not.

[ESTHER, *sinking on hassock beside her father's chair, listens intently and with exhibition of deepest interest and emotion to* BEN-HUR's *story*]

BEN-HUR Nor will I vex your ears with tales of my three years' death in life, for so long wore I the chains of the galleys. But Heaven was kind to me, and even in that darkness it drew upon me a friendly eye. Arrius, the duumvir, of all the Romans the only one for whom, in the Last Judgement, I pray that mercy may be found, looked upon me one day with compassion. He heard me, and believed in my innocence; and that night—a night of battle—he bade them leave me unfettered. We were crushed, by a ship of the enemy. All my fellows, ironed and helpless, went down cursing their gods; but I, by the favour of mine, won to a fragment of floating wreck, and saved myself—and Arrius.

ESTHER [*murmuring fervently*] Heaven be praised!

BEN-HUR [*gratefully to* ESTHER] I thank thee! From that night I was no longer a slave, save to the kindness of Arrius, who adopted me as his son. He would have made of me a Roman, and a Roman soldier; and fain was I to learn of the conqueror how I might, haply, conquer in turn. Hence the garb in which thou seest me. Nothing did he deny me, save the one thing my heart most hungered for—leave to search for my people. That, with more than a father's jealousy, and with all his Roman pride, he forbade. And so close were the bonds in which he held me that, while he lived, Rome was my prison. He is dead—and my search is begun. And now, speak. Hast thou aught to tell me? Or must I fare farther?

SIMONIDES Strange—most strange—is this tale thou tellest.

BEN-HUR And thou dost not credit it?

SIMONIDES I say not that. But, were I assured past all doubt of its truth, nothing could I tell thee of thy lost ones.

BEN-HUR [*despairingly*] Nothing?

SIMONIDES Nothing—as Heaven is my witness.

BEN-HUR [*turning away*] Oh, then I may bid thee farewell.

SIMONIDES Yet stay. One question. Hadst thou ever a friend called Messala?

BEN-HUR [*bitterly*] A 'friend'?

SIMONIDES And hast thou reason to suppose that from him thou mightst learn—

BEN-HUR [*interrupting*] Oh, if thou knowest where I may find him, tell me not of mine enemies—let Heaven deal with them as it will—but give me to meet this false, false friend, to whom I charge all my woes!

SIMONIDES Standeth thy account so with him?

BEN-HUR [*almost fiercely*] What dost thou know of him?

SIMONIDES Patience! Nothing do I know but this: the new consul, Maxentius, will celebrate his arrival with games, and among those who will make sport for him in the circus there is said to be one Messala, a Roman.

BEN-HUR Here? In Antioch? [*He whirls towards the door*]

SIMONIDES Stay! Thou knowest not if it be he.

BEN-HUR That will I soon learn.

SIMONIDES And if it be, what wilt thou do? Be not rash.

ESTHER [*with deep solicitude moving towards* BEN-HUR] Oh, I pray thee, do be advised! Heed my father!

SIMONIDES [*warningly*] Esther!

[*She returns to the side of her father's chair*]

BEN-HUR I thank thee again, daughter of Simonides. The good will thou showest me is as a draught from an angel's cup to one who dieth of thirst in the desert. But thy father's confidence I have not won. Why, then, should he have mine? God reward thee! I must about my mission.

[*Exit* BEN-HUR, *door C.*]

ESTHER [*appealingly to her father as* BEN-HUR *vanishes*] My father—

SIMONIDES [*instantly becoming alert*] Silence! Malluch! [MALLUCH *springs from behind the hangings*] Quick! Follow that man! Lose him not from thy sight! If he meet this Messala, be thou there to see. And bring me word of his every act, his every speech—yea, his every look. Dost understand?

MALLUCH I do, good master.

SIMONIDES Fail not!

[*Exit* MALLUCH *hastily, door C.*]

SIMONIDES [*to* ESTHER] Well, now! What wouldst thou say?

ESTHER O my father! Dost thou believe him?

SIMONIDES But what sayest thou?

ESTHER Seemed he not truthful? His words—his looks—

SIMONIDES Ah! It is plain how he seemeth to thee. He hath won thee—with the pity of his tale and the fervour and the comeliness of his youth.

ESTHER O my father! [*She casts herself down beside him, embracing him*] Be not angry. Have I offended, I pray thee forgive me.

SIMONIDES [*recovering his self-control*] Peace, poor innocent! It is I should ask forgiveness of thee. But now, art thou brave? For I, too, have a tale to tell—not of Zion and its peace [*picking up the paper from the arm of the chair, and, after the next sentence, sadly laying it down again*]—for those now mine eyes may never see. But the Lord determineth. Esther, canst thou tell me what day this is?

ESTHER What day? Woe's me, my father! Dost thou think I could ever forget it?

SIMONIDES The twentieth day of the fourth month! This day, five years ago, my Rachel, thy mother, fell down and died. Oh, to me she was as a cluster of camphyre in the vineyards of Engedi! And where was ever her like to be found? Princes were fain to do her honour. And yet—yet—possess thy soul, O Esther!—she was a bondswoman.

ESTHER [*in intense surprise*] My mother?

SIMONIDES And I—I, too, was a slave.

ESTHER [*almost incredulously*] Thou, a slave? O my father!

SIMONIDES 'Was'? Nay, I am—if the tale of this youth be true.

ESTHER [*breathlessly*] It cannot be!

SIMONIDES Yet further—since the child followeth the condition of the parent, if I be not free from my bondage, thou, even thou, my precious one, in all thy modesty, thy purity, and thy beauty, art a slave.

ESTHER [*wildly, rising*] A slave—I—to whom?

SIMONIDES To whomsoever can prove himself heir to the Prince of Hur. [*She turns away, as if dazed*] Now canst thou wonder that I was slow to admit his claim?

ESTHER Why hast thou kept it from me?

SIMONIDES Hold me not to blame. Ere thou wast of an age to comprehend, the House of Hur was blotted out. I thought it extinct. What need, then, to tell thee?

ESTHER Oh, strange doth it seem, my father! And hard—hard—for thee!

[*Again she sinks down beside him, and puts an arm about him*]

SIMONIDES For me? Hast thou no fear for thyself?

ESTHER He who hath so loved his mother and sister, and who still so loveth their memory, cannot be base at heart, my father. Surely, he will set us free.

SIMONIDES Hast thou such faith in him?

ESTHER And he will acknowledge and reward thy faithfulness, and maintain thee in honour. Can he do less?

SIMONIDES [*laying his hand on* ESTHER'*s head*] And what will he do for thee? [*She drops her face in his lap*] Come—thou shalt decide. One test hath the Lord provided. If he knoweth Messala, and Messala knoweth him, then shall I know that he is indeed the son of Hur. But shall he know? Or, if know he must, must he know all?

ESTHER [*rising*] I pray thee, have pity!

SIMONIDES To thee do I leave it, for thine will be the sacrifice. And oh, bethink thee well! Today thou hast his respect, and his pleasant words, and his kindly looks. But how shall it be when thou standest before him not as the heiress of Antioch, but dowerless, and his thrall?

ESTHER [*in anguish*] Make not my task too hard!

SIMONIDES Cruel I must be to save thee from sorrow and disappointment yet more cruel. Put not thy trust in princes.

ESTHER Then in Heaven will we put our trust.

SIMONIDES [*half-aside*] It is Heaven's own voice. [*To* ESTHER] Then if he be the son of Hur, he must know—all?

ESTHER He must know. [*She throws herself into his arms*]

    [*Curtain*]

Scene 2

[SCENE: *The Grove of Daphne.*[80] DISCOVERED: *A troop of young girls crossing from L. to R.—following these, a troop of boys. All are in festal array, and trip to the music of the following song*]

CHILDREN [*singing*]

        For today we take and give;
        For today we drink and live;
        For today we beg or borrow.
        Who knoweth of the silent morrow?

[*Exeunt, R., the children. Enter, L., a troop of women, carrying garlands*]

WOMEN [*singing*]

        Daphne, through this haunted grove,
        Where thou fledst the fair Apollo—
        Where the song and sigh of love

[80] The numbering of this scene and the scene to follow differ between the printed programme and the text. This discrepancy arises because Scene 2 in the playscript is merely a 'carpenters' scene', briefly played before a down-stage backcloth, whilst the more elaborate temple setting, 'The Heart of the Grove', is set upstage behind the painted drop.

Breathe from ev'ry leafy hollow—
Wander we, and fain would prove
Whether still the god will follow.

[*Enter, L.,* BEN-HUR. *The women look back towards him, beckoning and waving their garlands enticingly*]

WOMEN [*singing*]

Whether still—
Whether still—
Whether still the god will follow.

[BEN-HUR, *pausing L. C., turns from the women impatiently*]

WOMEN [*singing, moving R.*]

Heigho! Heigho!
Ho, for the revels of Daphne!

[*Exeunt the women, R.*]

BEN-HUR What pagan rites are these? And where is one who will answer me a question?

[Enter L., MALLUCH]

BEN-HUR Ah! Good friend—a word.

MALLUCH At thy service.

BEN-HUR Canst thou tell me whither this road leads? And who are these that follow it?

MALLUCH Thou art a stranger in Antioch?

BEN-HUR I confess it.

MALLUCH And thou hast never heard the adage, 'Better be a worm, and feed on the mulberries of Daphne, than a king's guest'?

BEN-HUR [*looking at him*] Then this is the Grove of Daphne?

MALLUCH In all the world, it is said, there is not its like. Art thou in quest of pleasure, seek no farther. Whatever thy heart's desire, thou mayst find it here. Of what art thou in search?

BEN-HUR I have been told of a course for chariots somewhere within these bounds. Dost thou know of such?

MALLUCH Thou askest after the stadium near the Fountain of Castilia?

BEN-HUR Whatever it be, it is said—in the khan where I lodge—that the champions who are to compete in the circus are accustomed to drive there daily.

MALLUCH And thou wouldst see them at their practice?

BEN-HUR If I might.

MALLUCH Come, I will be thy guide.

BEN-HUR Good! Thou shalt not be the loser [*putting his hand to his purse*].

MALLUCH Thy thanks will be enough. Shall there be no coin current
but the Roman [*with gesture refusing proffered fee*]?
[BEN-HUR *regards* MALLUCH *for an instant questioningly, then
warmly proffers his hand*]
BEN-HUR Take, then, my thanks. By thy speech thou art of Judaea.
MALLUCH I was born within a stone's throw of the market-place in
Jerusalem.
BEN-HUR So much the better! Let us on! [*They move towards R.*]
MALLUCH [*turning to Ben-Hur*] And by the shortest course?
BEN-HUR I pray thee.
[*Exeunt. Change of Scene*]

Scene 3

[SCENE: *The heart of the Grove—Temple of Apollo.* DISCOVERED:
*A procession entering from R. and passing into temple—troops of boys
and girls, as in Scene 2; priests of Daphne; worshippers, bearing
offerings; singing girls and Devadasi,*[81] *etc.*]
CHORUS [*singing*]

>Daphne! Daphne! Whilst above,
>Beams the Sun-god in his power,
>Still the earth his warmth shall prove;
>Still the bee shall seek the flower,
>And the bird his mate; and love
>Still shall be the maiden's dower.
>Follow we
>Bird and bee,
>Whilst the earth is still in flower!
>Heigho! Heigho!
>Ho, for the bridals of Daphne!

[*Last in this section of the procession are a youth and maiden,
who follow, he eagerly, she reluctantly. She turns back; he, in dumb
show, entreats her. She breaks away from him, as if to escape. Enter
from R., second section of procession, headed by singing girls. Following these, Eros, shepherds and shepherdesses, youths carrying hoops
of flowers, etc. The singing girls intercept the flying maiden*]

---

[81] 'Devadasi'. one of Wallace's anachronisms. The term refers to female devotees of
a Hindu god, who dance in that god's temple. Wallace uses the term to mean temple-
dancer.

CHORUS [*singing*]

> Prithee, maiden, why so coy?
> What is here to hurt or harm thee?
> What to vex thee, or annoy?
> What to flutter, or alarm thee?
> Eros—rosy little boy!
> Let his smiling looks disarm thee!

[*Pantomime—the maiden and Eros—the maiden yielding.*
CHORUS [*singing*]

> Cometh here
> One as fair
> As Apollo's self to charm thee!

[*The youth springs forward and clasps the maiden's waist. Instantly the other youths, carrying hoops of flowers, erect over the pair a moving bridal bower*]
CHORUS [*singing*]

> Heigho! Heigho!
> On to the Temple of Daphne!

[*Exeunt all into temple. As the last of the procession vanishes in the temple, enter from R. MALLUCH and BEN-HUR, MALLUCH first*]
MALLUCH Thou art now in the heart of the grove.
BEN-HUR [*pointing to temple*] And this?
MALLUCH The Temple of Apollo.
[BEN-HUR *gazes about him, as if yielding to the fascination of the scene.* MALLUCH *continues*]
MALLUCH Seem not the worshippers a happy throng? Shall we enter?
BEN-HUR [*with start, and shudder of aversion*], O mother! Tirzah! Cursed be the moment, cursed the place, in which I yield myself happy in your loss! [*Recovering himself, glances at* MALLUCH] Come! The stadium!
[*He seizes* MALLUCH *by the arm, and hurries with him towards L. Exeunt* BEN-HUR *and* MALLUCH, *L. Change of Scene*]

Scene 4

[SCENE: *The Fountain of Castalia. Fountain, L.C., as far to the front as practicable, stadium curving from R.2 to L., passing in front of fountain.* DISCOVERED: *The revellers of Scenes 2 and 3 trooping*

*on, escorting the youth and maiden who were the central figures of
Scene 3*]

CHORUS [*singing*]

> Now the blissful rites are said,
> Happy mortal, clasp thy treasure!
> Not by Hymen are ye wed,
> But by Eros, god of Pleasure.
> Haste, and ere his reign is sped,
> Quaff the cup, and tread the measure!

[*The maiden again shows coyness, but joins with the youth at last in
the wild abandon of the dance which follows*]

CHORUS [*singing*]

> For a day,
> While we may,
> Quaff the cup and tread the measure!
> Heigho! Heigho!
> Ho, for the revels of Daphne!

[*A wild dance, led by the Devadasi, in which all the revellers join.
Pressing forward through the throng,* MALLUCH *and* BEN-HUR, *who
have entered a moment earlier at back, appear on the edge of the
course*]

MALLUCH The stadium! Here runs the course [*pointing it out*].

[*Exeunt, R. and L., Devadasi and revellers, save for a group of the
latter, who throw themselves on the sward up stage*]

BEN-HUR But we are late. There is not a wheel in sight.

MALLUCH Patience! We are in time for thy purpose.

BEN-HUR [*turning on him suspiciously*] And what thinkst thou is my
purpose?

MALLUCH Well, thou wouldst have a look at the champions—[BEN-
HUR *assents with a look*] which I can all but promise thee; and I take
it thou wouldst gain some knowledge to aid thee in the laying of
thy wagers.

BEN-HUR Thou hast a shrewd wit. The betting is heavy?

MALLUCH As never before.

BEN-HUR And who the favourite?

MALLUCH The Roman, of course, and at whatever odds thou wilt.

BEN-HUR Hath he such fame?

MALLUCH Prodigious. And his horses—last year they won him in the
Circensian, at the Circus Maximus.

BEN-HUR [*aside*] Then it is Messala beyond doubt.

MALLUCH Thou hast been a frequenter of the circus?

BEN-HUR I have heard the grind of wheels.

MALLUCH In Rome?

BEN-HUR In Rome.

MALLUCH And thou hast never seen this Messala?

BEN-HUR I said not so.

MALLUCH So sure is he of the victor's crown, he hath pledged it already—or so it is reported.

BEN-HUR [*aside*] How like him!

MALLUCH And it is said he hath staked his all upon the issue—both fame and fortune.

BEN-HUR 'His all'? Then, if by chance he were to lose—

MALLUCH His worst enemy could not wish him completer ruin.

BEN-HUR Ah! And thou thinkst there is none to withstand him? But look [*looking and pointing off R.2.*]!

MALLUCH [*looking off R.2.*] The horses of Ilderim the Generous, a sheikh of the desert from beyond Moab.

[*Enter Arabs, leading two of Ilderim's horses*]

BEN-HUR What fire! What action!

[*The horses, led in front of* BEN-HUR *and* MALLUCH, *pass out R.U.E.* BEN-HUR, *following them with admiration, continues to comment*]

BEN-HUR What a pair for yoke-steeds!

MALLUCH I see thou hast knowledge of horseflesh.

[*Exeunt Arabs and horses, L.U.E.*]

BEN-HUR There are but two?

MALLUCH Nay—four. [*He points off R.2.*]

[*Enter, R.2, Arabs, leading the other two of Ilderim's steeds*]

BEN-HUR [*admiringly observing them*] What a pair for trace-mates! Good friend, I have been in the stables of the Emperor, but never saw I horses like these. Why are they not in harness? Will they compete?

[*Exeunt horses, the Arabs leading them, L.U.E. Enter, R.2,* KHALED. *He carries a banner pendant from a spear.* MALLUCH, *instead of replying to* BEN-HUR's *question, calls his attention to* KHALED]

MALLUCH This may tell thee.

KHALED Men of the East and West, hearken!

[*The revellers up stage come forward, and others enter, R. and L. All stand listening to* KHALED]

KHALED The good Sheikh Ilderim giveth greeting. With four horses, sons of the favourites of Solomon the Wise, he hath come up against the best. Needs he most a mighty man to drive them. Whoso will take them to his satisfaction, to him he promiseth enrichment for ever. So saith my master, Sheikh Ilderim the Generous.

[KHALED *passes out L.U.E.*]

REVELLERS [*laughing and applauding*] Lo! Lo! Come away!

[*The revellers scatter, and exeunt R. and L.*]

BEN-HUR [*to* MALLUCH] Why the proclamation, friend?

MALLUCH It means that in the arena the Arab hath no skill. Moreover, his horses are untrained. On the sand and under the saddle they are swift as young eagles and docile as doves. But who is he that will break them to traces?

BEN-HUR Yet it might be done. [*Turning aside*] If it be true that Messala hath staked his all upon this cast! And if, with these, I might contend against him! [*Turning again to* MALLUCH] Thou knowest this Sheikh Ilderim?

MALLUCH I have met him. Why dost thou ask?

BEN-HUR [*after brief pause*] For no good reason. An idle thought. But the course is deserted. Shall we see no more?

MALLUCH The hour is not yet late.

BEN-HUR By this light the day is waning.

MALLUCH It is in the shades of evening they drive. Bide we a little longer. I would have thy judgement on the Roman.

BEN-HUR What? Thou too—

MALLUCH Though no gamester, I have been known to take a hazard. And meanwhile here is something to amuse thine eyes [*looking and pointing off L.U.E.*].

[*Enter, L.U.E., a camel, led by a Ethiopian and bearing in a howdah on its back* BALTHASAR *and* IRAS]

BEN-HUR [*looking*] What have we here?

MALLUCH Some princely visitor from Ophir or the Nile. By the equipage, Pharaoh's self.

BEN-HUR [*seeing* IRAS] And Pharaoh's daughter! But was ever a daughter of the Pharaohs so fair?

[*The camel approaches the fountain and halts*]

BALTHASAR [*to* BEN-HUR] My son! Canst thou tell me if these waters be sweet?

BEN-HUR [*approaching and making reverence*] Like thyself, noble stranger, I am new to these scenes. But here is one who may answer thee, [*Indicating* MALLUCH].

MALLUCH No sweeter waters flow. This is the Fount of Castalia.

IRAS Castalia! I will look upon it.

[*She claps her hands. The Ethiopian comes to the camel's side.* IRAS *speaks to* BALTHASAR]

IRAS Give me the cup.

[*She takes cup from* BALTHASAR, *and, assisted by the Ethiopian, descends from the howdah*]

BEN-HUR [*to himself, observing her*] Is it not Sheba's queen—she that bedazzled Solomon?

IRAS [*tripping towards the fountain, suddenly pauses, hesitates, drawing back her skirt*] So famous a fount, and so careless the keeping! The waters have o'errun the marge.

BEN-HUR [*springing forward*] May not I serve thee?

IRAS If thou wilt.

[*Ben-Hur takes the cup from her hand, and, stooping, fills it at the fountain. The swelling strains of the orchestra indicate the approach of the returning revellers. Their song is heard at a distance, but sounding louder and nearer*]

> Haste! and ere his reign be sped,
> Quaff the cup and tread the measure.

[BEN-HUR, *having filled the cup, presents it to Iras*]

IRAS [*taking the cup, lifts it, smiling upon him, and speaks*] I thank thee.

[*Enter instantly, R. and L., the revellers*]

REVELLERS [*singing*]

> For a day,
> While ye may,
> Quaff the cup and tread the measure!

[*Linking hands, they weave a wild dance about the fountain and the group beside it, continuing their song*]

> Heigho! Heigho!
> Ho, for the revels of Daphne!

VOICES [*without R.2*] Beware! Beware!

REVELLERS Have a care!

[*Sound of approaching hoofs and chariot-wheels without, R.2. Enter, R.2, a chariot drawn by four horses—two white, two black—and driven by* MESSALA. *Behind* MESSALA, *in the chariot, stands* DRUSUS. *The revellers fly before the chariot with shrieks of terror, and exeunt up R. and off L.* IRAS *retreats to the side of the camel, which stands in the middle of the course*]

BEN-HUR [*to* MESSALA, *and springing in front of the chariot*]

Hold! Look where thou goest! Back! Back!

[*He seizes the bridles of the horses and pushes them so far back that* DRUSUS *is tilted out*]

BEN-HUR Dog of a Roman! Carest thou so little for life?

MESSALA [*springing from the chariot*] Drusus, take thou the reins. [*Crossing in front of the chariot, he advances on* BEN-HUR] Who is this, that—

[IRAS *utters a cry of alarm*]

BALTHASAR [*stretching forth his hand from the howdah*] Forbear!

[*As* BEN-HUR *and* MESSALA *come face to face,* MALLUCH *steps between them.* BEN-HUR, *at the same instant, recognizes* MESSALA]

BEN-HUR [*half-aside*] Messala! I thank thee, Heaven!

[*He turns again fiercely towards* MESSALA. MALLUCH *again interposes*]

BALTHASAR [*calling, and leaning from the howdah*] Peace! In God's name! I adjure you both. Stain not thy soul with violence, brave youth—thou that hast so nobly protected the helpless! And thou that hast been saved from crime, take our forgiveness and depart!

[*A brief pause.* BEN-HUR, *restrained by* BALTHASAR'*s words, stands glaring upon* MESSALA, *who gazes as fixedly upon him. But in* MESSALA'*s looks there is doubt and perplexity*]

MESSALA [*with sudden change of manner and a light laugh*] Perpol! Grey hairs have their privilege.

[*He crosses in front of* BEN-HUR *and addresses* IRAS]

MESSALA But if I bow, it is to thee, O fair one! And by our old mother Earth, I saw not you or your camel. Say, then, that I am forgiven. By Pallas, thou art beautiful! I wonder what land can boast herself thy mother? The sun of India is in thine eyes; in the corners of thy mouth Egypt has set her love-signs.

[IRAS, *standing mute beside the camel, casts down her eyes.* BEN-HUR, *watched closely by* MALLUCH, *with difficulty restrains himself.* MESSALA *continues to* IRAS]

MESSALA No word? Cruel as beautiful! Ah, well! Yet, if Apollo get thee not, thou shalt see me again. Not knowing thy country, I cannot name a god to commend thee to; so, by all the gods, I will commend thee to—myself.

[*He again crosses in front of* BEN-HUR, *returning to his chariot*]

BEN-HUR [*In hoarse, half-whispered utterance, striding forward as* MESSALA *passes him*] Stay!

[IRAS *instantly springs to* BEN-HUR'*s side, and lays her hand upon his arm.* MESSALA *as instantly turns again, facing* BEN-HUR]

MESSALA What is thy quarrel with me? Have I seen thee before? Or wouldst thou shine as a protector of beauty?

IRAS [low, to BEN-HUR] For my father's sake! For mine!

MESSALA [again laughing lightly] None the less, fair mistress, thou wilt smile upon me yet.

[He returns, R.C., and remounts his chariot]

IRAS [to BEN-HUR] Heed him not!

BEN-HUR [to himself] Should I let him go?

[MESSALA, taking the reins from DRUSUS, drives towards L.U.E.]

MESSALA [in parting salutation to IRAS] Till another day!

[Exeunt MESSALA and DRUSUS in chariot, L.U.E.]

BEN-HUR [in extreme agitation, stepping apart from IRAS and forgetful of her] O Thou that hast led me to him, teach me now, for Thou knowest my cause, how I may humble the mocker, how bring the spoiler low?

IRAS Thou hast made an enemy—and through thy kindness to a stranger.

BEN-HUR No enemy have I made.

IRAS Then hast thou found one.

BEN-HUR Long lost. And for that it is I who should give thanks. But forgive me now if I take my leave. An urgent duty claimeth me.

IRAS Ah! But at least thou wilt not disdain to make a friend?

BALTHASAR And thou wilt not refuse an old man's blessing? Come near, my son.

[BEN-HUR approaches and bows his head before BALTHASAR, who continues]

BALTHASAR I know not the motive that prompted thee; but well today hast thou served the stranger, and, in the name of the one God, I thank thee. I am Balthasar, the Egyptian. I am far from mine own land, and my power to serve thee is slight; but there is one hard by, in the Orchard of Palms, whose favour may be a buckler to thee. Visit me there, if thou wilt, in the tent of Sheikh Ilderim, whose guests we are, and I promise thee welcome in his name.

BEN-HUR [in surprise] Ilderim? Sheikh Ilderim?

[Enter, L.U.E., ILDERIM, running]

BALTHASAR Look! Even now he is here to confirm my words.

BEN-HUR [aside] Is not this more than mere chance?

ILDERIM What is this I hear? Ye have been in peril? And from the Roman?

BALTHASAR Come! I would have thee know our preserver, [pointing to BEN-HUR as he speaks].

ILDERIM Now, by the splendour of God! [*He grasps* BEN-HUR*'s hands*]

BEN-HUR Put me not to blush, I pray you.

ILDERIM I know not thy name, but, whoever thou art, account me doubly thy debtor. Tell me how I may do thee good, for some return shalt thou have of me, as I am Ilderim the Generous.

BEN-HUR [*aside*] Cometh this fortune from above or below? [*To* IL-DERIM] And thou art Sheikh Ilderim the Generous, known even in the palace of Caesar?

ILDERIM So am I called.

BEN-HUR And thine the horses I saw led by? And for thee the proclamation for a driver I heard but now?

ILDERIM Such proclamation hath been made for me.

BEN-HUR Then, O Sheikh—if, indeed, I have found favour in thy sight—one boon will I beg of thee.

ILDERIM Name it.

BEN-HUR Let me drive thy horses in the games.

ILDERIM [*amazed*] Drive my horses? Thou?

BEN-HUR Think not my claim so presumptuous. Much might I tell thee that I will not, for what were words without proof? But this I say, that in Rome I am not unknown.

ILDERIM In Rome? Then thou, too, art a Roman?

BEN-HUR Arrius, son of the duumvir. On the records of the palaestrae thou wilt find the name, and for these three years the winners in the Circus Maximus have held their crowns at my pleasure. But this is Antioch; and here there is none to vouch for me. So I pray thee, put my skill to the trial. Let me but harness thy racers, and stretch the reins above them. Thou hast eyes; stand by and see.

ILDERIM So might I judge of thy skill, doubtless.

BEN-HUR But thou wouldst have some surety for my will? Listen, then. Thou mayst trust me. I will win for thee—not for thy gold, not yet for glory, but for a prize more precious—revenge.

ILDERIM By Allah! Though I love not thy race, thy face and words take hold on me. But is there no one in Antioch to speak for thee?

BEN-HUR No one.

ILDERIM Yet did I not see thee this day in the house of Simonides?

BEN-HUR [*surprised*] Thou sawest me? It may be so; I was there, though I saw not thee.

ILDERIM Who is this with thee?

[*Crossing in front of* BEN-HUR, *he advances towards* MALLUCH, *who stands* R. MALLUCH *looks warningly on* ILDERIM, *and puts his finger to his lips.* ILDERIM *pauses and utters a low ejaculation aside*]

ILDERIM So!

BEN-HUR [*alluding to* MALLUCH] We met for the first time within the hour. Have I not said? There is none to vouch for me.

ILDERIM [*turning to* BEN-HUR *with decision*] Come. I will take thee at thy word. I will see thee handle my stars of the desert, and tame them to the yoke, if thou canst. [*He offers his hand, which* BEN-HUR *grasps warmly*] Meanwhile, thou shalt abide with me, along with these whom thou hast befriended.

BEN-HUR But I need not so trespass upon thy bounty.

ILDERIM 'Bounty'?

BEN-HUR Thy dowar is near. My days I may spend with thee, but the khan will serve me well as a lodging.

ILDERIM The khan? While the tents of Ilderim are spread?

BEN-HUR Truly, I would rather it were so till it be proven that I am no impostor.

ILDERIM What modesty is this? And in a Roman! [*He turns to* IRAS] Mayhap, fair daughter, he will come at thy bidding.

IRAS [*stretching out her hand to* BEN-HUR] Wilt thou not?

[BEN-HUR *hesitates for an instant longer; then, stepping quickly forward, he takes her hand and bows over it, lifting it to his lips*]

ILDERIM Come, It is agreed. To the dowar!

[*Enter instantly, R. and L., the revellers (including Devadasi). They fill front of stage, whirling in a wild dance to the music of the song, which herein follows.* IRAS, *assisted by* BEN-HUR, *remounts the howdah*]

REVELLERS [*singing*]

> Spin! Arachne, spin!
> Gladness and madness and woe!
> For, howsoever the game begin,
> Ever it endeth so.
> Burning madness and freezing woe—
> Tempest and frost and fire—
> These, all these, shall the mortal know,
> That meeteth his fate by the fountain's flow,
> And findeth his heart's desire.
> This is the price that his soul shall pay
> For love, that liveth a night and a day!
> And this is the path that all must go
> That drink of the wells of Daphne.
> Spin! Arachne, spin!

[*Through the evolutions of the dancers, the camel is seen departing, towards L.U.E., led by the Ethiopian;* BEN-HUR *and* ILDERIM *walking on either side.* BEN-HUR, *as he goes, looks up at* IRAS, *who smiles down upon him.* MALLUCH, R., *outside the circle of dancers, watches the departing group. Curtain*]

ACT IV

Scene 1

[SCENE: *Interior of the tent of* ILDERIM. *Tent-flap at back raised, giving view of landscape—curtains R. and L., beyond which glimpses are had of other compartments of the pavilion—rugs, divans, and other suitable furniture and furnishings.* DISCOVERED: ILDERIM, IRAS, *and female slaves—they form a group in the doorway of tent, all looking outward. Beyond, in the open, Arabs come and go, running, at intervals—suggestions of a crowd—shouting and cheering heard at curtain. Those in the doorway gaze out eagerly and excitedly—*IL-DERIM *stands a little in advance of the group, just outside the tent-door*]

ILDERIM [*at curtain, shouting*] Back! Stand back! Give him free course. He hath them. Look! The four as one! By the splendour of God, he hath them!

[*Cheering without, at back, off L.*]

ILDERIM But now for the turning! Will he hold them?

BEN-HUR [*shouting without, at back, off L.*] Ho, Atair! Rigel! Antares![82]

ILDERIM They come—and shoulder to shoulder.

[*Cheering without, at back, off L., rising, swelling, and sounding nearer. Trampling of hoofs and rush of chariot-wheels.* BEN-HUR *sweeps past the tent-opening in chariot, driving the four bays. He crosses from L. to R. A crowd of Arabs follow in his course, running and cheering*]

ILDERIM Now, by God's splendour! [*He turns to the women behind him and cries*] Have ready the leben![83] We will feast tonight! [*He turns and rushes out, shouting*] Enough! Unyoke them! The work is done!

[*Exeunt the female slaves through curtains, R.* IRAS *turns from the doorway and comes down*]

IRAS What strength he hath! What mastery! And what conceit in his mastery! It were a mercy to break him of it, as he hath broken the horses of Ilderim.

ILDERIM [*reappearing outside door, and calling back*] Say that I await him! Let him not delay!

---

[82] Ilderim's four chariot horses are named for stars: Antares in the constellation of Scorpio, Rigel in Orion, Atair in Aquilae, and Aldebaran in Taurus.

[83] An Arab beverage made from soured milk.

[*At a sign from him, slaves, who accompany him, lower the tent-flaps.*
He enters the tent, and comes down towards IRAS *exultantly*]

ILDERIM Hast thou such horses on the Nile?

IRAS And has thou such drivers in the desert?

ILDERIM Thou hast a woman's eyes—but thy father—he hath not yet arisen?

IRAS Dost thou think to charm him with horsemanship? Leave him to his sleep, and his visions.

[*Enter* BEN-HUR *through tent-door, C. He is in racing garb, and flushed from his exercise*]

ILDERIM [*meeting* BEN-HUR *with outstretched hands*] Come!

BEN-HUR Well, thou hast seen. What sayest thou?

ILDERIM Son of Arrius, I account the day already won. I had hoped, but never had I believed, that thou couldst make good thy words. By the splendour of God! I have known kings who governed millions of men, and yet could not win the respect of a horse. And that thou, in four short days, shouldst have so tamed to thy hand these, the kings of their kind—

BEN-HUR Their blood is royal, else my task had been hopeless. But now, Sheikh, no more practice. Whether for good or ill, their training is finished. Tonight, rest.

ILDERIM For horse and man!

BEN-HUR And tomorrow—

IRAS Victory!

[BEN-HUR *and* ILDERIM *turn towards* IRAS. BEN-HUR *bows in acknowledgement of her speech*]

ILDERIM [*to* IRAS] Thou hast taken the word from my lips.

IRAS [*with low courtesy, half-mockingly*] I pray thee forgive me, most noble Arrius, that I intrude with a stolen phrase, and one that must be stale to thee.

BEN-HUR [*taking her hand and bending over it*] Nay, but forgive me, that I saw thee not. I thank thee for thy wish.

IRAS To one who hath known the praise of Rome, how stupid must seem the compliments of a barbarian [*again with low courtesy*]!

BEN-HUR Thou art merry. [*He turns to* ILDERIM *and again addresses him*] Yet one more word. [*To* IRAS] I pray thee, pardon me.

IRAS [*nettled, with a toss of the head*] As often as thou wilt.

BEN-HUR [*to* ILDERIM] Again, today, there was a stranger in the field.

ILDERIM [*startled*] Another?

BEN-HUR Khaled hath him in charge, and I have asked that he be brought here, for I would view him more closely. But whether or not I know him, let me warn thee once more, good Sheikh: from this till the trial look well to what thou hast, for there is not treachery to which the Roman will not stoop.

IRAS Thou canst say so of thy countrymen?

[BEN-HUR, *turning towards* IRAS, *answers her only with a bow. He continues to address* ILDERIM]

BEN-HUR [*to* ILDERIM] Guard thy horses both by night and by day.

ILDERIM By the splendour of God, I will set a hedge of spears about them.

[*Enter, through tent-door, C., Khaled, the Arab, who appeared as herald in the Grove of Daphne*]

ILDERIM Ha! Khaled!

KHALED The stranger—I have brought him.

ILDERIM Let us see him.

[*Exit* KHALED]

BEN-HUR [*to* IRAS] Wilt thou remain?

IRAS And why not? Since thou hast proven me to be invisible!

[*Re-enter* KHALED, *bringing* DRUSUS]

KHALED [*to* DRUSUS] Enter! Move quickly!

DRUSUS [*to* KHALED] I thank thee, good fellow, for thy courtesy. [*To* ILDERIM] The Sheikh Ilderim—if I mistake not?

ILDERIM Welcome—if thou comest as a friend.

DRUSUS [*seeing* IRAS] Ah! And the fair Egyptian!

[*He bows with the exaggerated politeness of the Roman exquisite*]

IRAS [*aside*] Where hath he seen me?

DRUSUS [*to* ILDERIM] Most illustrious Sheikh, oft have I heard of Arab hospitality, but truly—if one may say it—thy people in their good offices are a trifle—hm!—profuse.

ILDERIM Thou hast some errand? Declare it.

DRUSUS An errand? Surely—else were I not here. [*Aside*] Would I were elsewhere! Briefly, then, I am commissioned to crave thy advice—in the matter of a wager.

ILDERIM A wager?

DRUSUS A question having arisen, in itself of no great import, but somewhat curious, and now of pecuniary interest to the extent of several sesterces.

ILDERIM And what question?

DRUSUS Touching the name of thy driver. [ILDERIM *and* BEN-HUR *exchange glances*] Now it is commonly held—indeed, it is so stated in the application for entry—that he is called Arrius, and is a Roman. But a certain noble youth hath laid odds—

[BEN-HUR *walks down and stands beside* DRUSUS. DRUSUS *pauses, and, turning, looks at him*]

DRUSUS Begging thy pardon—

BEN-HUR Say on.

DRUSUS Mayhap I address the party?

BEN-HUR To thy purpose.

DRUSUS [*ill at ease, but attempting to preserve his show of nonchalance*] I say, it is wagered by a certain noble youth—

BEN-HUR [*interrupting him*] Thou art a friend of Messala's. I saw thee with him in his chariot at the Fountain of Castalia.

[IRAS *gives a sign of comprehension*]

DRUSUS [*as if moved to deny the charge*] I?

BEN-HUR And it is in his interest thou art here. Plain speaking were best.

DRUSUS H'm! Ha! Why, as thou sayest—[*Aside*] Jupiter, thou aidest the brave. Help me now. As thou sayest, plain speaking mayhap were best. But were it also the safest?

BEN-HUR So thou speakest the truth.

DRUSUS [*to* ILDERIM] I have thy pledge?

ILDERIM Thou hast it.

DRUSUS Then, in brevity, this was the half of mine errand: to learn if thou wouldst avow thyself to be rightfully called Arrius—[*He pauses for an instant and glances at* BEN-HUR] And since to that thou hast no reply to make—

BEN-HUR None.

DRUSUS I will even acquit myself of the other half.

[*He crosses and bows before* IRAS]

DRUSUS Adorable princess! My friend Messala sends thee his compliments upon thy beauty, and humbly begs that in the circus tomorrow thou wilt strengthen his heart by wearing these, his colours.

[*He presents to her a knot of ribbon, scarlet and gold, which she takes half-unconsciously, in her amazement*]

BEN-HUR Insolent!

[*He makes a stride towards* DRUSUS, *but instantly restrains himself*]

DRUSUS [*turning quickly*] By *thy* leave, noble Sheikh, I will take mine leave.

[*Exit through door C.* KHALED *permits him to pass, but looks inquiringly at* ILDERIM]

ILDERIM [*in wrathful amazement*] Heardst thou ever the like?

BEN-HUR Yet harm him not. He hath thy pledge.

ILDERIM And lest I forget it—[*To* KHALED] See him beyond the bounds, and quickly.

[KHALED *springs out through tent-door C.*]

ILDERIM Oh, spake not there Rome itself, its arrogance and its impudence! Son of Arrius, hardly can I believe thou art a Roman.

[*He rushes out through door C.*]

BEN-HUR [*to* IRAS] And thou hast taken his gift!

IRAS Why not?

BEN-HUR Canst thou not see the insult in his compliments?

IRAS What is that to thee?

[*She places the knot of ribbon against her breast coquettishly and defiantly.* BEN-HUR *turns away with an offended gesture*]

IRAS Hear and behold him, Isis! Thou talkest like my father.

BEN-HUR Would, indeed, that I speak like him! Then, perhaps, I could win thee to listen.

IRAS But tell me. What is thy feud with Messala. And what this question about thy name?

BEN-HUR Who told thee I have a feud with Messala?

IRAS Thou—at the Fountain of Castalia—not only by look, but by word. Thou hast met him before. He is noble, is he not?

BEN-HUR It is so said of him.

IRAS And rich?

BEN-HUR Yes.

IRAS And wicked?

BEN-HUR That also is in his list of attractions.

IRAS [*laughing*] Now I know thou hast some grudge against him. He hath crossed thee—in love, mayhap.

BEN-HUR [*after slight pause*] Yes, in love the most holy. [*Iras laughs lightly*] Let me hope thou wouldst not laugh, didst thou know.

IRAS So solemn! But will it please thee so much if I yield this little trophy?

BEN-HUR It will please me.

IRAS Only that?

BEN-HUR What more should I say? It is for thine own sake I ask it.

IRAS And not for thine? Go! It is not true. Thou wouldst play the tyrant, and I will not humour thee.

BEN-HUR I beseech thee—

IRAS No!

BEN-HUR Then if I confess that it is for my sake also?

IRAS Oh, rare condescension!

BEN-HUR That it hurts me like a blow to see thee so lightly endure such disrespect. Put it away! For thou shalt—[*He moves as if to seize the badge from her hand*]

IRAS [*checking him, with sudden haughtiness*] Oh! Oh!

[*Enter through door C.*, MALLUCH, *letter in hand*]

MALLUCH [*saluting Ben-Hur*] My master Simonides sends thee greeting. And I have here a letter for the Sheikh Ilderim. Canst thou tell me where I may find him?

BEN-HUR [*astonished*] Thy master? Simonides? Art thou not he who was with me in the Grove of Daphne? [MALLUCH *inclines his head*] And thou art in the service of Simonides?

[*Enter hastily, door C.*, ILDERIM]

ILDERIM Ha! Malluch! A letter from thy master [*taking letter which* MALLUCH *extends to him*]?

BEN-HUR And ye two know each other?

[ILDERIM *smiles, stroking his beard*]

ILDERIM Doth it surprise thee that one who cometh in Roman garb should meet with distrust from those not Romans; or that they should lay their wits together to prove him, but conceding him their faith? But content thee. If thou hast been spied upon, all that hath been learned is to thy credit. And listen now to this.

[*Reads letter*] 'O Friend, assure thyself first of a place in my inner heart. Of the youth in thy dowar,[84] calling himself the son of Arrius, I have already written, assuring thee of his trustworthiness. With him must I now speak on a matter of such concern that it may not be entrusted to writing; wherefore tonight I will make bold to visit him in thy hospitable tent. To thee and all thine, peace. What should I be, O my friend, but thy friend. Simonides.'

BEN-HUR [*astonished*] Simonides would speak with me?

ILDERIM So he saith.

[BEN-HUR *looks inquiringly at* MALLUCH]

MALLUCH With his daughter, he is now upon the road, and should be near at hand.

BEN-HUR [*with increased astonishment*] With his daughter?

[MALLUCH *turns to* ILDERIM]

MALLUCH There is no answer, noble Sheikh?

ILDERIM None, save that they shall be most welcome.

[*Exit* MALLUCH, *door C.*]

IRAS [*aside*] So! There is a daughter? [*To* BEN-HUR] Thou art in high favour, it seems. Both wealth and beauty come to pay thee their court. How long hast thou known this merchant Simonides and his—daughter?

---

[84] See n. 9.

[*Enter* BALTHASAR, *through curtains, L.* BEN-HUR *hastens to his side and supports him*]

BEN-HUR Good Balthasar!

BALTHASAR My son!

BEN-HUR [*assisting him to divan, L. C.*] Thou hast slept? Thou art refreshed?

BALTHASAR [*sinking on divan*] And thou hast been at thy practice? What goodly gifts are youth and strength! How precious beyond compare!

BEN-HUR When put to worthy use. Truly, venerable father, in thinking upon thy life's quest, and the steadfastness of thy faith and thy purpose, I ask myself if I be not as the fool who turneth aside from following a star to grasp at a bauble.

BALTHASAR Thou speakest from the heart?

BEN-HUR As my soul liveth, thy words of last night abide with me, and gladly would I hear more.

[IRAS *shows weariness and ill-concealed disdain*]

BALTHASAR And gladly will I tell thee more. And gladly, too, if it might be, would I have thee for a companion on the journey that I soon must take.

ILDERIM Wilt thou leave us, then?

BALTHASAR One more stage hath my pilgrimage. Long hath been my time of waiting and wandering since I fared with Gaspar and Melchior, and, led by the star, we three, from the three ends of the earth, found in the manger of Bethlehem, the Holy Child, before whose throne all kings shall bow. Thirty and more years ago! But never hath my faith wavered. And now the Child is a man. Soon, if ever, He must declare himself, and stand forth and reign. And He will. A voice telleth me the hour is at hand.

BEN-HUR And where now wilt thou seek Him?

BALTHASAR Where but in the land of that people to whom the promise was first given. There, on the slopes of Galilee or by the Jordan, shall I find Him. [*As if inspired*] He is there now. Standing in a door, or on a hilltop, only this evening He saw the sun set, one day nearer the time when He himself shall become the Light of the World.

BEN-HUR [*reverently*] May thy faith be confirmed!

ILDERIM [*with equal reverence*] The one God grant it!

[*Enter door C.,* KHALED. *He holds aside the tent-flap. Enter* MALLUCH, *instantly following* KHALED. *Voices are heard without*]

BALTHASAR [*to* ILDERIM] Ye have visitors.

[ILDERIM *goes to door of tent*]

BEN-HUR [*grasping* BALTHASAR's *hand*] We will speak of this again.

ILDERIM [*speaking out through door C.*] Enter—in Allah's name!
    [*Enter* SIMONIDES *and* ESTHER *at back in palanquin.* SIMONIDES
    is borne into the tent by slaves, and placed on divan, R.C. ESTHER
    closely follows]

ILDERIM And may his name be praised, I have thee at last beneath my
roof!

SIMONIDES [*returning* ILDERIM's *greeting*] Peace be with thee!

ILDERIM [*greeting* ESTHER] Gentle daughter!

SIMONIDES [*to* BEN-HUR] God's blessing on thee!

ILDERIM Good Simonides, this is Balthasar, of whom thou hast heard
me speak.

BALTHASAR [*to* SIMONIDES] The peace of the Lord be with thee!

SIMONIDES And with thee!

ILDERIM [*presenting* IRAS] And this, his daughter—and this, good my
friends, is Esther, the daughter of Simonides. [IRAS *surveys* ESTHER
haughtly but curiously] And now are we all known, one to another.

SIMONIDES Not yet. For he whom ye have known as Arrius, and a
Roman, is neither a Roman nor Arrius.
    [*General surprise*]

ILDERIM Not a Roman?

SIMONIDES But of mine own race, and by name and title Judah, son
of Ithamar, Prince of the House of Hur.

IRAS [*half aside*] A prince!

ILDERIM Said I not, in my heart—

BEN-HUR [*almost incredulous*] I am acknowledged then?

SIMONIDES Thank not me, but this girl at my side [*half turning to*
ESTHER, *who drops her face*]. And after her, thine enemy. Messala hath
recognized thee. Thy name is posted this night on all the walls of
Antioch.

IRAS [*aside*] What strange romance is this?

SIMONIDES [*to the company*] The history of the young man and all the
wrongs he hath suffered is for another telling. Now, son of Hur
[*turning to* BEN-HUR]—thou hast a claim for justice—a mightier
never went to man or Heaven; but beg it not, nor seek it with the
strong hand. View it as a commodity in the market, and forthwith—
purchase it.

BEN-HUR [*bitterly*] Purchase it? And wherewith?

SIMONIDES With gold. What else?

BEN-HUR It is true the Roman left me not a beggar, but as against
the wealth of my foes—

SIMONIDES Thou canst buy them and sell them—thou canst bid against Caesar himself. And since wealth is a means to every end, there is no dream of thy heart that thou canst not now realize, for thou art the richest subject in the world.

BEN-HUR Do not mock me.

SIMONIDES Esther, give me the papers. [*She gives him papers. To* BEN-HUR] Thou hast heard of me as thy father's friend. I was more, and yet less. Together we traded by land and sea, and our gains were as great as the Lord's bounty. But he was the principal; I, but the agent. All I had was his while he lived. All I have is thine now. Take, and read! [*He offers* BEN-HUR *a paper*] Or, if thou hast not patience for the items, read at least the summing up. [BEN-HUR, *with gesture, declines the paper*] No? Then, Malluch, do thou read.

MALLUCH [*taking the paper, reads*] 'Moneys in hand, and estimated value of ships, camels, horses, warehouses, and merchandise in transit and in store, held by me, Simonides, in trust for the Prince of Hur—six hundred and seventy and three talents.'

[*He returns the paper to* SIMONIDES. *General amazement*]

ILDERIM Six hundred talents!

IRAS A kingdom's worth!

SIMONIDES To that add the palace of Hur in Jerusalem, purchased since the list was prepared; and where thou wilt find thine old nurse, Amrah, installed as keeper.

[*He offers* BEN-HUR *a second paper, the deed with seal, shown in Act III, scene* 1]

BEN-HUR [*incredulous, taking the paper half-unconsciously*] And this is true that thou tellest me?

SIMONIDES Speak I falsely, Esther? [*To* BEN-HUR, *laying his hand on* ESTHER's *head as he speaks*] But again let me confess it—to me thou owest no thanks. Here is the monitor, whose voice—

ESTHER No! No! Thou shalt not say it! [*To* BEN-HUR] If ever a moment he hath doubted or questioned what was his duty, it was but for my sake. Freely doth he yield it, and with thanks to Heaven that he can restore to thee thy right.

BEN-HUR Have I so railed against my fate, and doubted the Most High, and cursed my kind, and yet such marvels were in store for me! And still such goodness exists on earth! Then, if thou dost not speak in jest, one thing, and one only, of all thou hast tendered me will I accept—the house of my fathers. That shall be mine. [*He presses the deed against his breast*] But all besides—and serve me now as a witness, Sheik-Ilderim—all else of which these papers make

account—ships, houses, merchandise, moneys—if right in them I
have, to thee, O Simonides, I give them back, and seal them with
loving gratitude to thee and thine for ever.

ILDERIM Worthily and nobly said!

SIMONIDES I see thy spirit, son of Hur; and I am grateful that thou
hast been sent to me, such as thou art. But I may not accept. Esther,
thou hast yet another paper.

[ESTHER *rises, half turns away for a moment, then tremulously but
resolutely hands to her father a third paper.* SIMONIDES, *taking the
paper, offers it to* BEN-HUR, *who wonderingly accepts it*]

SIMONIDES Thou hast not yet all the account.

BEN-HUR [*reads*] 'Statement of the servants of Hur: Amrah, keeper of
the palace—in Jerusalem; Simonides, steward, in Antioch'—[*He
pauses, then reads slowly, and with emotion*] 'Esther, daughter of Simonides'—[*He looks at* ESTHER, *whose head is bent upon her breast*]
Servants?

SIMONIDES Slaves, should I have said? For thy father's slave was I.

BEN-HUR [*glancing at Esther*] It cannot be.

SIMONIDES Again, Esther, wilt thou vouch for me?

BEN-HUR [*with burst of emotion*] Then do I free thee.

SIMONIDES That canst thou not; for look, young master, the awl-mark
in mine ear [*showing it*]! A slave for ever—by the law of Moses!

BEN-HUR [*with increased emotion*] Then, if serve me thou wilt, may I
not name thy place and reward? And thou, Esther [*he crosses to
her*]—for, in reverence, may I not call thee so?—upon thee, at least,
there is no ban that I may not break. Dost thou think I could hear
thy name coupled with terms of servitude? Or that I could rob thee
of thy patrimony? Hear now what I will do! I will open again the
doors of that darkened house in Jerusalem; there, where my fathers
dwelt, thy father shall dwell, the steward of all I possess. [*He turns
and addresses Simonides*] Wilt thou accept the trust? [SIMONIDES *bows
his head.* BEN-HUR *continues to* ESTHER] And thou, in place of that
Tirzah whom I have lost, shall be the sunbeam to lighten its
gloom—no servant, but dear to me, and as honoured as mine own
father's daughter. Shall it not be so?

[ESTHER *stands with bowed head, agitated*]

SIMONIDES [*leaning forward, regarding her anxiously*] Speak, daughter of
Rachel!

ESTHER [*to* BEN-HUR, *struggling with emotion*] Oh, think me not un-
mindful of thy great goodness, nor judge of me unkindly; but, if
answer thee I must—

BEN-HUR Thou canst not refuse?

ESTHER Where my father goeth, there will I go; and where he abideth, there will I abide. But since thou canst not change his condition, I pray thee seek not to change mine. Let me be to thee but as thy servant.

> [*Drawing back, with low obeisance and bowed head, she suddenly turns, casts herself down beside her father, and, embracing him, buries her face in his bosom.* SIMONIDES *caresses her approvingly and pityingly.* BEN-HUR *gazes upon her*]

IRAS [*to* BEN-HUR, *half aside*] Thou art answered.

> [*Then, turning away, with a low laugh, she goes to door C. and parts the curtains, but pauses, looking back with mocking smile*]

ILDERIM Prince of Hur, I give thee joy. And to thee, Simonides, and to thy daughter, I give praise for honesty all but passing the virtue of man. And now—for I know that ye have found in each other not master and servant, but friend and friend—ye shall sit together at my table, and break bread, and seal your friendship after the fashion of the desert.

SIMONIDES That much will I not refuse thee, good Ilderim; but my stay must be brief.

ILDERIM Thou wilt not return before morning? The sun hath already set.

SIMONIDES But the moon hath risen. And this night must I be again in Antioch about my young master's business.

ILDERIM I will not contend with thee.

> [*He claps his hands. Enter, through curtains, R., female slaves*]

ILDERIM Come then—the meal is spread.

> [*Exit* IRAS *through door C., with a backward glance at* BEN-HUR *who alone observes her departure.* ILDERIM *continues without break*]

ILDERIM And wherein my fare falleth short, ye shall have for reflection the talk of one who hath seen strange things [*indicating* BALTHASAR]. Good Balthasar, wilt thou lead the way?

> [*Exit* BALTHASAR *through curtains, R. Exit, following* BALTHASAR, SIMONIDES, *borne by slaves.* ILDERIM *addresses* ESTHER]

ILDERIM Thou wilt sit with us? See to her, Malluch.

> [*Exit through curtains, R.,* ESTHER, *attended by* MALLUCH. *Exeunt through curtains, R., the female slaves.* ILDERIM *addresses* BEN-HUR, *who stands apart, as if in a waking dream*]

ILDERIM And thou—

BEN-HUR Give me a moment's grace, I pray thee.

ILDERIM I understand thee. Great good fortune, like evil, doth oft for a time seem past belief. But assure thyself—it is real. Allah grant thee wisdom to use it well.

BEN-HUR [*echoing his words*] 'To use it well'.

ILDERIM We shall expect thee.

[*Exit* ILDERIM *through curtains, R.*]

BEN-HUR Wealth, boundless wealth, and 'wealth is a means to every end'. Spake he the truth? Means, then, to compass justice and vengeance not only for myself, but—dare I think of it?—mayhap for my mother, my sister—my whole race. Oh, vision too dazzling! And Esther—that to her I should owe it all! How sweet her face, how pure, how fair! Like a lily against the other's gorgeous beauty. And yet, were that other at the feast, would I linger?

[IRAS *is suddenly heard singing 'The Lament'.* BEN-HUR *pauses, arrested by the sound*]

BEN-HUR The nightingale! [*The song of* IRAS *swells and sinks*] Of what—for whom—doth she sing? [IRAS *executes a brilliant passage*] Splendour—and power—and passion!

[*Enter, door C., the Ethiopian. He stands dumb, just within the door.* BEN-HUR *turns to him*]

BEN-HUR Well? [*The Ethiopian extends to him the knot of ribbon last seen in* IRAS's *hands*] For me? [*He seizes it eagerly*] The badge of Messala! She hath resigned it—and at my bidding! [*He turns again to the Ethiopian*] And she awaits me?

[*The Ethiopian bows.* BEN-HUR *comes down, communing with himself in extreme agitation*]

BEN-HUR Since she hath so stooped from her pride, can I do less than acknowledge her graciousness? [*Speaking quickly over his shoulder to the Ethiopian*] Say that I come.

[*Exit instantly the Ethiopian, door C.*]

BEN-HUR Can I do less? Yet stay! [*He turns towards door*] The word is spoken. How shall I make my excuses here [*looking towards curtains, R.*]? I, for whom the feast was spread? What blackness of ingratitude? But may I not return—and before I am missed?

[*He crosses towards R., and pauses for an instant, as if listening to voices beyond curtains*]

BEN-HUR Balthasar telleth his tale again; and I should be there to hear. [*The song of* IRAS *again rises without*] But oh, thou rarer voice!

[*He goes quickly to door C., parts the curtains; then hesitates for an instant*]

BEN-HUR Forgive—

[*The last word is uttered in a half-whisper of entreaty towards curtains, R. Instantly he whirls and vanishes, door C. Stage dark. Through the period of darkness, the singing of Iras is heard. It concludes just before the lights are turned on for following scene*]

Scene 2

[SCENE: *Orchard of Palms—lake and grove of palms by moonlight. Roadway crossing from R. to L., front.* DISCOVERED: IRAS, *reclining on trunk of fallen palm, L.C. In one drooping hand she holds a lyre; near her,* BEN-HUR, *half reclining, leans towards her*]

BEN-HUR Hast thou no songs but those of the Nile?

IRAS Of what should I sing? Of Judaea's holy river? Thou seest—I know much of thy land. I might even count thee its hills and its dales, and tell thee the names of its villages.

BEN-HUR It is a fair land.

IRAS To its own people. But now I understand thee.

BEN-HUR In truth?

IRAS And thy interest in my father's tale. Shall I read thy thoughts?

BEN-HUR If thou hast such power.

IRAS I mean not thy thoughts of the moment, but those that lie deeper, nearest thy heart.

BEN-HUR That were witchcraft—

IRAS Last night, when my father rehearsed his story, a strange light shone in thine eyes; today again it shone there; and thus do I interpret it. When he that is to be King of the Jews shall come to his own, he will have need of soldiers. And thou hast been bred to arms. [BEN-HUR *turns away his face*] Look not away! Thou hast visions of prowess—of leadership—of honours won in his cause—perhaps—who knoweth?—of dominion at the King's right hand.

BEN-HUR [*aside*] Art thou, indeed, a sorceress?

IRAS Have I not read thee aright?

BEN-HUR And if a man were to dream such a dream, would he be wise in thy sight or foolish?

IRAS And why wouldst thou know?

BEN-HUR [*with passion*] Because, for all thy mocking smile, thou surely wast born to inspire great deeds; because, when I look in thine eyes and listen to thy voice, all things seem possible; and, given but a word from thee, earth would have no horizon that could bound my hopes. [*He leans nearer, and his arm enclasps her waist*] O Egypt! Egypt!

Heaven that have given thee so fair a form cannot have denied thee a soul. 'Thy lips are like a thread of scarlet.' I love thee.

IRAS Now it is thou that mockest.

BEN-HUR I love thee. Say that for thee I may strive in the lofty path thou hast painted; then, if the King hath crowns in his gift, one will I win, and place it—here [*he kisses her upon the brow*].

IRAS And all this thou wouldst do for me?

BEN-HUR For thee.

IRAS And for me only? Not for the glory or the favour of any other, human or divine?

BEN-HUR May not one love thee and yet own allegiance to duty?

IRAS 'Duty'?

BEN-HUR To his people? To Heaven?

IRAS Listen. There was once a woman who was loved—one only—a queen of my race. For her a great soldier forgot his duty, forsook his people, forswore his gods. For her he dared, and was fain not to win kingdoms, but to cast them away. Ah; that in truth was love—and of such a love I dream. Wouldst thou do as much for me?

[BEN-HUR *stands speechless, torn with conflicting emotions. He glances backward*]

IRAS No! Already thine eyes turn backward. And a man's whole heart will I have, or—none. Go! Thou art waited for.

[*Turning from him, she claps her hands. A shallop glides on from L. In the stern sits the Ethiopian, wielding a single oar*]

BEN-HUR And where wilt thou go?

IRAS Wherever the bark may take me. [*Stepping into the boat, she throws herself down in the bow*] Farewell!

BEN-HUR [*with sudden mad resolve, catching up the harp, which she has left on the bank*] Stay! Thou shalt not go alone.

IRAS Ah! But thy duty?

BEN-HUR [*passionately*] Already hast thou charmed me from it past forgiveness and past return.

IRAS And Heaven?

BEN-HUR [*stepping into boat*] Is where thou art. Now, if a spell thou knowest, O Egypt, to slay remorse and stifle care, take thy harp and weave it.

[*Sinking on the thwart facing her, he extends the harp, which she takes, laughing in low tones lightly. The Ethiopian wields the oar. The shallop glides off R. As it vanishes, the chords of the harp are heard, fading in the distance. Enter L.I. MALLUCH. He walks slowly,*] *looking backwards. Enter, L.I.* SIMONIDES *and* ESTHER, *in litter borne by slaves.* ILDERIM *walks beside litter*]

SIMONIDES [*speaking as litter enters*] Strange words, and well worth the pondering. But the hour grows late, and we take thee too far. [*Litter halts, L.C.*]

MALLUCH Shall I go ahead, good master?

SIMONIDES Go. We follow thee.

[MALLUCH *exits* R. SIMONIDES *continues to* ILDERIM]

SIMONIDES And now get thee back to thy guests. It well may be that in Balthasar thou entertainest a true prophet—but of that we will talk hereafter.

ILDERIM Ye will not have a brace of spears for convoy?

SIMONIDES What, within sight of the city walls? Say to our young master we were sorry not to await his return.

ILDERIM It is he who will most regret it.

SIMONIDES Doubtless he hath good reason—which concerneth not us. Each to his own, and all to God, who hath us in His keeping. Peace be with thee [*offering his hand*].

ILDERIM [*taking his hand*] A safe journey.

[*The song of* IRAS *rises in the distance.* ESTHER *glances out across the lake.* ILDERIM, *after a brief pause, speaks*]

ILDERIM It is the Egyptian. She is abroad upon the water.

[*The song continues, the group listening.* ILDERIM *again speaks*]

ILDERIM Shall not youth have its day?

[ESTHER *buries her face in her hands*]

SIMONIDES My daugher, thou art ill.

ESTHER No, no!

SIMONIDES We tarry too long. The air is chill. Give thee good-night.

ILDERIM Good-night! And Allah avert all evil!

[ILDERIM *turns, and exit, L.I. The litter, at a signal from* SI-MONIDES, *moves towards* R.]

ESTHER [*imploringly*] Yet stay—my father!

SIMONIDES And wherefore?

[*The litter halts,* R., *near entrance.* ESTHER, *turning her head, looks out across water*]

SIMONIDES What wouldst thou see? Oh, look not!

[*The shallop, now farther from the shore, drifts on in the full glare of the moon, masked by foliage on bank till it approaches* C. IRAS *still reclines in the bow, one hand trailing in the water.* BEN-HUR, *grasping her other hand, inclines towards her in an attitude of rapt devotion. The Ethiopian, as before, in the stern, slowly wielding his oar.* ESTHER *utters a moan, and covers her eyes with her hands*]

SIMONIDES Malluch! On!

[*The litter, with its bearers and occupants, moves off R.; the shallop, with its occupants, C. Quick Curtain*]

ACT V

Scene 1

[SCENE: *Exterior and entrance of the circus at Antioch. On the wall, near C., a banner, displaying the programme of the race (see novel, book 5, chapter 10*[85]*).* DISCOVERED: *A procession entering from R., to music, and passing off through great arched gateway, L.I.— citizens (men and women) crowding, R. front—another smaller group L. front. In the latter group, half-concealed,* DRUSUS. *As the last of the procession disappears into circus, the citizens press forward, thronging stage. The main current of the crowd follows the procession, flowing in through gateway, but there are stragglers, who, lingering and gathering in groups, give diversity to the movement.*

Note: Those that exeunt into circus cross at back and reappear as newcomers when required. Many of the citizens wear knots of ribbon—the Roman faction displaying the colours of MESSALA *(scarlet and gold); the Jewish faction the colours of* BEN-HUR *(white)*]

CITIZENS [*shouting as procession vanishes*] Lo! Lo!

1ST CITIZEN [*shouting*] Maxentius! Long live the Consul Maxentius!

2ND CITIZEN [*shouting*] Long live Antioch! Long live the games!

1ST CITIZEN [*shouting*] Long live Messala! The Roman! The Roman!

CITIZENS [*Roman faction, shouting*] Messala! Messala! The Roman!

2ND CITIZEN [*shouting*] Ben-Hur! Ben-Hur!

CITIZENS [*Jewish faction, shouting*] Long live Ben-Hur!

[*Enter with crowd, which continues to pour on from R.,* CECILIUS, *with two or three Roman youths*]

---

[85] 'I. A four of Lysippus the Corinthian—two greys, a bay, and a black; entered at Alexandria last year, and again at Corinth, where they were winners. Lysippus, driver. Colour, yellow.

II. A four of Messala of Rome—two white, two black; victors of the Circensian as exhibited in the Circus Maximus last year. Messala, driver. Colours, scarlet and gold.

III. A four of Cleanthes the Athenian—three grey, one bay; winners at the Isthmian last year. Cleanthes, driver. Colour, green.

IV. A four of Dicaeus the Byzantine—two black, one grey, one bay; winners this year at Byzantium. Dicaeus, driver. Colour, black.

V. A four of Admetus the Sidonian—all greys. Thrice entered at Caesarea and thrice victors. Admetus, driver. Colour, blue.

VI. A four of Ilderim, sheik of the Desert. All bays; first race. Ben-Hur, a Jew, driver. Colour, white.'

CECILIUS By Bacchus! Rivers of people! [*Espying* DRUSUS, *he comes to him*] What? Drusus—thou here? Messala—thou hast seen him? He is safe to win?

DRUSUS So say my tablets.

CECILIUS [*half-drunkenly*] Who hath coin of the realm to wager? Rome against the world! [*Lifting and twirling purse*] Lucre, and to spare, on the Roman!

2ND CITIZEN [*coming forward*] A hundred shekels on Ben-Hur!

CECILIUS Shekels? Thou garbage-eater! Go to, lest Abraham arise and smite thee.

2ND CITIZEN [*producing purse*] But wilt thou take my wager?

CECILIUS And what know I of thy shekels? Coin of the realm, said I.

2ND CITIZEN Ha! Ha! Thou ass! Cease thy bray!
    [*Citizens, Jewish faction, laugh derisively*]

CECILIUS [*to* DRUSUS] Come, shall we in?

DRUSUS I pray thee, excuse me.

CECILIUS Ha! Thou art on duty? In the service of Eros? Give this day to Fortuna. [*To his companions*] Come, friends! Messala! Messala!

ROMAN YOUTHS [*with* CECILIUS, *shouting*] Messala! The Roman!

CITIZENS [*Jewish faction, shouting*] Ben-Hur! Ben-Hur!
    [*Exeunt into circus* CECILIUS *and companions, and, following them, citizens*]

DRUSUS [*leaving his post*] Cecilius is right. A fool's errand. She will not come. And Messala is an idiot. I will quote him his own adage.
    [*Enter from door in wall, L.C.*, MESSALA. *He is in racing garb, over which he wears a toga*]

MESSALA Ha, Drusus—well? Thou hast not seen her?

DRUSUS All the world is here but Egypt.

MESSALA And thou hast kept watch?

DRUSUS Like the variest gander that ever sentinelled Rome. But dost thou know what hour it is? By Phoebus, thou shouldst now be in thy chariot, not masquerading here.

MESSALA Contain thy soul, good Drusus. See her I must—if but once more, and come she will, by all my omens. But look [*turning up stage*]! Here, at least, is one who shall masquerade no longer. [*He points to the banner on wall*]

DRUSUS Ha! The noble Arrius!

MESSALA [*reading derisively from the inscription on banner*] 'Ben-Hur—a Jew—Driver.'

DRUSUS Thou hast plucked him of his plumes. Thou hast laid him bare.

MESSALA Name and race—and the record shall follow. Slave of the galleys, eh?

DRUSUS But confess—had I not prompted thee—

MESSALA I own it, good Drusus. I owe thee much. Something there was in his face when I met him in the Grove of Daphne—something that pricked my memory—yet could I not be sure till I had heard thy tale, of Arrius, and the slave whom he adopted.

[*Enter citizens of both factions, R.*]

DRUSUS [*drawing* MESSALA *aside*] Soft! If they should recognise thee—

MESSALA What of that? Dost thou think I have no friends here?

CITIZENS [*Roman faction, shouting as they pass*] Messala! Messala! The Roman!

MESSALA [*aside to Drusus*] Hark!

CITIZENS [*Jewish faction, shouting as they pass*] Ben-Hur! Ben-Hur!

DRUSUS [*aside to* MESSALA] And hark to that!

[*Exeunt citizens into circus*]

DRUSUS He, too, hath his friends.

MESSALA So be it!

DRUSUS All the others are forgotten. Thy contest is with him.

MESSALA And even so would I have it.

DRUSUS Yet forget not! As the son of Arrius, in the palaestrae he was unmatched. He played with the blue-eyed giants from the Rhine, and the hornless bulls of Sarmatia, as they were willow wisps.

MESSALA A truce to thy croakings! I tell thee, Drusus, in the arena today I will humble him in the dust; in the game of love, too, will I break and beggar him.

DRUSUS [*rolling his eyes and throwing up his hands*] 'Love'?

MESSALA And after—but look!

A VOICE [*without, R., calling*] Make way! Make way!

MESSALA [*looking off R.*] Ah—see!

DRUSUS [*looking off R.*] A litter!

MESSALA And beside it—the Ethiop! Her attendant genius! She is here!

[MESSALA *and* DRUSUS *retire to shelter of pillar, R. front, where they remain just within view. Enter from R. citizens, men and women, scattering as they advance before a litter, which enters, borne by slaves. The curtains of litter are closed. Within are* IRAS *and* ESTHER. *Beside the litter walks the Ethiopian*]

A VOICE [*without, as litter enters*] Make way! Make way!

[*Enter, hastily, from R.,* MALLUCH, *following litter*]

MALLUCH [*calling to bearers of litter*] Hold, hold there! The litter cannot enter. [*The litter halts, L.C.*] The master bids you to wait.

IRAS [*suddenly draws back the curtain and looks forth. She is gorgeously attired—face and neck bare*] Whose master?

MALLUCH My master—the merchant Simonides.

IRAS And the Prince? Where is he?

MALLUCH His duties detain him. Will it please you to alight?

IRAS A goodly reception, truly!

[*Assisted by the Ethiopian, she alights from the litter. On her bosom she wears a knot of white ribbon*]

MESSALA [*admiringly, aside to* DRUSUS] Antony's own charmer!

DRUSUS [*aside to* MESSALA] But look! On her bosom—the white!

MESSALA [*aside to* DRUSUS] Pluto take her!

IRAS [*turning and speaking to* ESTHER, *who is yet within the litter*] Well—dost thou hear? We have arrived.

[ESTHER *appears—the curtain which has concealed her being drawn aside by* MALLUCH—*and, assisted by* MALLUCH, *she shrinkingly alights. She is modestly garbed and veiled*]

MESSALA [*aside to* DRUSUS] Another! Who is she?

DRUSUS [*aside to* MESSALA] I know not.

IRAS [*to* ESTHER] It had been common courtesy, in thy gracious lord, is his time indeed so precious, to greet us, at least by proxy. Must we stand here waiting like water-carriers?

[*Exeunt, R., the bearers with litter. Of the citizens who have entered, preceding and following the litter, some have passed into the circus. Others stand about, gazing curiously upon* IRAS. *She notes them*]

IRAS What a stange people! Saw they never a woman's face before? Come, show them thine—for their great wonder.

[*She approaches* ESTHER *and makes movement as if to remove her veil*]

ESTHER [*shrinking back, with protesting gesture*] Oh, I pray thee!

IRAS [*observing her*] Why, thou dost not wear his colours. Dost thou not wish him to win? To be sure, he will have no easy task. Hast thou seen Messala? He is beautiful as Apollo.

MESSALA [*aside to* DRUSUS, *exultantly*] Hearest thou?

A VOICE [*without, R.*] Make way! Way!

MESSALA [*aside to* DRUSUS] What next?

A VOICE [*without, R.*] Way for the merchant Simonides.

MESSALA [*aside to* DRUSUS] Simonides?

DRUSUS [*aside to* MESSALA] The Midas of Antioch.

MESSALA [*aside to* DRUSUS] One might think it were Caesar. O wealth, what a power thou art!

[*Enter, R., slaves, bearing litter in which sit* SIMONIDES *and* BAL-THASAR]

SIMONIDES [*calling to his bearers*] Stay! Malluch!

[*The litter halts near C.*]

MALLUCH [*coming forward quickly*] Good master—

SIMONIDES Ah! Ye are here. The tablets! [*He takes tablets from* MAL-LUCH] Thy pardon, good Balthasar. [*He writes hastily*]

DRUSUS [*aside to* MESSALA] See—with him—the wizard of the fountain!

SIMONIDES [*continuing to write*] Thou hast secured our places, as I bade thee?

MALLUCH Near the Porta Pompae, next to the seat of the Consul.

SIMONIDES And the litter?

MALLUCH Thine may enter—no other.

SIMONIDES It is well. Thou knowest where to find Sanballat [*finishing writing, and tearing off leaf of tablet*]?

MALLUCH Yes, master.

[*Enter door in wall, L.C.,* ILDERIM, *hastily*]

SIMONIDES [*to* MALLUCH, *seeing* ILDERIM] One moment. Good Ilderim.

ILDERIM [*saluting the occupants of the litter*] Peace to you both!

MESSALA [*aside to* DRUSUS] Thy friend, the Sheikh!

SIMONIDES Thou art from the stalls?

ILDERIM And I bring thee a message. Ben-Hur sends thee greeting, and will see thee, if he may, before the race.

SIMONIDES Bid him to think only of his coming trial. All is well? Thou art assured?

ILDERIM [*with conviction*] If Allah forget us not, the victory is won.

SIMONIDES Good. Thou wilt join us?

ILDERIM Later, if I may. But now I must back to my desert-born. I leave them not till the summons hath sounded. [*Going*]

SIMONIDES [*calling after him*] Thou knowest where to find us?

ILDERIM [*turning at door, L.C.*] Allah be with us! And Apollyon hang on the wheels of the Roman!

[*Exit* ILDERIM, *hastily, door in wall, L.C.*]

SIMONIDES [*to* MALLUCH, *giving leaf from tablet*] Now! This to Sanballat. And haste! Bid him to add it to his fund, and use it as he may.

[*Exit hastily* MALLUCH, *R.I.,* SIMONIDES *addresses* BALTHASAR]

SIMONIDES Even in thy land, O Balthasar, we were given the warrant to despoil our enemies. [*To the bearers*] Come! Let us on! [*Turning to* ESTHER *and* IRAS] And ye, my children, follow us closely.

[*The litter moves towards circus entrance. Enter hastily, door in wall, L.C.,* BEN-HUR. *He, like* MESSALA, *is in racing garb*]

BEN-HUR [*checking the advance of litter*] Stay!

[*The litter halts*]

IRAS   Ah! The Prince!

> [MESSALA *and* DRUSUS *draw farther back, R., becoming invisible to audience, and remain so until* BEN-HUR*'s exit*]

BEN-HUR   [*with deep emotion*] Good Simonides! I have but time to crave thy forgiveness and thy blessing; and withhold them not from me, I pray thee.

SIMONIDES   My forgiveness, Prince of Hur?

BEN-HUR   For that I forsook thee last night, so rudely, in the tents of Ilderim—and allowed thee to depart without a word.

SIMONIDES   The time and ways of Ben-Hur are his own. Not to me need he render account. Nothing have I to forgive—but, for my blessing, thou hast it freely.

BEN-HUR   [*disappointedly, recognizing the coldness in* SIMONIDES' *tone*] Ah. And thou, Esther—[*turning to her*] Thou, too, wilt forgive me, nor think me wholly ungrateful? Without thy good will I may not win. My fault lieth heavy upon me. Say that it is forgotten—and that thou dost wish me well.

ESTHER   Be sure I wish thee well.

BEN-HUR   But with thy lips only thou sayest it. Lift up thine eyes and look upon me.

ESTHER   [*with feeling and fervour, gazing in his face*] Oh, canst thou doubt? With all my heart, I pray that good fortune may be thine— today, and ever.

BEN-HUR   O honest soul! I thank thee.

SIMONIDES   [*calling*] Esther!

> [*She crosses to the litter, and takes her father's hand. Exeunt into circus bearers with litter containing* SIMONIDES *and* BALTHASAR. *Exit also* ESTHER, *walking beside litter, still grasping her father's hand. The Ethiopian remains standing near the entrance to circus.* BEN-HUR *turns to* IRAS, *who moves forward from R.C. to follow litter. He stays her with lifted hand*]

IRAS   So! Thou hast eyes for me—at last.

> [BEN-HUR *regards her with gloomy brows. He speaks at last in constrained tones*]

BEN-HUR   And I would ask a favour of thee.

IRAS   Thou beginnest graciously. Well?

BEN-HUR   That thou wilt veil thy face.

IRAS   [*surprised, incensed*] And why?

BEN-HUR   Because it is not modest to go so uncovered. Because I would not see thy beauty the target for ten thousand bestial eyes.

> [*As he speaks the passion in his voice grows in intensity*]

IRAS And who hath made thee the arbiter of manners? Or the daughter of the merchant the model of fashion?

BEN-HUR That is thine answer?

IRAS Unless thou canst give me a better reason.

BEN-HUR [*passionately*] I will give thee one. Thou wearest my colours, and I would not blush for thee.

IRAS Sayest thou so? That were easily helped.

[*She tears the knot of white ribbon from her bosom and casts it from her.* BEN-HUR *recoils*]

IRAS What more? To please thee, I yielded the scarlet; now, at thy bidding, I surrender the white.

BEN-HUR And with as little regret? [*She shrugs her shoulders. He continues*] Less, mayhap. And thou art she who but last night—

IRAS Well—wherein have I changed? Did I promise to guard what thou callest my beauty solely for the delight of thine eyes? A queen thou wouldst make me—and for what? To sit and mope in a darkened chamber, and receive homage only from thee?

BEN-HUR Why did I not leave thee the scarlet?

IRAS Ah! Why not, indeed? Scarlet becometh me well.

BEN-HUR Thou canst avow it. And to be admired and desired—to be flattered by the fool and the libertine—to draw upon thee the common public stare—is more to thee than to be honourably worshipped?

IRAS Thou growest wearisome. What wouldst thou have?

BEN-HUR I would have thee so esteem thyself, and see thee so esteemed by others, that thy beauty might be all but forgotten, through reverence for thy purity and modesty. But that thou canst not understand? Were it my last request, of that thou couldst give me no hope?

IRAS Why, good Ben-Hur, thou art beside thyself. Mistake me not for the other. I am not thy slave.

[*He seizes her hands, gazes in her face—for an instant—then, with a hoarse cry, casts her off, turns, and rushes out through door in wall, L.C.*]

IRAS Fool! [*She looks after him*]

MESSALA [*springing from his hiding, and bowing low before her, as she turns at the sound of his steps*] Beauteous Egypt! Start not! Fly not! Hear me—but a word. Messala am I. Did I not swear by the Fountain of Castalia thou shouldst see me again? Thine eyes have pierced my soul. [*She moves as if to go*] Stay—hear me—for thou must. Cleopatra art thou; and I, of the blood of the Caesars. Here, then, is thy quarry! A smile—but one! It is a Roman that begs.

[*The eyes of* IRAS *rove wildly, resting for an instant on the placard on the wall, then on* MESSALA. *As she meets his look, she averts her face. Feigning surprise and indignation at his proposal, she betrays— by the methods of the coquette—that she is impressed by, and entertains, it.* MESSALA, *springing forward, seizes her hand and presses it to his lips. With a low cry, she withdraws her hand, and—with a backward look—exits hastily into circus. Exit, following her, the Ethiopian*]

DRUSUS [*springing from his hiding*] Foiled! Defeated!

MESSALA [*exultantly*] Not so! By all the gods, good Drusus, she is mine—mine—dost thou hear?

[*Enter citizens, R. Enter* CECILIUS *and Roman youths, from circus*]

DRUSUS [*to* MESSALA] Beware!

CECILIUS [*recognizing* MESSALA] Ha! Messala! And thou art dallying here, while we bet our good gold upon thee!

MESSALA Cecilius! Beshrew thy tongue!

1ST CITIZEN [*recognizing* MESSALA] Messala. Look, it is he.

CITIZENS [*crowding about* MESSALA *and his companions*] Messala! Messala! The Roman!

[*Enter, R.,* SANBALLAT]

MESSALA [*to* CECILIUS] Now see what thou hast done. [*To crowd, striving to pass*] Good friends, I pray you, give me leave.

SANBALLAT [*forcing his way through the crowd, and confronting the Romans*] Romans! Most noble Romans! I salute you. It came to me that there was great discomfort, because offers on Messala were going without takers. The gods must have sacrifices. Here am I. Odds first—amounts next. What will you give me?

DRUSUS [*to* MESSALA] Here is sport. Out with thy tablets!

SANBALLAT Come, what odds? The Consul is in his seat.

CECILIUS What odds? Two to one.

SANBALLAT What? Only two? And yours a Roman?

DRUSUS Take three, then.

SANBALLAT Three, say you? Only three? Give me four.

CECILIUS Shadrach, thou lookest needy. If four will avail thee, take it.

SANBALLAT Five—give me five, for the honour of Rome—five.

[*Shouts of derision from the Roman faction of the crowd*]

DRUSUS Ha, ha! And when thou art brought to book, what wilt thou wager? A *denarius* Five let it be!

SANBALLAT If Caesar die tomorrow, there is one to take his place. Give me six.

[*Louder shouts of derision and laughter from the crowd*]

MESSALA [*stepping forward*] Come then! Six be it! Six to one! The difference between a Roman and a Jew! And now, the odds being settled, the amount—and quickly!

[SANBALLAT, *smiling, writes quickly on tablet, tears off leaf, and hands it to* MESSALA. MESSALA *takes it, glances at it, amazed*]

DRUSUS Read.

MESSALA [*reading*] 'Twenty talents'. [*The Romans exchange amazed glances*] Thou knave! Where hast thou twenty talents? Show me.

[SANBALLAT, *still smiling, produces and hands to* MESSALA *another leaflet—the one given by* SIMONIDES *to* MALLUCH. MESSALA *glances at it and stands speechless*]

CECILIUS Read—read!

DRUSUS [*seizing the paper from* MESSALA, *reads*] 'The bearer, Sanballat, hath now to his order with me fifty talents, coin of Caesar. (Signed) "Simonides".'

CECILIUS 'Fifty talents!'

CITIZENS [*amazed*] 'Fifty talents!'

CECILIUS A trick! A trap!

DRUSUS By Hercules, the paper lies. Who but Caesar hath fifty talents? Down with him!

MESSALA Stay! [*To* SANBALLAT] The sum is great—but I take thee.

[*He writes hastily on tablet, tears off leaf, and gives it to* SANBALLAT]

SANBALLAT Good! Romans, another wager, if you dare. Five talents against five talents, that Ben-Hur will win.

DRUSUS Down with him! Down with the insolent white!

CITIZENS [*Roman faction, shouting*] Down with him!

SANBALLAT [*shouting above the tumult*] My offer holds till the race is run. I may be found near the seat of the Consul. Peace to you all.

[*Exit, hastily, into circus. A trumpet sounds without—in circus.* MESSALA, *leaving his companions, springs through door in wall, L.C.*]

CITIZENS [*all shouting*] To the arena! To the arena!

[*They rush towards entrance of circus, and exeunt, shouting and struggling for precedence. With them go* DRUSUS, CECILIUS, *and companions. Throughout the commotion the trumpet sounds—a succession of sharp, quick calls. Stage dark. Through the period of darkness the tumult of the crowd heard—shouts of 'The Roman!' 'The Roman!' 'Jove with us!', and 'Ben-Hur!' 'Ben-Hur!' Then the thunder of hoofs and wheels*]

Scene 2

[SCENE: *Interior of circus—race in progress*[86]]

BEN-HUR [*shouting to his steeds*] On, air! On, Rigel! Antares! Oho, Aldebaran!

[*The wheel rolls from* MESSALA'*s chariot, and* MESSALA *falls as* BEN-HUR *draws past him. Stage dark. Change: lights up.* BEN-HUR, *standing in his chariot before Consul's seat, receives the victor's crown;* ILDERIM *caressing his horses;* MALLUCH *also near horses.* SIMONIDES, ESTHER, IRAS, BALTHASAR, *and* SANBALLAT *in box above, in characteristic attitudes. Shouting—cheering—trumpet-calls. Curtain*]

---

[86] The numbering of the scenes in Act V differs between the New York and London programmes. The New York programme and printed text treat action before the backcloth as a continuation of Scene 2; the Drury Lane programme treats it as a discrete scene. See my introduction to *Ben-Hur* and the illustrations of the chariot-race sequence.

ACT VI

Scene 1

[SCENE: *Apartment in the palace of Hur in Jerusalem. Door C. in flat—door L.C.—great window R., giving view of Jerusalem—sunset effect. Suitable furniture and furnishings.* DISCOVERED: SIMONIDES *in great chair, C.—two servants standing near—before him another servant, head covering in hand*]

SIMONIDES [*to the last-named servant*] Thou wilt find, in the booths near the Tower, soldiers of the guard who have been relieved from duty. Take this purse [*giving him purse*] to loosen their tongues; but use thine own tongue only for questioning. Be discreet: learn what thou canst, and bring me report quickly.

[*Exit servant, hastily, door C.*]

SIMONIDES Without Malluch, I am as an arm without a hand. [*To another servant*] Now, place me nearer the window.

[*The servant wheels his chair near window, R. Enter* ESTHER, *door L.C. Exeunt servants, door C.* SIMONIDES *to* ESTHER]

SIMONIDES Come! Feast thine eyes with mine.

ESTHER [*embracing him*] Dear father!

SIMONIDES [*returning her caress*] My little one! See! The city beautiful. [*Kneeling beside his chair, she gazes out with him across the city*] Even so fell the sun upon it in the evenings of that long ago when I, from the market-place, looked up to the palace, and envied those who dwelt herein. But happiness abideth not always in palaces?

ESTHER [*with effort to conquer sadness*] It is fair. It is beautiful.

SIMONIDES Yet rather wouldst thou it were Antioch.

ESTHER How canst thou say so? I am happy here.

SIMONIDES Think not I have failed to read thy heart, or that mine own hath not bled for thee. And had I held fast to what I had—

ESTHER No, no! For then had I been unworthy [of] a look from him, and without pride in thee.

SIMONIDES Thou art thy mother's daughter—and would I could give thee better comfort! But this only can I bid thee hope: that the spell of the Egyptian hath been broken, and that his eyes are now turned to loftier things.

ESTHER What more could I desire? But what is this mission on which he hath gone? May I not know?

SIMONIDES He hath gone, with Malluch, to Galilee, there to see and judge of him whom the people say is the Messiah. Thou hast heard of the mysterious man?

ESTHER His name is on all tongues.

SIMONIDES And of the throngs that attend him? And the miracles he is said to have wrought? Thou knowest, Esther, I am slow of belief, but if this in truth be He of whom the prophets have spoken, and whose star Balthasar followed, to what better cause could a son of Hur devote his life and his fortune?

ESTHER And Judah—doth he believe?

SIMONIDES I await his report. Tonight I expect him.

ESTHER This night?

SIMONIDES And a strange report—strange, and it may be terrible— must I make to him.

ESTHER [*wonderingly*] My father?

SIMONIDES A rumour hath come to me—it is yet to be confirmed— that when, of late, at the coming of Pilate, the doors of the prisons were opened, there were found in the Tower of Antonia, in a secret cell, two women, who had been so long immured that even the keepers knew not their names.

ESTHER Two women?

SIMONIDES They were freed. But the doom of leprosy, contracted in their prison house, was upon them.

ESTHER Heaven have mercy!

SIMONIDES They were driven from the gates, and whither they have gone no one knoweth.

ESTHER And thou hast thought—

SIMONIDES How can I choose but think that these may be the lost ones?

ESTHER God in His goodness forbid! But oh, my father, can it be that Amrah knoweth?

SIMONIDES Amrah?

ESTHER I had meant to tell thee. Now these three days she hath acted so strangely, weeping and praying as she goeth about her tasks. And every morning she hath asked me for leave to go from the house with a basket of food—

SIMONIDES [*eagerly interrupting*] Where? To whom?

ESTHER She will only say that it is for the afflicted. But this I know— she goeth far. And once she spoke of the Vale of Hinnom.

SIMONIDES Hinnom? The city of the lepers! Let me see her. Send her to me.

[ESTHER, *rising, turns towards door. Enter, door C.*, MALLUCH, *in riding-dress*. SIMONIDES, *turning his head, sees* MALLUCH]

SIMONIDES Eh? Who is there? Malluch?

MALLUCH It is I, good master.

SIMONIDES Ben-Hur? Where is he?

MALLUCH He is close at hand. We have journeyed all day with the Nazarene.

SIMONIDES [*surprised*] With the Nazarene?

MALLUCH But He hath turned aside to Bethpage, where He will pass the night; and Ben-Hur hath tarried with his swordsmen.

ESTHER His swordsmen?

MALLUCH He bade me press forward, and tell thee to expect him.
[*Clatter of horse's hoofs heard without, off R.*]

SIMONIDES He shall be welcome. And hark! Even now—
[*The clatter of hoofs ceases suddenly without, R.*]

ESTHER [*who has hastened to window, looking out and down*] It is he.
[*Enter Amrah, door C.*]

AMRAH [*in extreme agitation*] Oh, good master! Good master!

SIMONIDES Amrah!

AMRAH I pray thee, forgive me that I come unbidden; but do I hear thou hast news of Judah?

SIMONIDES He is here. His foot is upon the threshold.

AMRAH Now blessed be the name of the Lord! [*Turning to go*]

SIMONIDES Amrah, remain.

AMRAH I obey, good master.

SIMONIDES [*to* ESTHER] Thou wilt stop and greet him?
[*Enter* BEN-HUR, *door C., in riding-dress.* SIMONIDES *greets him*]

SIMONIDES Welcome back to thine own house!

BEN-HUR [*grasping* SIMONIDES' *hand*] Peace to thee, Simonides! And to thee, sweet Esther, peace!
[ESTHER, *with head bowed, gives him her hand, which he raises reverently to his lips*]

BEN-HUR Amrah! Good Amrah!
[*Turning to* AMRAH, *he extends his hands, which she seizes and kisses fervently*]

AMRAH O gracious master! Thou hast come again, and in safety? God be praised!

BEN-HUR Go now, Malluch, and get thy rest.

MALLUCH Thou wilt need me no more?

BEN-HUR No more this night
[*Exit* MALLUCH, *door C.* BEN-HUR *turns to the others*]

BEN-HUR Well! Ye are waiting to hear?

SIMONIDES Wilt thou not first rest and be refreshed?

BEN-HUR Thine ears are impatient. Malluch hath told thee nothing?

SIMONIDES Save that the Nazarene is at Bethpage.

BEN-HUR Tomorrow He will enter Jerusalem.

SIMONIDES So soon!

BEN-HUR He will enter it, but not in state; with thousands, but not with an army.

SIMONIDES Then hast thou—

BEN-HUR I have brought with me three legions of Galileans; but they may return as they came. There will be no swords drawn. Here is no King.

SIMONIDES No King?

BEN-HUR Upon the throne of Solomon He will never sit.

AMRAH [to BEN-HUR] It is of the Nazarene thou speakest, master?

BEN-HUR It is of Him.

SIMONIDES The reports were false.

BEN-HUR Again thou judgest too quickly. But first let me tell thee. He is of Nazareth, and I, too, was once in Nazareth. I passed through it a prisoner—bound, dragged in the dust at a horse's heels. And there, while my guards halted at the well, and I lay fainting and unpitied, a boy whose face I have never forgotten placed a cup of water to my lips, and laid his hand upon my head in blessing. That face I have seen again. It is the face of the man—if He be a mere man—who resteth tonight at Bethpage.

ESTHER How wonderful!

BEN-HUR The same eyes, so full of pity, so mystic, so far-seeing! The same brow, about which a halo seemed to shine! But the face of a king! No! Meek, with the meekness of a woman! Sorrowful, with the foreknowledge of a martyr! The face of one born not to rule, but to suffer and, I fear, to die!

SIMONIDES And so fadeth our dream!

BEN-HUR [with intense sadness and dejection] Our dream of an earthly kingdom—of great deeds to be done, and sacrifices to be made, in a cause in which the worthiest might become more worthy, and even the errors of a wasted life might, haply, be redeemed! Yet, have I not told thee all. Of what I must now report, judge as thou mayest. For myself, I can but say that I am lost in wonder, daring neither to believe nor to disbelieve what mine eyes have seen.

SIMONIDES And what hast thou seen?

BEN-HUR I have seen the lame made to walk; the blind to see; the deaf to hear—by the laying-on of His hands. I have seen lepers cleansed and made whole—

AMRAH [*tremblingly eager*] 'Lepers!' 'Lepers', didst thou say, master?

BEN-HUR So that their flesh was as that of little children.

AMRAH [*falling upon her knees and seizing hold of his garments*] Master! Good master—

BEN-HUR [*disregarding her*] And more—I have seen the dead raised.

ESTHER The dead?

BEN-HUR By His mere word of command. Now who is this? And what is He, who can so overrule the laws of nature, or deceive the senses of all beholders?

AMRAH But tell me, tell me again, master—thou hast truly seen lepers made whole?

BEN-HUR Again I tell thee, I have seen it, Amrah.

AMRAH And with thine own eyes? [*Rising*] Thou hast seen it—thou hast seen it!

[*She hurries out, door C.*]

SIMONIDES [*calling after* AMRAH] Amrah! Wait without. I would speak with thee. [*To* BEN-HUR] Well, hast thou more to tell us?

BEN-HUR Tomorrow—tomorrow—

[SIMONIDES *claps his hands. Enter servant, door C.*]

SIMONIDES [*turning again suddenly to* BEN-HUR] But Balthasar? Thou hast seen him? Doth he still believe?

BEN-HUR [*dropping his eyes*] A great grief hath befallen him. His daughter hath deserted him.

SIMONIDES Iras—fled?

BEN-HUR And with Messala.

SIMONIDES [*to servant*] Bear me to the antechamber—[*Calling as he disappears*] Amrah!

[*Exit* SIMONIDES, *wheeled out by servant, door C.* ESTHER *stands for a moment irresolute; then turns towards door*]

BEN-HUR [*a tender accent in his voice*] Sweet Esther, go not yet. If thy heart can hear, I would speak to it.

ESTHER [*regarding him in surprise*] Mine?

BEN-HUR I have had a fever, Esther, which flung me into a delirium, and gave me to see visions, all empty, but of mighty hold upon me. In manly wise, I admit the Egyptian wove a spell about me. She had a serpentine power of fascination that took away my reason. I could see the right, but could not turn from the wrong. Were I less

subject to beauty, O Esther, I should not come to thee with the
speech I have now to tell.

ESTHER [*agitated, and with bent head*] Oh, I pray thee!—

BEN-HUR [*taking her hand*] I have to tell thee now, Esther, that the
glamour is gone, and I see with my natural eyes. Her beauty had
in it a taint of poison; thine is the beauty of the rose just breaking
into bloom, pure of itself, and doubly pure of the morning dew
upon it. Oh, sweet Esther, I love thee!

[*He puts his arm about her, but she draws from him*]

ESTHER Thou lovest—me?

BEN-HUR And long ago I loved thee. But I knew not mine own
heart—I knew it not.

ESTHER Oh! And dost thou know it now?

BEN-HUR For time and for eternity I know it. No spell of sorcery is
this, but a worship that hath grown with the days and the months,
and shall grow in strength and in holiness for ever.

ESTHER But think—think upon thy station—and mine!

BEN-HUR Speak not such words, for I will not hear them! As far art thou
above me as the angels. Esther, so deep mine unworthiness, I scarce
dare hope that my prayer will reach thee, or that thou canst forgive—

ESTHER 'Forgive'?

BEN-HUR But thou wilt? Thou dost?

ESTHER Oh, and what have I to forgive? Thy happiness hath been
mine only care, and the one burden of my prayer, since the day
when first I saw thee.

BEN-HUR Mine own!

[*He clasps her in his arms. Enter, door C.,* IRAS, *heavily veiled.*
BEN-HUR *and* ESTHER *recoil from the Intruder*]

BEN-HUR Who art thou? [IRAS *drops her veil*] Iras!

IRAS [*to* ESTHER, *with mocking smile*] I see thou hast kept thy bird well
in hand.

BEN-HUR Shameless!

[ESTHER *hurries to door, C.* BEN-HUR *calls after her*]

BEN-HUR Stay! Go not—

[*Exit* ESTHER, *door C.* BEN-HUR *again addresses* IRAS]

BEN-HUR And thou comest here?

IRAS Son of Hur! I have heard of a custom of the dice-players. When
the game is ended, they consult their tablets and make up their
accounts. We two once played at a game—

BEN-HUR And thou hast the hardihood to recall it? Between us there
is nothing to be said.

IRAS Be not so sure. For, by my tablets, thou art in my debt. Nor is that all. Thou hast played, it would seem, at yet another game [*surveying him*]. Booted and belted! A sword at thy side! But be these the trappings of a captain of Israel? Leader-in-chief of its armies? [BEN-HUR *turns away. She laughs, ironically*] And thou wouldst have shared thine honours with me! Well, tell me, O Prince of Jerusalem! Hast thou found Him? The King so long foretold? And when shall the power of Rome be broken?

> [BEN-HUR *turns, as if to answer indignantly, but again turns away. She continues*]

IRAS I went yesterday to see your dreaming Caesar. Amongst his attendants, I looked for one figure with a promise of royalty—a horseman in purple, a chariot with a driver in brass, a stately warrior behind an orbed shield. It would have been—oh, so pleasant!— to have seen a Prince of Jerusalem and a cohort of the legions of Galilee! [*She laughs heartily*] Instead of a Caesar, helmed and sworded, I saw a man with a woman's face and hair, riding an ass's colt, and in tears. The King; the Son of God! The Redeemer of the world!

BEN-HUR [*with dignity*] Daughter of Balthasar, if this be the game of which thou hast spoken, take the chaplet—I accord it thine. But thou hast a further purpose. To it, I pray thee, and briefly!

IRAS Briefly, then, I would save thee—if I may.

BEN-HUR Save me?

IRAS [*with vindictive forcefulness*] Thou hast here, tonight, three trained legions of Galileans to seize the Roman governor and enthrone the son of the carpenter of Nazareth. Suppose this were told to the Lord Sejanus!

BEN-HUR And thou wouldst tell it?

> [IRAS *replies with significant gesture.* BEN-HUR *folds his arms and speaks*]

BEN-HUR Well?

IRAS And hast thou no more to say?

BEN-HUR Thou hast some price to put upon thy silence. I wait to hear it.

IRAS [*after slight pause, with sudden change to seductive pleading*] Call it not a 'price' that I would exact. O noble Prince, thou hadst once a friend—

BEN-HUR Messala?

IRAS He did thee wrong, but deeply hath he deplored it.

BEN-HUR Is it so?

IRAS Forgive the past—as he hath forgiven. Admit him again to thy friendship, and restore the fortune he lost in the great wager. To thee the amount is as nothing, but to him—Oh, take counsel of thy generous heart, and save him from poverty—which to a Roman, nobly born, is more odious than death.

BEN-HUR And did Messala send thee to me on such an errand—to beg?

IRAS [recoiling, angrily] 'To beg'—

BEN-HUR And only for this? Not for forgiveness—for that word was a lie upon thy lips—but for a paltry handful of gold! For alms!

IRAS 'Alms'?

BEN-HUR A fitting request! And sent by a fitting messenger!

IRAS [in fury] Thou drinker of lees! Feeder upon husks! To think I could love thee, having seen Messala! And thou canst so despise his plea! Then let me tell thee—not once alone, but fourfold shalt thou make restitution. Even the kissings of my little finger that thou hast taken from him shall be paid for, and that before tomorrow noon, or thou shalt settle with the Lord Sejanus.

BEN-HUR Then with the Lord Sejanus must I settle. Once for all, no favour do I ask or expect. And to Messala nothing will I give.

IRAS Nothing?

BEN-HUR No, not even my curse. Instead of that, I send him thee, whom he shall find the sum of all curses.

IRAS Thou! Thou! And thou darest—

BEN-HUR I have spoken.

IRAS Oh, but thou shalt repent of this!

[She turns and rushes towards door, C.]

[Enter SIMONIDES, wheeled in by servant, door C.]

SIMONIDES [to IRAS] Hold! Hear first a word from me.

[IRAS stops. SIMONIDES continues rapidly, and the whole scene from this forth should be played with the utmost rapidity]

SIMONIDES Thou speakest of the Lord Sejanus. Here I hold his pledge and Caesar's [lifting and shaking paper], signed and sealed, promising me vengeance on the despoilers of the House of Hur. One thing only hath been lacking to my case—proof of the fate of the mother and daughter. That proof have I now secured.

BEN-HUR [with raised hands, and staggering as if struck] Thou knowest?

SIMONIDES Prepare thyself. [To IRAS] And thou—hear my witness. Then, to Messala, if thou wilt, and bid him match his charge against mine. [Turning his head, calls] Amrah! Come!

[Enter, door C., AMRAH, followed closely by ESTHER]

SIMONIDES Tell now thy tale.

AMRAH [*throwing herself at* BEN-HUR*'s feet*] O master! Master!

BEN-HUR [*wildly*] Speak!

AMRAH I cannot. [*To* SIMONIDES, *imploringly*] Speak thou for me.

SIMONIDES They live, Ben-Hur.

BEN-HUR They live!

SIMONIDES But rejoice not, for there be fates worse even than death. From a loathsome dungeon, loathsome and infected, they have come forth—lepers.

BEN-HUR Lepers? God of my fathers!

SIMONIDES They were driven from the gates. Amrah hath found them—Amrah hath fed them. She hath the secret of their hiding.

BEN-HUR [*to* AMRAH] Speak! Where are they?

AMRAH [*clutching his garments*] I dare not tell thee.

BEN-HUR Dare not?

AMRAH I am pledged to them.

BEN-HUR [*dragging* AMRAH *to her feet*] But not against me, who have sought them so long.

AMRAH O master! Master!

BEN-HUR Where may I find them? Where, I say?

AMRAH In a tomb in the Vale of Hinnom.

BEN-HUR To see them! To save them!

[*With a cry of horror, he rushes out, door C.*]

AMRAH [*calling after him*] But, master, the Nazarene!

[AMRAH *reels, is caught and, for an instant, supported by* ESTHER]

ESTHER [*also calling*] Judah!

[*Leaving* AMRAH, ESTHER *comes down towards the now cowering* IRAS]

ESTHER Oh, thou vile woman!

SIMONIDES [*checking* ESTHER*'s advance, turns to* IRAS *and points towards door*] Go!

[IRAS, *with face bowed in abject defeat, moves towards door. Tableau. Curtain*]

Scene 2

[SCENE: *A hillside. Tomb (practical) L., clump of foliage set R. Path leading off and up R.2. Time: early morning. Enter from the tomb the* MOTHER *of* BEN-HUR.

Note: In this scene she and TIRZAH *appear as lepers—physical appearance and dress in accordance—appropriate music.*]

MOTHER [*standing in doorway of tomb, and looking out over the landscape*] Another day! [*She falls to her knees*] O Lord, how long! [*She calls*] Tirzah! But why should I waken her? Why may she not sleep for ever? After so many years—so many—buried from the light of the sun, to be upraised again for this!

[*Enter from tomb,* TIRZAH]

TIRZAH Didst thou call me?

MOTHER To sleep again, dear, for Amrah hath not come.

TIRZAH I would not sleep. I cannot. The tomb is so dark. It mindeth me—

MOTHER Of that other tomb that engulfed thy youth. [*She clasps* TIRZAH *in a tearful embrace*] O my poor Tirzah! My martyred one! So sinned against and afflicted! So cruelly, foully robbed of all the joys that were thy due!

TIRZAH Why dost thou weep, my mother? Surely it is pleasant to see again the blue of the skies, and the light on the hilltops, and the green trees. And soon Amrah will be here, with news of Judah. For so many mercies, should we not be glad?

MOTHER [*again fervently embracing* TIRZAH, *with eyes uplifted*] We should be glad. We will be glad. O Thou that doest all things well, I thank Thee that Thou hast given to this child a heart less bitter and rebellious than mine. Come then! Let us speak of Judah. He hath gone on a journey, but will soon return. Said not Amrah so?

[*Enter* AMRAH, *L.I., hurriedly, bearing basket*]

TIRZAH She is here. Amrah! Amrah!

AMRAH O my sweet Tirzah! O my mistress! Then he hath not found you?

MOTHER Who hath not found us? But come no nearer! Unclean, unclean!

[AMRAH, *rushing towards them, falls on her knees before the* MOTHER *of* BEN-HUR *and clasps her arms about her. The* MOTHER *of* BEN-HUR *recoils in horror and endeavours to free herself*]

MOTHER Amrah! Back! What hast thou done?

AMRAH But, mistress, hear me!

MOTHER Now thou hast touched us, thou, too, art unclean.

AMRAH I care not.

MOTHER Thou carest not? Now thou canst never return to thy master. Thou canst bring us no more word of him. Oh, thou false, thou wicked woman!

AMRAH [*still clinging to her skirts*] I am not false—I am not wicked. O mistress, if you will but hear me! I bring you good tidings. There is One who can cure you—and even now He is near.

MOTHER [*incredulously and pityingly*] Poor Amrah!

AMRAH No! No! As the Lord liveth—thy Lord and mine—I speak the truth! He is now at Bethpage, but soon will He pass by.

MOTHER Who will pass by?

AMRAH The Nazarene, and He cureth all who come to Him. O mistress, let us go and meet Him!

MOTHER And who hath told thee all this?

AMRAH Judah. Now wilt thou believe me?

MOTHER Then he hath returned?

AMRAH Last night he came.

MOTHER Where is he now.

AMRAH O mistress, mistress, he went forth to find you.

MOTHER And thou hast told him?

AMRAH How could I deny him? O mistress, he commanded me. Yet would he not bide till I had told him all. For scarce had I named the Vale of Hinnom, when forth he rushed. He would wait for no more. Then, with the morning light, I came.

MOTHER And now, through all the tombs of the valley, touching and breathing their infection, doth he search for us?

AMRAH Mercy! Pardon!

MOTHER O Amrah! Amrah!

AMRAH Yet why should we fear? There is cure for all. Oh, haste! Eat a little, to give you strength—and let us go.

MOTHER Thou sayest that Judah hath told thee. What—what hath he told thee? This Nazarene—what and whence His power?

AMRAH I know not. Some there be who call Him the Messiah. This only do I know: He cureth the sick, He even raiseth the dead. Judah hath seen it all—seen lepers cleansed and made whole again, so their flesh was like to that of little children.

MOTHER Who could do this but the Messiah? And thou sayest He is near?

AMRAH Today He will enter Jerusalem. And see! By this path we may reach the road from Bethpage, by which He will come, [*pointing back*].

A VOICE [*off L., distant, calling*] Hillo! Hillo!

MOTHER Hark! Someone cometh. Let us hide ourselves [*taking TIR-ZAH's hand and moving towards door of tomb*]!

TIRZAH But if it should be Judah? Wouldst thou not see him?

MOTHER O my poor Tirzah, knowest thou not—canst thou not understand—that him of all men must we avoid? Come! Come!

[*The three women conceal themselves behind clump of bushes, L.*]

MALLUCH [*without, off L., distant, calling*] Hillo!

BEN-HUR [*without, off L., near, answering the hail*] Ho!

    [*Enter* BEN-HUR, *L.I. He is haggard, and staggers with fatigue and despair. His dress is disordered*]

BEN-HUR 'In a tomb in the Vale of Hinnom,' said she. Yet here doth the Vale of Hinnom end, and is there, in all its length, a charnel-vault where misery may hide that I have left unvisited? [*Spying the tomb, L.*] Another!

    [*He rushes to the tomb, enters, and reappears with despairing look and gesture*]

BEN-HUR No one! O Amrah, hast thou played me false—or art thou crazed—as I? [*He falls upon his knees*]

MALLUCH [*off L.I., calling*] Hillo! Master! Master!

    [*Enter* MALLUCH, *hurriedly, L.I.*]

MALLUCH Ah! At last have I found thee?

BEN-HUR [*staggering to his feet*] Malluch! What dost thou here?

MALLUCH [*hurrying towards him, and supporting him*] The whole night long have I searched for thee.

BEN-HUR Hast thou? And I—I have searched for years.

MALLUCH Thy quest hath been in vain?

BEN-HUR I am accursed. For some great sin am I punished, Malluch. Again the earth hath swallowed them. For surely—oh, surely—all the outcast, piteous shapes which haunt this vale of horrors have I seen. But they—

MALLUCH It may be thou hast passed them in the darkness. It must be so. Come! I have horses near.

BEN-HUR Whither should I go?

MALLUCH Thy strength is spent, and thou art torn and bleeding. Thou canst not wander thus.

BEN-HUR Under no roof, across no threshold, will I go while they are houseless!

MALLUCH Thou shouldst not say so. [BEN-HUR *reels*] See! Thy limbs fail thee.

    [BEN-HUR *sinks backwards to sitting position on stone, held and prevented from falling by* MALLUCH]

BEN-HUR [*faintly*] Let me but rest a little.

MALLUCH But not here; for illness is upon thee. Thy grief and all thou hast borne of late, and suffered, have overtaxed thee. Come!

BEN-HUR I tell thee, no!

MALLUCH Then promise me but this—that thou wilt bide here till I return with Amrah. Own, good master, that now I speak in reason. With her guidance, we soon may find them—if her tale be true.

BEN-HUR Malluch, thou art right. Thou showest me my folly. Had I but stayed to question her more closely! Why did I not? Oh, I have played the madman—if, in truth, I be not mad!

MALLUCH [*soothing and continuing to support him*] Nay! All will yet be well.

BEN-HUR [*faintly*] Go!

MALLUCH And thou wilt bide? [BEN-HUR*'s head droops*] Ah! Little need to ask! Master!

[*He lowers* BEN-HUR *to a reclining position on the stone, and hastily places his hand upon his heart*]

MALLUCH No! God be praised! It is not death, but sleep. Nature's best balm! [*Gently, but swiftly, he covers Ben-Hur with cloak*] Oh, Heaven keep him—and grant him happier waking!

[*Exit* MALLUCH, *running L.I. Music. The three women reappear from their hiding, the* MOTHER *leading,* TIRZAH *clinging to her. All their speech in this scene is in suppressed tones, but little above a whisper. They noiselessly move a step nearer to* BEN-HUR]

MOTHER [*falling on her knees*] Oh, look! How pale! How still!

TIRZAH And see—he hath been weeping!

MOTHER [*with hands outstretched towards* BEN-HUR] Dost thou mourn us so?

TIRZAH [*with anguished movement, as if drawn towards the sleeper*] Oh, if we might but comfort him!

MOTHER [*staying* TIRZAH] No! No! Unclean! Unclean! Oh, blessed sleep, that giveth us the boon of looking on him!

TIRZAH See how little changed—so little—

MOTHER [*bitterly*] And we! [BEN-HUR *stirs in his sleep*] Hush!

BEN-HUR [*calling in his sleep*] Mother! Mother! Tirzah!

MOTHER [*to* TIRZAH] Speak not! Answer not, for thy life!

TIRZAH [*uncontrollably sobbing*] My brother!

MOTHER [*rising in anguish and terror*] Oh, we must hence!

[*The sound of a multitude singing heard from back, distant. This music, now low, now loud, is continued till end of Act*]

AMRAH Mistress! Dost thou not hear?

MOTHER Is it the choiring of angels?

AMRAH These must be they that follow the Nazarene. Come! Come! Lest we be too late!

MOTHER Yes! Come, Tirzah!

TIRZAH [*who has sunk to her knees*] Oh, go thou, my mother, and leave me.

MOTHER Leave thee? And what were the gain to me, if I were healed and not thou?

AMRAH [*assisting the* MOTHER *to lift* TIRZAH *to her feet*] My little one—lean on me.

TIRZAH And thou thinkst there is a hope?

MOTHER Came not the message from Judah? Courage, for his sake.

AMRAH [*supporting* TIRZAH *and moving with her towards R.2.*] Come! Let us haste!

MOTHER [*going last, and looking back*] A hope—and if it be quenched—Oh, my son, our eyes have seen thee for the last time on earth!

> [*Exeunt, the three women, by path R.2. The drop becomes transparent, disclosing view of the Mount of Olives, with Jerusalem in the distance. The singing is heard nearer. Enter, R., a multitude, singing. An answering strain is heard from a multitude L.—the latter as yet invisible.* AMRAH *and the mother and sister of* BEN-HUR *appear, lower R., and seek to go up towards the Mount with the throng, but are repulsed, with gestures of horror and loathing. Enter, L., a second multitude, descending the Mount, singing and bearing palms. Those who have come from the R., pause.* AMRAH *and the two lepers, facing the second multitude, kneel, C. Suddenly, from above, a dazzling radiance pours upon the kneeling women; the palms wave, the anthem swells and touches its culmination, the drop becomes opaque, but the chanting continues, again distant, and low*]

BEN-HUR [*waking, and springing to his feet*] Ah! Whence is this heavenly music? And they—stood they not here? Was it a trick of the brain?

> [*Enter hurriedly, L.I.,* MALLUCH, *accompanied by* ESTHER. *She is veiled.* BEN-HUR *goes quickly towards them*]

BEN-HUR Malluch! But this is not Amrah. [ESTHER *throws aside her veil*] Esther! Thou—here?

ESTHER [*throwing herself into his arms*] O Judah!

MALLUCH I met her, good master, by the well of En Rogel.

ESTHER And he prayed me to turn back, but I would not. Ah, how thou hast suffered [*seizing his hands*]!

BEN-HUR It is nothing—but Amrah?

ESTHER An hour since she left the house. She fled from me.

BEN-HUR And even now, mayhap, she is with them.

ESTHER [*listening intently*] It may be. But Judah—what sound of singing is it I hear?

BEN-HUR Dost thou hear it? Then it is no fancy.

ESTHER What is no fancy? Judah! Thine eyes are wild.

BEN-HUR Listen! A moment since, whilst here I lay, I could have sworn they stood beside me—but oh, how changed! They whispered together; and I called to them—but they wept, and vanished. Still, with mine eyes I followed them; and I looked, as it seemed, on the Mount of Olives; and a great multitude, bearing palms, and chanting—such harmony as this! And they, too, the beloved, were there, but the people shunned them. Then, on the heights above, I saw Him—the Nazarene! The new light of the world! He came towards them—such pity on His face as shone on me by the well, of old. They knelt—they implored Him—and again I saw even such a miracle as met my sight by the wave of Galilee. He spake, and their affliction fell from them; in health and in strength and in comeliness, they arose; and I awoke, and they were not. Oh, was it but a vision of sleep—false, like so many another?

ESTHER Vision it was, but it was not false. O Judah, Heaven hath sent thee this token. Thou shalt see it confirmed.

[*The sound of the chanting increases*]

ESTHER Hark! The chanting! It cometh nearer!

[*Enter, hurriedly,* AMRAH, *by path,* R.2.]

MALLUCH Look—Amrah!

BEN-HUR It is she.

AMRAH [*espying* BEN-HUR, *and running towards him*] O Master! Master! Joy! Thy mother—Tirzah—

BEN-HUR Thou hast been with them?

AMRAH [*falling on her knees, and clutching* BEN-HUR *'s garments*] And the Nazarene—they have met Him—they are healed!

BEN-HUR Oh, have the heavens opened?

AMRAH The Lord hath wrought it. Mine eyes have seen it.

BEN-HUR [*lifting* AMRAH *to her feet*] Praised be His name! But take me to them, that I, too, may see!

AMRAH Come then!

[*She leads the way towards R.2.*]

BEN-HUR [*encircling* ESTHER *with his arm*] Come! Come!

[*He leads her quickly towards R.2.,* MALLUCH *following*]

AMRAH [*at foot of run, R.2.*] They are near.

BEN-HUR [*to* ESTHER] O day of gladness—thrice blessed—that giveth me mother, and sister, and thee!

[*Exeunt all, R.2.*]

Scene 3

[SCENE: *The Mount of Olives, with view of Jerusalem, as shown in* BEN-HUR's *vision.* DISCOVERED: *The multitude, as in the vision. The whole concourse comes down towards front, singing, palms waving —the* MOTHER *of* BEN-HUR *and* TIRZAH, *restored, walk in the van. Enter, R. front,* AMRAH, BEN-HUR, ESTHER *and* MALLUCH. *Recognizing his mother and* TIRZAH, BEN-HUR, *with a cry of joy, rushes to meet them. He embraces them—then, turning, he draws* ESTHER *into the group, and she, too, embraces and is embraced by the* MOTHER *and* TIRZAH *in turn.* BEN-HUR, *his mother,* TIRZAH, ESTHER *and* AMRAH *fall upon their knees,* AMRAH *a little apart from the others;* MALLUCH, *standing by, reverently bows his head. The words of prayer are chanted. At its conclusion, the music swells into a joyous and triumphant strain. The characters rise. Curtain*]

THE CHARIOTEERS
Originated and Produced by

Marshall Moore

The timing of *Ben-Hur*—performances in America from 1899 and in London from 1902—coincides with the moment that popular entertainment comes to a fork in the road. Straight ahead is further development of the stage play. Leading to one side is the faint trail of cinema. The stage history of *Ben-Hur* and *Ben-Hur* 'borrowings' is brief. The history of *Ben-Hur* motion pictures continues up to 1959, but in each instance the first stage and filmic ventures after the Klaw and Erlanger production reveal much about the current perception and reception of toga drama.

In late November of 1905 the London Coliseum introduced its programme for the following fortnight: eleventh on the programme, directly following the screening of 'No. 10. American Bioscope, with latest Motion Pictures', was a concluding dramatic sketch entitled *The Charioteers*. An account of this sketch, reported in the *Era*, leaves small doubt that Drury Lane's *Ben-Hur* has been its inspiration—the characters' names alone confirm this source—and also it draws upon a painting that had earned notoriety for its sado-masochistic sensationalism at the Royal Academy's 1888 exhibition:

The prestige of this world-famous palace of amusement has been more than sustained by the production of *The Charioteers; or, A Roman Holiday*. Roman history, with its many lurid pages descriptive of the tortures and the doing to death of Christian martyrs, has served the purpose both of the novelist and the dramatist. One of the most successful of modern plays, *The Sign of the Cross*, owes much of its popularity to the thrilling scenes illustrative of the sufferings of the Christians who died 'to make a Roman holiday'; and the same theme has been delicately yet effectively handled in the new and elaborately staged production at the Coliseum. In the first scene we have most artistically and effectively realised the celebrated picture by [Herbert Gustave] Schmalz, [Faithful unto Death] 'Christianae ad Leones'.[87] It is the fatal entrance to the arena, and the roar of lions eager for their prey adds another

[87] Although the females in Schmalz's painting are nudes, there is no evidence that any performers were unclothed in the stage version.

pang to the sufferings of the rope-bound Christian maidens who are shortly to be cast amongst the hungry wild beasts. The young martyrs have to bear in silent agony the taunts and jeers of the Pagan crowd—it is all a part of the cruel day's amusement. Esther, the daughter of Salanes, a rich Jew, stands apart from the rest. Her beauty has made her the object of general admiration and remark. She has won the love of Judah, a young Hebrew, but Marcus, a Roman warrior, has also been strongly attracted by the handsome Christian maiden, who has now been converted to Christianity, and is now calmly awaiting a terrible death. Salanes, as a last expedient to save his beloved daughter from the terrible lions, throws out a suggestion that the rival lovers should compete in a chariot race, the stakes to be the life of Esther. Judah boldly offers the challenge, and it is at once accepted. The chariot race is a triumph of realism, to which no verbal description can do justice. The excited crowd, the eagerness to witness the trial of skill, the keenly contested race itself with four-horsed chariots—all these elements go to make up a wonderful spectacle that could only be successfully produced on a large stage, and with perfectly trained supernumeraries. The result of the race is, of course, a foregone one—Judah is declared the victor, and Esther's life is saved.[88]

The narrative thread of this sketch, listed in the playbill as 'A Sensational, Dramatic and Musical Wordless Spectacle' and promising the spectacle of 'THREE FOUR-HORSE CHARIOTS RACING AT FULL SPEED ON THE WHIRLING STAGE', was sung by one of the actors who fulfilled, within the drama, the role of a centurion. An orchestral score by Walter Slaughter accompanied the action. This production, probably lasting under twenty minutes, was in two scenes, the latter utilizing the Coliseum's large revolving stage and, again, a pair of treadmills and a moving backcloth based on the background to Schmalz's painting.

It would be easy to dismiss *The Charioteers* as a piece of minor toga drama, but not before considering a further point. If we seek links between the performance of melodrama on the stage and its appearance in the early silent film, one of these links has to be the music-hall sketch. Performed under the '18-minute rule', a quasi-legal convention that held dramatic playlets to a maximum performance time of twenty minutes,[89] and viewed in close proximity to 'Bioscope' motion pictures, the dramatic sketch cut action down to the barest essentials

[88] *Era*, 2 Dec. 1905.

[89] John Lawson advertised his appearance in a dramatic sketch as 'Humanity—in 18 minutes'. Within this time-span, he performed the role of a Jew who had married a Gentile woman who was being unfaithful to him. Lawson's character encountered his rival and had a ferocious fight, partly on a stairway, destroying much furniture and ending with the rival being thrown from a balcony. Lawson concluded his act by stepping to the footlights and singing 'Only a Jew'.

of plot and to a minimum of characterization. In this context it is also useful to reconsider *The Charioteers*, performed immediately after the screening of an assortment of films, and to recall that it is silent, 'a musical, wordless spectacle', with a narrative provided by accompanying song (also printed on the 'Pink Sheet' inserted in the Coliseum's programme). The effect of such narrative devices is not dissimilar to inter-titles in silent films. It is further useful to remark on the manner in which the characters Esther, Judah, and Marcus are morally identified—made 'morally legible' to the theatre's audiences. Finally, it is helpful to note that, even as *The Charioteers* was being performed at the Coliseum, film distributors were advertising the following motion picture: '*The Christian Martyrs*: Arena with Nero witnessing the binding of Christians on the Cross, who are then devoured by the lions. March-past of Gladiators. Also shows Daniel in the den of lions. Most thrilling. About 450 ft/The subject £11 5s.'[90]

Both the dramatic sketch and the early film are short, narrative, usually performed with small casts, supported by orchestral accompaniment, and—often—seen within minutes of one another by the same audiences. It is unlikely that we shall ever be able to confirm that one form has directly influenced the other, but we may insist that audience expectation of film melodrama was conditioned by prior familiarity with the music-hall dramatic sketch.

The text of *The Charioteers; or, A Roman Holiday* is taken from the programme and 'Pink Sheet' for the London Coliseum of 8 December 1905, which describes how the 'wordless spectacle' was to follow Chung Ling Soo, 'the great Chinese Magician', the O' Learys, 'Oriental Acrobats', *Fenella*, 'an Original Operetta', and 'American Bioscope, with latest Motion Pictures'. The programme acknowledged the lyrics by Roland Carse and the music by Walter Slaughter. The cast and settings (with designers) for the production were as follows:

Judah, a young Hebrew	Mr A. CLIFTON ANDERSON
Marcus, a wealthy young Roman	Mr OSCAR ADYE
Salanes, a wealthy Christian Jew	Mr KEINO JOHNSTONE
Esther, his daughter (a Christian martyr)	Miss BILLIE DOYLE
Sheikh el Shelibi, an Arab owner of horses	Mr R. MANSELL
Centurion	Mr VERNON COWPER

[90] Advertisement in *Era*, 1 July 1905, by Pathé Cinematographic Co., High Holborn, London.

Herbert Gustave Schmalz, *Faithful Unto Death: Christianae ad leones*, 1888, the
painting "realised" in *The Charioteers* at the London Coliseum, 1905.

Tableau 1: The Entrance to the Arena:
'Faithful unto Death' (Christianae ad Leones) The Challenge—
Acceptance! (Jas. A. Hicks).

Tableau 2: The Arena: The Race (Cecil E. Hicks).

Tableau 3: The Triumph of the Victor

Period: AD 50

The 'pink sheet' that accompanied the programme then reproduced
the following lyrics: CHORAL INTRODUCTION
It is holiday in Antioch, and the circus is crowded
ROMAN, ATHENIAN, SYRIAN, JEW,
Eagerly witness the pastimes provided,
Such as the fierce Pagan populace knew.
Athletes contesting their skill and endurance,
Martyrs by Lions—mid scoffing and jeers—
Torn to death ruthlessly in the Arena,
Followed by races with Charioteers.

[*Curtain rises, disclosing the entrance to the arena*]
'Faithful unto death' (Christianae ad Leones)

The Christian maidens wait their doom,
Imprison'd 'midst surroundings gay,
While hungry lions angry roar
Portents the hideous fate in store
For those refusing to adore
The Pagan Gods in Pagan way.

T'ward the arena—passing through
The people, callous, heartless, gay
Their eyes upon their victims rest
With ribald joke and scornful jest,
And flauntingly their joy attest
That this is Roman holiday.

CENTURION'S ANNOUNCEMENT
In the arena are the Christians placed,
'The Lions their spoil impatient wait;
'Within the circus get ye all with haste
'If ye'd behold the Christians' fate.'

JUDAH'S ARRIVAL
'Tis Judah—a Jew, tho' Roman bred,
Beholding his fair Esther's fate,

He fearlessly approaches her he loves
And offers her protection.

SHEIKH EL SHELIBI'S CHARIOTEER TORN BY LIONS
And now behold a dire disaster.
The Roman Charioteer of the Sheikh el Shelibi
(The only driver feared by Marcus)
Mangled by Lions, to which he cast the Christians,
Now lies a useless mass—a terrible example
Of man's inhumanity to man—
And he being thus disabled for the race
The Sheikh is sore distressed.

SHEIKH (TO JUDAH)
'Beheld I not thyself this very day,
'At practise drive a chariot with well skill'd hands?'

JUDAH
' 'Tis so. In Rome's arena have I driven oft
'The racers of the Emperor himself.'

SHEIKH
'List then to me. The winner in the final race today
'Lay twixt the ROMAN and my Charioteer.
'If thou wilt take my driver's place,
'And win the race against that Roman cur,
'I will bestow on thee estates and gold
'Enriching thee for ever.'

JUDAH'S CONDITIONS OF ACCEPTANCE
JUDAH (TO MARCUS)
'This is the woman I love, yet thou hast bought her,
'And by law she is thine.
'Than she should be a plaything for thee, I would rather
'Her fate to the lions consign.
'On these terms only do I this race contest;
'That should I lose, she to the lions be thrown,
BUT, should I win, grant me but this request,
'To claim her liberty—and she to be mine own.'

[*They move into the circus*]

IN THE ARENA
THE RACE! THE RACE! See how they bound along,
And how each noble Charioteer
His plunging steeds doth deftly steer

And govern their wild career
With muscles trained and strong.
Like ribbons lie the loosened reins,
The lithe long lashes swish through the air
The foaming horses onward bear.
See Blue advances! White beware!
Now 'tis the Red one gains.
The ROMAN wins! The Greek lacks pace!
He falls behind! The ROMAN's won!
NO! See how straight the ARABS run!
They gain! They gain! The ROMAN's done!
The JEW has won the race.

[*Second tableau*]
VICTORY! Victory! Triumphant all above,
The JEW remains, and thus attains
The woman of his love.
Humbled in his pride,
Laurel crowns the victor's brow
Freedom crowns his bride.

BEN-HUR
(*Film, 1907*)
Produced by the Kalem Company

Lew Wallace had been dead for two years when, in 1907, *Ben-Hur* was first adapted for the screen. The film was exhibited commercially in eastern American cities until an injunction, claiming infringement of copyright, was brought against the film-makers. All further showings of *Ben-Hur* were abandoned, and the film itself was supposedly destroyed in 1912, after the makers, the Kalem Company, failed in their appeal against the Klaw and Erlanger management and Harper Brother publishers before the US Circuit Court of Appeals. Fortunately, not all the film was destroyed. Enough footage survives to provide some indication of the Kalem production and their methods as well as a view into other and earlier toga dramas.

The Kalem production, it was claimed in court, advertised their film 'under the title *Ben-Hur*, Scenery and Supers by Pain's Fireworks Company. Costumes from Metropolitan Opera House. Chariot Race by 3rd Battery, Brooklyn. Positively the Most Superb Moving Picture Spectacle ever Produced in America. Sixteen Magnificent Scenes . . . etc . . . With ta[l]king titles, culminating in "Ben Hur Victor".'[91] What the Appellate Court's summary, the advertising copy, and the surviving film[92] reveal is that Wallace's novel was broken into sixteen sequences or scenes and filmed in and around Coney Island. The surviving chariot-race sequence shows that a portion of the mid-stage scenery from Pain's *The Last Days of Pompeii* (q.v.) was carried a half-mile from the fireworks theatre in Manhattan Beach to the Brighton Beach Racetrack, where, on the west side of the course, it was re-erected.[93] Other pieces of the same setting, filmed on the same site, might have been used in other sequences. The seashore was

---

[91] From the opinion of Mr Justice Holmes, 'The *Ben-Hur* Case', *Bioscope*, 22 Feb. 1912.

[92] Seeking copyright in 1907, Kalem, observing the specified conditions, deposited an opaque paper print of their *Ben-Hur*. By the mid-1950s most of the prints had deteriorated, but 93 feet (about $2\frac{1}{2}$ minutes' viewing) of the chariot-race were salvaged: Library of Congress Paper Print Collection, FLA 4991.

[93] See illustrations on pp. 98–9.

nearby for the galley episode. Supernumeraries made the short journey as well, some of them, it would appear, bringing their costumes and property banners with them. Other costumes (it is not evident which costumes nor the production from which the costumes were taken) were brought from the Metropolitan Opera House in Manhattan. The chariots and their horses came from a local National Guard artillery battery. It was a pastime of these artillery units and local fire-engine companies to hitch chariots to the teams trained to draw cannons and caissons or fire apparatus, and, with drivers costumed as 'Romans', to hold exhibition races at the nearby Dreamland Hippodrome. A film, made in 1905,[94] shows the races: a parade of riders and their attendants in Roman costume, several chariot-races, some 'cowboy' races, 'Roman riding' (i.e. controlling two unsaddled horses whilst the rider stands with one foot on the back of each), and conventional races with jockeys up. There is nothing to indicate that the actors in the principal roles of Judah and Messala were in any way skilled performers. Their acting is perfunctory, although with gestures taken from stage performances, and it is likely that these two men were members of the artillery battery who had been coached in movements and gesticulation. There were no retakes. What did it matter that a dog ran in front of the camera to chase after the horses? Film and time and the co-operation of the participants were precious.

[94] Ibid., FLA 5058.

THE BARBARIAN INGOMAR

Directed by D. W. Griffith

When, in 1908, the American director D. W. Griffith made *The Barbarian Ingomar*, he was both extending the life and altering the nature of an early toga play. *The Barbarian Ingomar*[95] is taken from a drama with a long and irregular history, first as a play supporting German culture in the face of French condescension, and later as a parable warning from Griffith about foreign immigration into America. The source for Griffith's film is *Ingomar, the Barbarian*, a play first seen in London at Drury Lane and Sadler's Wells in 1851. But this *Ingomar* is an unauthorized translation by Maria Lovell from German of Friederich Halm's *Son of the Wild (Sohn der Wildnis)*, written in 1846 for Viennese audiences. Apart from language, Halm's and Lovell's plays are similar. Each enacts the consequences that ensue when Myron, an armourer living in the Graeco-Roman colony of Massalia—later to be Marseilles—leaves on a journey to seek work. Whilst travelling, he is captured by a tribe of barbarians, the Alemanni, and held to ransom. When word of Myron's capture reaches Massalia, the frightened citizens refuse to come to his assistance, pleading a technicality: Myron has been captured outside the district. His daughter Parthenia now seeks assistance, but the only promise of ransom comes from Polydor, a wealthy old man, who will exchange ransom for Parthenia's hand. Parthenia now determines to confront the barbarians herself. She goes to their camp, where Myron has been forced to execute servile tasks, and confronts the barbarian chief, Ingomar. Ingomar and the other barbarians are struck by her beauty. Myron concludes a bargain with Ingomar: he will leave Parthenia as a hostage and seek ransom. Myron gives Parthenia a dagger to guard her honour. Ingomar is moved to declare his passion for Parthenia, but his tribesmen are less honourable and abduct her to sell her to slavers. Ingomar rescues Parthenia in a bloody fight and conveys her to Massalia. Because they now love one another, they marry, and Ingomar, pre-

[95] Ibid., FRA 0180 (305 feet).

viously an untamed woodsman, attempts to become a respectable citizen and farmer. In these efforts he is thwarted by Polydor and the other citizens of Massalia, who, continually comparing their own Roman virtue and civilization with Ingomar's barbarianism, act with hypocritical deceit and self-interest. When the barbarians attack, Ingomar, although he has ample opportunity to despise the Massalians, none the less helps to rescue the town. The townspeople now celebrate his loyalty, but, although the play ends happily, Ingomar's and the audience's respect for the people of Massalia has been contaminated.

The conflict here is not Christians against pagan Romans, but barbarians against Romans. Both 'Roman' and 'barbarian' are coded terms. As Halm appears to have intended, the play may be read as a comment on French-German relationships in the 1840s. The complacent bourgeois Massalian/French, shopkeepers and artisans, still prating about their revolutionary purity and culture, patronize the Alemanni/German people, who are no less honourable or less civilized than they. Translated to London and the 1850s, it retains Halm's antipathy to the *petit bourgeois*, and quietly questions British xenophobic nationalism —and, equally, the equivalent nationalism of other Europeans—surrounding the Great Exhibition in Hyde Park.

Lovell's play was soon published in both London and New York by Samuel French and entered the American repertoire. *Ingomar, the Barbarian* continued to be played on both sides of the Atlantic. Henry Irving, in his apprentice days in the English provinces, played the roles of Myron and another Massalian. In 1883, with the Lyceum Theatre leased to the American producer Henry Abbey, the role of Parthenia was chosen as one of the parts in which to introduce Mary Anderson. Opposite her, as Ingomar, was J. H. Barnes. Under Augustin Daly's management, Mary Anderson subsequently reintroduced *Ingomar, the Barbarian* to American audiences, bringing a young William Terriss from London as her Ingomar. Whilst the play was considered outmoded by London audiences, Americans were undeterred by its overt sentimentality. It was still being performed in metropolitan New York throughout the 1890s. The costumes worn by the actors in Griffith's *Ingomar* look very like the costumes of contemporary stage productions of the play, and it is reasonable to assume that such a wardrobe, readily available, was hired for the occasion.

It may have been at one of the New York performances that Griffith made the acquaintance of *Ingomar, the Barbarian*. In 1908, when he came to adapt it, he was prepared to make changes to the narrative.

At first inspection, it would appear that Griffith has done nothing more than invert the title and, perhaps because at that time he was making films no longer than a reel in length, shorten the play by eliminating Acts IV and V. Thus the film ends at the end of Act III, when, having rescued Parthenia from abductors who now intend to gang-rape her, and having then returned her to her home in Massalia, Ingomar is given consent to marry a delighted Parthenia. But there are further differences. Whereas both Halm and Lovell are even-handed in their depiction and condemnation of barbarians and Massalians, Griffith remains partial to the Massalians, who are no longer shopkeepers but a single, wealthy, patrician Roman family. These people, Romans, are civilized, standing up to the crudeness of the barbarians. Ingomar, the personification of the alien other, has to be instructed in gentle civilized ways and in honourable ways before he can be a fit husband to Parthenia. Parthenia and Myron are to be his tutors. Not until Ingomar has rejected barbarian behaviour, overcome the rapists, and rescued Parthenia, is he welcomed into a Roman home.

What Griffith has created in this *Ingomar* is a parable and warning about immigration in the early 1900s. According to Barabara Tuchman, 'America was in a period of unprecedented expansion. The population increased by 50 per cent from fifty million to seventy-five million in the years 1880–1900.'[96] Immigration into the United States, previously a few hundred thousand persons annually, peaked in 1896 and again in 1907, when it reached 1,285,000 immigrants, many of them from Southern and Eastern Europe.[97] Many of the immigrants were Roman Catholic; many were Jews. Fears generated by these record figures had rejuvenated membership in both the American Party, which had opposed Roman Catholic—especially Irish—immigration in the 1850s, and the Anti-Imperial League, which fretted about the extension of the American hegemony to Catholic Cuba and the Philippine Islands. Whilst much anti-immigration sentiment understandably came from American urban workers who feared competition from newer arrivals, some patrician Americans contributed to the debate. Theodore Roosevelt, a descendant of early Dutch settlers and American president between 1901 and 1909, expressed these views in a polemical book[98] and, in his second term of office, supported the establishment of a Congressional Committee on Immigration to address the problem of 'new immigrants' from Eastern and Southern Europe.

[96] Tuchman, *The Proud Tower*, 119.
[97] Cf. the Annual Reports of the US Immigration Service.
[98] *American Ideals* (New York, 1897, 1902).

Griffith, too, is aware of[99]—more likely, a sharer in—these anxieties.
He has translated the older, more established Americans' (the patrician
Romans') fear of being overrun by outlandish, different, 'other' immigrants (barbarians) into a statement of reassurance to his American audience. His film, simultaneously, is a warning to these newer
immigrants: before they can be accepted, they must—and will—
renounce their barbarian practices. They must, in Roosevelt's term,
become 'Americanized' (for 'Americanized' read 'civilized'), rejecting
the characteristics which stamp them as different from earlier generations of Americans. Then, and only then, will they be welcomed into
American homes. Only then will their sons and daughters intermarry.

The 'text' of *The Barbarian Ingomar* is a sequence-by-sequence synopsis
of Griffith's film, accompanied by photographs taken from individual
frames of this film.

EPISODE 1: *A Garden Setting in Massalia (Graeco-Roman Marseilles)*
Myron prepares to leave on a journey. He says farewell to his wife
Actea and to his daughter Parthenia. Myron, accompanied by Lykon,
a friend, leaves.

EPISODE 2: *The Garden of Myron's Home*
Parthenia sits alone, pining for her father. She is visited by Polydor, a
crabbed, elderly man, who offers her a life of wealth if she will accept
his offer of marriage. When Parthenia contemptuously refuses him,
Polydor responds with threats.

EPISODE 3: *The Forest*
A pathway. Two armed barbarians take up positions of ambush and
spring out as Myron and Lykon pass. Myron is captured, but Lykon
escapes.

EPISODE 4: *Myron's Garden*
Actea and Parthenia are relaxing when Lykon arrives with the alarm-
ing news of Myron's capture. Actea and Parthenia are distressed and
cry out. Their cries bring Polydor, who comes to learn what is causing
the commotion. When he is informed that Myron is being held
for ransom, he refuses to assist and departs, leaving the family dis-
traught.

[99] Given Griffith's subsequent translation of fear of 'the other' into more overt racism
and support for the Ku Klux Klan in *The Birth of a Nation* (1915), 'aware' may be an
inappropriately generous term.

EPISODE 5: The Barbarian Camp in the Forest
Two barbarians, Ambivar and Trinobantes, quarrel over dice. Ingomar, chief of the Alemanni, is disturbed by their quarrelling and tries to end the dispute. Five more barbarians enter, bringing Myron as their captive. Myron is brought before Ingomar, who informs his captive that ransom must be paid. Myron proudly refuses to pay and is thrown to the ground by Ingomar, forced to gather firewood for the bandit camp-fire, and is then hustled off into captivity.

EPISODE 6: The Forest: The Scene of Myron's Capture
Lykon and Parthenia come to the forest to try to find and rescue Myron.

EPISODE 7: The Barbarian Camp
Parthenia and Lykon enter the barbarians' camp. Lykon leaves, but Parthenia, seeing Ingomar, approaches him to demand her father's liberty. Ingomar produces empty money bags and insists on payment of ransom. Myron then offers to get ransom, leaving Parthenia as hostage. He brings out a dagger from his clothing, first threatening himself and then Parthenia if his faith should be broken. He then gives the dagger to Parthenia. She, in turn, threatens herself with the dagger. Myron leaves. Ingomar makes a gesture towards Parthenia, who again raises the dagger defiantly.

EPISODE 8: The Barbarian Camp
Parthenia is alone. Ambivar enters and attempts to woo her. Parthenia's response is to threaten herself with her dagger. Ingomar now enters and drives Ambivar away. Ingomar returns to court Parthenia himself. She, in consternation, again threatens herself with the dagger, and Ingomar, frustrated, threatens her with his sword. He then relents. It is now apparent that Ingomar and Parthenia are attracted to one another. Ingomar goes off, leaving Parthenia alone. Ambivar, Samo, and Novio now enter and seize Parthenia, who faints into Ambivar's arms. They rush off with her.

EPISODE 9 (a sequence of 5 separate intercut shots): The Forest
The barbarians, carring Parthenia, flee, with Ingomar in pursuit. At one point the abductors lay a false trail to mislead Ingomar and are, at first, successful. Ingomar retraces his steps, finds the barbarians' route, and resumes his pursuit.

EPISODE 10: A Clearing in the Forest
The three barbarians enter, still carrying Parthenia. The semi-conscious girl is tied to a tree, and Ambivar tries to force himself upon her. She refuses him and is threatened.

EPISODE 11: *The Forest*
Ingomar runs through the forest, pursuing Parthenia's abductors. He discovers the barbarians, and a combat with swords ensues. Ingomar drives off Novio and Samo and kills Ambivar. He then releases Parthenia, who at first is frightened by his declaration of love. Ingomar kneels, offering her his sword hilt first. Parthenia, moved by this act, bids him rise, and together, hand in hand, they walk (into the camera) towards Massalia.

EPISODE 12: *The Garden in Massalia*
Myron, Actea, and Lykon are in despair over their failure to raise the ransom money to reclaim Parthenia; their misery is mocked by Polydor. Parthenia and Ingomar enter. There is joy at the family's reunion. Ingomar now asks for Parthenia's hand. At first there is consternation, but Parthenia pleads with her parents, who give their consent. Parthenia and Ingomar embrace, whilst her approving parents look on.

Episode 1 (*a*)

Episode 1 (*b*)

Episode 2 (*a*)

Episode 2 (*b*)

Episode 3

Episode 4

Episode 5 (a)

Episode 5 (b)

Episode 7 (a)

Episode 7 (*b*)

Episode 7 (*c*)

Episode 8 (*a*)

Episode 8 (b)

Episode 9 (a)

Episode 9 (b)

Episode 10

Episode 11 (*a*)

Episode 11 (*b*)

Episode 12

AFTERWORD

The Barbarian Ingomar, a five-act drama compressed into nine minutes' viewing time, offers the merest foretaste of toga films to follow, and barely suggests that stage plays might be translated effectively into motion pictures. With hindsight, we know otherwise. Theatre pieces became films, and silent toga films, intelligible without recourse to language (apart from easily replaced inter-titles), reached wide and appreciative international audiences. However, although British and American plays and novels, such as *The Sign of the Cross* and *Fabiola*,[100] were quarried to provide subjects for films, there are marked changes in the production and in the content of these subsequent films. It is not within the scope of this study to pursue and to explain these changes, but events associated with these developments may be sketched briefly. Apart from *The Last Days of Pompeii* (abridged into a pyrodramatic spectacle), *The Charioteers*, and *The Barbarian Ingomar*, the toga dramas in this volume are full-length entertainments, and whilst the films of 1907–8—*Ben-Hur* and *The Barbarian Ingomar*—fall well short of these entertainments in duration, the growing popularity of motion pictures, and improvements to the technologies of film-making, made it inevitable that longer films would be made and exhibited.

Many of these full-length films would be toga pieces; even more of them would be Italian. Cinema historians[101] are in general agreement that, between 1911 and 1915, the making of large-scale art films moved to Italy, and they are equally agreed that the motion picture which first confirmed the high quality of such Italian work was Enrico

---

[100] Taken from Nicholas (later Cardinal) Wiseman's *Fabiola; or, The Church of the Catacombs* (1854), *Fabiola* narrates the youth and martyrdom of St Sebastian at the hands of Roman persecutors, and the conversion of Fabiola, a wealthy Roman girl, to Christianity. At the instigation of the actor-manager Edmund Tearle, *Fabiola* was dramatized by the Revd Arthur Whitley and the actress Kate Clinton as *From Cross to Crown* (1897), and remained in Tearle's repertoire through 1907.

[101] David Robinson, *World Cinema* (London, 1973); Liz-Anne Bowden (ed.) *The Oxford Companion to Film* (London, 1976).

Guazzoni's *Quo Vadis?* (1913). Between 1901 and 1908 there had been two, perhaps even three, versions of *Quo Vadis?* by French film-makers (notably Ferdinand Zecca, who filmed *Quo Vadis?* twice) dramat-izing Sienkiewicz's novel for the screen. Despite the ambitious scope of Zecca's second version, none of these films appears to have been more than a brief success. With Guazzoni's *Quo Vadis?*, it was differ-ent. The film, reputedly with a cast of 5,000 actors and 30 lions, was distributed widely in America, where it was credited with inspiring D. W. Griffith to attempt large epic films, and in Britain, where distribution rights for the film were publically auctioned for a record £6,700. In the same year, world audiences had a choice between three rival Italian versions of *The Last Days of Pompeii*. Mario Caserini's *Nero and Agrippina* was also produced in 1913; Giovanni Pastrone's *Cabiria* followed less than a year later.

Cabiria is not, within the intended meaning of Chance Newton's phrase, a toga drama. Rome's opponents are Carthaginians, not Chris-tians, but the adroit and spectacular reworking of Roman history for current social and political motives opens the subject of Roman im-perial expansion to other uses. The technical achievement of *Cabiria* is outstanding for that date. American studios continued to make toga films, but when Frederick Thomson made *The Sign of the Cross* (1914) for Famous Players–Lasky, he imported Italian actors and scenic artists. Thomson's American Marcus Superbus (William Farnum) was op-posed by an Italian Tigellinus (Giorgio Majeroni), and an American Nero (Sheridan Block) had an Italian courtier (Rienzo de Cordova).

Whilst films of *Quo Vadis?* and *The Last Days of Pompeii* point to a persistent tradition of dramas with Christians and Romans as antagon-ists, *Cabiria* offers a more precise index to the value and purpose of Italian motion pictures set in the ancient Roman world. Nationalism had become a pronounced strain in Italian political thinking since unification in 1861, and, as in Britain and America, rhetoric and images of Republican Rome were evoked to establish continuity between a historic past and a modern present, even if the modern republic included a king as titular head of state. Ancient Rome on film, therefore, represented modern Italy. As the Roman Republic was followed by the Roman Empire, so Italy rebuilt its former trading colonies, especially in North Africa—but with mixed success. Italian forces and Italian colonists had been defeated and expelled from Abyssinia in 1896. Before that date and continuing into the twentieth century, there were sporadic efforts to establish Italian colonies in Tunisia and Libya, with the most ambitious of these campaigns beginning in 1911. *Cabiria* coincides with the Italian campaign to retake Libya, the site of ancient Carthage destroyed by Rome in the Second Punic War. The analogy between past and present is clear: Rome is destined to dominate Carthage, whatever that city and its territory might be named and whosoever its present rulers, in this instance the Ottoman Turks, might be. *Cabiria* speaks to its Italian audiences as analogy and prophecy. In capturing coastal lands and key Libyan cities, Italy had achieved most of its political and military objectives before the film was released.

There was a further reason for Italian film-makers to eschew dramas founded on Roman–Christian conflict. The decision of the Italian parliament to subsume the city and suburbs of Rome into the Italian secular state and to deny the Vatican's jurisdiction for this territory was to produce a political breach unresolved until 1929. Whereas toga drama, as we have come to understand it, hints at eventual resolution between Christian and Roman, contemporary Italian politics offered meagre expectation of reconciliation. Italian evocations of internal conflict therefore chose other metaphors from the past. Pasquali's *Spartacus; or, The Revolt of the Gladiators* (1913) enacts a rebellion led by Spartacus, a Thracian chief captured and made to serve as a gladiator for Roman spectacles. When, opposing Roman corruption, weakness, and cruelty, he leads a popular revolt and captures Rome, Spartacus does not take revenge, but—now as a Roman—unifies the discordant factions. The modern parallel to Spartacus, easily understood by Italian audiences, is Garibaldi, whose rebellion helped to create the modern Italian state.

By the mid-1920s the making of toga films had returned to the Hollywood studios—some films to be made in Europe, or partly in Europe, with American capital, but with the ideological content geared to the tastes and perceptions of American audiences. Roman and Christian persevered as implacable adversaries, but their subliminal identities changed with political and social movements: now 'New Deal' Romans, now anti-McCarthy or anti-Communist Christians, now homophobic Romans and gay Christians, and every now and then parody Romans and Christians. The metaphor lived. It still does.

A Select Filmography of Toga Films

The following filmography is not an exhaustive directory of toga films nor a catalogue of films on the subject of Romans and their Empire. Rather, it lists key toga films which are thought, or known, to have survived in their entirety or in part. The listings identify producers, directors, and performers of these films, and the locations of extant prints. The films chosen are chiefly motion-picture versions of stage plays referred to in this study, but in some instances I have included motion pictures which do not enact conflict between Romans and Christians but between Rome and other internal elements. These films, in articulating a scenario of opposition and resistance to a dominant political or sexual culture, have acquired a contemporary significance and status.

Androcles and the Lion (1950)

Production: RKO
Director: Chester Erskine
Print: ?

LAVINIA	Jean Simmons
ANDROCLES	Alan Young
CAPTAIN	Victor Mature
FERROVIUS	Robert Newton
CAESAR	Maurice Evans
MEGAERA	Elsa Lanchester

The Barbarian Ingomar (1908)

Production: American Mutoscope & Biograph Company
Director: D. W. Griffith
Print: Library of Congress

PARTHENIA	Florence Lawrence
INGOMAR	Harry Salter

Ben-Hur (1907)

Production: Kalem Film Company
Director: Sidney Olcott
Print: Chariot-race only, Library of Congress

Ben-Hur (1925)

Production: Metro-Goldwyn-Mayer
Director: Fred Niblo
Print: Kevin Brownlow Productions, Ltd., London, Mondadori Video, Milan

BEN-HUR	Ramon Navarro
MESSALA	Francis X. Bushman
ESTHER	May McAvoy
MOTHER OF HUR	Claire McDowell
TIRZAH	Kathleen Key
IRAS	Carmel Myers
SIMONIDES	Nigel de Brulier
SHEIKH ILDERIM	Mitchell Lewis
SANBALLAT	Leo White
ARRIUS	Frank Currier
BALTHASAR	Charles Belcher
MADONNA	Betty Bronson
AMRAH	Dale Fuller
JOSEPH	Winter Hall

Ben-Hur (1959)

Production: Metro-Goldwyn-Mayer
Director: William Wyler
Prints: Video widely sold, British Film Institute

BEN-HUR	Charlton Heston
MESSALA	Stephen Boyd
ESTHER	Haya Harareet
MOTHER OF HUR	Martha Scott
TIRZAH	Cathy O'Donnell
SIMONIDES	Sam Jaffee
SHEIKH ILDERIM	Hugh Griffith
ARRIUS	Jack Hawkins
BALTHASAR	Finlay Currie
PONTIUS PILATE	Frank Thring

Cabiria (1914)

Production: Italia Film
Director: Giovanni Pastrone
Print: Mondadori Video, Milan

CABIRIA	Lidia Quaranta
SOPHONISBA	Almirante Manzini
FULVIO	Umberto Mozzato
MACISTE	Bartolomeo Pagano
ARCHIMEDES	Enrico Gemelli
MASSINISSA	Vitale DeStefano

Fabiola (1917)

Based on Cardinal Wiseman's novel *Fabiola; or, The Church of the Catacombs* (1854) and Arthur Whitley's and Edmund Tearle's toga play *From Cross to Crown* (1897). See also *Sebastiane*.

Production: Palatino Films
Director: Giovanni Pastrone
Print: Centro Sperimentale di Cinematografia, Rome

Friends, Romans, and Leo (1916)

Production: Conquest Pictures (Thomas A. Edison)
Director: Alan Crosland
Print: Library of Congress (Kleine Collection)

PLENTO MORPHEUS	Ray McKee
LEO	William Fables
MULIUS CAESAR	William Wadsworth
MYRIA	Juanita Fletcher
LIARUS BUNKO	Harry MacDonough, sen.

The Last Days of Pompeii (1913)

Production: Ambrosio Films
Director: Arturo Ambrosio
Print: Centro Sperimentale di Cinematografia, Rome

The Last Days of Pompeii (1913)

Production: Pasquali Films
Director: Ernesto Pasquali
Print: Centro Sperimentale di Cinematografia, Rome; fragment in Kleine
    Collection, Library of Congress

The Last Days of Pompeii (1926)

Production: Fert-Pittaluga
Directors: Carmine Gallone and Amleto Palmeri
Print: Museo Nazionale del Cinema, Turin; Centro Sperimentale di Cinemato-
    grafia, Rome

NYDIA	Maria Corda
IONE	Rina de Liguoro
GLAUCUS	Victor Varkoni
ARBACES	Bernhard Goetzke
CALENUS	Emilio Ghione
APECIDES	Victor Evangelesti
OLITHUS	Ferruccio Biancini

The Last Days of Pompeii (1959)

Production: Italy-Spain-Monaco-United Artists
Director: Mario Bonnard
Print: ?

NYDIA	Barbara Carroll
JULIA	Annemarie Baumann
IONE	Cristina Kaufman
GLAUCUS	Steve Reeves
HIGH PRIEST	Fernando Rey

The Life of Brian (1979)

Production: Handmade Films (George Harrison, Denis O'Brien, John Goldstone)
Director: Terry Jones
Designer: Terry Gilliam
Print. Video/CBS-Fox

WRITTEN BY AND STARRING (IN MULTIPLE ROLES): Graham Chapman, John Cleese, Terry Gilliam, Eric Idle, Terry Jones, Michael Palin.

WITH (MOSTLY IN MULTIPLE ROLES): Gwen Taylor, Carol Cleveland, Sue Jones-Davis, Kenneth Colley, Terence Baylor, Bernard McKenna, Neil Innes, John Case, John Young, Andrew MacLaughlan, Chris Langham, Charles McKeown, Charles Knode, Spike Milligan, George Harrison.

Quo Vadis? (1913)

Production: Cines
Director: Enrico Guazzoni
Print: Cineteca, Milan; Centro Sperimentale di Cinematografia, Rome

PETER THE APOSTLE	J. Gizzi
NERO	C. Cattaneo
POPPAEA	O. Brandini
TIGELLINUS	C. Moltini
URSUS	B. Castellani
LYGIA	Leah Giunchi
VINICIUS	A. Novelli
CHILO	A. Mastripietri
EUNICE	A. Cattaneo
PETRONIUS	G. Serena

Quo Vadis? (1925)

Production: Unione Cinematografica Italiana-First National
Director: Arturo Ambrosio
Print: Cineteca, Milan; Centro Sperimentale di Cinematografia, Rome

NERO	Emil Jannings
LYGIA	Lillian Hall Davis
POPPAEA	Elena Di Sangre
DOMITILLA	Elga Brink
EUNICE	Rina de Liguore
VINICIUS	Alphonse Fryland
URSUS	Bruto Castellani

CHEILON CHEILONIDES	Gino Viotti
TIGELLINUS	R. Van Riel
PETRONIUS	Andree Habay

Quo Vadis? (1951)

Production: Metro-Goldwyn-Mayer
Director: Mervyn LeRoy
Print: Video widely available

VINICIUS	Robert Taylor
LYGIA	Deborah Kerr
NERO	Peter Ustinov
PETRONIUS	Leo Genn
PETER	Finlay Currie
PLAUTIUS	Felix Aylmer
POMPONIA	Nora Swinburne
URSUS	Buddy Baer
POPPAEA	Patricia Laffan
EUNICE	Marina Berti

The Robe (1953)

Production: 20th Century-Fox
Director: Henry Koster
Print: ?

MARCELLUS GALLIO	Richard Burton
DIANA	Jean Simmons
DEMETRIUS	Victor Mature
PETER	Michael Rennie
CALIGULA	Jay Robinson
JUSTUS	Dean Jagger
PILATE	Richard Boon
MIRIAM	Betta St John
PAULUS	Jeff Morrow
EMPEROR TIBERIUS	Ernest Thesiger
JUNIA	Dawn Adams

Sebastiane (1976)

Production: Megalovision-Cinegate
Director: Derek Jarman
Print: British Film Institute

SEBASTIAN	Leonard Treviglio
SEVERUS	Barney James
MAX	Neil Kennedy
JUSTIN	Richard Warwick
CLAUDIUS	Donald Dunham

ADRIAN	Ken Hicks
ANTONY	Januz Romanov
MARIUS	Stefano Massari
JULIAN	David Finbar
LEOPARD BOY	Gerald Incandela
EMPEROR DIOCLETIAN	Robert Medley
DANCER	Lindsay Kemp and Troupe

The Sign of the Cross (1914)

Production: Famous Players–Lasky
Director: Frederick Thomson
Prints: American Film Institute, Libary of Congress (last half only)

MARCUS	William Farnum
NERO	Sheridan Block
TIGELLINUS	Giorgio Majeroni
GALABRIO	Charles E. Verner
PHILODEMUS	Rienzo di Cordova
BERENIS	Ethel Gray Terry
DACIA	Ethel Phillips
POPPAEA	Lila Barclay
FAVIUS	Morgan Thorpe
STEPHANUS	Ogden Child
MERCIA	Rosina Henley

The Sign of the Cross (1932)

Production: Paramount Pictures
Producer and Director: Cecil B. DeMille
Prints: British Film Institute, Library of Congress

MARCUS	Fredric March
NERO	Charles Laughton
TIGELLINUS	Ian Keith
GLABRIO	Ferdinand Gottschalk
DACIA	Vivian Tobin
POPPAEA	Claudette Colbert
ANCARIA	Joyselle Joyner
FAVIUS	Harry Beresford
TITUS	Arthur Hohl
STEPHANUS	Tommy Conlon
MERCIA	Elisa Landi

The Silver Chalice (1955)
Production: Warner Brothers
Director: Victor Saville
Print: Warner Video (USA)

HELENA	Virginia Mayo
DEBORRA	Pier Angeli
SIMON	Jack Palance
JOSEPH	Walter Hampden
MIJAMIN	Joseph Wiseman
LUKE	Alexander Scourby
PETER	Lorne Greene
ADAM	David J. Stewart
LINUS	Herbert Rudley
NERO	Jacques Aubuchon
IGNATIUS	E. G. Marshall
AARON	Michael Pate
BASIL	Paul Newman
HELEN (as a girl)	Natalie Wood
BASIL (as a boy)	Booth Colman

Spartacus; or, the Revolt of the Gladiators (1913)

Production: Pasquali Films
Director: Ernesto Pasquali
Print: Library of Congress; Centro Sperimentale di Cinematografia, Rome

Spartacus (1959)

Production: Universal International
Director: Stanley Kubrick
Print: Restored film on general release

SPARTACUS	Kirk Douglas
MARCUS CRASSUS	Laurence Olivier
VAVINIA	Jean Simmons
GRACCHUS	Charles Laughton
BATIATUS	Peter Ustinov
JULIUS CAESAR	John Gavin
HELENA GLABRUS	Nina Foch
TIGRANES	Herbert Lom
GLABRUS	John Dall
MARCELLUS	Charles McGraw
CLAUDIA MARIUS	Joanna Barnes
DAVID	Woody Strode
ANTONIUS	Tony Curtis

.